Planning and Urban Growth in the Nordic Countries

STUDIES IN HISTORY, PLANNING AND THE ENVIRONMENT

Series editors   *Professor Gordon E. Cherry,*
University of Birmingham

Professor Anthony Sutcliffe,
University of Leicester

1   The Rise of Modern Urban Planning, 1800–1914
Edited by Anthony Sutcliffe

2   Shaping an Urban World
Planning in the twentieth century
Edited by Gordon E. Cherry

3   Planning for Conservation
An international perspective
Edited by Roger Kain

4   Metropolis 1890–1940
Edited by Anthony Sutcliffe

5   Arcadia for All
The legacy of a makeshift landscape
Dennis Hardy and Colin Ward

6   Planning and Urban Growth in Southern Europe
Edited by Martin Wynn

7   Thomas Adams and the Modern Planning Movement
Britain, Canada and the United States, 1900–1940
Michael Simpson

8   Holford
A study in architecture, planning and civic design
Gordon E. Cherry and Leith Penny

9   Goodnight Campers!
The history of the British holiday camp
Colin Ward and Dennis Hardy

10   Model Housing
From the Great Exhibition to the Festival of Britain
S. Martin Gaskell

11   Two Centuries of American Planning
Edited by Daniel Schaffer

12   Planning and Urban Growth in Nordic Countries
Edited by Thomas Hall

13 From Garden Cities to New Towns
    Campaigning for town and country planning, 1899–1946
    Dennis Hardy

14 From New Towns to Green Politics
    Campaigning for town and country planning, 1946–1990
    Dennis Hardy

Forthcoming Titles

The Garden City
Past, present and future
Edited by Stephen Ward

Planning Europe's Capital Cities
Edited by Thomas Hall

Planning and Urban Growth in the Nordic Countries

Edited by Thomas Hall

E & FN SPON

An Imprint of Chapman & Hall

London · New York · Tokyo · Melbourne · Madras

UK	Chapman & Hall, 2–6 Boundary Row, London SE1 8HN
USA	Chapman & Hall, 29 West 35th Street, New York NY10001
JAPAN	Chapman & Hall Japan, Thomson Publishing Japan, Hirakawacho Nemoto Building, 7F, 1-7-11 Hirakawa-cho, Chiyoda-ku, Tokyo 102
AUSTRALIA	Chapman & Hall Australia, Thomas Nelson Australia, 480 La Trobe Street, PO Box 4725, Melbourne 3000
INDIA	Chapman & Hall India, R. Seshadri, 32 Second Main Road, CIT East, Madras 600 035

First edition 1991

© 1991 Thomas Hall

Typeset in 10/12½ pt Times by
Rowland Phototypesetting Ltd, Bury St Edmunds, Suffolk
Printed in Great Britain by Clays Ltd, St Ives plc

This book was commissioned and edited by
Alexandrine Press, Oxford

ISBN 0 419 16840 0

British Library Cataloguing in Publication Data
Planning and urban growth in the Nordic countries.
  1. Scandinavian countries. Town planning
  I. Hall, Thomas
  711.40948

  ISBN 0-419-16840-0

Library of Congress Cataloging-in-Publication Data
Planning and urban growth in the Nordic countries / edited by
  Thomas Hall.—1st ed.
    p.   cm.—(Studies in history, planning, and the
environment)
  Includes bibliographical references and index.
  ISBN 0-419-16840-0 (USA)
  1. City planning—Scandinavia—History.   2. Urbanization—
Scandinavia—History.   I. Hall, Thomas, 1939–
II. Series.
HT169.S27P53   1991
307.1′216′0948—dc20   90-10341
                                                                CIP

CONTENTS

Preface
– ix –

Contributors
– xiii –

1. THE NORTH – DOES IT EXIST?
Thomas Hall
– 1 –

2. URBAN PLANNING IN DENMARK
Bo Larsson and *Ole Thomassen*
– 6 –

3. URBAN PLANNING IN FINLAND AFTER 1850
Mikael Sundman
– 60 –

4. URBAN PLANNING IN NORWAY
Erik Lorange and *Jan Eivind Myhre*
– 116 –

5. URBAN PLANNING IN SWEDEN
Thomas Hall
– 167 –

6. CONCLUDING REMARKS:
IS THERE A NORDIC
PLANNING TRADITION?
Thomas Hall
– 247 –

Subject Index
– 261 –

Index of Towns and Areas
– 265 –

Index of Persons
– 269 –

PREFACE

The purpose of this book is to provide a survey of the development of urban planning in the Nordic countries, with particular emphasis on the period since the middle of the nineteenth century. We have focused in particular on the following questions:

- Around the beginning of the present century there was a radical change in perceptions of planning in most parts of Europe. This has been described by Anthony Sutcliffe in *Towards the Planned City* (1981). When and how did this shift from pre-industrial to 'modern' planning occur in the Nordic countries?
- What were the legal frames for planning, and how has planning legislation changed during the period in question?
- How have plans been made and approved, and by whom? And how has the planning system been organized at different times?
- How has planning been affected by societal developments in the different countries?
- What urban ideals have influenced the design of the plans?
- To what extent have the authors of the various plans been inspired by projects of their colleagues in the other Nordic countries, and to what extent have they sought models and ideas from outside these countries, and if so from where?
- What concrete effect has planning had on the physical development of Nordic towns?

The term 'planning' first appeared a little over a hundred years ago and is used today to cover a wide range of activities. However, the chapters which follow are concerned chiefly with detailed physical planning. It has not been possible to make a systematic study of more comprehensive planning, for example concerning communications, or the disposition of large areas of land for various purposes or their protection against exploitation.

In writing the separate chapters we have inevitably encountered various problems of selection and demarcation. Some of these should be mentioned here.

We have addressed the physical growth of the towns only in so far as this has been of immediate relevance to planning. Housing policy and the design of buildings are examples of related fields which are sometimes difficult to distinguish from planning as such. Moreover, a country's planning operations are inevitably bound up with its political conditions and administrative structures (an excellent account of this with reference to Great Britain appears in Gordon Cherry's *The Politics of Town Planning* [1982]). Thus the question arises as to how much background is required in order that a reader, lacking knowledge of the social organization of the Nordic countries, may find the descriptions here instructive and meaningful. Each author has struck his own slightly different balance, depending on his particular premises and special areas of interest and on the specific problems and developments in his own country.

The choice of examples has also raised some problems of principle. What should we choose: examples that are 'average' or 'typical' of normal plans and projects, or 'show cases' which have caused a stir, possibly even abroad, because they have broken with tradition and been regarded as innovative and original? In the first instance, how do we decide what is typical? And in the second, how do we avoid harping on the same worn-out themes, perhaps serving to reinforce old values and judgements inherited from earlier writers, often the very people who first reported on the projects in the professional press? There are no clear-cut answers to these questions.

Something should also be said about the editor's role. The first reaction of anyone responsible for a book of this kind is probably to hope that contributors will adopt a uniform design, making for easy reading and ready comparisons. Originally my idea was that all the chapters would follow a similar pattern, but I soon realized how very unrealistic such an approach was. To begin with, this kind of constraint would prevent the authors from exploiting their own special interests and knowledge; moreover conditions differ in all sorts of ways in the four countries, which makes it difficult to follow the same pattern in describing developments in planning there. Authors and editor thus agreed on a compromise: although each author adopted his own approach and chronological structure, the aim was still as far as possible to discuss the same questions and to present comparable material. We may not always have succeeded in this, but we hope that our readers will nevertheless be able to form a picture of certain similarities and differences, and of the distinguishing features of the four countries in a planning context.

One further comment should be made as regards the focus of the different chapters. When I was first asked to edit this publication, Anthony Sutcliffe's book, which describes the breakthrough of modern planning in England, France, Germany and the United States, had recently been published, and it was intended at first that the present book should be a kind of Nordic counterpart, i.e. that the emphasis would be on planning as such rather than on design or the shape and content of plans, and that our account should concentrate on the decades around the turn of the present century. But my co-authors proved to be more interested in urban planning ideas and the design of the plans; moreover, it did not seem sensible to let an account of Nordic urban planning stop at 1915. The Swedish chapter, however, comes closer to the original idea than the others: one fairly long section is devoted to planning legislation and the planning system, and the period 1860–1910 is given comparatively greater prominence.

Our source material consists chiefly of earlier studies, in some cases our own. In addition three of the authors, Erik Lorange, Ole Thomasen and Mikael Sundman have taken an active part in the processes which they describe. The first two are also professors of planning. All the contributors have previously written widely on the topics discussed here.

In writing these chapters and in our editorial discussions of the texts, we have been careful to see that all facts are adequately supported. Our decision not to include notes depended on the language factor: practically all our sources are written in one or other of the Nordic languages. Moreover, access to most of the sources is difficult for anyone outside the Nordic countries. It thus seemed unnecessary to burden the book with a note apparatus. Instead we have included an annotated bibliography to each country.

There may not always seem much point in describing and analysing plans which the reader cannot see. However, the number of illustrations in a book of this type has necessarily to be restricted. We have therefore had to reject many pictures which we would like to have included.

This book has received financial support from several sources. It would not have been possible for me to fulfil my editorial function, or to write the Swedish chapter, without the economic support I have received from the Swedish Research Council for the Humanities and Social Sciences. The Letterstedt Society has helped to cover our expenses, and the Nordisk Kulturfond has paid for the translation.

A great many people have participated in producing this book. Of these I would particularly like to thank Nancy Adler, our translator and constantly patient English-language mentor.

REFERENCES

Cherry, G. E. (1982) *The Politics of Town Planning*. Harlow: Longman.
Sutcliffe, A. (1981) *Towards the Planned City: Germany, Britain, the United States and France, 1780–1914*. Oxford: Basil Blackwell.

Thomas Hall
University of Stockholm

CONTRIBUTORS

THOMAS HALL has been employed by the Swedish Research Council for Humanities and Social Sciences as a research fellow. Currently he is head of the department of Art History at Stockholm University. His main research field is urban planning in various periods. His publications include a doctoral thesis on the mediaeval development of Stockholm and further *Mittelalterliche Stadtgrundrisse, Versuch einer Übersicht der Entwicklung in Deutschland und Frankreich* (2nd ed., 1980), '. . . *on a national scale', Studies on the Redevelopment of Stockholm's City Centre* (1985), *Planung Europäischer Hauptstädte, Zur Entstehung des Städtebaues im 19. Jh.* (1986). In 1989, he was awarded the prize 'critic of the year' by the National Association of Swedish Architects for his articles on current planning and building issues.

BO LARSSON is an architect, employed as a lecturer at the Institute of Town and Landscape Planning at the School of Architecture at the Royal Academy of Fine Arts in Copenhagen, and he is also practising as a town planning consultant. He has worked for the town planning office in Malmö, Sweden, and he is one of the authors of the plan for the new town of Alsike near Uppsala, Sweden. His research work includes a comparative analysis of comprehensive planning and the design of dwelling areas and urban renewal projects in the four Nordic metropolitan areas (Copenhagen, Helsinki, Oslo and Stockholm). He has published several papers, reports and articles on planning in Danish and Swedish periodicals.

ERIK E. LORANGE is an architect and former professor of Urban Planning at the Oslo School of Architecture (retired 1986). From 1947 to 1950 he was deputy director in the authority responsible for the replanning of the war-damaged towns. From 1950 to 1965 he was Chief Planner in Kristiansand, and from 1965 he was head of regional planning in the county of Vestfold, until his appointment as professor in 1971. In 1962, while on leave from Kristiansand, he worked as a UN Town Planning Adviser on slum clearance and redevelopment in Singapore. His books include *Regional tenkning* (1977), *Byen i landskapet – Rommene i byen* (1984) and *Historiske byer* (1990). He has published numerous articles on planning in Nordic periodicals.

JAN EIVIND MYHRE is a historian, currently employed at the Historical Institute, University of Oslo. He has published several books on Norwegian urban history, and has recently published a general history of Oslo (Kristiania) 1814–1900, *Hovedstaden Christiania* (*Christiania, the Capital*), Oslo, 1990.

MIKAEL SUNDMAN is an architect and has been employed at the Helsinki Town Planning Office since 1971. He has also been a lecturer at the Institute of History of Architecture at the Helsinki School of Architecture and at the Helsinki College of Industrial Design. He has written extensively on urban planning, for instance *Stages in the Growth of a Town* (1982).

OLE THOMASSEN is an architect and former professor at the Institute of Town and Landscape Planning at the School of Architecture at the Royal Academy of Fine Arts in Copenhagen. He is a former head of the Master Planning Office of Copenhagen. He was visiting professor in urban planning at the Technical High School of Norway in Trondheim in 1955 and in Nairobi in 1969–70. He has published several works on planning.

1

THE NORTH – DOES IT EXIST?

Thomas Hall

In this book we have tried to describe the main lines in the planning history of Nordic towns. We should therefore perhaps start by discussing what is meant by 'the North' or 'the Nordic countries' today, and to indicate some of the chief events in the history of this part of the world.

The concept of 'the North' includes Denmark together with the Faröe Islands, Finland, Iceland, Norway and Sweden ('Scandinavia' includes Denmark, Norway and Sweden only). With their 22.7 million inhabitants (1984), the Nordic countries have a fairly modest population, but they cover an area more than twice the size of any single West European country. Does 'the North' exist as a social, cultural and political unit, or is it simply an honorary title, an idea lacking any real substance? There is no clear-cut answer to this question. It is possible to identify parallel or similar features between the Nordic countries as well as differences, and to point out areas of effective collaboration and others in which contact is weak or even non-existent.

PARALLELS AND DIFFERENCES

Let us disregard Iceland and the Faröe Islands in the present context and limit ourselves to Denmark, Finland, Norway and Sweden. In many respects the four countries look back on a shared history, albeit one frequently touched by armed conflict. They have similar political systems and a similar political culture, although Finland has a president who possesses real power, while Denmark, Norway and Sweden have retained their royal families as a political ornament. The languages, apart from Finnish, are also closely related. Swedish is still an official language in Finland and for a minority of the population it remains the mother tongue, but the proportion of Finns unable to speak any Swedish appears to be increasing rapidly.

Working through the Nordic Council, an advisory co-operative body elected by the Nordic parliaments, and the Nordic Council of Ministers, which is concerned with collaboration at government level, much has been achieved in harmonizing legislation and activities in many areas of society. Among the most important and spectacular results have been that Nordic citizens may live and work in any of the Nordic countries without special permits on the same conditions as the country's own citizens and with rights to the same social benefits. To cope with more run-of-the-mill co-operative activities, over a hundred different units have been set up to cover most aspects of society. Examples in the area of planning and building are Nordplan (the Nordic Postgraduate Planning Institute), an institute located in Stockholm for the further education of planners, and the Nordic Institute for Regional Policy Research. Apart from the more official types of collaboration there is also a good deal of close co-operation between political groups, trade unions and other non-commercial organizations, while many Nordic firms operate in two or more of the four countries.

But there are also obvious differences between the Nordic countries. This even applies to their geography. Denmark is predominantly flat. Norway's landscape, rising to an average height of about 500 metres, is dominated by fjords and mountains; the only fairly large areas of unbroken lowland are to be found around the Oslo and Trondheim fjords. Finland has a broad and fairly flat coastal plain, behind which lies a plateau covered in lakes to the south, and to the north a high mountain landscape. Sweden includes a variety of landscape types: along the border with Norway lie mountains which gradually give way to lower wooded regions towards the coast; to the south of this area there are both mountainous and wooded regions and plains, while the far south consists of a sedimentary plateau like Denmark's. As a direct result of these geographical conditions, Denmark is densely built-up, while the other countries include extensive deserted areas, and except in certain regions are sparsely built; this situation causes major problems in regional policy.

On defence and foreign policy the Nordic countries have adopted different lines. After the Second World War attempts were made to establish a defensive Scandinavian pact, but with their recent memories of the defencelessness of the Nordic countries, Norway and Denmark decided to join NATO. For Finland a good stable relationship with the Soviet Union was and still is felt to be the overriding goal; in 1948 Finland had to agree to the so-called 'pact of friendship and mutual military aid'. Sweden has maintained her traditional policy of non-alignment, which also has important implications for Finland and thus for the North as a whole. These diverse bloc affiliations were the main reason for the most notable setback to

Nordic co-operation to date, namely the failure to establish an economic union in NORDEK in 1970. Negotiations about a customs union broke down as early as the 1950s, but it was possible in any case to abolish barriers to trade within the framework of the European free trade organizations, although Denmark – unlike Sweden and Norway – followed England into the European Community.

Relations between the European Community and those Nordic countries, which so far have remained outside, have long been in the melting-pot, and a solution can presumably be expected in the early 1990s. Perhaps as a result of perestroika even Finland will be able to join in the European cooperation to an extent that would have been unthinkable only a few years ago.

The similarity between the Nordic languages is another area where more might have been expected, in this case in facilitating the exchange of information and cultural contacts between the countries. In fact, however, Danish, Norwegian and Swedish are too similar to be taught as 'foreign' languages in school, but are still sufficiently dissimilar to make reading more arduous. In any sizeable bookshop in the Nordic countries you will generally find shelf after shelf of books in English, and at least one of literature in German and French. But you will probably find very little in the other Nordic languages. If any of the literature of the other Nordic countries is included at all, it will probably be in translation. Similarly foreign programmes on television or at the cinema are predominantly non-Nordic. A plan for distributing the domestic television output in each other's countries has met with powerful opposition, particularly in Sweden. You can generally find newspapers from the other Nordic countries at any major outlet, but they are expensive. And the coverage in the media of developments in the other Nordic countries is pretty scant; only major events get a mention. In the Stockholm daily newspapers, for example, British domestic policy receives far more attention than current policies in the neighbouring Nordic countries.

This relative lack of interest in the other Nordic countries is not restricted to the mass media. Most artists, researchers and various professional experts are likely to have better contacts outside the North than with their Nordic colleagues, and many university courses give Nordic material short shrift. This probably has something to do with the other Nordic countries being neither 'home' nor 'abroad'. To anyone seeking contact beyond their own borders, the countries outside the North probably offer more of a contrast to conditions at home and are thus more interesting than the next-door neighbours in the North.

Finally it should be remembered that southernmost Denmark and northernmost Norway are about as far from one another as Denmark is from North Africa. Such great distances are naturally also accompanied by variations in living patterns: for example, Denmark is more 'continental' in atmosphere than the rest of the North.

There is thus something of a paradox in the idea of 'the North'. Both success and failure have marked the various attempts at unity: in many areas the Nordic countries have collaborated closely, in others their plans for co-operation have never got beyond the blue-print stage. We can perhaps conclude that the keen interest in the idea of the North, which leading politicians of various shades have evinced, has resulted in a collaborative apparatus whose actual content does not always correspond to intentions.

Is it possible, then, to speak of a Nordic urban planning tradition? We shall address this question in the concluding remarks. Without anticipating this discussion, we would nevertheless suggest here that no other group of states in Europe lends itself as well as this one to a common study in a single context.

UNIONS AND WARS

The history of each country is touched upon in the respective chapters. But something should perhaps also be said about the history of the North and the Nordic concept. Over the centuries that succeeded the end of the Viking age, the countries now known as Denmark, Norway and Sweden emerged as loosely organized states. The oldest and most advanced was the Danish kingdom which included large parts of present-day Sweden. Norway included Iceland and Greenland as well as Bohuslän, the present Swedish county north of Göteborg. Sweden's interest was turned towards the east, and during the thirteenth century Finland came under Swedish dominion. Fighting naturally occurred now and then among the three kingdoms, but there does not seem to have been any really deep or permanent conflict between them.

The idea of co-operation in the North seems to be almost as old as the Nordic kingdoms themselves, and it was even fairly easy to achieve in various personal unions, since the social structure, the language, the religion and the legal systems of the three countries were very similar. During the period when the Nordic kingdoms were establishing themselves, several unions occurred in various combinations but none of them lasted very long. This had more to do with the generally insecure position of the kings than with any fundamental opposition to the idea of union. Nevertheless a union was established in 1380 between Denmark and Norway, which was to persist until the beginning of the nineteenth century and which made Norway at least a *de facto* vassal of Denmark. In 1397 the three countries were united in the 'Union of Kalmar', by agreeing on a common regent in what remains one of the most controversial and fascinating events of the Middle Ages in the North. The fifteenth century was dominated by conflict between the Danish-Norwegian kings who periodically ruled Sweden and various Swedish constellations which saw their interests threatened by the aspirations of the union kings. Mediaeval union ambitions came to a dramatic end in the 'Stockholm Bloodbath' of 1520. The Danish King Kristian II captured Stockholm and then had about eighty of his leading opponents beheaded at the time of his coronation, to which they had been invited with an amnesty in prospect. The result of course was to rally the populace to the Swedish cause; within a couple of years Kristian had been expelled and an independent Swedish kingdom established. It was three hundred years before · the idea of a pan-Nordic union was raised again.

The sixteenth, seventeenth and eighteenth centuries are a dark period in the history of internal relations in the North. The two powers, Denmark-Norway and Sweden (with Finland), were ruthless opponents in war and diplomacy, neither of them hesitating to collaborate with its neighbour's enemies elsewhere. During these wars the border provinces suffered widespread devastation. At the beginning of the period Denmark was the stronger, but during the seventeenth century the emphasis shifted and Denmark-Norway lost the coastal counties bordering on Sweden. In the end the boundaries between the three countries had acquired their definitive form. The frequent wars served to buttress negative attitudes between Denmark and Sweden – attitudes which continued to affect historiography into modern times and which persisted in the school books of both countries for a very long time.

The Napoleonic wars had dramatic consequences in the North: the two powers which had existed since the Middle Ages were split into four. As a result of the Treaty of Tilsit in 1807, Alexander I was given a free hand in the North and Sweden was compelled to cede Finland to the Tsar, under whom it became an autonomous dukedom. The loss of Finland was one of the main reasons why in 1810 Sweden chose the French marshal Jean-Baptiste Bernadotte as heir to the Swedish throne (he was subsequently known in Sweden as Karl Johan). But Berna-

dotte recognized the political and military impossibility of reconquering Finland. Instead he succeeded in getting the allied enemies of France to agree to the incorporation of Norway with Sweden; in 1814 Denmark was forced to agree to this, but was allowed to retain Iceland and Greenland. In this way these two countries were separated from Norway. Norway, on the other hand, was not prepared to accept the settlement and in 1814 proclaimed itself a constitutional monarchy on – for the times – liberal lines (the Eidsvoll Constitution). This triggered a Swedish attack in what proved to be the last war between any of the Nordic states. An agreement was reached before much fighting had taken place, however, whereby Norway accepted Karl-Johan as their king in return for recognition of their new constitution.

During the nineteenth century the prevailing nationalistic and liberal currents affected relations between the Nordic countries in several ways. During the second half of the century resentment in Norway at the enforced union with Sweden was growing, although the country was autonomous in every way except as regards foreign policy. After various 'episodes' in which both the countries were driven by pride and prestige, the union was dissolved in 1905 to the relief of both parties. In Finland nationalism revealed itself in opposition to the policy of Russification which was periodically launched from St Petersburg, and in attempts to break with the cultural heritage from Sweden, the former mother country, and to discover a Finnish identity.

Although Norway and Finland were inclined to emphasize their distinctive historical and cultural character and particular political interests, 'Scandinavianism' showed another face: it stressed the common elements in the history and cultural development of the Scandinavian countries, often invoking the Union of Kalmar and calling for political collaboration with a view to establishing a united Scandinavian state. Scandinavianism was strongest in

Denmark. In Sweden it was supported with great enthusiasm in university circles, but even other groups were influenced sporadically by Scandinavian ideas. Norway was far less interested, while in Finland any pan-Nordic movement was precluded on political grounds.

The acid test of Scandinavianism came with the Danish-German conflict regarding Schleswig and Holstein. The Danes counted on military support from Sweden-Norway. During the 1848–49 war some Swedish-Norwegian troops were sent to help the Danes, but they took no part in the actual fighting. Their task was limited to the defence of Denmark proper. In 1863 Denmark adopted the so-called November Constitution, which in practice meant making Schleswig part of Denmark, and this time the expected Swedish-Norwegian help was not forthcoming. After a series of military setbacks the Danes were forced to cede Schleswig, Holstein and Lauenburg to Prussia, and Scandinavianism had lost its credibility. Nonetheless it had evidently helped to dispel a good deal of the suspicion which had been accumulating for so many centuries, and towards the end of the nineteenth century the foundations were laid for the more recent collaborative arrangements, for example by establishing a Scandinavian postal union. Nordic conferences and congresses on various topics, including meetings between architects, also became common. In such events Finland, too, would often take part.

The budding labour movement, with its internationalistic bent, was also quick to establish inter-Nordic contacts.

During the First World War the Scandinavian countries remained neutral. The common policy was expressed in identical declarations of neutrality and in the meetings between the three kings in Malmö in 1914 and in Kristiania in 1917. For Finland the fall of the Tsar brought liberation from Russia. After the war Denmark regained the Danish-speaking part of Schleswig.

During the 1920s Nordic collaboration made little progress but during the 1930s interest revived, not least because of the growing threats from outside. Among other things regular ministerial meetings began to be held at this time. Finland was also more closely involved than before. From 1940 to 1945 Norway and Denmark were occupied by the Germans and Finland had to fight two wars with the Soviet Union. Sweden did not get drawn into the war. Finland suffered most and was compelled to cede extensive areas to the Soviet Union, as well as having to pay heavy war damages.

The Second World War seems to have promoted a sense of community among the Nordic countries which had not existed before, thus laying the foundations for the co-operative enterprises briefly outlined here. A milestone was the establishment of the Nordic Council in 1952.

2

URBAN PLANNING IN DENMARK

Bo Larsson and Ole Thomassen[1]

PRE-INDUSTRIAL BEGINNINGS

Compared to the other Scandinavian countries, Denmark is small and without any great contrasts in its landscape. It has no mountain ranges or vast forests, no uninhabited areas or complex lake systems such as Finland, Norway and Sweden all possess. In area Denmark is less than 10 per cent the size of Sweden and about 12–13 per cent of Finland or Norway, although its population of five million is bigger than that of either of these two countries. Denmark is intensively cultivated with dwellings almost everywhere. No house is ever very far from its neighbour, but on the other hand most urban communities are fairly small. There are only about twenty urban agglomerations with more than 30,000 inhabitants, and of these one, the capital city in the eastern corner of the kingdom, accounts for more than one-third of the total urban population.

Denmark's most characteristic feature is that it consists of several islands – the largest being Sjælland and Fyn – together with the Jylland peninsula connecting the country with continental Europe. Nowhere in Denmark is the distance to the coast more than 50–60 km. Denmark consists of lowlands and gentle slopes; the highest point is 173 m above sea level. Man has shaped the landscape by cultivating the soil, planting forests, lining the roads with trees and securing the coasts against the natural forces of the sea.

Although relatively small in a Nordic context, Denmark's development and settlement patterns have been determined by certain characteristic topographical features. Almost everywhere the coast provided occasion for early settlement, even where the sea is rough as it is along the west coast of Jylland. Most of the coast here has been formed, by water and wind, into broad sandy beaches with long parallel spits of sand, but with limited opportunities for farming to supplement fishing. Conditions were different along the long fjords and rivers cutting inland in eastern Jylland and on the larger islands. Here the soil was very fertile, and fishing and agriculture could develop prosperously side by side. At the head of the fjords early settlements could develop more safely than along the open coast, and communications by waterway and river to the interior of the country were good.

Some of the earliest Danish towns such as Hedeby, Roskilde, Haderslev, Næstved, Ålborg and Randers, grew up at the heads of the various deeply penetrating fjords. They were at one time seaports, and also marked the confluence of the oldest roads of the interior. Other early towns such as Ribe, Århus and Odense developed at river estuaries or on

1. Bo Larsson is the principal author of this chapter. However, Ole Thomassen prepared the original outline and has continuously supervised the work.

navigable rivers. Some of these towns appear to have been planned structures, but most of them have developed spontaneously as small communities based on fishing and agriculture. In the ninth century Hedeby was surpassed by the new coastal settlement of Schleswig which became one of the main trade centres in the Baltic region.

Around 1100 there were at least twelve settlements in Denmark that could be described as towns according to the conditions of the times. In many of the earliest towns a considerable part of the original street pattern has survived. The patterns varied: there might be a small agglomeration of buildings protected by a primitive semicircular rampart as at Hedeby and Århus, or a town could be built along a system of roads leading to a river-crossing as at Randers, or there might be a central core with buildings along a radial road system such as Slagelse, or often there were single roadside towns on the coast with narrow passages to the shore. The buildings, single or in rows, were built in the available materials – wood, clay or mud and wattle combined. Archaeological reconstructions have given us some impression of the appearance of the original townscapes. In the tenth century Ribe developed to become an important North Sea harbour.

This was also the time when the Danish provinces were being successively united, combining the power of several lesser chieftans to form a single country. This was followed by an early attempt to establish a national defence plan against internal enemies as well as foreigners coming by sea. The long coastline in particular was vulnerable to pirate attack. The fortresses of Copenhagen, Kalundborg and Vordingborg were built to provide a triangle of defence for Sjælland, while the fortresses of Malmö in Skåne and Nyborg on Fyn were also erected to protect the important west-east road from Ribe and Jylland across Fyn and Sjælland to Roskilde, Lund and the provinces east of Øresund, which at that time were Danish. The foundation

of Copenhagen as a major town was also part of the royal 'regional' policy. Its aim was to make Copenhagen a permanent settlement and market-place, based on the autumn herring markets on both sides of Øresund which attracted merchants from all over northern Europe.

The political stabilization of the country and the reinforcement of the military defence of the littoral were followed in the thirteenth century by a rapid increase in the number of towns. The new towns, encouraged by the favourable terms of trade as well as the royal town-planning policy, were generally close to the coast and their sites were chosen with a view to the combined possibilities of production and trade. This urban development was also an effect of the German colonization of the Slavonic regions east of the Elbe, starting with the foundation of Lübeck in the middle of the twelfth century. Over the next two centuries hundreds of new towns and settlements south and east of the Baltic reinforced the trade links between many of the Danish towns and the new colonized areas. Lübeck surpassed Schleswig in importance and was soon the main centre for trade and navigation in the Baltic and one of the leading Hanseatic towns.

During the twelfth century about ten agglomerations were granted town privileges, and during the thirteenth century more than forty towns were founded. Almost half the towns that lie today within the present borders of Denmark were granted town status between 1100 and 1300. Many of them were protected by castles and fortifications. In some towns the church was built as a fortress. Many of them grew up on older roads, which then became their main streets. Along these streets the buildings were densely packed, with continuous façades. Gardens and stores faced on to the back streets, parallel to the main street. In many coastal towns the main street was parallel to the coastline and usually connected with the docks and harbours by narrow cross-alleys. The first market-places were formed by a broadening of the

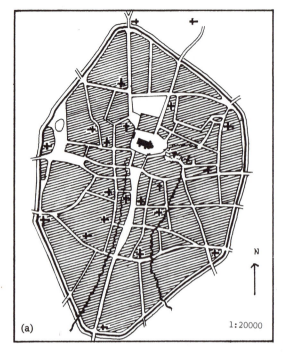

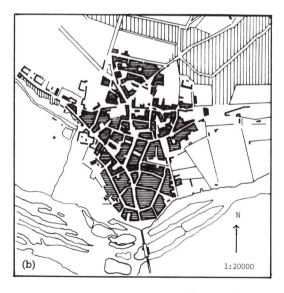

Figure 2.1. Mediaeval towns.
(*a*) Lund around 1300 with many churches and a surrounding wall (Lund is now Swedish). *Source*: Based on a map by Ragnar Blomquist (1946), published in Authén Blom (1977).
(*b*) Randers in 1860. *Source*: Based on *Trap Danmark* 1860s.

street in front of a church, or by a street crossing, or a fork.

German town-planning principles began to influence Danish towns towards the end of the thirteenth century. The market-place was given a more dominant position. The street system was more regular than before, and the buildings were grouped in blocks with dense structures on all sides. The location of the church was often subordinated to the street system, with the church placed in one of the regular blocks. The town hall was generally built in the market square.

The fourteenth century was on the whole a period of economic stagnation and few towns were founded. In the fifteenth century conditions improved, and the king supported the Danish merchants in their competition with the Hanseatic League. In 1422 towns were granted monopoly rights to trade, crafts and navigation. The importance of Øresund as an international thoroughfare was growing steadily as new types of ships made navigation safer round Skagen at the northern tip of Jylland. This also meant the decline in the importance of Ribe and later of Lübeck as centres of trade and navigation, while cities such as Malmö, Ålborg and Odense were expanding. The development of the Øresund area was promoted by Copenhagen's status as the royal capital, encouraging the development of Helsingborg and the founding of the new town of Landskrona. The importance of Helsingør increased considerably as a result of the Øresund toll. Kronborg Castle and several monasteries were built. Helsingør developed according to a gridiron plan, in continuation of the original thirteenth-century street pattern.

In the sixteenth century the royal power, now much strengthened, was behind the foundation of a few new towns. In Hillerød and Skanderborg, for instance, agglomerations grew up round new castles built to serve the king and his court as they travelled round the kingdom. But it was in the seventeenth century, mainly during the reign of Christian IV, that the most important additions to the mediaeval town pattern were made. The king tried to encourage Danish trade by founding new towns as commercial centres and fortifications at the same time. The Renaissance concept of town planning now became influential in Denmark: the street plan had to follow a strict geometrical pattern and the town had to be surrounded by fortifications, which were designed according to the latest military technology and with an aesthetic application of the geometrical principles.

Among the most important examples of seventeenth-century town planning were the fortified towns of Fredericia in Jylland and Kristianstad in Skåne, the scholarly centre for noblemen at Sorø on Sjælland, and above all the major additions that were gradually being made to Copenhagen. These last consisted of the new districts of Bremerholm (1606) and Christianshavn (1617), the extended fortification system and the districts of Frederiksstaden after 1640 and Frederiksholm after 1660, and in the two last decades of the century also the extension of the Christianshavn ramparts round a new naval harbour. In the 1630s dwellings were built for the marine soldiers. Many of these rows of houses are still in use as dwellings today, with the addition of a second storey.

Fredericia was founded in 1649 and located at the most important road junction in the country. The town was destroyed by the Swedish in 1657. As the replanning and rebuilding was beginning in the 1660s, Denmark had already lost the provinces east of Øresund on the Swedish mainland, and the government was considering moving the capital to the new and now centrally located town. However, these plans were abandoned. Nevertheless Fredericia grew, having acquired a reputation as a place of refuge for foreign or threatened groups such as Jews, Roman Catholics or members of the Reformed Church. With its regular gridiron street layout and its well-preserved fortifications Fredericia is the most typical Renaissance town to be seen in Denmark today. Christianshavn

and Kristianstad were built according to the Dutch pattern, with mercantile buildings along canals. Several other towns besides Kristianstad were built in provinces that were later separated from Denmark.

Towards the end of the seventeenth century Denmark's economic situation weakened, while the economic and political power was becoming concentrated in fewer hands and fewer towns. Many towns lost much of their importance and declined, while larger ones such as Copenhagen and Ålborg prospered. The colonial wars between England and France gave more scope to Danish free trade, encouraging the development of strong commercial capitalism and economic centralization to the capital city.

The king favoured Copenhagen and granted it sole rights to a substantial part of the country's foreign trade. During the eighteenth century several monumental buildings were constructed and squares were laid out, for example Christiansborg Castle, Amalienborg Castle, and the square known as Kongens Nytorv. In Frederiksstaden, one of the new parts of the town, Baroque and Rococo palaces were built as well as new mercantile houses. After three great fires in the mediaeval part of the town – one of them after the English bombardment in 1807 – many of the streets were regulated and new buildings erected.

It was also during the eighteenth century that the first real industrial agglomeration was founded: Frederiksværk grew up round a cannon foundry with royal privileges, which was to become a major export enterprise. The cannon were part of the lucrative 'triangular trade' in iron goods, slaves and sugar. The sugar from the West Indies and other goods from Denmark's growing foreign trade arrived in the new warehouses and factories in Christianshavn and the other expanding harbour areas, which were an important element in the centralization of Copenhagen's urban development.

Another type of settlement, the well-preserved

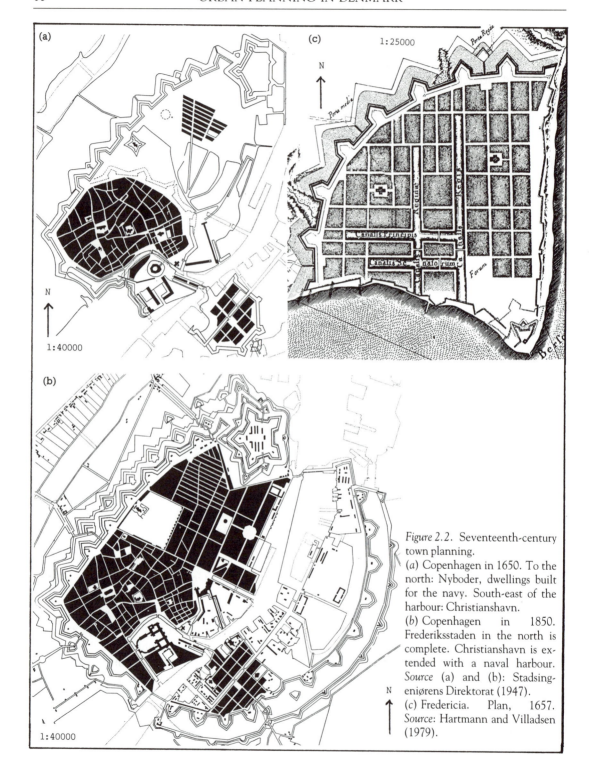

Figure 2.2. Seventeenth-century town planning.

(*a*) Copenhagen in 1650. To the north: Nyboder, dwellings built for the navy. South-east of the harbour: Christianshavn.

(*b*) Copenhagen in 1850. Frederiksstaden in the north is complete. Christianshavn is extended with a naval harbour. *Source* (a) and (b): Stadsingeniørens Direktorat (1947).

(*c*) Fredericia. Plan, 1657. *Source*: Hartmann and Villadsen (1979).

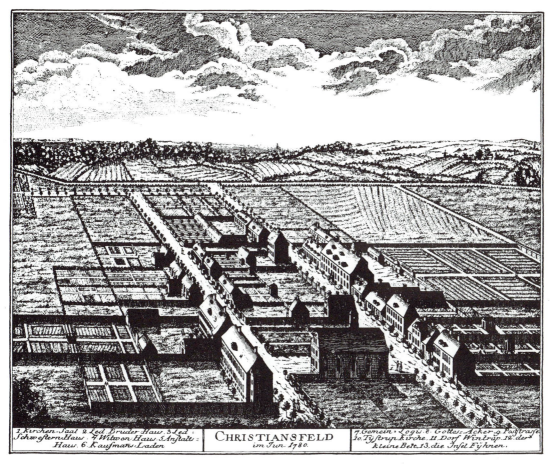

Figure 2.3. A village from the period 1770–1850. Christiansfeld. A Hernhutian settlement, founded in 1772. Print from 1780. *Source*: Hartmann and Villadsen (1979).

and homogeneous village of Christianfeld, was founded by the Herrnhutians in South Jylland in 1771–73. It was built along two parallel streets and has several splendid buildings, but was never granted town rights. Among the few new urban settlements of the century we should also mention Hørsholm.

Among the most remarkable planning activities of this period were the royal highways in North Sjælland and the planned system of castles and manor houses in the region. Near Copenhagen, Frederiksberg Castle was the centre of a system of roads. This eighteenth-century investment in royal building and road construction has greatly influenced the later urbanization of North Sjælland. Most of the royal highways of the eighteenth century are important main roads today.

In 1801 more than half the urban population of Denmark lived in Copenhagen. At that time the capital had 100,000 inhabitants. The city continued to grow, and in 1850 had a population of about 150,000 living within the seventeenth-century fortifications. The exploitation of the plots within the city boundary had been rapidly increasing. New storeys were added to existing houses along the streets, and new buildings were erected in the courtyards. Population

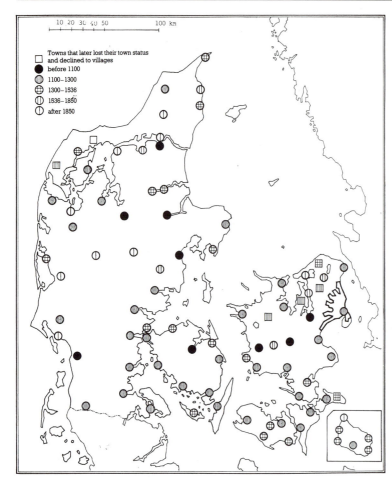

Figure 2.4. The Danish urban system.

(*a*) The age of the Danish towns (within the present borders of the country). Most towns were founded before 1536. *Source:* Based on several sources, for example Lorenzen (1947–1957).

density consequently reached alarming proportions, and hygienic conditions deteriorated. A severe cholera epidemic struck the city at the beginning of the 1850s.

Buildings from the first half of the nineteenth century are still a typical feature of the streets in the old part of the city. Classical architecture with light-coloured façades and little ornament predominated. In many provincial towns such as Odense, Nyborg and Varde classical buildings are still a dominant element in the townscape.

Many small and medium-sized towns were growing slowly but steadily. The north Jylland fishing village of Fladstrand had become an important harbour, and was renamed Frederikshavn. The last town to be founded during the Age of Absolutism was also the first factory town, Silkeborg. The paper manufacturer, Drewsen, established several enterprises here. Dwellings for his employees were built round the factories, so that Silkeborg was planned from its start in the 1840s according to a gridiron street layout.

The first railway, between Copenhagen and Roskilde, was inaugurated in 1847, thus opening a new era in urban and industrial development.

The following sections deal with five rather well-defined historical periods. Each begins

Figure 2.4.
(*b*) The urban system and the railways. The majority of the communities with more than 1000 inhabitants (1983) are located along the railways. Many of them developed as railway communities. *Source*: Based on population statistics and older railway maps.

with a general introduction to the period, followed by discussion of the metropolitan area, the three major cities of Århus, Odense and Ålborg, and of the other provincial towns. In this way it is possible to compare the planning development in Copenhagen with that of other cities and towns of the country.

1850–1915: NEW CONDITIONS FOR URBAN GROWTH

Important political and economical changes took place in Danish society in the middle of the nineteenth century. In the new constitution of 1849 the former absolute and feudal state was replaced by a liberal system. Trade and production were freed from old regulations, and the trading privileges of the towns were abolished. There was a breakthrough in industrial production, based largely on agricultural products and production for the agricultural industry. Animal production for the export market represented a growing proportion of rural industry as a whole. Of great importance in this context was the agricultural co-operative movement, which not only promoted rational rural production, but also helped to spread sections of the industry, such as dairies and slaughterhouses, to the new expanding villages and towns. The agricultural sector became integrated into the commodity and market economy, based on the towns and railway junctions. The rapid development of banking and the introduction of joint stock companies both helped to encourage this modernization of industry including agriculture. The new banking firms, the commercial and industrial companies and the public administration made a noted impact on the physical appearance of Copenhagen and other towns with their office complexes, factories and various other buildings.

From the mid-1800s most towns were linked together by a combination of state-owned and privately financed railways. Along the railway lines the new stations gave rise to growing settlements, and these new communities played an important role as service centres for the agricultural sector. The investment in railways, new harbours, steamships and new ferry routes (including rail ferries) brought the different parts of the country increasingly close to one another. Eventually it became possible to reach any part of the country from Copenhagen in a single day.

The mechanization of agriculture freed a large section of the rural workforce, and this in turn was an important prerequisite of subsequent urbanization. The urban population as a whole increased by about 800,000 during the period 1850–1915. As they were the main junctions of the transportation network, the bigger cities grew faster than the smaller ones. Copenhagen increased by 330,000 inhabitants and the three largest provincial cities – Århus, Odense and Ålborg – by about 100,000 together. In 1915 several provincial towns (for example the east Jylland fjord towns) had around 15–20,000 inhabitants, but most towns were still small, with fewer than 5,000. After 10–15 years many new railway communities had become as big as the smaller towns, and they enjoyed a comparably high level of services. But only a few agglomerations were granted town status during this period.

Apart from the railway communities the urban pattern – except in some more recently founded towns – was almost the same as during the late Middle Ages. The settlement pattern of the rural districts, however, had altered after the land reform at the beginning of the nineteenth century and the changes in the agricultural economy. Farmland was redistributed and many farmsteads moved from the villages into the open country.

The rapid urbanization of this period was generally characterized by a lack of comprehensive planning. There were some general regulations for building construction and site planning, dealing with fire security and the height of buildings in relation to streets etc, but there was no overall planning for urban development. Most town extensions were a result of the successive subdivision and sale of private farmland to provide building lots for single-family or multi-family housing. Public planning was primarily concerned with the layout of streets and with infrastructure following the sale of property. On publicly owned land it was possible to designate parcels of land for public buildings of various kinds. But it was the planning and development of railways and harbours and the sale of private land which largely determined the structure and pattern of growth in the towns. Very often the new streets connecting the railway station with the old urban core became major shopping streets. At the same time the appearance of many towns began to change considerably due to developments in the industrial production of building materials. Smaller buildings in clay and half-timber were replaced by larger houses built in brick.

Copenhagen

In Copenhagen there was, as we have seen, strong pressure to extend urban development outside the seventeenth-century fortifications. In 1852 the military restrictions on building between the artificial lakes round Copenhagen and the royal causeway Jagtvej, 2 km further out, were abolished, and the area was opened up to exploitation. Few restrictions were imposed and some of the new suburban areas were very densely developed with blocks of flats for the working classes. Most of these buildings were five or six storeys high, with two-room flats and meagre sanitary installations. The flats were often intended to accommodate eight people or more. In other areas building speculators erected more spacious and better equipped dwellings for the affluent.

In 1856 the military functions of the fortifications around Copenhagen were abandoned, and the demolition of the town gates began. In the following decade several proposals were made for the use of the wall area and the area

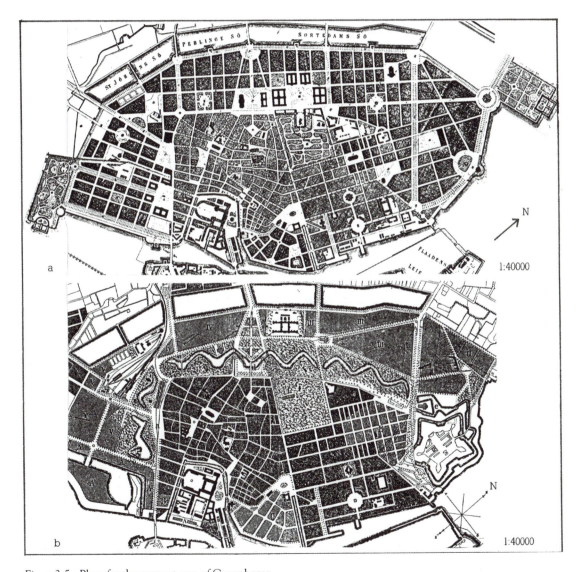

Figure 2.5. Plans for the rampart area of Copenhagen.
(*a*) C. Seidelin's plan of 1857, covering the rampart area with dense blocks. *Source*: Holm and Johansen (1941).
(*b*) F. Meldahl's plan of 1866 with a park belt along the old fortifications. *Source*: Hartmann and Villadsen (1979).

between the fortifications and the artificial lakes. These plans ranged from covering the whole area with regular blocks, squares and public buildings, to transforming most of it into parks. The final 1872 plan (revised in 1885) was a compromise, dividing the area into parks, public institutions and dense blocks. The plan showed some resemblance to the Ringstrasse plan in Vienna; both involved a system of ring boulevards. In 1867–69 the area had been sold by the military authorities to the municipality of Copenhagen, and in 1873 the selling of plots to private builders began. On the Christianshavn side the walls were preserved, and parts of them were later opened for recreational use.

The area outside the former Vesterport or West Gate was gradually integrated into the commercial and administrative city centre. Here the new town hall, the Tivoli park and the main railway station were located. Certain parts of the new blocks, for example Rådhuspladsen and Søtorvet, were given a more elaborate architectural design. Some plans for urban renewal in the old part of the city were designed as part of larger architectural projects, for example in Frederiksgade and Kongens Nytorv. Around the turn of the century a great many buildings in the old town were replaced by business and office buildings. In the smaller side streets, however, most of the architecture of the classical period was preserved.

As early as the 1850s a philanthropic housing policy for the working classes was launched, with the building of small units consisting of two-storey houses surrounded by green areas. This policy was initiated by the Medical Society (with Emil Hornemann and Frederik Ferdinand Ulrik in the van), and under the influence not only of Edwin Chadwick's 1842 *Report on an Inquiry into the Sanitary Condition of the Labouring Population in Great Britain*, but also of the contemporary housing ideas and town-planning schemes being realized in other European countries. From the late 1860s onwards this housing reform movement was taken

up by the better-paid workers, who began to organize themselves into building associations which erected low-rise housing in different parts of Copenhagen. The areas consisted of terraced houses in the *Kartoffelraekkerne* ('Potato Rows') near the eastern end of the artificial lakes round the centre of the city. However, this type of housing did not provide a model for policy in the following decades, and the working classes generally had to accept dense dark blocks without healthy open spaces.

Towards the end of the century the building legislation began to enforce tougher restrictions regarding sanitary conditions, density, light, etc., although the requirements were still fairly modest. One of the results of the new laws was the building of long narrow blocks rather than the earlier deeper blocks with buildings in yards behind. Some of the first residential areas for the upper bourgeoisie were now being developed to the north along the Øresund coast.

The building associations mentioned above gradually became societies for home-owners, oriented more towards the middle class. After the turn of the century several garden suburbs (for example Vigerslev) were built, based on ideas culled from Camillo Sitte and Raymond Unwin.

These ideas also began to influence the design of block dwellings while at the same time a national Romantic style of architecture favouring heavy red brick houses became common. Buildings of this type grouped together for visual effect and with a more conscious approach to the architectural design of streets and squares can be found at Danasvej in Frederiksberg, at Amagerbro and elsewhere. Among the most important architects of this period were Charles I. Schou, Ulrik Plesner and Martin Nyrop.

Plans for expanding the railway system and the harbour determined several important aspects of Copenhagen's structure. The central railway station was moved twice, and the railway tunnel finally built under the boulevard that had replaced the fortifications round the historic town, combined with new tramways from the suburbs, provided the growing city with a major new transportation system. Later this system, together with the railway ring round the expanding suburbs, made it possible to plan the overall traffic facilities more efficiently, and important industrial areas were located along the railway in conjunction with the extension of the harbour to the north and south. These early stages of modern Danish town planning were dominated by the dynamic personality of Charles Ambt, city engineer from 1886 to 1902, who was closely involved in the work on the harbour and the railway system. He was also responsible for the development of the new sewage net in the capital.

In 1901 several large districts were incorporated into Copenhagen, which consequently tripled its area, and seven years later an international competition was held to plan the new parts of the town. The competition entries were strongly influenced by the new planning ideals introduced in Britain, Germany and elsewhere in Europe. All the award-winning projects showed a clear reaction against dense, high-rise urban development. They favoured the garden-suburb concept, and in the limited area of multi-storey housing they introduced an open green space in the interior of the blocks.

Many of the projects located industry separ-

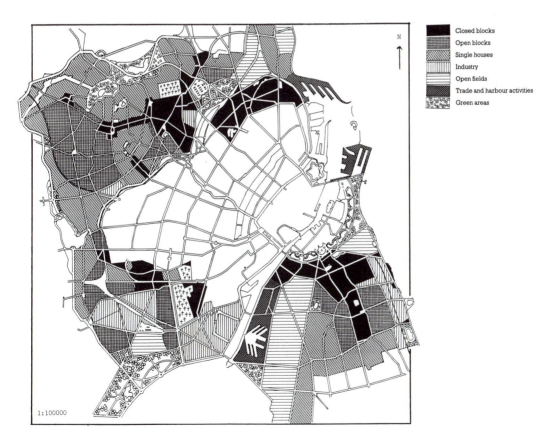

Figure 2.6. Structural planning of Copenhagen at the beginning of the twentieth century.
The second-prize project in the Copenhagen town planning competition of 1908, designed by Aage Bjerre. *Source:* Based on Stadsingeniørens Direktorat (1942).

ately in fairly large well-serviced areas, others suggested classifying streets according to different functions and facilities. Some projects made very detailed architectural proposals, while others presented a combination of land-use proposals and traffic solutions to provide a framework for later detailed planning.

The first prize went to a proposal produced by Carl Strintz, a city engineer in Bonn, who was much influenced by Camillo Sitte. His plan was very detailed, providing a carefully designed street network with squares and parks. The second prize was awarded to a rather different type of entry, a zoning plan based on a rational system of main roads with special zones for different functions or types of buildings. This plan was in many respects ahead of its time, and it was to be of crucial importance to the future development of Copenhagen, and even of other cities. The author of the plan was Aage Bjerre, a municipal town-planning engineer in Copenhagen, who was later appointed head of city planning and engineering in the capital. In this post he strongly supported various ideas taken from the different competition projects.

Århus, Odense and Ålborg

Between 1850 and 1915 Århus, Odense and Ålborg became the principal centres in their regions with populations of 45–75,000. Of the three, Ålborg was most obviously industrial, with major enterprises largely located near the harbour and railway. Small home-based workshops and medium-sized factories were also to be found in otherwise predominantly residential areas. Ålborg was a good natural harbour in its fjord, Limfjorden. In Århus, as in Copenhagen, the port was extended by reclaiming land round the old harbour. Odense acquired better conditions for navigation after the canal from the fjord was opened in 1803.

There were no comprehensive plans for the physical development of suburbs. The towns grew spontaneously along existing roads, where the breaking up of former farms gradually made way for new suburbs. Working-class districts were built in all the larger towns in Denmark, although they were not as congested as in Copenhagen. Typically they consisted of blocks of two- to four-storey buildings, with small workshops in some of the yards and private gardens in others. These districts were situated close to the old urban core. The side streets of the old towns also contained many working-class dwellings. As in Copenhagen, new single-family houses were built outside the denser urban areas. In Århus the districts to the north (Risskov) and south (Højbjerg) attracted larger single-family homes for the upper classes on account of the hilly scenery and the seaviews. Other suburbs of a more working-class character began to appear in the west during the 1890s (Åbyhøj, Viby). On the hills south-west of Ålborg, where there is a beautiful view towards the fjord, the garden suburb of Hasseris grew up.

In these towns, too, the commercial centres were largely redeveloped. Older houses of modest dimensions along the shopping streets were replaced by tall buildings, a mixture of commercial, office and residential complexes, often with ancilliary buildings with yards behind. This renewal was particularly extensive in Ålborg. Narrow alleys disappeared and the old-fashioned nature of the town was replaced by a more contemporary big-city character. The narrow rivers, the Østerå and the Vesterå, were built over by new main streets in the town centre. The Østerå was covered by the new main thoroughfare, Østergade-Boulevarden. The new street was lined with massive brick buildings. The various districts now began to be differentiated into distinct zones: shopping and business streets and back streets in the old town centres, working-class districts, middle and upper-class districts, and quite extensive industrial, harbour and railway areas. As in Copenhagen, tramway systems were established in Århus and Odense.

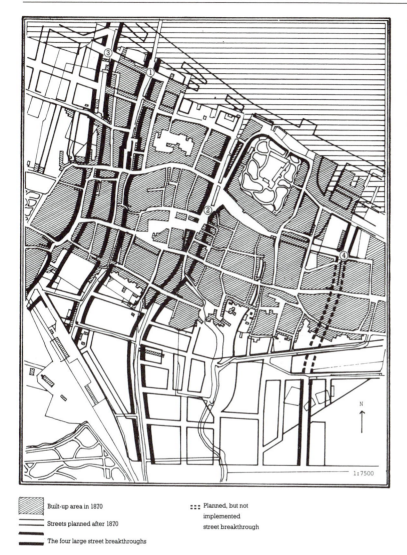

Figure 2.7. Street plans in Ålborg, shown on a map from the 1870s. *Source:* Based on *Trap Danmark* from the 1870s and later maps. (1) Vesterå; (2) Østerå-Boulevarden; (3) Vesterbro, 1933 (cf. p. 27); (4) Dag Hammarskjöldsgade (cf. figure 2.23).

Built-up area in 1870

Streets planned after 1870

The four large street breakthroughs

::: Planned, but not implemented street breakthrough

1:7500

N

Other Provincial Towns

Three important new towns were developed during the nineteenth century: Silkeborg, Esbjerg and Herning. They had different backgrounds. As was mentioned above, Silkeborg grew up round a paper mill, while Esbjerg was founded by the government in 1866 as a new harbour for the west coast. Herning evolved more spontaneously, due to certain favourable conditions. The cultivation of the Jylland heath led to a strong economic upswing in the surrounding region. The town was an important railway and road junction, as well as being the centre of an extensive textile industry. While Herning grew out along the old main roads without any town-planning concept, Silkeborg and Esbjerg evolved on the basis of gridiron plans. They are among the few Danish towns built from the start according to a fixed regular street layout.

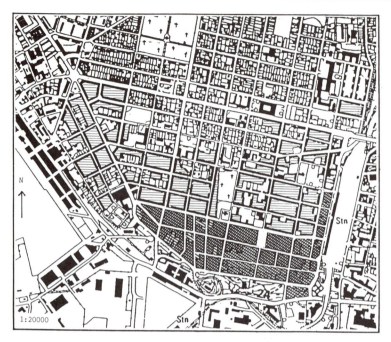

Figure 2.8. The central parts of Esbjerg today. The first stage of the gridiron plan (the darker hatched area) was approved in 1870. *Source:* Based on Hartmann and Villadsen (1979) and the topographical map of Denmark 1:25,000.

The new railway communities grew apace. By the turn of the century most of them had populations of about 500–1,000. These new settlements consisted mainly of single or two-storey brick houses. The main street, near the station, was often typically urban with houses in unbroken rows sometimes rising to more than two storeys. There was no planning and the communities were sometimes invoked as ugly examples of unplanned development. The national society *Bedre Byggeskik* (Better Building) campaigned for stricter architectural standards for new construction, and in 1909 the Association of Architects launched its 'battle against ugliness', building a 1:1 scale model of a small railway community in connection with a big national exhibition in Århus. This was an early example of the kind of urban design in which the social functions of a community are consciously reflected in the design of its buildings. The houses were constructed with a view to their specific functions, but they were all subject to a common style with features stemming from older Danish architecture. This exhibition and other similar events influenced the further development of the railway communities, not least the design of various public buildings such as railway stations, post offices and schools.

Many smaller towns were unable to compete either with the more rapidly expanding towns or with the new railway settlements. Some which had formerly enjoyed a certain importance now found themselves outside the main railway and navigation system (for example Nysted and Præstø). Their only additions consisted of a few new streets, some minor factories, and so on. Others grew more rapidly, with suburbs first growing along and later between the main roads (Nykøbing Mors, Middelfart, etc).

Several medium-sized provincial towns grew into 'mini-cities', with working-class districts consisting of low blocks of flats and residential areas for the richer classes. In the town centres new business buildings were erected and new industrial districts developed round the harbours (Randers, Vejle, Horsens, etc).

By the end of the nineteenth century new public buildings and parks featured as an important element in many provincial towns.

1915–1945: INCREASING STATE INTERVENTION IN THE ECONOMY AND PLANNING

In response to a severe building crisis before the First World War and to the growing shortage of dwellings during the war, the government and some of the local authorities launched a social housing policy around 1918. The state provided low-interest loans, and public and non-profit housing was encouraged. Several public housing associations were started. During the 1930s state intervention in the economy and in construction and planning increased. In Denmark, as elsewhere, attempts were made to solve the problems of the Great Depression by adopting a Keynesian policy for dealing with crisis. The fact that, as part of its employment policy, the government initiated the construction of several new roads and bridges had major implications for urbanization and the development of a nationwide communications system. The largest bridges were the Storstrøm Bridge (between Sjælland and Falster) and the Lillebælt Bridge (between Fyn and Jylland). Plans for bridges between Denmark and Sweden (at Copenhagen and Helsingør) were also discussed but were postponed. The railway network was fully developed by about 1930, by which time some minor lines had in fact already been closed down. Motorization was increasing slowly but steadily, and the main-road system was improved and asphalted.

During this period migration into the towns continued. Municipalities that had already been expanding most rapidly continued to do so. During the 1930s Greater Copenhagen had one million inhabitants, and the urban areas of Århus, Odense and Ålborg over 100,000 each. Many towns attained populations of 25–30,000 inhabitants. Most railway settlements also continued to grow.

In 1922 the Danish Town Planning Institute (*Dansk Byplanlaboratorium*) was founded as a semi-private organization with a library and a workshop for various activities such as discussion groups, planning, publications and courses. One of its aims, following Geddes' teaching, was that plans should be preceded by the collection of data and an analysis of the problems, and that better planning legislation should be encouraged. The first Town Planning Act (*Byplanloven*) appeared in 1925. But not until 1938 was it made obligatory to draw up both general and comprehensive plans for every town or community of more than 1,000 inhabitants. However, this obligation was not fulfilled to the same extent everywhere, and a special national committee for town-planning issues – the *Kommitterede i Byplansager* – was set up under the Minister for Housing. This committee had both advisory and supervisory functions, and under the leadership of competent architects and planners it worked successfully to improve the quality of town planning.

During the 1920s the public and non-profit housing associations had been in the van of town-planning developments. New concepts of urban design evolved: blocks with green open courtyards, terraced houses, and garden suburbs with single-family homes. Neo-classical architectural ideals were combined during this period with national Danish traditions. In the 1930s, the age of functionalism, a fundamental idea was to reinforce the human and social goals of housing policy. In Denmark these ideas were connected with the inception of a welfare policy. Here functionalism did not have the close links with the cubist style that it had in many other European countries. Most houses were build in red or yellow brick with pitched roofs. The houses were generally characterized by attention to detail and a high level of craftsmanship. The layout of of the towns was gradually altering. Closed and semi-closed blocks were being replaced by a freer and more open approach. A new type of urban design was emerging, much influenced by collaboration with landscape and garden architects, the best known being G. N. Brandt and

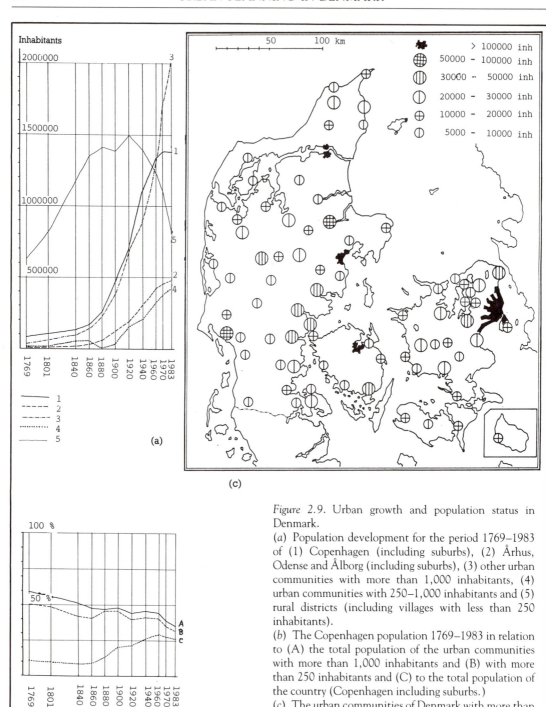

(a)

(b)

(c)

Figure 2.9. Urban growth and population status in Denmark.

(a) Population development for the period 1769–1983 of (1) Copenhagen (including suburbs), (2) Århus, Odense and Ålborg (including suburbs), (3) other urban communities with more than 1,000 inhabitants, (4) urban communities with 250–1,000 inhabitants and (5) rural districts (including villages with less than 250 inhabitants).

(b) The Copenhagen population 1769–1983 in relation to (A) the total population of the urban communities with more than 1,000 inhabitants and (B) with more than 250 inhabitants and (C) to the total population of the country (Copenhagen including suburbs.)

(c) The urban communities of Denmark with more than 5,000 inhabitants (1983). *Source*: Based on population statistics and Institut for By- og Landskabsplanlægning (1978).

C. Th. Sørenson. Housing and other buildings were planned and located in green areas, allowing for the direction of the sun. Less interest was shown in the street layout or the urban character, or in variety. Light and air were the key concepts. During the 1930s buildings were often placed strictly parallel with one another, but during the 1940s urban design became more irregular and varied.

In the 1930s the government launched a policy of public housing renewal. The general aim was to clear old congested and unhealthy areas, and to replace them by modern buildings and to concentrate on light and air. Only a few urban renewal projects had been completed before Denmark became involved in the Second World War.

Copenhagen

After the First World War the new principles of urban design were mainly realized in Copenhagen, largely by non-profit and public housing associations. Much care was devoted to comprehensive neighbourhood and site planning, and to the design of buildings and open spaces.

In the Arresøgade area the planners strove to attain varied street patterns. Until 1930 streets were still regarded as the most important feature of the townscape. But in contrast to earlier traditions, the same care was now being devoted to the courtyard façades as to the street front. Buildings were to look just as attractive when viewed from their common courtyards. The yards in the new closed blocks grew from being fairly small (Borups Allé and Struenseegade, 1919–20) to some considerable size (Hornbækhus, 1922). The new site planning of this decade had something in common with contemporary planning for housing areas in Holland by Berlage and others, but in Denmark it developed with strong neo-classical overtones.

During the 1930s the closed blocks were gradually replaced by more open structures which let more sunshine into the courtyard. Many staircases were now entered from the yard rather than from the street. The Bispebjerg district includes many forms of building that are typical of this period, ranging from large closed blocks to U-shaped and L-shaped arrangements or detached parallel buildings. The district has examples of late classical architecture (around Grundtvig church), as well as early functionalist buildings and a park type of development influenced by the Arts and Planning School *Bauhaus* in Dessau. Ryparken and Blidahparken are further examples of typical functionalist park-like developments. Among the major architects of the period were Ivar Bendtsen, Thorkild Henningsen, Edward Heiberg, Paul Baumann and Knud Hansen.

Public housing also included single-family homes, and terrace houses were introduced mainly as a result of the influence of the British housing tradition. Pioneering examples were Bakkehusene (1921) and Vibevænget (1922). Brønsparken (1940) is a terrace-house block for lower-income groups, where careful planning made space possible for a large number of dwellings within a relatively small area. After 1940 it became more common to make comprehensive plans for somewhat larger housing areas, often consisting of several types of house (for example Glumsøparken and Humlevænget). However, the planned development of larger and more independent urban units was not envisaged. Most projects involved limited additions to existing built-up areas. As a result of the developments outlined here Copenhagen grew successively beyond its municipal borders, and in the suburban communities, mainly to the north, areas with terrace houses and blocks of flats were built to a higher standard of planning.

Gradually Copenhagen's inner city was renewed. Considerable expansion of the central business district became possible when the central station was moved to its present site and an area to the north-west of the new station be-

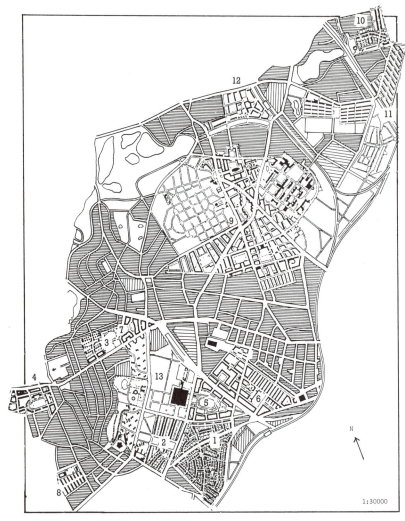

Figure 2.10. North-west Copenhagen with Bispebjerg, Bellahøj
and other blocks.
(1) Grøndals Vænge garden suburb (1914–20), (2) Bakkehusene
(1921),   (3)   Bavnevangen
(around   1920),   (4) Brønshøj
Torv (1920s), (5) Genforenings-
pladsen (1920s), (6) Vibevænget
(1922), (7) Parkstykket (1930s),
(8) Brønsparken (1940), (9) Bispebjerg (1930s and 1940s), (10)
Studiebyen (a project developing
new types of garden houses,
around 1920), (11) Ryparken
(1932–35), (12) Kantorparken
(1939–40) and (13) Bellahøj
(1950–52).
Source: Based on the topographical map of Denmark
1:25,000, with buildings shown
in the areas mentioned only.

came available. Between 1911 and 1928 several projects were worked out for developing this area. The earliest included winding streets and irregular blocks, while later plans had a stricter and more rational character. Neo-classical ideals were enjoying a renaissance at the time. In the end a fairly strict plan based on regular blocks was approved, but the development of the area proceeded rather slowly and was not completed until the 1970s. Most of the buildings in the area are standardized offices in an 'inter-national' style.

During the 1930s Knippelsbro (the older bridge over the harbour) and Torvegade were widened to make a broad thoroughfare between the city centre and the island of Amager. This was a continuation of the Ny Østergade-Bremerholm artery through the old part of the city that had been started forty years earlier. Along the north side of Torvegade, buildings – some of them 300 years old – were demolished to make way for functionalist five-storey blocks of flats. Traffic planning was cited to motivate the expropriation and demolition of slum areas.

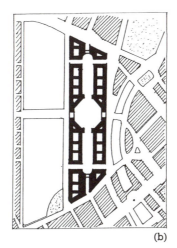
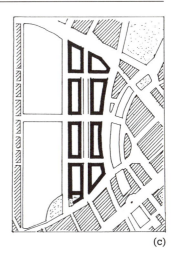

1:20000   (a)   (b)   (c)

Figure 2.11. Three plans for the old railway site at Vesterport, Copenhagen.
(a) Plan by the municipality of Copenhagen 1912, based on the first-prize plan in a town planning competition in 1910, by Egil Fischer, Holger Rasmussen and O. K. Nobel.
(b) Plan by Carl Petersen, Ivar Bendtsen and Edvard Thomsen, 1920.
(c) Plan by Edvard Thomsen, 1928, finally approved by the municipality.
Source: (a), (b) and (c): Based on Holm and Johansen (1941).

Christianshavn – a notable part of the old city – was much affected by the new thoroughfare, one of whose results was an increase in the density of traffic in the central and mediaeval parts of the city.

The Slum Clearance Act of 1939 provided new opportunities for redeveloping old quarters. The first area chosen for renewal included several blocks along Adelgade and Borgergade in the northern seventeenth-century part of the old city. Many buildings in this area were in very bad condition and lacked sanitary installations. Many of the inhabitants were poor and had considerable social problems. There was little understanding for the idea of preserving old buildings of historical interest in the area. So the aim was to replace the buildings as well as many of the inhabitants. This large-scale renewal project was launched in 1939 but was then interrupted for several years by the war, and was only completed in a somewhat changed and reduced form around 1970. The new buildings included tenement houses, business premises

and office buildings, and the density was fairly high.

The far-sighted city-planning competition of 1908 was not followed by any master plan for the municipality of Copenhagen (as required by the new planning legislation). Developments were controlled by a municipal land policy and easement clauses. Many years before the competition and the incorporation of new areas into the town, the municipality had bought up large tracts of open farmland to prevent uncontrolled urban development in the new districts. By selling land on long-term leasehold to housing co-operatives and social housing associations, the municipality was able to control the quantity of urban development and to buy back the property sold seventy to ninety years later. The repurchase price was to be the original selling price of the land plus the value of the buildings.

A successful planning policy was also implemented for parks and recreation areas. Mainly on the initiative of the Copenhagen city engineer, Olaf Forchhammer, new parks were

Figure 2.12. The first regional plans of the Copenhagen area.
(a) The regional traffic plan of 1926. *Source:* Egnsplan-rådet (1971) (supplied with the railway plan).
(b) The regional green plan of 1936. *Source:* Egnsplan-rådet (1971).

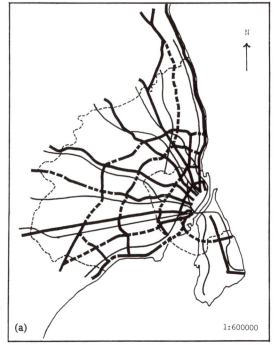

A proposed suburb railway system
Existing roads
Proposed roads

(a)   1:600000

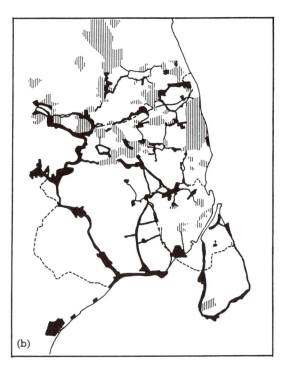

Proposed green areas
Existing green areas

(b)

connected to one another by a system of green corridors, with paths for cycling and walking. The system of main roads was also improved. A new by-pass, the Tuborgvej ring road, was constructed through the new parts of the city. The road was part of a major traffic plan for a larger region, worked out in 1926 by a team appointed by the Association of Danish Engineers (*Dansk Ingeniørforening*). The plan also included suburban railways, some of which were realized. The first electric suburban railways ('S-trains') came into operation in the 1930s, promoting the development of new suburbs along the railway lines in a finger-like radial development rather than in concentric circles as before. This provided part of the basis for the post-war regional plans.

The 1926 traffic plan was the first step towards a regional plan for Greater Copenhagen. In 1928 the Danish Town Planning Institute initiated the first regional planning committee, although without any legally formalized authority, and in 1936 this committee proposed a plan for future green areas in the Copenhagen region. It was recommended that the new park system in the central municipality should be extended to embrace a regional park and path system. This plan provided a basis for an important move towards active nature conservation policies in the region in the years to come, and many of the paths for walking and cycling were laid out during the Second World War as part of a policy to remedy unemployment.

Århus, Odense and Ålborg

In Århus rebuilding of the central railway station and renewal of the area to the north began in the 1920s, and new major traffic arteries were constructed here as well as in other towns. During the 1930s the inner part of Århus was surrounded by a ring road connecting all the main roads leading out of the town. In the urban core the new main street, Åboulevarden, was constructed over a river. New business build-

ings and blocks of flats were erected along the street.

In Ålborg a new artery, Vesterbro, was cut through the old town in 1933 and connected to the new bridges over Limfjorden. Vesterbro was winding and varied, lined with five-storey functionalist brick buildings. This road construction led to the large-scale demolition of buildings, some of which were only thirty or forty years old (cf. figure 2.7).

The change over from large closed blocks to open blocks and park districts is clearly illustrated in Århus (the Søndre Ringgade and the Marselis Boulevard district) and in Ålborg (around Sjællandsgade). These areas exhibit town-planning qualities resembling contemporary housing developments in Copenhagen.

In Odense housing was dominated by single-family homes. Immediately south of the city centre large residential areas were planned. The street network here was designed to be both rational and varied. In Århus and Ålborg new residential districts of varying social status were also developed. Hasseris outside Ålborg was extended, as were the residential districts along the coast near Århus.

Other Provincial Towns

Most provincial towns were still dominated by the old main streets. Only in the larger provincial towns, for example in Esbjerg, Randers, Horsens and Fredericia, are there any examples of the closed or open square blocks from the inter-war period. Nor were many flats being built in a parkland setting during this period here. In many provincial towns, however, non-profit housing associations built smaller blocks of flats and terrace houses. If it occurred at all, development in the smaller and medium-sized towns consisted mainly of detached houses. Many of the minor towns stagnated, merely adding some detached houses along the highways leading into the towns.

Most of the railway station settlements also

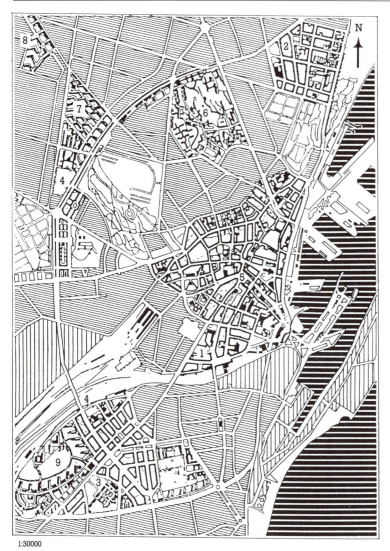

1:30000

Figure 2.13. Town planning in central Århus. (1) The district north of the railway station with the new town hall – today there are plans to develop the railway area with new buildings; (2) dense blocks of flats from around 1900 (Trøjborg); (3) the Marselis Boulevard district from the 1930s and 1940s; (4) the ring-road, flanked by inter-war buildings; (5) Åboulevarden, a street covering a little stream; (6) the university, planned by Kay Fisker and others, 1931–46; (7) Mølle-vangen, 1950s; (8) Præstehaven, 1939–41; and (9) Skanderborg-vej, 1960s. *Source*: The topographical map of Denmark 1:25,000 with buildings shown in the areas mentioned and in the old town only.

grew slowly but steadily; some reached populations of a few thousand. Among those which expanded the most are Grindsted, Skjern and Haslev. Skjern achieved town status in 1959 – the youngest in the country – eleven years before a municipal reform abolished the official term 'town'. Grindsted grew up in the middle of the Jylland heathland as a junction of six railway lines. Today only one of these is left, and that only as a goods line.

Ringsted is one of the few smaller towns, where a comprehensive town plan was prepared. The town was squashed between property owned by the church and the Classical school. After the railway was opened at some distance from the old urban core, the town developed haphazardly on the only land available for urban development. It was not until 1917 that the convenient area between the old town centre and the railway station previously held by the church became open to urban development. After a town-planning competition for this area in 1919, the winning project by Steen Eiler Rasmussen and Knud H. Christiansen was adopted. This involved closed blocks along the street axes between the market square and the station. West of the church, on the slope towards the river Ringsted, single-family houses were planned. The market square was to be redesigned to give the old church a more dominating position. However, implementation was rather slow and was not finished until the 1960s, and the plans were successively altered from closed to open blocks.

After the First World War the government followed the Esbjerg example, planning new harbours on the west coast of Jylland. In 1917 it was decided that the construction of two new harbours, Hirtshals and Hanstholm, was to go ahead. Hirtshals was to be tackled first, and as in Ringsted a town-planning competition was held in 1919, and the same architects won the first prize. The winning plan was inspired by the first English garden cities, and was based on a regular system of streets. The land was owned by the state, and land speculation was to be avoided. The government sold land to private developers, however, in order to finance the construction of the harbour. The town plan has been revised several times, and has only been realized in part.

In 1923 a town-planning competition was also held for Hanstholm. Again the prize-winning project was influenced by contemporary classi-

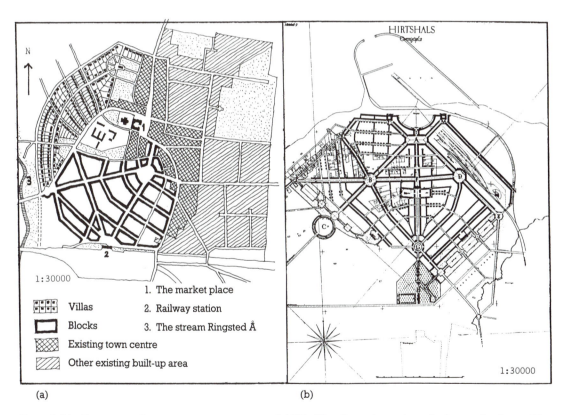

(a) (b)

Figure 2.14. Two town planning competitions around 1920. The first prize projects both won by Steen Eiler Rasmussen and Knud H. Christiansen.
(a) Ringsted, 1919. *Source:* Based on *Architecten Maanedshæfte* (1919).
(b) Hirtshals, 1922. *Source:* Hartmann and Villadsen (1979).

cal geometrical town-planning ideals, but the development of both the harbour and town of Hanstholm was delayed for several decades.

1945–1960: ECONOMIC EXPANSION AND INDUSTRIAL HOUSING

During the 1950s mechanization in the agricultural sector increased production and exports, and reduced employment. And yet agricultural production accounted for a decreasing share of Danish exports. Industrial employment was growing but was distributed unevenly over the country.

Round several towns new industrial estates were developing along modern ring roads. Motorization had not yet reached a level at which its serious consequences were obvious. The segregation and differentiation of traffic systems was still fairly limited, and there were relatively few parking spaces at shopping centres. These were designed in fairly small units and were closely integrated in the site planning, often with shops and dwellings in the same building.

During the Second World War few dwellings were built, but in the 1950s housing activity expanded again. Many towns began to extend beyond their municipal boundaries and weekend cottage communities appeared along the coast. The 1949 Regulation of Built-up Areas Act (*Byreguleringsloven*) required that special zones for urban development should be defined round the larger towns, to prevent uncontrolled urban growth and to preserve farmland and recreational resources. The towns were not allowed to extend outside these fixed limits. In urban areas embracing more than one municipality, the different local authorities had to co-operate in their planning activities.

Public and non-profit housing continued on a large scale, with rents within reasonable reach of most people. The government supported the development of industrial building methods, but traditional brick construction was nevertheless still predominant. Typical of many of the new settlements were their park landscaping, their terrace and their cluster housing. Development units were generally larger than during the inter-war period, but much care was still devoted to the details of the urban design. Most new urban areas were planned with a view to functional differentiation in land use, as prescribed by the Town Planning Act of 1938. Many new housing areas were planned as neighbourhood units with social institutions and commercial services, in the spirit of British new town planning. Experiments in new forms of collective living were also made. Only a few of the new urban units functioned entirely in accordance with the original intentions, but many were given a physical environment of high quality.

Many buildings from this period have a rather traditional Danish character, differing from most contemporary building in the other Nordic countries. But by about 1960 industrialized prefabrication and a more cosmopolitan approach to architecture was beginning to have a greater environmental impact on Danish urban development.

Copenhagen

In 1947 a regional planning committee presented its famous 'Finger Plan' for the development of Greater Copenhagen. The idea was that the capital should be extended in 'fingers' along the radial railway lines, which would mean reinforcing and regulating development trends already established earlier. Around the suburban railway stations urban units of about 10,000 inhabitants were to be developed. The major radial highways were to be built along but outside the 'fingers'.

Central Copenhagen was to remain the principal regional centre, relieved by a string of business and industrial estates outside the dense city area, along the circular railway and a proposed inner ring road. At the crossings between

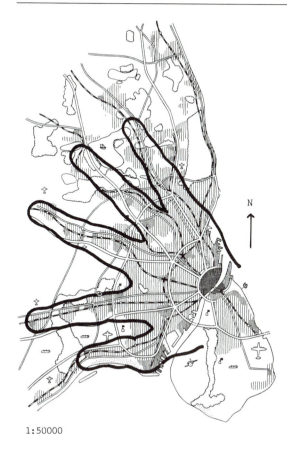

1:50000

Figure 2.15. The 'Finger Plan' of Greater Copenhagen, 1947. Darker areas: centres and industrial sites. *Source:* Rasmussen (1952).

(*byudviklingsplan*) and as such served to guide the local authorities in their zoning for urban growth. However, it proved impossible to prevent more widespread urban development, especially in the northern parts of the region, and the green wedges were eventually narrower than was intended. Also, a good deal of suburban development took place outside the regional limits of the 'Finger Plan' area.

In 1954 the municipality of Copenhagen worked out a preliminary General Plan for the central municipality in the region, based on the 'Finger Plan'. The General Plan found the municipality of Copenhagen to be almost entirely built-up, but in great need of urban renewal. The mediaeval parts of the city were to be preserved by reducing commercial development and controlling the permitted building density. Commercial activities were to expand outside this district. Existing plans for widening the streets in the old town were cancelled, but it was proposed that a larger thoroughfare along the ring of artificial lakes should surround the old city, linking the major radial roads from the suburbs. The dense residential quarters outside the commercial city centre were to be redeveloped in stages and made less compact, to begin with by demolishing old buildings and constructing new ones less densely. At that time no desire had been expressed to preserve these densely built quarters.

The preliminary General Plan never led to a final plan. It was mainly an analysis of the planning problems in Copenhagen, and a presentation of preliminary planning principles. The plan had more importance as a subject for debate among planners than as a plan for actual development. However, an important result of the plan was the reduction in building rights and the abandonment of the street-widening plans in the mediaeval city centre; both of these proposals were approved by the city council in 1959. This was followed by yet greater restrictions on major traffic and the limitation of parking in the old town core. Through traffic was

this express way and the suburban 'fingers', large service and production centres were planned, while between the 'fingers' wedges of green were to be kept. Two of the radial roads, Hareskovvejen and Hørsholmvejen, had been planned earlier as 'excursion roads' in the green zones, and these were now upgraded to become primary radial motorways.

Without any regional authority to assume responsibility for implementing the new comprehensive planning schemes the 'Finger Plan' had no actual legal basis, but in accordance with the 1949 Regulation of Built-up Areas Act the plan proposal was transformed into a zone plan

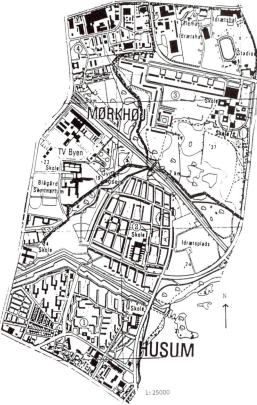

Figure 2.16. Housing areas in Greater Copenhagen from the 1950s and 1960s.
(1) Voldparken by Edvard Thomsen, 1950; (2) Tingbjerg by Steen Eiler Rasmussen and others, begun in 1956; and (3) Høje Gladsaxe by Hoff & Windinge, Juul Møller and Agertoft and Alex Poulsen, 1966. North of Høje Gladsaxe a part of (4) Gladsaxe industrial area, planned in the 1940s. *Source:* The topographical map of Denmark 1:25,000.

transferred outside the area, which made it possible successively to establish several pedestrian precincts (for example, Strøget in 1962).

The non-profit housing associations were still in the lead when it came to developing new types of urban design. New blocks of flats were grouped in informal arrangements in green areas (for example Voldparken, Hvidovreparken and Kildevænget), or in more closed and regular forms (Tingbjerg, Glostrup Vestergård). High-rise industrialized housing was introduced in Bellahøj. This housing estate

consisted of twenty-eight tower blocks grouped in green surroundings. In other localities too (Sorgenfri, Brøndbyøster) high-rise houses were the favoured form. High-rise housing, however, never became as common in Copenhagen as in Swedish cities like Stockholm and Göteberg. Many areas had a combination of high and lower buildings, or a mixture of flats, terrace houses and bungalows. In Søndergård Park different types of terrace houses and semi-detached family homes were built. The private gardens were often very tiny, while the open spaces were combined to form a common green area between the groups of dwellings. As part of the 'Finger Plan' new suburban units were built around the S-train stations, for example in Brøndbyøster and Glostrup to the west, Herlev and Ballerup to the north-west, and at Sorgenfri to the north. The buildings were generally higher and the density greater near the station than on the periphery of these suburbs. At Lyngby and Hjortekær new suburban units were built along a planned S-railway to Nærum. However, this line was never constructed and the suburbs were served by the motorway to Helsingør instead.

Provincial Towns

Several of the larger provincial towns also grew beyond their municipal borders between 1945 and 1960, and these towns drew up development plans in co-operation with neighbouring municipalities. The Ålborg area produced such a plan in 1948 and the Århus area in 1954. Here, too, the Regulation of Built-up Areas Act provided certain opportunities for controlling urban development. New main roads were drawn on the maps, and the planners generally aimed to preserve green belts between the different parts of the towns. The plans presupposed the redevelopment of large sections of the older town areas. In Århus and Ålborg new streets cutting through old quarters were delineated. The municipality of Århus proposed a main street through the city centre, from the Town Hall to Nørreport. In a wide zone along this street the old buildings were to be demolished and replaced by modern business complexes.

However, only a small part of this plan was carried out. Various models for urban expansion were discussed in Århus, for example linear urban structures, finger-like structures,

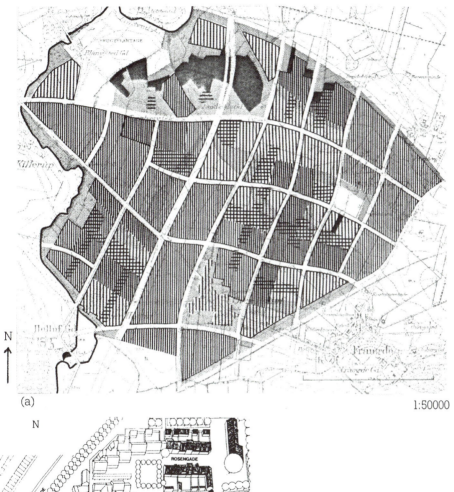

(a)   1:50000

(b)   1:3000

Figure 2.17. Town planning in Odense – some examples.
(a) The Milton Keynes inspired plan for south-east Odense, 1973. Mixed functions put into a large-scale gridiron plan. Source: Dispositions-plan for Odense Sydøst, 1973.
(b) The H. C. Andersen quarter – a conservation area separated from the town centre by Thomas B. Thriges gade. Source: Svensson (1981).

or satellite towns. In the end a further concentric development with an extended 'finger' towards the west was chosen.

The towns were extended a little at a time: in Ålborg, Odense and Århus only a few largish and comprehensively planned areas were added during the period in question. Most new dwellings were single-family houses and bungalows, but some areas of low-rise building and flats were also built. In Århus the new quarters of Møllevangen (L-shaped buildings) and Vorrevangen (mixed development) were added. Vorrevangen represents an early example of traffic segregation, with small culs-de-sac and extensive green areas. Other urban units with mixed flats and terrace houses were built in Odense (Højstrup) and Ålborg (along Hobrovej).

In most small and medium-sized towns

growth during the 1950s was modest. The existing towns were extended with the addition of detached single-family houses, and a few areas with flats and terrace houses. New bypasses were constructed outside some of the towns, and industrial estates were often planned along them. Some examples of new residential areas from this period should be mentioned: Kingoshusene in Helsingør (architect Jørn Utzon), Klostermarken and Fælledvej in Roskilde, and Kildemark in Næstved.

Two very interesting development projects in Denmark were initiated in this period, based on and organized by two new and fast growing private industrial enterprises. Near Odense where the fjord had been deepened, a big new shipyard, Lindøværftet, was established in 1957 by one of the most prosperous multi-purpose enterprises in Denmark. And concomitant with

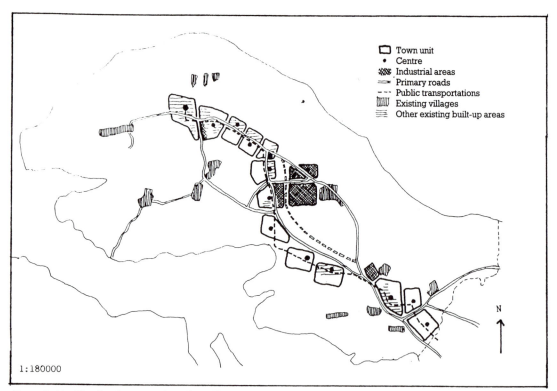

Figure 2.18. The development plan of Nordborg on Als 1973, around the Danfoss industrial complex. *Source:* Based on *Forslag til dispositions-plan for Nordborg kommune,* 1973.

the growing employment in the shipyard a new urban unit, Munkebo, was planned and built by the corporation for its workers and other employees. This separate suburb of Odense consisted mainly of rented bungalows, and it included institutions and commercial services also built by the shipyard owner.

The second new enterprise was started in 1933 on the island of Als near the German border by a farmer's son, who ran a small-scale plant producing expansion valves in part of his father's house. This enterprise developed at an almost explosive rate to become the great Danfoss Company. During the 1940s and 1950s production prospered. Each year the number of employees increased by 20–25 per cent. Residential areas for the company's employees were built in the neighbouring villages: Nordborg, Langesø, Havnbjerg and elsewhere. In the 1960s this whole district had about 9,000 inhabitants, but the company actually employed over 10,000 people. Many of the workers commuted from Sønderborg and even further away. This is an example of a single company that has profoundly changed the commuting pattern and the urban development of a whole region. If a large enterprise like Danfoss was to have been located according to a formal regional plan, it would probably never have been located on Als.

1960–1975: PROSPERITY, OPTIMISM AND RAPID URBAN GROWTH

Around 1960 the Danish economy was experiencing the start of a boom period. The 1960s were prosperous and economic activity reached a peak around 1970. During the 1960s planners were very optimistic about the future. A steadily rising standard of living was regarded almost as a law of nature. Most towns counted upon substantial urban expansion and big investments were made in communications systems. Better harbours and modern ferries linked Copenhagen and Sjælland to Fyn, Jylland, Sweden and Germany. Once again, however, the ambitious plans for a bridge over Øresund were postponed. The road network was expanded and improved, and new expressways were opened. The landscape was restructured by the new highways and motorways, while historical roads were often down-graded or cut off. Most local railways – except in the metropolitan area – were closed and replaced by bus services, while use of the main railway lines was intensified. In many town centres large areas were occupied by bus terminals. Tramways were abolished throughout the country – in Copenhagen, Århus and Odense – and replaced by buses. Public transportation was to a great extent subordinated to private motor transport. In many cities the street structure and the traffic pattern changed. In residential areas and in the central and local business districts, pedestrian precincts and culs-de-sac were introduced. But this was often combined with new streets cutting through the older parts of the town and the building of new by-passes and vast parking areas. Distances within the urban areas were greater than before, and people became increasingly dependent on private cars. Motorization increased to about one car per three inhabitants. Expanding traffic space, increasing social and commercial services, demands for areas for recreation and future expansion and demand for lower building densities resulted in the rapid growth of urban land use per inhabitant.

The smaller average size of households and the rapid urbanization contributed to a high demand for new dwellings. Industrial housing began to take over, and the building industry became concentrated in fewer and bigger units. These large building firms exercised a considerable influence on town planning, and urban design was affected by the demand for quick construction and thus for prefabricated buildings.

Big areas of 'catalogue' bungalows grew up round the bigger cities. Many rural settlements or railways communities became dormitory towns for commuters to the larger towns. The economic boom meant that more and more people were buying second homes. Before the 1970 Urban and Rural Zoning Act (*By- og landzoneloven*) there were few restrictions on the apportioning of plots for weekend cottages in rural districts, and an increasing stretch of the coast was occupied by weekend and vacation cottages.

As a result of an administrative reform in 1970, almost 1400 municipalties were merged into 275, and twenty-three counties (*amter*) were reduced to fourteen. The economic principle was that each economic region in the country should form a single county, and every urban agglomeration of at least several thousand inhabitants should constitute a single municipality together with its surrounding rural area. The legal distinctions between towns and rural communities were abandoned. Together with the Planning Law Reform in the 1970s, this created new conditions for town and country planning. Already in the 1960s a national physical development plan had been initiated, mainly at the level of ideas. The 1962 Zone Plan divided the country into zones for urban expansion, agriculture, nature conservation etc. Regional planning activity was also introduced outside the metropolitan region on local initiatives.

The social functionalism of the 1950s was partly replaced by a more technocratic attitude in the 1960s. The new parts of the towns were being more obviously developed as separate districts characterized by different functions, building types and social classes. Many older town centres developed as specialized shopping and service districts, while smaller production units and dwellings had to move away. Land rents rose rapidly in the central areas, and the concentration into large units and chain organizations in the retail and service sectors resulted in town centres of ever-increasing uniformity. Accessibility by car, the need for parking areas, and commercial expansion were often

regarded as more important than cultural, social and environmental qualities, in both old and new centres.

At the beginning of the 1970s new development tendencies appeared: urban expansion decreased, as did the rate of housing construction. Fewer economic resources were available for the construction of new roads and other traffic facilities, and motorization was no longer increasing. At the same time there was growing opposition to the planning practice of the 1960s. Around 1970 some displacement of urban growth from larger to smaller towns, and from earlier expansive regions to more remote ones, began to be noticeable. This was due partly to a restructuring process in industrial production, to state subsidies for the development of peripheral regions, and to the existence of a more stable workforce and a lower wage level in those regions.

Copenhagen

The 1947 'Finger Plan' was based on the assumption of fairly limited growth in the Copenhagen region. But actual urban expansion soon exceeded the limits set by the plan. Furthermore, it was unevenly distributed. In the attractive affluent northern parts of the metropolitan region there was widespread urbanization and considerable extension of the urban zones. The green wedges thus grew narrower, and the preservation of many qualities of the landscape was threatened. In the southwestern part of the region, on the other hand, urban development was slower than expected. The 'monocentric' structure of the capital resulted in heavy economic and traffic pressure on the city centre. Extensive industrial and other types of enterprise moved out of inner Copenhagen, while offices came to occupy a growing proportion of the central areas.

New regional plans for the Copenhagen area sought to alter this development pattern, still on the assumption of rapid future urban growth. After much discussion had taken place in a joint technical committee to achieve a new regional planning strategy, a second regional plan was approved by the politicians in 1962. This plan aimed to concentrate most urban growth into two 'fingers' towards the west and south-west, and to establish two new centres in order to relieve the pressure on the city centre. In the south-western finger along the Køge Bay a new linear urban structure for 150,000 inhabitants was planned, supported by a special law. New suburban centres were planned at Lyngby in the northern area and at Høje Tåstrup to the west. The development of the northern centre was the most successful, due to the relatively affluent and dense population in the area.

The Third Regional Plan of 1973 was to be implemented by the newly organized regional administration for greater Copenhagen. The plan was based on 'transportation corridors' and 'junction centres'. Regional functions and new industrial and service areas were to be located in 'activity zones' along the transportation corridors north-south and east-west in the region, to serve both the existing 'Finger Plan' area and a new proposed development to the west. At four major junctions, regional centres were planned. Høje Tåstrup was promoted as one of these. The Regional Plan referred mainly to development zones outside the finger plan area. Within the finger-plan area development was to be limited and the plan contained few proposals for the future development of built-up areas, for example most parts of the municipality of Copenhagen.

The 1973 Regional Plan also included a number of proposals from the 1960s: bridges or tunnels were to cross Øresund to connect Helsingør with Helsingborg and Copenhagen (Dragør) with Malmö (Limhamn). A new international airport was planned on the island of Saltholm, linked to the Copenhagen-Malmö bridge. A large new urban district was planned on West Amager, the vast area reclaimed from the sea in the 1940s south of the central part of Copenhagen.

In the city of Copenhagen the 1954 General Plan (see p. 31) was followed by a number of plan proposals in the 1960s. A system of expressways would traverse the municipal area, and large parts of the dense nineteenth-century districts required redevelopment. An underground rail system was planned. The urban centre was to be improved and promoted to become an efficient economic centre for Scandinavia to compete with Hamburg. West Amager was planned and designed as an entirely new urban structure to occupy a key position and in the international metropolis, linked to the old city centre, the Øresund bridge and the new airport, a new harbour and the regional motorway system.

However, many of the ambitious plans of the 1960s and early 1970s were postponed or abandoned. The cost proved too high and the plans for expansion unrealistic. The Øresund bridges were postponed, the existing Kastrup airport was extended rather than being replaced, and there was both popular and political pressure to restrict urban development on West Amager and to turn the area into a large recreation zone for the nineteenth-century districts of the town.

In the city centre, however, there was considerable building activity. New offices, business premises and hotel buildings were erected over a fairly large area, but there was no total redevelopment of whole city districts as in Stockholm. In 1968 a city expansion plan included a proposal for the total renewal of the inner Vesterbro area near the central railway station, but this plan too was postponed. In the vicinity of the earlier railway station area, however, the expansion of the central business district begun during the 1930s was completed.

Urban motorways (new radial roads and a new ring road) were constructed in the suburban areas; but in the municipality of Copenhagen only a few of these plans were ever realized. The population of this municipality

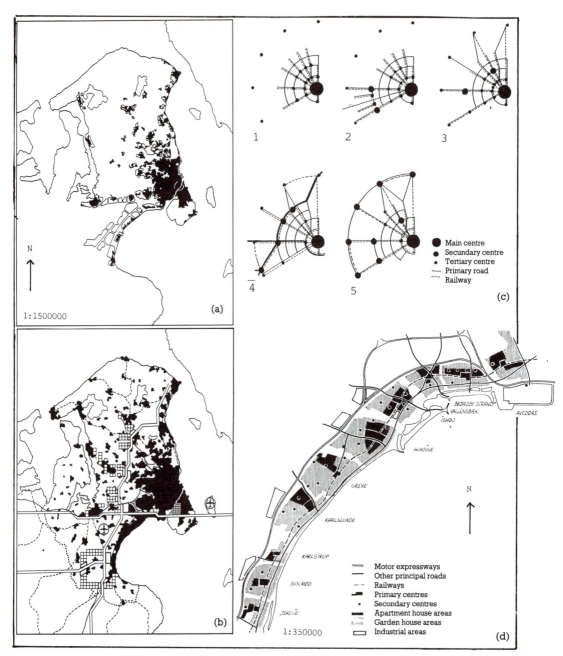

Figure 2.19. Copenhagen regional planning in the 1960s and 1970s.

(*a*) The 'Principal Outline of a Regional Plan' from 1960, aiming to concentrate the growth towards the west. The plan of 1962 was a compromise with growth also towards the north. Authors: Roy Draiby and others. *Source:* Based on a map in the Principal Outline of a Regional Plan, 1960.

(*b*) The regional plan of 1973 with transportation corridors and new development areas. *Source: København – partiernes udtalelser til §6-redegørelsen,* 1980.

(*c*) Schematic illustration of the regional plans of Greater Copenhagen. (1) The 'Finger Plan', 1947; (2) the 'Principal Outline', 1960; (3) the first stage plan, 1962; (4) the regional plan, 1973; and (5) actual status, 1987. *Source:* Based on Rasmussen (1974) and other sources.

(*d*) The Køge Bay plan, 1966. *Source:* Skriver (1984).

had fallen since 1954. Traffic had stagnated and there was no longer any need for new large roads, only for some expansion of major roads on Amager. The capacity of several existing roads was increased in the 1960s, however, partly at the expense of bicycles, pedestrians and buses. The proposed underground rail system was never realized, but the capacity of the existing rail network was increased as a result of certain technological innovations.

After 1970 large-scale redevelopment projects were launched in the dense nineteenth-century parts of Copenhagen, supported by a new law on urban renewal. During the 1970s the redevelopment plans aimed to combine demolition, reconstruction and modernizing strategies. In many blocks the courtyard buildings were pulled down, to leave a large common open space to replace the former small dark yards. But the public housing associations which were putting up new flats in these areas called for more widespread demolition, in order to obtain larger continuous building sites. Many redevelopment plans were criticized because of the extensive demolition involved. At the beginning of the 1970s many quarters revealed a picture of empty lots, delayed reconstruction, and many older buildings in a bad state of decay. Local citizen groups began to react, demanding a different approach to redevelopment with less demolition and more public local influence on the process.

In the period in question much of the urban expansion towards the west and south-west took place, mainly as a result of comprehensive zone planning. New suburbs arose towards Roskilde and Køge, and also in the northern part of the region. High-rise houses were built in larger units than ever before. The non-profit housing societies developed new types of industrially-constructed small houses, for example in Albertslund. The new suburban units were generally built in connection with the S-train stations and the local shopping and service centres, and they included schools, nurseries,

leisure-time institutions and large green areas. To a great extent motor traffic was segregated from pedestrians and cyclists.

But in many new suburbs the housing estates were too large and built too quickly, generally with a few types of house only, 'crane track siting', little variation, and poor architectural and environmental quality. The population was often dominated by low-income groups and a skewed age distribution, and the open spaces were generally rather carelessly planned. In many ways the social housing of the 1960s represented a step backwards in quality compared to the 1930s and 1950s. In the comprehensive planned development of the Køge Bay area, however, attempts were made to attain a higher quality in the environment by better co-operation between the overall planning and the site-planning of the public housing associations.

At the beginning of the 1970s the State Institute of Building Research (SBI) held a competition on dense and low-rise housing. Inspired by this, many social housing associations and housing enterprises developed new types of industrialized, low-rise, dense housing areas. Thus 'Galgebakken' in Albertslund was built according to a fairly regular plan and with a limited number of housing types, but the design and the size were such as to encourage social contact; among other things the buildings were grouped round small common open spaces and narrow alleys. At about this time there began to be a gradual shift away from fairly regular plans with a few types of houses only, to more irregularity and a greater variety of house types. Some areas had a cubistic look, while elsewhere, for instance in 'Gadekæret', Ishøj, the planners aimed at winding varied streets and sloping roofs like those to be seen in the small provincial towns.

The dense, low-rise housing competition also provided inspiration for the development of planning processes, which included the participation of the inhabitants, the users, in the design process. Groups of private or public

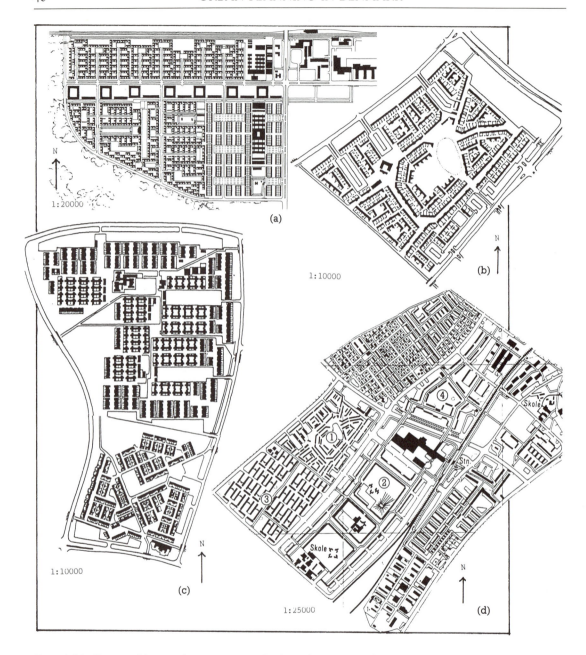

Figure 2.20. Dense and low-rise housing units in the Copenhagen region from the 1960s and 1970s.
(*a*) Albertslund South, 1966 by Fællestegnestuen (Thyge Arnfred, Viggo Møller Jensen). *Source:* Jørgensen (1979).
(*b*) Galgebakken, 1974 (the northern area) by J. P. Storgaard, Hanne Marcussen and others, and Hyldespjældet, 1976 (the southern area) by Ole Birch and others. *Source:* Information brochure from Vridsløselille Andelsboligforening.
(*c*) Gadekæret, 1977 by KBI. *Source:* Information brochure from Vridsløselille Andelsboligforening.
(*d*) Central Ishøj with the dwelling units Gadekæret (1), Vejlebroparken (2), Strandgårdsparken (3) and Vildtbanegård (4). *Source:* The topographical map of Denmark 1:25,000.

housing companies constructed new homes in co-operation with the users, and great attention was paid to common facilities. 'Skråplanet', built in 1973, is one of the first of such housing areas.

The later dense, low-rise housing estates often exhibit considerable environmental quality and a high level of community among the inhabitants. In these areas academics and the middle classes often predominate, while the inhabitants of the more traditional flats are largely working class. Many of the residential estates – both large and small – have been planned as relatively independent units, not connected with the neighbouring suburbs in any organic way. Around 1970, however, attempts were also made to improve the design of areas consisting of multi-storey blocks of flats. In Farum a very dense, multi-storey terrace house complex was built with a view to combining the advantages of the family house and the block of flats. The flats are collected round common covered spaces, and they all have outdoor terrace gardens. Traffic and parking areas, however, prevent direct contact with the ground and the open spaces between the houses.

In this period, however, most housing construction in the metropolitan area (and in the country as a whole) consisted of bungalows and other single-family detached houses in relatively unplanned areas. This was a result of the rising standard of living, of industrialized build-

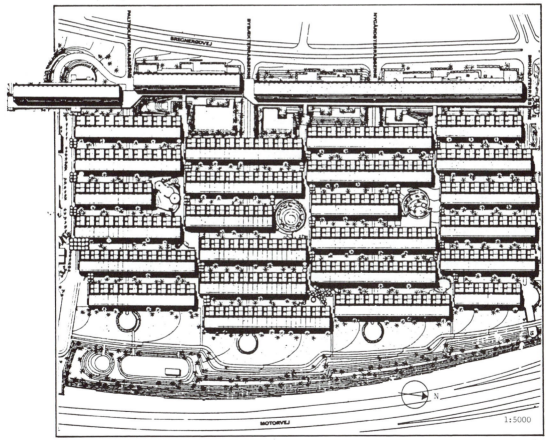

Figure 2.21. Residential area in Farum, Copenhagen region. Farum Midtpunkt 1970–74. Dense, terraced blocks by Fællestegnestuen (Thyge Arnfred, Viggo Møller Jensen). *Source:* Faber (1977).

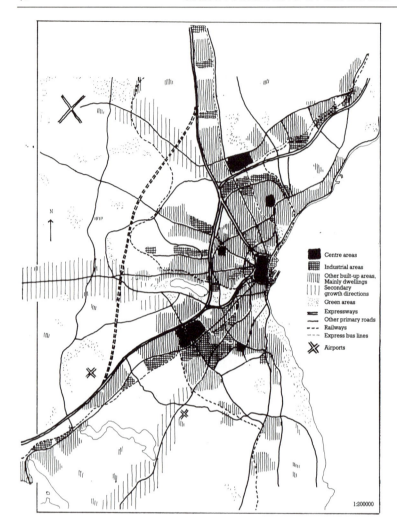

Figure 2.22. The development plan of Århus 1966. *Source:* Based on *Egnsplan for Århusegnen,* 1966.

ing production and of increasing motorization. Widespread one-family housing areas developed in the Copenhagen region, frequently as dormitory towns without workplaces and far from the necessary services. Typical examples of bungalow areas from the period 1960–75 are to be found in the north-western part of the Copenhagen region. From about 1975 the building of bungalows began to decline. Real incomes were not increasing as before, the cost of living was rising rapidly and the demand for single-family houses fell.

The municipalities in the region differ con-

siderably from one another. Some communities favour large-scale public housing activity while others go in almost entirely for private housing, depending on the political stance of the municipality concerned. Public and non-profit housing associations predominate in the Køge Bay area, the 'finger' development towards Roskilde and the north-west finger towards Ballerup. The social segregation tendencies and the economic inequalities between the municipalities in the metropolitan region are obvious. Special problems faced the municipality of Copenhagen because of its declining population over the last two decades, and its growing proportion of low-income groups and pensioners. The municipality has tried to solve this problem by increasing the volume of housing construction for the higher-income bracket.

Århus, Odense and Ålborg

By the beginning of this period, Århus, Odense and Ålborg had expanded far outside their town boundaries, and during the 1960s plans for the new urban areas were worked out in collaboration with the neighbouring communities. In connection with the municipal reform the municipalities of Århus, Odense and Ålborg incorporated all their suburbs as well as their

immediate rural surroundings. The district plans for greater Århus indicate urban growth in fingers along the main radial roads, particularly along the E3 motorway towards Skanderborg and Randers. Proposals were made for an inner circular expressway round the urban core and an outer by-pass motorway outside the city. Radial motorways were to give access to the urban core. Two auxiliary centres were planned: Lisbjerg in the north, and Tranbjerg in the south. Rapid and continuous urban growth was expected.

The road system was adjusted to the increasing level of motorization, although many of the plans were never realized. In the urban centres new streets through the city area and new park-

(a)   1:7000

(b)   1:7000

Figure 2.23. Ålborg plans from the 1970s (cf. figure 2.7).
(a) The proposed street breakthrough, Dag Hammarskjöldsgade, which was stopped.
(b) The present situation with the new community centre to the right. *Source* (a) and (b): Svensson *et al.* (1981).

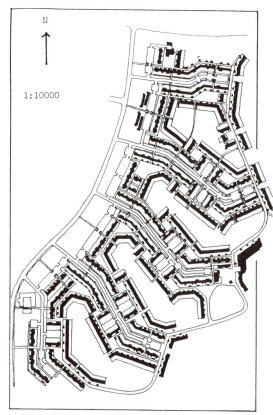

N

1:10000

Figure 2.24. A housing area in Århus.
Håndværkerparken, 1983, by Arkitektgruppen i Århus,
Svend Hansen, and others. *Source*: Nygaard (1984).

ing spaces were planned, resulting in severe encroachment on the environmental quality of the old city. Few of these streets through the towns were built, due partly to the withdrawal of state funds for the purpose. In Odense the broad artery, Thomas B. Thriges Gade, slashed through the old town centre like an open wound, and the H. C. Andersen quarter was cut off from the rest of the city centre (see figure 2.17). In the late 1980s a 'healing of this wound' was discussed, by overbridging the artery with new blocks. In Ålborg several years of discussion stopped plans for a new through road, and a new civic hall was built where the street had been planned. The expressway round the city centre of Århus was never built.

Major co-ordinated action characterized the plans for the area south-east of Odense and east of Ålborg at the beginning of the 1970s. These areas were planned to include new universities, regional facilities, dwellings and industrial estates. In both cities the expansion zones were based on large grid-iron systems inspired by Milton Keynes in England. The universities were planned on the same scale as small towns. However, urban growth was slower than expected and the new university buildings and many other regional facilities stand isolated in open fields outside the cities (see figure 2.17).

Big new industrialized housing complexes were erected. Some areas were designed on rectangular lines following the building-crane tracks (Gjellerupparken in Århus, Vollsmose in Odense), while others were characterized by a more varied garden-type development (Langenæs in Århus, Frydendal in Ålborg). Long rows of uniform houses were typical. Bungalow areas spread outside Århus, Odense and Ålborg into the surrounding villages, where the building of 'catalogue' houses predominated.

During the 1970s the municipalities increasingly learned to consider conservation as an important element in their plans for urban renewal. Sometimes this assumed the form of picturesque modernization at rather high cost, for example the H. C. Andersen quarter in Odense. In some towns decaying low-rise housing for the working classes was transformed into attractive homes for the higher-income groups. In other areas, such as Sjællandsgade in Århus and Vesterbro in Odense, the local population took an active part in attempts to carry out relatively inexpensive renovations.

Other Provincial Towns

Many medium-sized towns were growing fairly well and wanted to promote further expansion. The establishment of 'alternative large cities' by linking neighbouring urban districts together had been discussed. One example of this was a draft proposal for combining the three towns of Vejle-Fredericia-Kolding, situated at one of the most important traffic junctions in the country, to create one big triangular city as a second national centre. Other possibilities were to connect towns in linear structures along main traffic routes. The urban connection of Hjørring with Hirtshals in north Jylland and Herning with Holstebro in north-west Jylland were discussed.

In Holstebro the municipal politicians found it more realistic to connect their town with Struer than with Herning. The Gullestrup area north of Herning was developed as the first stage of such a linear formation. The aim of these linear structures was to promote economic development in the respective regions. However, apart from Gullestrup none of the plans was realized.

Most towns were planning large industrial

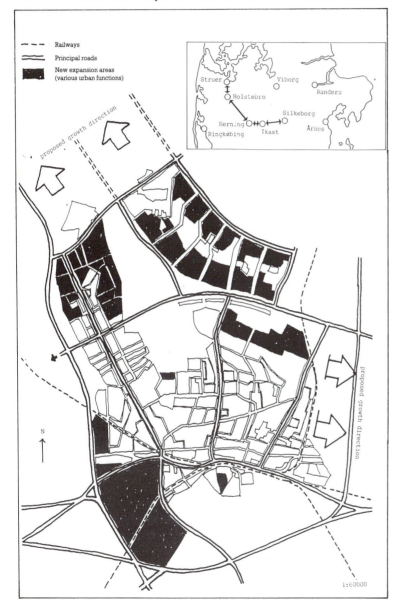

Figure 2.25. Development plan of Herning, 1969 and proposed development axes. *Source:* Based on *Herning Dispositionsplan,* 1969.

estates and other expansion areas on the out-skirts. But the competition between towns was keen, and any realistic considerations con-nected with the implementation of this growth were neglected. In Roskilde, for example, there were plans to surround the new university cen-tre with considerable urban expansion. Howev-er, this idea was never realized and the universi-ty is still isolated in an open field quite a long way from the town, a monument to the wreck of the original plans. The government-initiated university project also meant a change in the master plan adopted by the municipal author-ities, as it altered the direction of the expansion of the town.

The town centres were to be transformed into more efficient regional centres, easily accessible by car and surrounded by wide access roads serving large parking places. The old high streets were converted into pedestrian pre-cincts in which retailing and other central functions were to be concentrated. Along the pedestrian precincts it was expected that new supermarkets and other business premises would replace many of the older buildings, and

most dwellings were to be moved away from the town core. Once the plans were implemented, the central part of the towns would consist mainly of pedestrian precincts or 'purchase corri-dors', with standardized buildings and shops surrounded by a wide belt of parking spaces and access roads, as in many United States suburban centres. The centre would be separated from the rest of the town by this wide traffic zone, and the small enterprises and gardens behind the business streets would disappear. The plans were often illustrated by drawings showing their future appearance. On these drawings rows of trees were frequently shown on the parking area, giving the impression that the shopping centre was surrounded by a green belt.

Typical examples of this kind of centre plan were produced for Holstebro in 1962, for Hillerød in 1963 and for Roskilde in 1969. The Holstebro plan was implmented in broad out-line since the local authorities had purchased large tracts of the central area, but similar plans for most other towns were only partly realized. In the 1970s the new centre plans were generally revised. Traffic areas were reduced, more

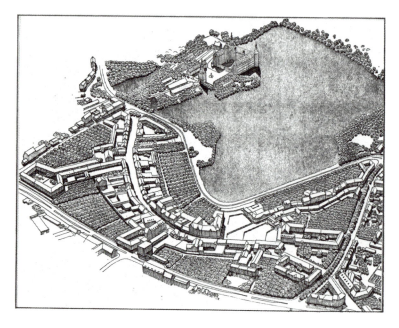

Figure 2.26. Planning the cen-tral district of a provincial town in the 1960s.
The centre plan of Hillerød, 1963. The town core merely con-sists of a 'retail corridor' and park-ing areas (shown with trees). *Source: Hillerød købstad. Center-plan, 1963.*

dwellings were allowed and more opportunity was allowed for the preservation of existing buildings and activities. Yet the centre plans often resulted in decay, widespread demolition behind the main shopping streets, and the loss of environmental quality. In Randers a large section of the old town was pulled down to make way for a new street, a bus terminal, various cultural institutions and business buildings. In several towns, however, this did not prevent most new retailing from establishing itself in new suburban centres.

In spite of the many centre plans, most older town cores are better preserved in Denmark than they are in Sweden and Finland for example, although this is generally due more to economic conditions than to preservation policies. An exception occurred in Helsingør, where a new suburban centre relieved the pressure on the old centre and where plans for the old core assumed as a matter of principle that all existing buildings and their functions should be preserved. The municipal planners established close co-operation with property-owners and residents in order to attain these goals. In some smaller towns, too, there had long been agreement between the authorities and the citizens that the old-town character should be protected (for example in Ribe and Tønder). Here special preservation plans were worked out. Similar plans were also made in other small remote towns, where there was little pressure on the old centre (for example in Svaneke and Ærøskøbing). The means for achieving these goals included protection orders on single buildings and direct conservation decisions taken by the municipal authorities and the Ministry of the Environment for certain sections of the town concerned.

Government plans for developing the harbour and town of Hanstholm were postponed for many years, but during the 1960s, after further investment in harbour construction, a new round of town planning quite different from the old one was finally initiated.

Hanstholm was planned as a residential town with the consequent segregation of pedestrians and vehicular traffic. The centre was located along a pedestrian precinct through the middle of the agglomeration. The first stage of the centre was opened, and the harbour also became an important fishing harbour and a ferry terminal. The township represented quite a successful part of the overall regional development policy in Thy (north-west Jylland), and in 1980 it had a population of 2,800.

1975–1990: PLANNING REFORMS AND MANIFESTATIONS OF CRISIS

The Danish economy was no exception to the worldwide economic recession which began in the mid-1970s. The recession and the rising rate of unemployment had the greatest impact in the metropolitan area. With some exceptions, urban growth stagnated in the whole country, and such expansion as there was took place in some of the smaller towns rather than in the major cities. This was largely due to a decline in the move away from the agricultural sector, a fall in industrial employment, and the decentralization of industrial units. The effects of the economic crisis also affected the public sector, which now began to try to cut costs in many fields.

In the 1980s a new urban growth began in Århus and in several minor towns in Jylland, but Copenhagen was still showing very slow development. Unlike Stockholm, Oslo and Helsinki there was no new expansion in Copenhagen in these years.

As a result of the new situation, economically and as regards urbanization, the number of new settlements fell, while more weight was placed on re-use and on the improvement and densification of existing built-up areas. Many housing units dating from the 1960–1975 period were subject to social problems, wear and tear, decay, poor environmental quality and problems of segregation. In the years to come a significant share of physical planning will be concerned with the improvement of such areas. Many garden suburbs also have problems: increasing cost of living, long distance to services, lack of stimulation in everyday life, and social isolation. Since many of the single-family houses were hard to sell, they often had to be sold by court order when the owner could no longer afford to live there. In the older parts of the towns, urban renewal consisted to a greater extent than before of the preservation of earlier buildings, but more houses than necessary were still being demolished. The few new urban areas were planned in such a way as to avoid the monotony of the 1960s and to create more variety. Priority was given to the building of low-rise, dense housing areas with local influence on the planning process and close links with existing services. Thus, in comparison with the 1960s, while government housing policy had less of a social character (less public housing, fewer cost regulations, more influence from market forces), the housing units were actually planned with more attention to the social life and the environmental quality of the areas in question. There was thus a contradiction between the government's policy and the aims of the urban planners, which meant that the better quality of the new dwelling units mostly benefited the middle class.

As a result of the planning reforms of the 1970s a coherent planning system now covers the whole country. Three new planning acts were approved in the 1970s: The Country and Regional Planning Act (*Lov om lands- og regionplanlægning*) 1973, the Act of Regional Planning in the Metropolitan Area (*Lov om regionplanlægning i hovedstadsområdet*) and the Municipal and Local Planning Act (*Lov om kommune- og lokalplanlægning*) 1977. Together with the 1970 Urban and Rural Zoning Act and the 1970 administrative reform the planning acts shaped a quite new situation for town and country planning. Major construction projects are now regulated by mandatory

local plans, and these in turn must accord with the municipal plan. All municipal plans must in turn be based on a comprehensive regional plan. In the metropolitan area, the regional plan should cover the municipalities of Copenhagen and Frederiksberg as well as the three neighbouring counties (*amter*), but in the rest of the country each county was enjoined to work out a regional plan.

By 1980 regional plans covering the whole country had been approved and in the late 1980s all municipal plans were finished. The regional plans define a system of service centres in each region, consisting of major regional centres and municipal and local service centres of various kinds. The State Planning Department (*Planstyrelsen*), at the beginning of the 1980s, combined the approved regional towns into a comprehensive map of Denmark, which could perhaps be regarded as a kind of national plan.

Outside the metropolitan area the regional plans will all be revised in the 1990s. In the metropolitan area a new regional plan was approved in 1989, but in 1990 the regional planning authority – the Metropolitan Council (*Hovedstadsrådet*) – was abolished. In the future there will be no comprehensive plan for the whole metropolitan area, but only plans for each of the three counties of the area in addition to the municipal plans for Copenhagen and Frederiksberg. This is a considerable step backwards in Danish planning.

According to the new planning reform, the public is to be involved in the local planning process as well as in planning at the municipal and regional levels. This is effected by way of meetings, study circles, information etc. An Act of Urban Renewal (*Byfornyelsesloven*) passed in 1983 is also based on the assumption of extensive joint consultation. However, experience to date indicates that the public debate generally leads to only limited local influence on the planning process.

Although the Danish planning system is well developed compared with many other countries, there are unsolved problems: the integration of physical planning with economic and social planning at the different levels leaves much to be desired. Relations between national sector planning and comprehensive physical planning still give rise to conflict. There is political disagreement about whether or not planning should be binding on development, and whether or not the planning process is too slow. Some people see the planning process as an unnecessary and bureaucratic obstacle that delays the various development schemes. Others see planning as an opportunity for the development of their own physical surroundings. The Ministry for the Environment is considering new ways of speeding up the planning process and making it more effective, but such efforts meet with opposition from many quarters. The fact that there were plans covering the whole of Denmark in the 1980s might, however, reduce the need for planning in the future. The basic planning work is already done, and future planning will mostly consist of smaller additions and changes in connection with development schemes and the accomplishment of new environmental and ecological planning aims. Several municipalities are now using the planning system as a tool in local politics, in order to improve conditions for business, tourism, etc.

Copenhagen

Confronted with stagnating urban growth and diminishing housing construction, the 1973 Regional Plan for the metropolitan area proved to be greatly over-dimensioned. However, the regional political authority – the Metropolitan Council (*Hovedstadsrådet*) – did not until 1989 deem it necessary to produce a new plan. Many individual parts of the 1973 plan had been postponed by then. Only one of the four new regional centres, Høje Tåstrup, had been realized, and the north-south transport corridor was postponed. Future developments in the region will be primarily located in the vicinity of the

railway stations – i.e. in a continued finger structure – and there will be continuing development of existing suburban centres (Lyngby, Hundige) as well as the town centres in the periphery of the region (Helsingør, Roskilde, Køge etc.). Thus, the 1973 Regional Plan, with its major transport axes and four 'junction centres', can be regarded as a parenthesis. The revised Regional Plan of 1989 can then be seen more or less as a continuation of the 1962 plan, albeit at a slower rate.

Since hardly any new areas are being planned at present, most of the rather sparse housing construction must be located in previously planned but not yet fully built-up areas or in existing areas. Despite this, the 1983 Regional Plan Supplement on construction in existing urban areas was a very general and not very precisely formulated programme. However, a growing proportion of regional housing was being located within the municipality of Copenhagen – which hoped to attract more, and more lucrative, tax-payers – but for a long time this expansion followed no approved general plan. Not until 1987 did the City Council approve a proposal for a comprehensive plan. The idea of such a plan had been postponed, while the construction of new houses continued. Many building projects were controversial, because they exploited green spaces and older industrial areas no longer in use. It seems that the City Council intended to carry out as many projects as possible, before any plan regulating future development was approved. To a great extent the present plan follows the existing land use and the current trends of the building market. It is a '*status-quo* plan', without clear vision and open to almost any possibility. Not least, there is a lack of vision of how the harbour area should be developed in the future; but many projects for different parts of the harbour area have been presented. A special committee presented in 1989 a planning concept for the whole harbour area, but the municipality of Copenhagen has not yet (1990) decided if this

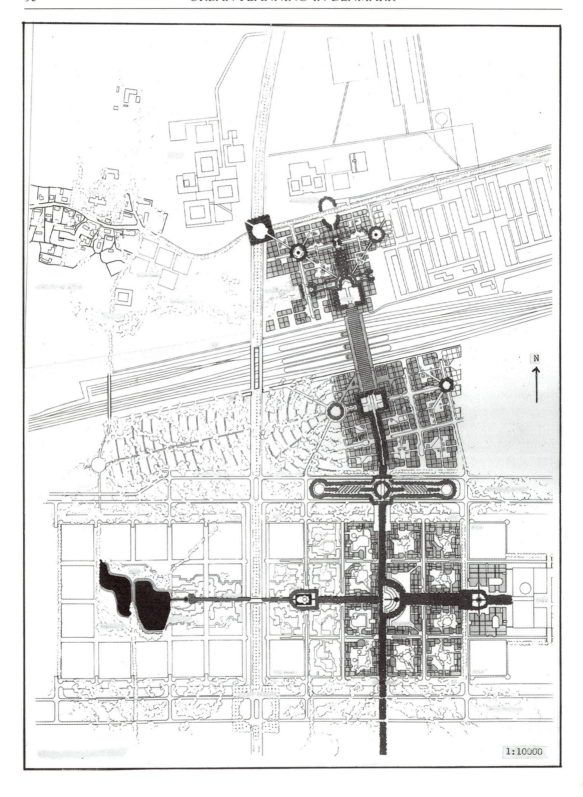

1:10000

Figure 2.27 (opposite). The first-prize proposal for the Høje-Tåstrup junction centre, Copenhagen region, by Jacob Blegvad, 1977. The first blocks and the railway station were built in the mid-1980s in neo-classicist and post-modern styles. *Source: Arkitekten'* No. 16, 1978.

Figure 2.28 (above). The 'Black Quarter' of Nørrebro, Copenhagen.
(a) 1841. *Source:* Aakjær *et al.* 1950.
(b) 1869. *Source:* Based on Hartmann and Villadsen 1969.
(c) 1969. *Source:* Based on the map of Copenhagen 1:5,000.
(d) After the redevelopment, 1970–1986. Pre-1969 buildings are shown in black. *Source:* Based on *Helhedsplan for Indre Nørrebro,* 1979.

concept should be followed. Private development schemes in the area are now being
approved without a general concept.

In the 1980s, urban renewal in Copenhagen
was on the increase, but it was criticized because
it allowed too much demolition and because the
new developments did not exhibit a sufficiently
high architectural environmental quality. Urban
clearance also resulted in a change in the
local population and a loss of social networks.
Opinions varied about town planning in
Copenhagen, and there were sometimes violent
conflicts between citizen groups and the municipal authorities, added to which the government continued to build offices in the city centre, even though this contradicted the intentions
of the regional plan and the urban renewal
plans. In the 1980s there was a clear tendency to
try to return to the traditional urban qualities
when planning new urban units. The winning
competition project of Høje Tåstrup (Jacob
Blegvad, 1977) was a pioneer work in this sense.
It was influenced by neo-rationalism and the
projects of the Krier brothers.

In many more recent suburbs, the social and
economic problems were increasing. Attempts
were made to solve these problems. In Albertslund Nord improvements were initiated. In
Tårnby, Gladsaxe and Rødovre new building
made the districts more dense and also more
varied. In Farum new methods of municipal
planning were tested, with a view to giving the
local population greater influence on the planning process. In the Fuglsang Park area the
school and the dwelling-houses were integrated
in a continuous urban design by 'Vandkunsten'.

Among the most successful results of regional
planning in the metropolitan area are the regional public transport system, including a uniform tariff system on all buses and trains in the
region, and the recreational planning which
includes extensive areas of forest and protection
for most of the green zones. In the west of
greater Copenhagen, broad green zones between the fingers were made more attractive by
the addition of artificial lakes and hills, forests,
and meadows for cattle breeding on old farmland purchased by the government. At Køge
Bay a new coastal park of about 500 hectares
has been constructed as a result of land reclama-
tion from the sea. New beaches, marinas and
green areas have all been created here. An

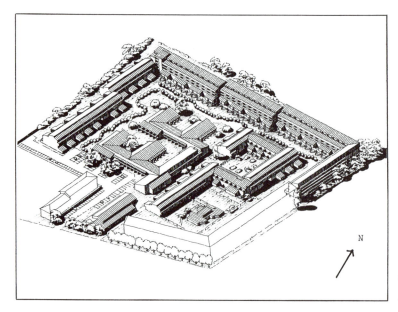

N

Figure 2.29. An example of
urban renewal on a former indust-
rial site.
Solbjerg Have, Frederiksberg
(Copenhagen), 1978–79. Fælles-
tegnestuen (Thyge Arnfred and
Viggo Møller Jensen), *Source:*
Arkitektur, No. 7, 1980.

important element in regional planning will be the regulation of the open country round the metropolis, including improved resource planning and the protection of environmental quality.

Århus, Odense and Ålborg

The three major provincial towns, Århus, Odense and Ålborg, are all facing problems in realizing the expansion plans drawn up during the 1960s, and early 1970s. In Århus the Lisbjerg and Tranbjerg centres have been postponed for the time being. The development of south-east Odense and east Ålborg is proceeding more slowly than planned, and the extension of the road system is also behind schedule.

The regional plans that touched on these three towns – the plans for the counties of Århus, Fyn and North Jylland – were approved by the government, like most other regional plans in the country, in 1980–81. In these three regions different structural alternatives were discussed with varying degrees of centralization/decentralization. In all three regions the discussion ended in a compromise that retained the town in question as the main regional centre with auxiliary centres, and defined the medium-sized towns as district centres. In these three counties, too, regional public transportation systems were established.

The regional plans were followed by discussions of the municipal plans, starting in 1982–83. Information about the municipal planning alternatives was sent to the citizens for their comments. One of the actions for the future was to rehabilitate the more recent areas with blocks of flats, and experimental projects involving user participation in the improvement process were undertaken in Århus and Ålborg. Experiments with new types of multi-storey dwelling houses are being carried through as well as ecological projects. In all three cities plans for the urban core were made in the 1980s.

Conservation in urban renewal and user participation are key concepts here.

Some parts of south-east Odense are now being developed. While the general plan for the area is large scale and regular, the local quarter plans are often dense and intimate, inspired by the small-town image. The Blangstedgård area was used as a building and dwelling exhibition in 1988.

Other Provincial Towns

In most minor provincial towns, municipal planning proposals started from the older master plans. However, expansion estimates were modified, road projects postponed or dropped, and the town centres were modernized more discreetly than was formerly intended. Most towns were only growing slowly, although there was a tendency for some of the smaller towns to grow more rapidly than the slightly larger ones.

The situation in the 1980s in the small and medium-sized towns can be illustrated by some examples. Herning, one of the youngest and most expansive Danish towns, had a large surplus of land available for development, the future of which was uncertain. In Fredericia only a few of the vast development areas projected in 1973 had been developed, but one large industrial complex had been established – the new central brewery belonging to De Forenede Bryggerier (Carlsberg-Tuborg), located at a central spot in the national transport system.

A planning competition for urban renewal in provincial towns in 1980 suggested how the older quarters of Esbjerg, Herning and Holbæk could be improved by preserving early buildings and adapting new building to the earlier structures so as to enhance the quality of the old elements in the townscape.

Køge, in the metropolitan region, is representative in many ways of town planning in the 1980s. In the 1960s large residential districts with single-family homes had been built as well as typical industrialized complexes with flats

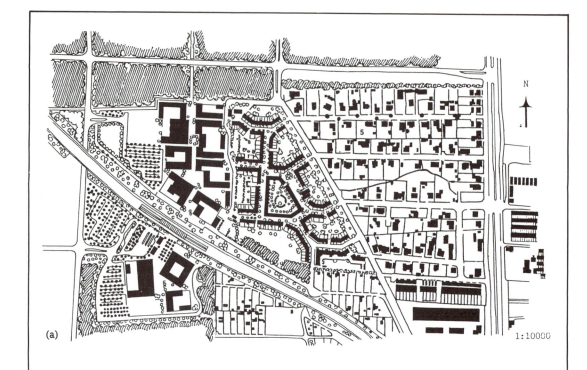

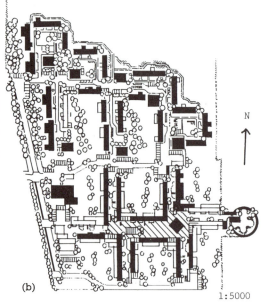

Figure 2.30. Two new urban units in Køge.
(*a*) Lynggården at Ølby station, 1983. A 'traditional' provincial town character with narrow streets and closed blocks. The new housing area (in the middle) links the garden suburb (right) to the new station (left). Architects: Karsten Vibild and others. *Source*: Based on *Arkitektur*, No. 8, 1983.
(*b*) Tinggården I and II in Herfølge, 1979 and 1984. Two small housing units, where new forms of local democracy and common facilities are being tried. Architects: Vandkunsten (Michael Steen Jonsen, Jens Arnfred and others). *Source*: Based on *Arkitektur*, Nos 7–8, 1979 and *Arkitektur*, Nos 5–6, 1985.

and parallel buildings. A 1971 centre plan had proposed new access roads and large parking areas squeezed into the blocks behind the shopping streets. This plan is now obsolete. The old city centre is to be preserved. New constructions in the town centre have been adapted to the old traditions, either in scale and form (the new Town Hall) or as a pastiche (the Parish Hall). A new station was erected in connection with the new S-railway from Copenhagen (part of the Køge Bay plan). Among the new housing areas, Tinggården represents a remarkable renewal of Danish housing traditions combined with a more informal architectural design, better physical organization to promote a sense of community, and broad individual freedom for the users. Tinggården by 'Vandkunsten' was a result of the SBI competition (cf. p. 39). In the Hastrup Vest district of Køge efforts have been made to plan a new urban area in a varied way and so as to create a town-like environment.

PROSPECTS

There are no obvious signs today of a revival in growth resembling that of the 1960s. The problematic market conditions and the restructuring of industrial production and of the service sector suggest that unemployment will remain high. This may result in greater social differentiation and more segregation in urban areas, and it will be important for urban planning, as well as social policy, to tackle the problems. Generally shorter working hours and unemployment will both mean that more people will remain at home in the residential areas during the day. This might provide opportunities for more activities, more life in the suburbs in the daytime. As part of a combined social and town-planning policy people in residential areas could perhaps be encouraged to take an active part in improving and planning their own surroundings.

Unless there is a rapid increase in immigration, the population of Denmark is likely to fall in the future. It has even been estimated that within 75–100 years from now the population of the country will have been halved unless the birthrate rises. It seems clear that the construction of new houses will be on a fairly limited scale in the future, compared with the situation fifteen years ago. It will probably be suggested in many cases that the over-large areas zoned for urban development but which are not required should be reallocated as rural zones again. There are thus good reasons for looking very carefully into the question of where building activity should be located in order to attain the best possible results. A slower rate of urban expansion need not mean that planning becomes less important. But the means of controlling building activity are still inadequate.

As regards the future of the smallest communities, there is great uncertainty. The 1979 National Planning Report recommended a concentration of the limited amount of urban growth in the somewhat bigger agglomerations with their better opportunities for providing an acceptable level of service. Many of the smallest communities may be obliged to choose between slow decline or dependence on service facilities in larger communities or towns. In the 1980s, however, many small communities, especially in Jylland, have had considerable growth.

In the late 1980s environmental problems were put into focus in the planning debate and efforts have been made to create ecological planning. The metropolitan Regional Plan of 1989 gave a very important place to ecological problems and to planning of non-built-up areas. Ecological town planning is perhaps more a question of building materials and techniques than of town layout. Around 1990 ecological town planning experiments were started in Esbjerg and Horsens, and plans for ecological urban renewal of Vesterbro, Copenhagen were worked out.

The continued restructuring of industrial production and the increasing use of computers in production and in administration and services may have far-reaching effects on urbanization.

Is the era of the large workplace over? Will we need large production sites in future? Will the role of urban centres as concentrations of workplaces be undermined? The future holds great uncertainty, but also many possibilities. Perhaps new techniques and increasing leisure may provide the opportunity for local citizens to become active participants in the creation of new towns. The planners must supply visions of a new and better urban future, not least of architectural values. But the problems will be great and spatial planning will have to be related to other more general social and political demands.

ANNOTATED BIBLIOGRAPHY

Aakjær, Svend et al. (1949–1950) *København før og nu*. Copenhagen: Alfred G. Hassings forlag.
A work in five parts describing the development and changes in the different parts of Copenhagen up to 1950. This work focuses on the period 1850–1950 and consists mainly of photographs, drawings and paintings, showing the successive changes in the features of the city. The changes are also described in texts and illustrated by old and more recent maps.

Arkitekten
The journal *Arkitekten* presents theoretical and ideological debates and discussions among architects and planners, the results of architectural competitions, and Danish and foreign examples of architecture and planning. It is edited by the *Danske Arkitekters Landsforbund* (Danish Association of Architects).

Arkitektur
The journal *Arkitektur* presents important works of architecture and town planning. The articles are generally written in Danish, English and German. This journal is edited by the *Danske Arkitekters Landsforbund* (Danish Association of Architects). *Arkitektur*, Nos 7–8, 1979 gives a good survey of Danish architecture and town planning 1904–1979.

Authén Blom, Grethe (ed.) (1977) *Urbaniseringsprosessen i Norden, I – III*. Oslo: Universitetsforlaget.
This work has three parts: 1. The Middle Ages. 2. The planned cities of the seventeenth and eighteenth centuries. 3. The first phase of industrialism. The different chapters in this history of urbanization in the Nordic countries describe the different countries (Denmark, Norway, Sweden) in their respective languages. The work focuses mainly on the economic and political life of the cities, but it also provides important examples of town planning in a social context.

Buhl, Ole (1941) *Socialt boligbyggeri. Udsnit af 15 års boligbyggeri*. Copenhagen: Foreningen Socialt Boligbyggeri.
In this book one of the public housing associations in Denmark *Foreningen Socialt Boligbyggeri*, presents most of its dwelling projects built during the period 1926–1941. Many of the projects represent the most progressive Danish housing architecture of the interwar period. They exemplify the development of Danish functionalistic architecture and the gradual change from closed blocks of flats to park-like urban design. The book was followed in 1987 by a presentation of the housing projects of *Foreningen Socialt Boligbyggeri* for the period 1942–1985.

Byplan
The journal *Byplan* (Town planning) is the main Danish review of urban research and town planning. Its articles discuss both implemented examples of town planning and ideas for future plans. Some are theoretical, others refer to planning practice. They deal with planning legislation and the politics of planning, as well as with æsthetic, social and technical aspects of town planning. This journal is edited by the *Foreningen af Byplanlæggere* (the Association of Urban Planners) and the *Dansk Byplanlaboratorium* (the Danish Town Planning Institute).

Danske byers udvikling (1972) Copenhagen: Kunstakademiets Arkitektskole, Henning Larsens B-afdeling.
A statistical survey of Danish urbanization from the late eighteenth century to 1965. The statistical information is presented in the form of easily readable maps and diagrams combining absolute and relative figures on population, economic life, etc. The captions stress important tendencies in different periods and make comparisions and rankings, but no deeper analyses. (Compare Matthiesen, 1985 and *Udvikling Danmark*, 1978.)

Dirckinck-Holmfeld, Kim et al., (1982) *Moderne dansk arkitektur / Modern Danish Architecture. Guide*. Copenhagen: Arkiték, Arkitektens forlag.
This guide to Danish architecture gives representative examples of Danish building and site plans in the post-war period. The main ideas and principles behind the different projects and plans are briefly referred to. The texts are in Danish and English. To

some degree this book overlaps with *Danish Town Planning Guide* (Svensson, 1981).

Egnsplanrådet (1971) *Regionplanlægning 1970–1975. Forudsætninger.* Copenhagen: Egnsplanrådet.

Egnsplanrådet (the Regional Plan Council) was the regional planning authority in the metropolitan area before 1973, when *Hovedstadsrådet* (the Metropolitan Council) was established. The 1971 publication was the background report to the regional plan of 1973.

Faber, Tobias (1977) *Dansk arkitektur.* Copenhagen: Arkitektens forlag.

This work presents the main features of Danish architecture from mediaeval times until the 1970s. While the book *Modern Danish Architecture* (see above) is a collection of examples with descriptive texts, *Dansk arkitektur* is a continuous historical text illustrated with examples. As in *Modern Danish Architecture* the examples mostly consist of individual buildings, but there are also examples of larger-scale site planning, such as residential districts and suburban units. The book is also available in German: *Dänische Architektur.*

Hartmann, Sys and Villadsen, Villads (1979) *Danmarks arkitektur. Byens huse Byens plan.* Copenhagen: Gyldendal.

This book is part of a series entitled *Danmarks arkitektur.* The book deals with town planning, urban design and urban architecture in Denmark from mediaeval times to the late 1970s. It focuses more on physical form and planning than the more general works of urban history or architectural history. It is a standard work on Danish town planning history. The captions are in both Danish and English.

Helkjær Jensen, Ruth and Jensen, Kr. Marius (eds.) (1976) *Topografisk atlas Danmark.* Copenhagen: Reitzels forlag.

An atlas with descriptive text, containing detailed maps of seventy-nine locations in Denmark, Greenland and the Faroe Islands. Most of the maps are fragments of the topographical map of Denmark 1:25000 (or 1:20000), but there are many examples of older maps showing the changes in the areas. Thus the atlas gives interesting illustrations of typical developments in the landscape, in the urban agglomerations and in the road network. English summary.

Holm, Axel and Johansen, Kjeld (1941) *København 1840–1940.* Copenhagen: Københavns kommune.

An historical survey of the transformation of Copenhagen from a pre-industrial capital city to a modern metropolis, edited by the municipal authorities of Copenhagen. One of the chapters deals with town and site planning, another with housing and building activity.

Institut for By-og Landskabsplanægning (1978) *Udvikling Danmark. Bind 1. Folketal.* Copenhagen: Kunstakademiets Arkitektskole.

A statistical survey of the population of all Danish urban agglomerations with more than 200 inhabitants from the late eighteenth century until 1975. Tables, maps and rankings. *Udvikling Danmark* is more detailed than *Danske byers udvikling* (see above) when it comes to the population figures and it includes more agglomerations. *Danske byers udvikling*, on the other hand, also contains figures on the economic structures of the towns.

Jørgensen, Lisbeth Balslev (1979) *Danmarks arkitektur. Enfamiliehuset.* Copenhagen: Gyldendal.

This book is part of a series entitled *Danmarks arkitektur*, and deals with single-family housing with the focus on the last 100 years. It includes presentations of larger urban areas or residential blocks and districts, dominated by single-family houses or dense low-rise houses. The captions are in both Danish and English.

Knudsen, Tim (1985) *Mod det planlagte København. Kampen for planlægningen 1840–1917.* Copenhagen: Københavns universitet.

An analysis of the beginning of modern town planning in Copenhagen: building regulations, the first social housing, transportation and sewage systems etc. This work stresses the roles of the professionals (engineers, architects, physicians) in the rise of modern urban planning.

Lebech, Mogens (1961) *Danske købstæder for 200 år siden og idag.* Copenhagen.

Published on the 200th anniversary of the Københavns Almindelige Brandforsikring (a fire insurance company) in 1961. The first part of this work contains reproductions of a great number of maps and bird's-eye views (copperplate prints) of most Danish towns in the eighteenth century. Pontoppidan's *Danske Atlas* (Danish Atlas) from the 1760s is reproduced with maps and descriptive texts. The second part of the work shows aerial photographs of most Danish towns in 1961, thus providing an opportunity for studying developments and changes in these towns over the 200 years.

Lemberg, Kai (1985) *Alligevel så elsker vi byen.* Copenhagen: Arkitektens forlag.
This book, written by the former head of the General Plan Office of the municipality of Copenhagen, deals with planning problems and planning practices in Copenhagen over the last two decades. It relates town planning to living conditions and everyday life in the city as well as to local politics.

Lorenzen, Vilhelm (1937) *Christian IV's byanlæg.* Copenhagen: A. F. Høst & sons, forlag.
A survey of town planning and urban architecture during the reign of Christian IV (1596–1648). Summary in French.

Lorenzen, Vilhelm (1947–1957) *Vore byer. Studier i bybygning. I–V.* Copenhagen: G. E. C. Gads forlag.
Vore byer (Our Towns) is published in five volumes, covering the periods 1536–1600, 1600–1660, 1660–1720, 1720–1814 and 1814–1870. It is the most detailed and broadest historical survey of Danish towns and cities between 1536 and 1870. Urban development is related to the general economic and political history of the country, and many towns are described in detail with maps and pictures. It is a standard work on Danish urbanization and town history and planning during this period.

Matthiesen, Christian Wichmann (1985) *Danske byers vækst. Atlas over Danmark.* Serie II, bind 3. Copenhagen: C. A. Reitzels forlag.
Like *Danske byers udvikling* and *Udvikling Danmark* this is a statistical survey of the development of the Danish urban agglomerations. It covers the period from the beginning of the nineteenth century until the 1980s and every urban community with more than 200 inhabitants. It contains population figures and economic statistics. It also attempts to analyse the dynamics of the urbanization process and the connections between the development of the urban system and the general economic development of the country. English summary.

Nygaard, Erik (1984) *Tag over hovedet. Dansk boligbyggeri fra 1942 til 1982.* Copenhagen: Arkitektens forlag.
A historical survey of Danish housing construction from 1942 to 1982. The author relates the building activity to the general economic, political and ideological development of the country. Thus building activity is related to cultural currents, housing policy, conditions in the housing market, technological innovations as well as to the development of town planning ideology. The account comprises individual buildings and plans for larger residential areas.

Olesen, Gunnar (1943) *Danske købstæder gennem tiderne.* Copenhagen: J. H. Schultz forlag.
A comprehensive history of Danish towns from the first mediaeval towns to the 1940s. The emphasis is on the functions of the towns in the country as a whole and on the everyday life of the towns. A good deal of attention is also devoted to the local administration and to the legislation concerning the towns. In this context the town layout patterns and physical planning are also described.

Rasmussen, Steen Eiler (1952) *Greater Copenhagen Planning. Status.* Copenhagen: Ejnar Munksgaard.
A description of the planning status of Greater Copenhagen around 1950 with the focus on the 'Finger Plan' of 1947. Available in English and Danish.

Rasmussen, Steen Eiler (1974) *København.* Copenhagen: G.E.C. Gads forlag.
A personal description of the urban development and planning of Copenhagen from mediaeval times until the 1970s. The different chapters of the book focus on different aspects of town planning. The book reflects the author's long experience of urban planning in the metropolitan region and is very well supplied with maps and photographs. The book is a standard work on Copenhagen planning.

Skriver, Poul Erik (1984) *Byerne langs Køge Bugt.* Copenhagen: Dansk Byplanlaboratoriums Skriftsserie, nr 28.
A historical survey of the urbanization along the Køge Bay, south of Copenhagen, with emphasis on the implementation of the Køge Bay plan after 1966.

Statens Byggeforskningsinstitut (1981) *Albertslund Syd og 10 nyere boligbebyggelser*, SBI-rapport 133. Copenhagen: Statens Byggeforskningsinstitut.
A comparative description of Albertslund Syd and ten more recent dense low-rising residential areas in Denmark.

Stadsingeniorens direktorat (1941) *København. De indlemmede distrikter. Byplanmæssig udvikling 1901–1941.* Copenhagen: Stadsingeniørens direktorat.
A detailed work on the development of the areas incorporated in Copenhagen in 1901. Numerous maps and photos. Several of the most renowned Danish residential areas are to be found among the districts developed in the incorporated areas in Copenhagen in the inter-war period. The book illustrates the implementation of several ideas proposed in the town planning competition of 1908.

Stadsingeniorens direktorat (1947) *København fra bispetid til borgertid. Byplanmæssig udvikling til 1840*. Copenhagen: Schultz forlag.
A detailed historical survey of urban development and town planning in Copenhagen from mediaeval times to 1840, richly illustrated with maps, plans and old pictures. Edited by the municipal authorities of Copenhagen.

Stadsingeniorens direktorat (1975) *København under borgerstyre*. Copenhagen, manuscript.
A detailed historical survey of urban development and town planning in Copenhagen 1840–1901. Together with *De indlemmede distrikter* and *København fra bispetid til borgertid* (see above) this work gives a thorough description of the urban development and planning of Copenhagen from mediaeval times to the 1940s. *Københaven under borgerstyre* has not yet been published in its final form, but a copy of the manuscript is available at the Danish Town Planning Institute in Copenhagen. The three books have been produced by the planning authorities of Copenhagen and represent an outstanding work on Copenhagen town planning history. So far no further section on planning in Copenhagen since 1941 has been produced.

Strømstad, Poul (1966) *Søerne*. Copenhagen.
A historical description of the creation of the artificial lakes around the central parts of Copenhagen, and of the town planning of the adjacent areas. A good deal of space is devoted to the planning of the former rampart and military areas between the mediaeval town and the lakes.

Svensson, Ole *et al*. (1981) *Dansk byplanguide / Danish Town Planning, Guide*. Copenhagen: Miljøministeriet, Planstyrelsen & Dansk Byplanlaboratorium.
A guide to Danish town and regional planning in the post-war period. A collection of examples with descriptive texts, referring to the main ideas and principles behind the different plans. This book gives a good survey of recent Danish urban and regional planning and of the contemporary planning problems and discussions in the 1980s. On the site planning of residential areas, the book overlaps to some degree with the guide *Modern Danish Architecture* (see above). Text in Danish and English.

Thomassen, Ole (1980) *Lyse dage og sorte nætter*. Copenhagen: Gyldendal.
A contribution to the debate on the planning problems of Copenhagen, describing brilliant and grim examples of urban planning and policy in the capital's history, and characterizing the problems and the possibilities of today.

Trap, J. P. (1858) *Kongeriget Danmark* (often referred to as *Trap Danmark*). Copenhagen: C. E. Gads forlag, 1st edition 1858 (5 volumes), latest edition 1958–72 (30 volumes).
Since the middle of the nineteenth century several editions of *Trap Danmark* have been published. *Trap Danmark* is a huge description of Denmark in many volumes, presenting every town, urban district, church, castle, etc. in the country. The town maps clearly illustrate the urban development and the descriptions of the towns give a good picture of industrial, commercial and cultural activities etc.

Villadsen, Christian *et al*. (1919) *De danske købstæder*. Copenhagen: Gyldendalske boghandel-Nordisk forlag.
A historical survey of the rise and development of the Danish towns from mediaeval times to the beginning of the twentieth century. This work deals with different aspects of urban history. One chapter concerns town layout and planning, and another concerns building traditions. Other chapters deal with manufacture, commerce, administration etc.

3

URBAN PLANNING IN FINLAND
AFTER 1850

Mikael Sundman

URBAN DEVELOPMENT AND PLANNING BEFORE 1850

For seven centuries Finland constituted an integral part of the kingdom of Sweden. In 1809 the country was incorporated into Tsarist Russia as an autonomous Grand Duchy and remained under Russian domination for more than a hundred years. Since World War I Finland has been a sovereign, politically neutral state with a market economy.

Finnish urban planning and development must therefore be considered part of the evolution of Sweden's history well into the nineteenth century. In his chapter Thomas Hall has described the general trends in Swedish urban development during that time. Here the intention is only to shed a little more light on the Eastern part of the realm.

Throughout Swedish rule Finland essentially remained a sparsely populated outpost. Large in area, the country supplied raw materials for building in the kingdom as a whole as well as food for the capital; it also served as a transit country for the trade with Russia and as a buffer against the Eastern military threat.

That the Eastern part of the realm was merely a sparsely populated outpost is exemplified by its having, in the Middle Ages, only six cities, six fortresses and six monasteries. The oldest urban communities still in existence, Turku (Åbo) and Viipuri (Viborg), both hail from the Swedish Crusades, which brought the region under Swedish dominion in the twelfth and thirteenth centuries. All other mediaeval cities are situated on the trade routes on the Baltic coast and in the south-western coastal area within Stockholm's direct sphere of influence. The Stockholm-centred economy served to curtail all urban development in Finland for a long period of time. Many potential city sites remained undeveloped in order to safeguard the trade interests of those cities already established, which were characterized by a marked German influence. As far as historians have been able to ascertain, at times as many as three-quarters of the burghers of Turku were German (see Gardberg, 1981).

Urban development was an important instrument of the economic policy of the crown during the sixteenth century. Trade and commerce were concentrated in the cities and with city burghers. In the middle of the century the policy of the crown focused on developing these cities only: Turku as the centre of the Eastern realm, Viipuri as the eastern trade and defence post, and the newly founded city of Helsinki (Helsingfors), centrally located on the southern coast. This city was intended to compete with and outmanoeuvre Tallinn (Reval) on the Estonian coast as well as to prevent illegal trade directly with Estonia from the countryside. However, the interest in developing Helsinki lessened when Sweden occupied Estonia a decade later, and the city remained an insig-, nificant provincial town.

The great planning drive of the seventeenth century was of particular importance for Finland. Trade in northern Finland was now aimed at future cities on the Gulf of Bothnia and, in particular, the energetic Governor General Per Brahe was instrumental in bringing about urban expansion in Finland. The number of towns trebled in a short time, and in the year 1668 there were as many as thirty urban communities. Trade interests, taxation, the northern and eastern defences and the administrative reform establishing different provinces formed the economic and political basis for urban development. Land surveyors educated to guarantee the economic interests of the crown were, during this period, responsible for urban planning on a scale which, relatively speaking, has never been surpassed. Twenty-two new city plans and twenty plans for regulating existing cities have been preserved from that time. A small number of Finnish cities such as Raahe (Brahestad), Kristiinankaupunki (Kristinestad) and Kokkola (Karleby) have retained the character of these new cities, a geometrically symmetrical gridiron plan of city blocks grouped around city squares and connected through streets of equal width (see Lilius, 1981 and Ranta, 1981).

The implementation of this grand programme of urban planning was a long time in the making. In part the programme was overambitious, and five cities remained undeveloped. There was not much new planning during the eighteenth century, when efforts were concentrated on planning and developing fortified cities and fortifications proper. Hall has commented on the implementation of plans for the radical city of Hamina (Fredrikshamn). The enlightened fortifications officer, Augustin Ehrensvärd, drew up elaborate city plans for

Helsinki and Loviisa (Lovisa). These plans contain many formal elements which demonstrate the evolution from the geometrical, relatively stereotype surveyors' plans towards the subtler and more dynamic ideals of classicism. The large-scale archipelago fortress of Viapori (Sveaborg) outside Helsinki was also notable as an urban environment built in stone, unique in a country dominated by wooden architecture. Russia had taken over the only old walled city Viipuri at the beginning of the century (see Lilius, 1981).

THE FINNISH TOWN BEFORE INDUSTRIALIZATION

In the mid-nineteenth century only about five per cent of the population of Finland lived in any of the thirty-two towns in the country. The towns were largely regular in design, with straight streets and more or less regular blocks, the result of constant prompting by the authorities in Stockholm over a period of more than 200 years (figure 3.1). Only Naantali (Nådendal), Porvoo (Borgå), Rauma (Raumo), Savonlinna (Nyslott), Tammisaari (Ekenäs) and Viipuri had retained part of their old irregular character.

The towns were built of wood. As late as 1842 nine towns still had no brick or stone buildings at all, and nineteen towns had no private houses in brick. Finnish towns possessed altogether 6,651 town houses of wood, but only 208 of brick (Gyldén, 1845), and of these last 180 were to be found in Viipuri, Turku and Helsinki. Due to regional differences in economic conditions the town houses in more northerly places such as Kajaani (Kajana) and Raahe were small modest buildings, while the wooden buildings in Helsinki, Turku and Hämeenlinna (Tavastehus) were quite distinguished looking in their bright Empire garb – a form of Russian-inspired classicism that was typical of the architecture of the Commissariat, (Intendentskontoret), the

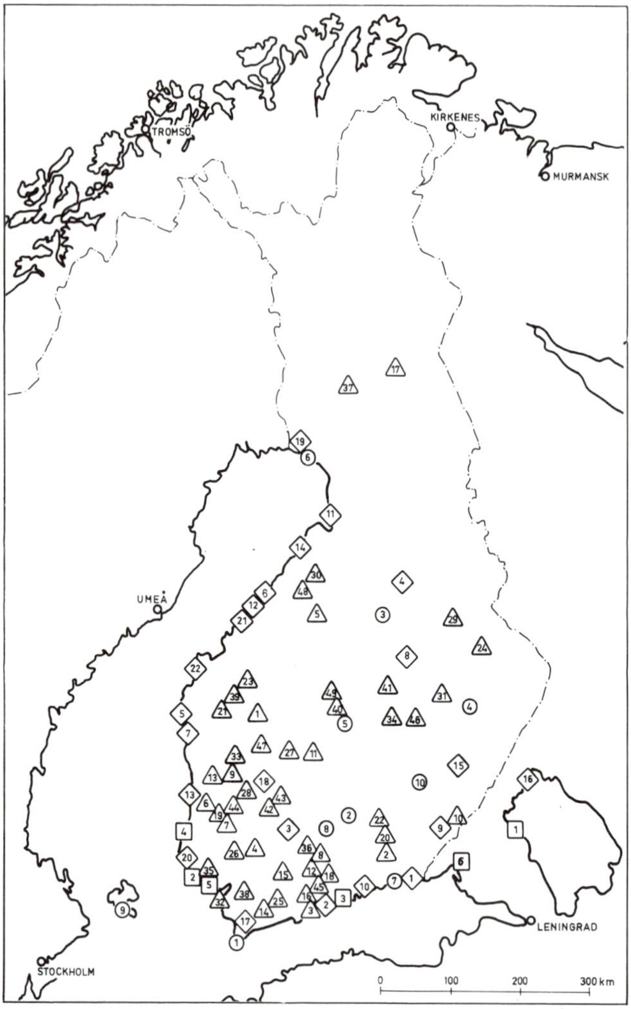

Figure 3.1. Finnish towns.

□ *Swedish period before 1500.* 1. Käkisalmi (Kexholm). 2. Naantali (Nådendal). 3. Porvoo (Borgå). 4. Rauma (Raumo). 5. Turku (Åbo). 6. Viipuri (Viborg).

◇ *Swedish period 1500–1809.* 1. Hamina (Fredrikshamn) 1721. 2. Helsinki (Helsingfors) 1550. 3. Hämeenlinna (Tavastehus) 1639. 4. Kajaani (Kajana) 1651. 5. Kaskinen (Kaskö) 1785. 6. Kokkola (Karleby) 1620. 7. Kristiinankaupunki (Kristinestad) 1649. 8. Kuopio 1782. 9. Lappeenranta (Villmanstrand) 1649. 10. Loviisa (Lovisa) 1725. 11. Oulu (Uleåborg) 1605. 12. Pietarsaari (Jakobstad) 1652. 13. Pori (Björneborg) 1558. 14. Raahe (Brahestad) 1649. 15. Savonlinna (Nyslott) 1639. 16. Sortavala (Sordavala) 1632. 17. Tammisaari (Ekenäs) 1546. 18. Tampere (Tammerfors) 1779. 19. Tornio (Torneå) 1621. 20. Uusikaupunki (Nystad) 1617. 21. Uusikaarlepyy (Nykarleby) 1620. 22. Vaasa (Vasa) 1606.

○ *Russian period 1809–1917.* 1. Hanko (Hangö) 1874. 2. Heinola 1839. 3. Iisalmi (Idensalmi) 1891. 4. Joensuu 1848. 5. Jyväskylä 1837. 6. Kemi 1869. 7. Kotka 1879. 8. Lahti (Lahtis) 1905. 9. Maarianhamina (Mariehamn) 1861. 10. Mikkeli (St Michel) 1838.

△ *Independent Finland 1918–* . 1. Alavus 1977. 2. Anjalankoski 1975. 3. Espoo (Esbo) 1972. 4. Forssa 1964. 5. Haapajärvi 1977. 6. Harjavalta 1977. 7. Huittinen (Vittis) 1977. 8. Hyvinkää (Hyvinge) 1960. 9. Ikaalinen (Ikalis) 1977. 10. Imatra 1971. 11. Jämsä 1977. 12. Järvenpää (Träskända) 1967. 13. Kankaanpää 1972. 14. Karjaa (Karis) 1977. 15. Karkkila (Högfors) 1977. 16. Kauniainen (Grankulla) 1973. 17. Kemijärvi 1973. 18. Kerava (Kervo) 1970. 19. Kokemäki (Kumo) 1977. 20. Kouvola 1960. 21. Kurikka 1977. 22. Kuusankoski 1973. 23. Lapua (Lappo) 1977. 24. Lieksa 1973. 25. Lohja (Lojo) 1969. 26. Loimaa 1969. 27. Mänttä 1973. 28. Nokia 1977. 29. Nurmes 1974. 30. Oulainen 1977. 31. Outokumpu 1977. 32. Parainen (Pargas) 1977. 33. Parkano 1977. 34. Pieksämäki 1962. 35. Raisio (Reso) 1974. 36. Riihimäki 1974. 37. Rovaniemi 1960. 38. Salo 1960. 39. Seinäjoki (Östermyra) 1960. 40. Suolahti 1977. 41. Suonenjoki 1977. 42. Toijala 1977. 43. Valkeakoski 1963. 44. Vammala 1965. 45. Vantaa (Vanda) 1972. 46. Varkaus 1962. 47. Virrat (Virdois) 1977. 48. Ylivieska 1971. 49. Äänekoski 1973.

The dates refer to the granting of town privileges. Names are given in their Finnish forms with the Swedish name in parentheses.

central building and planning authority, until the mid-nineteenth century.

The closed and stable organization – social, economic and architectural – which these towns represented began to disintegrate around the middle of the last century, due in part to the rapid growth in population (see table 3.1). Growth was greatest in the rural areas and among the non-property-owning classes. A proletariat was emerging. Migration within the

Table 3.1 Population and occupational distribution in Finland, 1840–1980

Year	Population		Population by industry (%)			
	Total	Percentage in towns and boroughs	Agriculture and forestry	Industry	Service industries	Others
1840	1,445,600	5.8	81.7	4.3	4.1	9.9
1850	1,638,900	6.2	81.0	4.3	4.3	10.4
1860	1,746,700	6.3	80.4	4.8	4.5	10.3
1870	1,768,800	7.5	78.1	5.1	4.8	12.0
1880	2,060,800	8.5	77.1	6.5	5.7	10.7
1890	2,380,100	9.9	74.7	8.0	6.2	11.1
1900	2,655,900	12.6	69.7	10.8	7.7	11.8
1910	2,943,400	14.7	65.8	12.1	7.6	14.5
1920	3,147,600	16.1	64.2	14.6	9.9	11.3
1930	3,462,700	20.6	58.2	16.4	11.9	13.5
1940	3,695,600	26.8	51.4	21.0	15.8	11.8
1950	4,029,800	32.3	41.5	29.2	22.1	7.2
1960	4,446,200	38.4	31.9	30.9	26.4	10.8
1970	4,598,300	50.9	17.6	30.1	33.6	18.7
1980	4,784,700	59.9	9.2	27.5	38.3	25.0

Sources: Peltonen (1982) and *Official Statistics of Finland*.

country had previously been hampered by strict rules regarding domiciliary rights, but these obstacles disappeared in 1865 with the new vagrancy regulations and the abolition of the 'lawful justification' requirement in 1883. Freedom of trade was introduced in 1879. This development took place more than thirty years after similar reforms had been introduced in the former mother country, Sweden (Lento, 1951).

The first manufacturing industries began to appear during the 1860s, often backed by foreign knowhow and capital. In 1857 steam sawmills were permitted and the first steam-driven machinery in manufacturing industry came into operation during the 1860s. In 1864 the law on joint-stock companies was introduced; private banking had started two years earlier. The wood-pulp industry, utilizing Finland's prime raw material, the forests, opened up during the 1880s. Traffic increased rapidly after the first steamboat began to ply the inland waterways in 1833. The important Saimaa Canal between the Gulf of Finland and the extensive eastern inland lakes was completed in 1856, and the first railway between Helsinki and

Hämeenlinna was open to traffic in 1862.

In terms of the land available, the towns were well placed to respond to the changing conditions of urban planning. By tradition the crown had donated a considerable amount of land to all new town foundations, and the tradition persisted during 'the period of autonomy', when Finland was a self-governing grand duchy under tsarist Russia. In 1856, for example, Alexander II commanded towns to be established in five places. In order to fulfill this injunction the Finnish Senate – which headed the central administration under the chairmanship of the governor general – had the right and the obligation to arrange donations of land to the future towns by compulsory purchase of land in the area.

Once the town plans had been approved, the land was transferred by the municipal authorities to private persons to build on. Land beyond the limits of the planned area was never sold, but citizens often leased land outside the planned area. This principle was not abandoned until 1943, when a new law allowed towns to sell areas of land outside the town plan with the

Table 3.2 Urban territories, 1842

	Tunnland within the town plan	Tunnland outside the town plan	Population 1843
Hamina (Fredrikshamn)	375	1,325	2,658
Heinola	80	5,177	955
Helsinki (Helsingfors)	376	3,045	13,175
Hämeenlinna (Tavastehus)	77	1,343	2,093
Jyväskylä	98	965	328
Kajaani (Kajana)	30	30,000	420
Kaskinen (Kaskö)	214	526	710
Kokkola (Karleby)	43	16,000	2,374
Kristiinankaupunki (Kristinestad)	66	4,378	2,226
Kuopio	160	2,319	2,161
Käkisalmi (Kexholm)	135	2,000	1,059
Lappeenranta (Villmanstrand)	15	80	616
Loviisa (Lovisa)	160	3,188	2,523
Mikkeli (St Michel)	67	1,619	181
Naantali (Nådendal)	23	624	571
Oulu (Uleåborg)	210	9,745	4,800
Pietarsaari (Jakobstad)	95	5,370	1,536
Pori (Björneborg)	168	5,480	4,927
Porvoo (Borgå)	165	2,689	2,767
Raahe (Brahestad)	86	3,649	1,845
Rauma (Raumo)	46	5,949	1,139
Savonlinna (Nyslott)	50	230	596
Sortavala (Sordavala)	106	2,000	759
Tammisaari (Ekenäs)	70	1,025	1,219
Tampere (Tammerfors)	169	425	1,936
Tornio (Torneå)	37	15,182	561
Turku (Åbo)	980	2,504	12,123
Uusikaarlepyy (Nykarleby)	24	3,042	1,076
Uusikaupunki (Nystad)	80	2,697	2,197
Vaasa (Vasa)	118	4,000	2,985
Viipuri (Viborg)	165	240	4,024

Sources: Gyldén (1845).
1 *tunnland* = approx. 1 acre

approval of the government (cf. Perälä, 1983).

In terms of planning technology, Finnish towns, in the mid-nineteenth century, were well equipped to deal with functional change. Planning activities were directed by the Commissariat, which in 1865 was reorganized to become the Public Building Board. It was to answer to the Senate, as the supreme authority, on all building operations in the country, and as late as the 1880s it still produced the plans for most public buildings and was responsible for all town plans. In 1848 planning activities had been decentralized and assigned to the county architects in the County Administration Board, but the Commissariat kept the central responsibility. As a result of the frequent town fires the

Commissariat and the towns themselves had acquired plenty of experience in rebuilding communities. Nor was it unusual for towns to be transferred from one place to another; Vaasa (Vasa) was transferred after a fire as late as 1852.

To begin with the architects, who were responsible to the Commissariat and later to the Public Building Board, were all foreigners, but Finnish architects were trained at the Commissariat in Helsinki or in Stockholm from the 1860s onwards, and after 1872 at the new Institute of Technology in Helsinki. Only in Turku was the town architect a municipal appointment. All the architects in the country were familiar with conditions in Sweden, and thus also with the situation in central Europe. It is perhaps rather strange that there was very little contact with St Petersburg and its Academy. In 1870 only one of the architects working in Finland had studied in St Petersburg.

After much preparation, a General Building Ordinance for Finnish towns was issued in 1856; it included directives for planning as well as building. It divided Finnish towns into four categories. In the first two, houses in the town centres were to be of brick, whilst in the two lower categories traditional one-storey wooden housing was tolerated. The main goal was fire safety. By stipulating the width of streets, by imposing a linear street pattern and a system of tree-lined avenues to divide the town into fire sectors, and by including planted areas between plots, it was intended to reduce the risk of fire. A certain tendency towards social differentiation can also be traced in these directives, according to which small plots for the less wealthy inhabitants were to be located towards the periphery of the town plan. The General Building Ordinance applied to all towns and became the planning norm for half a century.

THE GRIDIRON PLANS OF THE
NINETEENTH CENTURY

Nineteenth-century Finnish town plans were based on the 1828 Turku plan (figure 3.2). In 1827 Turku had suffered the worst fire disaster on record in the Nordic countries; over 2,500 buildings were reduced to ashes. Planning started from scratch, without reference to former conditions of ownership. The Governor General, who presided in the Senate and represented the Tsar in Finland, took an active part in the planning work, and C. L. Engel, head of the Commissariat, produced the plan.

The street network, which replaced the irregular organic structure of the old town, was laid out on a rigorously rectangular basis, broken only in the blocks around the cathedral (founded at the end of the twelfth century). The streets were generally 18 m wide, but three streets were 24 m wide. These main thoroughfares ran north-west/south-east and connected the banks of the river Aura that divides the city into two equal parts. They were intended as boundaries to the fire sectors in the town. The street network made minimal concessions to topography. A great many streets stopped abruptly where the lie of the land did not permit them to go any further. The explanation was that the building of Helsinki on similar terrain had given rise to heavy costs which, this time, were evidently to be avoided.

The regular gridiron of the city blocks was relieved by the tree-lined avenues along the river Aura, the park between the cathedral and the river, and the two large squares in the northern part of the town. This system of public spaces was consistently emphasized by the broad thoroughfares linking the various open places and the major arteries to form a coherent unit. The two mediaeval monuments, the castle and the cathedral, one at each end of the town, were linked by a single stretch of road north of the river. In accordance with the ideals of neoclassicism, the area round the church was left open and laid out as a park – a contrast to the dense building which had surrounded the cathedral before the fire.

Plots fell into three size groups. The largest

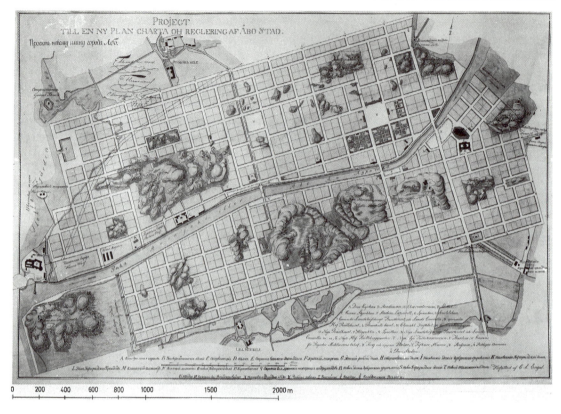

Figure 3.2. Turku, town plan by C. L. Engel, 1827.
This plan became a guiding example during the first part of the nineteenth century. The arrangement of the blocks immediately south of the square (x) shows how important green spaces were to become, both as a fire precaution and as a feature of the townscape. The town was built according to the plan. *Source*: The National Archives of Finland, Helsinki.

were close to the river, and the smallest furthest out towards the boundary on the north and south sides of the town. The rest of the town consisted of plots of more or less the same size. For three of the normal blocks, alternative building solutions were set out in detail. The emphasis on green spaces between the houses is striking, and was certainly due partly to the fire precautions and partly to the neo-classical preference for free-standing houses.

The public buildings were located in a zone between the church and the castle, following the line of the river. There is no sequence of open places or any axial perspective. Nonetheless there are suggestions of an axial design. The

University Observatory up on its hill and visible all over the town, provides a dominating accent in the townscape and a focal point for four of its streets. That no space was reserved in the plan for industry within the borders of the town is hardly surprising. Nevertheless the plan does reveal an incipient industry: the shipyard by the fortress.

The distinguishing features of this plan are rationality in the structure of the blocks, the fire precaution measures, and social differentiation. Aesthetic ambitions are revealed in a desire to vary the buildings in the individual blocks, and in the careful location of the public buildings. The public spaces are

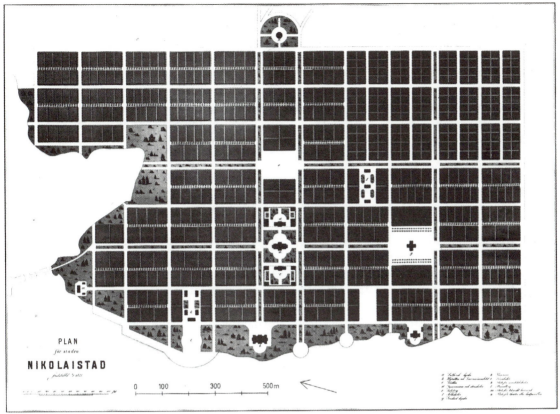

Figure 3.3. Vaasa, town plan by C. A. Setterberg 1855. Fire breaks and monumentality have shaped the urban structure, which is divided by broad tree-lined esplanades. Public buildings are located at the intersections of these main thoroughfares, the most important of them functioning as visual foci in the street vistas. The shoreline has largely retained its natural shape. Small plots for the poorer classes were located at the edge of town. The town was built according to the plan. *Source:* The National Archives of Finland, Helsinki.

defined by free-standing buildings in uniform style and size, surrounded by a wealth of greenery.

Engel's plan for Turku became an important prototype for the general building ordinances, and for the extensive planning operations launched during the 1850s by the Public Building Board (Lilius, 1981). The Board's first major project was the work of Carl Axel Setterberg, originally from Sweden, but then county architect in Vaasa county. In 1853 Setterberg presented his first proposal for rebuilding Vaasa after its destruction by fire. His final plan, dated 1856, reveals a desire to take Engel's rationalistic principle one step further (figure 3.3). The direction of the streets, the block divisions and the fire breaks have all been planned with a view to saving space, making the most efficient use of investments, and achieving maximum fire safety. The urban structure is divided by five tree-lined avenues, each 42 m wide. Within this overall system, the blocks are surrounded by streets, 15–18 m wide, which by and large cut right through the town. The residential blocks are cut in half by a 15-metre wide fire street lined with double rows of trees. Each plot is then also separated from its neighbour on the same street by a 6-metre wide alley. This hierarchic system was realized on a meagre scale, partly for economic and partly for aesthetic reasons, the idea being to create an urban space that was both more closed and more vertical than before (Lilius, 1983).

The places where the public buildings and institutions were gathered together had the same clear connection with the main thoroughfare as in the Turku plan. A new feature is that the north-south avenues cut through the middle of the open places rather than running along their sides. The two main churches, the Lutheran and the Orthodox, each marked the mid-point in their own squares, and were thus lying on the central axis of the avenue. Further, the court of appeal was located axially at the end of the avenue connecting the cemetery (furthest to the east), the market square and the church square. The free-standing public building provided a focus and structure in the otherwise uniform pattern of the blocks. All the streets except this avenue had the sea as a backdrop. The relation between the enclosed street space and the open landscape was also accentuated by the natural treatment of the continuous shoreline park. The coast was allowed to retain its natural outline, and with as little alteration as possible attractive recreation grounds were created along the waterfront. This conception of the town plan, combined with the romantic neo-gothic architecture which Setterberg adopted in his public buildings and several of the private mansions, reveals the kind of overall painterly effect he was striving for.

In addition to this, the social differentiation in the urban structure was clearly marked. The smallest plots were collected in a uniform 'working-class' district at the south-eastern end of the town. The streets and blocks here formed a pattern twice as dense as elsewhere. Otherwise, three plot sizes were consistently employed: large plots for the wealthiest residents, with brick houses round the market square and along the avenues running north-south, medium-sized plots along the intermediate streets between the avenues or in the blocks along the east-west avenues, and finally small plots furthest out on the edge of the town.

The plan contained no suggestion of the new demands imposed by steamer traffic, the railway or incipient industry. This lack of adequate allowance for the major prerequisite of urban expansion was a consistent feature of planning even as late as the 1880s, and can be seen, for instance, in the Finnish town plans of Setterberg's fellow-countryman, the versatile G. Th. P. Chiewitz.

After going bankrupt in Sweden, Chiewitz moved to Finland and was appointed county architect in Turku. Strict avenue plans for Pori (Björneborg) and Uusikaupunki (Nystad) can be traced to him. In 1860 he made a plan for the new town of Maarianhamina (Mariehamn), which shows his liking for enclosed street spaces to complement the open aspect of the avenue system. The plan closely resembles a model plan for a Swedish railway town by the Swedish architect A. W. Edelsvärd, which was published in 1859 (cf. p. 188 and Lilius, 1983).

Among the town plans that follow the requirements of the general building ordinances we should also mention the 1858 plan for Hämeenlinna by Albert Edelfelt at the Commissariat in Helsinki. There are two new features here, compared to the Vaasa plan. All the streets were tree-lined, and in combination with the system of fire breaks this guaranteed a markedly green overall effect. And the green aspect was further increased by the second novelty, namely the dense planted areas in the fire squares in the middle of the blocks. This theme was to recur in many of the plans dating from the second half of the century, for instance in Uusikaupunki, Sortavala (Sordavala), Kemi and Nurmes. The substance of the Finnish gridiron plans and their aesthetic qualities were the work of architects from Sweden, or at least trained there. But there are also signs of the influence of St Petersburg. Extensive urban planning activities had been launched in the Russian capital after the administrative reforms of the 1780s. New administrative centres in the provinces called for new plans. Between 1784 and 1836 the Tsar approved 416 complete town plans. At first this work came under the 'Commission for the Building of St Petersburg and Moscow', but after 1793 planning was decentralized to the local governments.

This vast modernization of the largely unregulated Russian urban structures can be divided roughly into two stages. Town plans during the first period up to about 1800 include complex axial arrangements, radiating street patterns and other themes familiar from the European Baroque. The second and more rationalistic period at the beginning of the nineteenth century leans towards simple gridiron plans, in which the structure of the blocks varies according to the demands of the topography. The most usual basic forms are the rectangle and the hexagon. Since the 1820s we find broad tree-lined avenues in many of the plans, while the composition of the open squares has been simplified. Public buildings, often freestanding, are located alongside or in the middle of the town squares. These plans were published in 1839 in the Russian statute book which was also available in Finland. In addition William Hastie, an English immigrant (known in Russia as Vassilij Ivanovich Gesti) had also written a pattern book for block plans which was distributed to all local governments in 1812 (Lindahl, 1974).

It is not known whether this pattern book was also available in Finland, but the similarity between the book and the planning principles adopted is striking. The emphasis on greenery, for instance in the dense vegetation in the fire squares within the blocks, is just one example. The author of a town plan will naturally want his plan to be accepted by the authority responsible for the final decision, so architects in Finland are likely to have kept themselves informed about the principles favoured in St Petersburg and in the various provinces. Nils Erik Wickberg has also pointed out that the emphasis on greenery in Engel's model Turku block was not his own idea but was the result of a demand from Governor General Zakrevski (Wickberg, 1973). And it is obvious that the Governor General, who in practice led the work on the town plan, would be familiar with the planning ideas and principles of the Russian state authorities.

When towards the end of the century industrial establishments began to affect town plans, plots were needed for the prompt provision of space to build homes for the necessary workforce. Thus many towns acquired special additional areas for workers' dwellings, for instance Helsinki, Pori, Tampere (Tammerfors) and Turku. From the point of view of urban planning, however, these areas are not particularly interesting. The gridiron plans were generally automatically extended to include an anonymous pattern of small plots for cheap houses.

The only plan to give any prominence to industry and transport was the town plan for Nurmes, far away in 'northern Carelia' (figure 3.4). The proposal was to divide the town into two halves. One, built round the market square and the Lutheran church, would fulfil the traditional function of the commercial centre, and the other would be an industrial town complete with workers' housing and areas reserved for industrial establishments in the neighbourhood of the Orthodox church and the tenement buildings.

As a result of a reform of municipal administration in 1873 the towns had acquired their own finance departments, whose tasks included supervising and managing urban building operations. Since around the same time the larger towns also created the new position of city engineer, it is not very surprising to find that even traditional urban-planning tasks in the towns slipped out of the hands of the architects employed by the national building authorities and into the hands of the city engineers (Åström, 1957). The architects had shown less interest in the needs of industry and transport than in the aesthetic design of the towns.

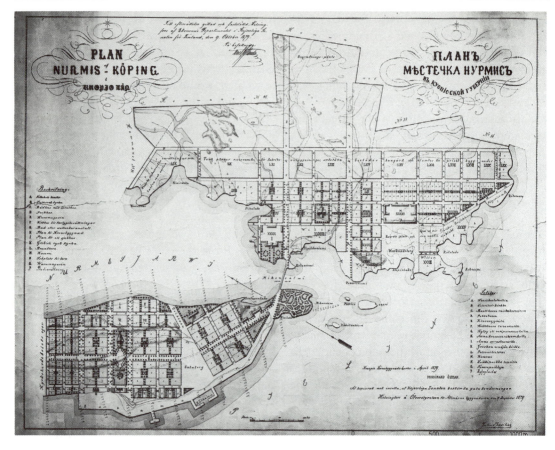

Figure 3.4. Nurmes town plan by Ferdinand Öhman 1879.
The idea was to create a commercial centre in the sparsely built region of north-east central Finland. The junction where highway and waterway converge provided the site for the new borough, which was to consist of a market town (bottom left) and an industrial town (above). Plot size was used as an instrument of social differentiation. Planted areas forming fire squares within the blocks were a standard feature of contemporary plans. The industrial section of the town was never built. *Source*: The National Archives of Finland, Helsinki.

The main town-planning tasks which occupied the attention of the engineers involved harbour and railway planning, the extension of existing town plans, and the regulation of the more ramshackle buildings round the old centres. Their position was enhanced after the reform of health and hygiene legislation, which in the 1870s linked town planning with the expansion of the public utilities.

By the turn of the century all boroughs and towns had been given gridiron plans in accordance with the requirements of the general building ordinances. But these plans had not met the actual requirements. Industry was located where ground happened to be available, often outside the plan boundaries. Nor was it possible to satisfy the demand for working-class dwellings within the planned area. Initiative and control were obviously being transferred increasingly from the central departmental level to the local authorities, which were nevertheless formally dependent on the pronouncements of the Public Building Board and confirmation by the Tsar. The aesthetic aspects of urban planning had been relegated to the background, while practical aspects and the consideration of the concrete needs of local industry and technological development now had pride of place. It is therefore not surprising that the demands which now arose for a more artistic approach to the urban environment, fell on fertile ground.

THE TURN OF THE CENTURY: AESTHETICS AND SPECULATION

Camillo Sitte's ideas reached Finland via Sweden. They inspired Lars Sonck, then 26 years old, to publish his own provocative views on planning and urbanism in the capital city. In an article in 1898 entitled *Modern Vandalism: Helsingfors Stadsplan* (Modern Vandalism: The Town Plan of Helsinki), he presents Sitte's ideas in light of the situation in the Finnish capital, severely criticizing the city's insensitive building, desolate streets and deserted squares. Sonck ends by demanding town planning competitions for Eira and Töölö (Tölö), both in Helsinki. The response was immediate and a competition for the Töölö plan was announced later that year, and in it the international currents were to acquire their Finnish interpretation. That Joseph Stübben was one of the judges in the later stages of the competition and Per Hallman from Sweden was the foreign expert, bears witness to an awakening interest in joining the general European debate (R. Nikula, 1981).

The competition became a struggle between new and old. The first prize was awarded to Gustaf Nyström, professor at the Institute of Technology, together with the city engineer Herman Norrmén (figure 3.5). The simple pattern of the blocks in their proposal was held together by star-shaped and radiating streets in the spirit of the large European cities. Sonck won the second prize with a wholly 'Sittian' project (figure 3.6). The public buildings were

juxtaposed to create complex place compositions and sequences. The residential blocks followed the contours of the terrain, the street vistas were closed except where they opened towards the parks. Small residential squares suggested a leaning towards rich sculptural effects in the handling of space. Plot width was generally greater than plot depth, as Sitte required. Sonck also developed Sitte's idea that 'no playground or public park should be open to the street', and suggested small public gardens inside the blocks. Instead of the great harbour buildings along the western shore included in the winning entry, Sonck proposed an extensive public park along the shoreline.

The Töölö competition ended in a compromise between the two award-winning proposals and launched a new phase in Finnish urban planning. The eleven entries submitted by single architects or by architect teams showed that a new planning generation was emerging in Finland, with the will and the ability to handle complicated urban-planning tasks. An indirect consequence of the competition was the establishment in Helsinki in 1907 of the office of municipal town-planning architect. The first holder of this office was Sonck's sparring partner, Bertel Jung.

The pugnacious Sonck continued to campaign for a better environment in an article, published in 1901, in which he discussed – or rather 'demolished' – Finland's small towns. He dismissed the gridiron plans of the previous generation of architects as desolate, and lacking in any element of the pleasant or beautiful. He even touched sarcastically on the social aspects of small-town life, declaring that 'a good deal of the proverbial drunkenness of the small town can be blamed on the dismal appearance of these linear villages'. As an alternative he drew a picture of small communities with compact centres surrounded by extensive areas with small houses in the greatest possible symbiosis with nature.

The social, economic and legal conditions

GUSTAF NYSTRÖM och HERMAN NORRMÉN.
Motto: *Etude.*
Första priset.

Figure 3.5. Töölö, winning entry in the 1899 town planning competition in Helsinki by Gustaf Nyström, professor of architecture, and Herman Norrmén, city engineer.
The streets largely follow the topographical conditions, while also allowing for the desired monumentality in the big squares where the streets converge. The great harbour installations bear witness to the commercial spirit that imbued planning towards the end of the nineteenth century. *Source*: Hallman (1900).

existed for building simple workers' housing as well as residential areas for the well-to-do. Land was available for sale round many towns, where former agricultural property tended to benefit from the increase in land values. As there was no law which allowed for official town planning on private land until 1932, the way was open for private planning and the sale of plots, without any regulations regarding the technical, hygienic or architectural quality of the buildings. Because of the high plot prices in the central districts, and the quality requirements and fire safety regulations for buildings within the town-plan area, immigrants from the countryside were economically unable to live in houses adapted to the building ordinances, and

were forced to settle in shanty-towns in peripheral areas. Outside the city limits there were few regulations as regards building or planning, and since a reform in 1864 it had been possible to divide the land and to sell off plots. Small speculators could thus make a profit by building wretched tenement blocks, and such areas grew up at random round many expanding industrial communities in the late nineteenth and early twentieth centuries. They had nothing at all in common with the ideal of the 'villa' estates envisaged by Sonck and others.

Garden suburbs could be established from 1898 onwards when a legal reform introduced the definition of a new concept, namely 'communities with a dense population'. Auton-

Figure 3.6. Töölö, town plan by Lars Sonck, awarded second prize in the competition in Helsinki in 1899.

The plan reveals a striving for variety and diversification in the urban structure. The plots are generally broader than they are long. Small public gardens are located inside the blocks. The public buildings are concentrated on the higher ground, where squares and open spaces succeed one another. The shore is reserved for recreation. *Source:* Hallman (1900).

omous associations were established, which bought land, planned the housing areas and sold the plots. It was round Helsinki with its relatively efficient railway network that such suburbs spread most rapidly (Harvia, 1936). Businessmen, bankers, senators and shipbuilders all became shareholders in companies of this kind, which tells us something of their speculative nature; the increase in land value in the larger towns had been obvious for a long time. That there was also a certain amount of idealism and a desire to create pleasant suburbs with small houses or to approach the question of urban space in the spirit of Sitte was generally due to the presence of some young architects among the shareholders of the companies.

Of the plans commissioned by these companies, the first (in 1901) was Sonck's modest but unusually thorough plan for Haaga (Haga), near the railway to the west of Helsinki (figure 3.7). The plan includes seventy-six house plots,

a railway station, a school, a hotel, a restaurant, a civic building and a caretaker's cottage. The street network is adapted to the topography. Sonck's architectural concept involves consistently locating houses as the background to the curving lines of the streets. A year before, Sonck had experimented for the first time with different housing patterns in the follow-up to the Töölö competition (Peltonen, 1983).

In the Eira town plan, which he created together with Bertel Jung and Armas Lindgren in 1905, Sonck finally succeeded in moulding his residential ideal into a firm overall composition (Brunila and af Schultén, 1955). For this district close to the open sea in southern Helsinki, the Public Building Board had produced a plan which did not match the ideals of these self-assured young architects. So the young men designed an alternative plan on their own initiative and at their own expense, and this was subsequently accepted as the official town plan.

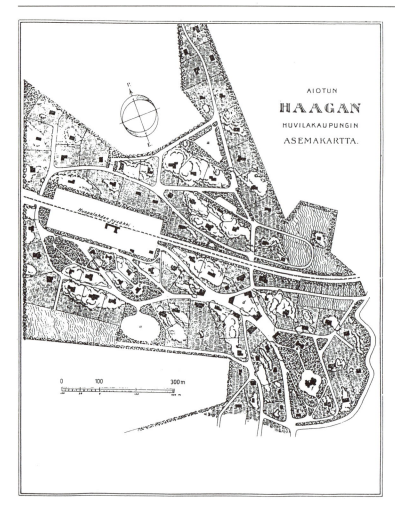

AIOTUN
HAAGAN
HUVILAKAUPUNGIN
ASEMAKARTTA.

Figure 3.7. Haaga villa suburb in the Helsinki region, plan by Lars Sonck 1901.
This small community on private land is both socially and physically a compact whole. The undulating street network has been designed as an integral part of the built environment, so that several of the larger villas have been located on high ground, providing a focal backdrop to the streets. The area was not built according to the plan. *Source:* Helsinki City Archives.

A novelty in this plan is the axiality which complements the free-standing or semi-detached mansions along the winding streets. Two controls served to supplement the plan: one was a special regulation that defined maximum heights for the cornices and roof-ridges on all eighty-seven plots, and the other was a remarkably detailed building ordinance which was established for the district and which regulated the design of the façades, landscaping, walls, and the space between the houses.

But Eira was a disappointment. The garden suburb character was obscured by skilful speculators, who managed to add low habitable ground floors and habitable attic floors to the officially two-storey buildings. Thus the houses really had four floors, and they have been called 'tenements in disguise' (Nikula, 1983) The discrepancy was only too obvious between the reality and the vision of an 'English' type of building which Sonck had launched in 1898 as his ideal for this area.

Perhaps the Eira town plan could be regarded as a spin-off from the bold ideas of Sonck and his friends for founding, planning and building a residential suburb for 'gentle folk' on the island of Kulosaari (Brändö). Plans for buying this island just east of Helsinki came to fruition in

1907, when a group of architects, engineers and businessmen joined to form the company AB Brändö Villastad. Here, perhaps, the speculative element was less noticeable than elsewhere. The pioneers of the project really got down to creating a setting for themselves and their own social class. The project was economically successful (Peltonen, 1983).

Sonck produced the original plan for Kulosaari in 1907. The house plots were grouped in blocks along gently winding streets, clearly distinguished as main and side streets and carefully adapted to the topography. The loosely-knit pattern of the blocks was held together in a firm structure by the skilful use of axial compositions. Along the straight street leading into town from the ferry in the west the eye was caught by a civic building with its slightly asymmetrical siting. On the slope behind, about 20 metres higher, stood another public building.

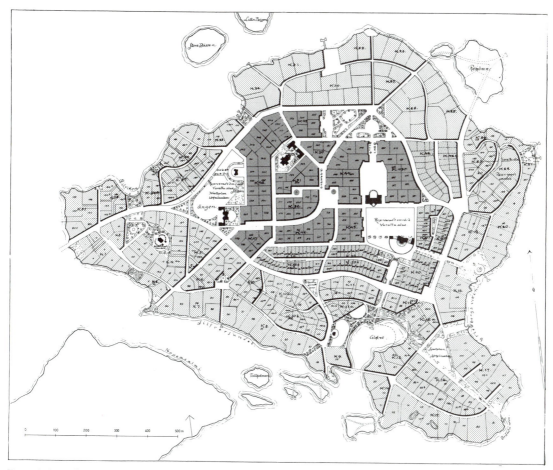

Figure 3.8. Kulosaari town plan by Lars Sonck 1909.
Kulosaari was an administratively autonomous villa suburb in the Helsinki region. The topography of this mound has been skilfully exploited, with high-rise blocks on the higher ground, surrounded by terrace houses (a novelty in Finland) and with villas towards the beaches. The crown of the hill has not been built, but three axes radiate out from it, linking the island with various important historical monuments on the surrounding islands. The area was built successively in accordance with revised plans, and intended for a prosperous social group. *Source:* Redrawn copy, Helsinki City Planning Office.

Thus the central hill, which dominated the scene topographically, also occupied a clearly defined position in the urban structure. Close to the crown of the hill there were two more public buildings, which also served as fixed points in a pattern of axial vistas: they set the residential area firmly in a broader spatial context. Further, a certain symbolism seems to be intended in the organization of the axes. The view towards the south-west ends in the central motif of the Viapori fort, namely the courtyard and the tomb of Field Marshal Ehrensvärd, the creator of the fort. The second axis points towards the main building of the great Turholm manor house, and the third – towards the north – focuses on Wik's royal stables with their echoes of mediaeval times. The hill from which these roads penetrate the historical surroundings of the town is known as 'Freemasons' Hill' (*Frimurarberget*), perhaps referring to the leisure interests of the Kulosaari pioneers. The crown of the hill, and the central point in the urban plan, has been left unbuilt – obviously inspired by Sitte's principle of 'keeping the middle empty'.

The plan was revised and radically altered by Sonck in 1909 (figure 3.8). The largest plots had sold slowly. The idea now was to replace the buildings planned for the inner town by terrace houses and multi-storey buildings. At the same time the fundamental concept of the town plan was changed. The tension was retained between a loose and topographically imposed pattern of blocks on the one hand, and strictly monumentalized axiality on the other, but a mediaeval touch – which had been wholly absent from the former plan – now seems to have been added in the small squares inserted between the blocks. Kulosaari continued to function as an exclusive, autonomous community right up to 1946, with its own town hall, its schools, tennis courts, sailing club, and its fashionable restaurant.

Sonck's enthusiasm and his many planning activities helped to spread his urbanistic ideals, with their Nordic roots and Sittean inspiration, among the architects of his own country. In the many competitions that were held – for Kuopio, Tampere, Vaasa, Turku, Jyväskylä, Mikkeli (St Michel) and Joensuu – these ideas were developed in the early years of the present century. They then spread further in the pages of the Finnish journal *Arkkitehti*, which was also published in a Swedish edition, thus guaranteeing dissemination throughout the Nordic countries.

SAARINEN AND THE MUNKKINIEMI-HAAGA PLAN

The English garden city movement soon became known in Finland through Raymond Unwin's *The Art of Designing Cities and Suburbs*. This book was presented to a Finnish audience as early as 1909, as a pioneering counterweight of 'the Viennese architects' enthusiastic cult of the mediaeval' and 'the learned pedantry of the coryphées of Cologne' (R. Nikula, 1981). It was the two architects Sigurd Frosterus and Gustaf Strengell who counteracted the violently romantic national architecture that flourished around the turn of the century with a more sober and international approach, and the same two drew attention to the town-planning debate in the Anglo-Saxon world. Strengell presented Hampstead Garden Suburb in two major articles in 1910. At the same time, from 1910 onwards, there was also a marked shift in interest away from garden suburbs towards the problems of the big cities and the monumentalizing urban ideals inspired by Otto Wagner's Vienna and by Berlin. Jung, town-planning architect in Helsinki, and his successor Birger Brunila were the leaders of this school. They spread their ideas in *Arkkitehti* and through the publicity which their bold monumental plans for the centre of Helsinki achieved in the national press. Concurrently, Eliel Saarinen launched his urban planning career with a theoretical discussion of the problems of the big cities which he presented in 1911 in an expert submission on the general plan for Budapest. This submission has since come to be regarded as Saarinen's manifesto, prefiguring his own later large-scale plans. He gained experience from the Canberra competition (second prize, 1911) and in the town planning competition for Greater Reval (first prize, 1912).

In the 1915 plan for Munkkiniemi-Haaga (Munksnäs-Haga) Saarinen merged the principles of garden city and big city planning (figure 3.9). The private company M.G. Stenius, in which Saarinen was a shareholder, had commissioned the plan, which sprang from two sources: the fact that Helsinki could no longer expand within its own boundaries, and the fact that Stenius possessed extensive land holdings north-west of Helsinki.

This plan, designed on a grand scale in Finnish and even in international terms, was the first modern master plan in Finland. It contains a theoretical section and a description (163 pages altogether), as well as the plan itself published in a beautiful colour plate. The theoretical section includes a survey of the history of town planning and of contemporary currents: Ebenezer Howard's ideas in *Garden Cities of Tomorrow* are discussed, and Unwin and Parker's Hampstead Garden Suburb is invoked as a good example of a modern environment. The plans for Letchworth, Port Sunlight and Bournville in England are also presented. This section of the plan also provides detailed population forecasts and land-use analyses for the different urban functions. There is also an aesthetic discussion of various elements in the urban space, as well as sections on building design and the legal aspects of implementation, and a discussion of the municipal organization which would handle building, public utilities, and the necessary services.

The plan itself presents a suburb consisting of large blocks of flats with uniform courtyards, terrace-house areas 'for different social classes',

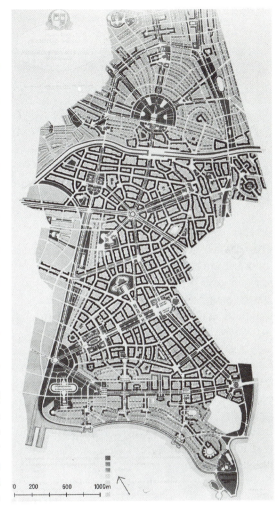

Figure 3.9. Munkkiniemi and Haaga, suburbs on private land north-west of Helsinki, proposed plan by Eliel Saarinen.
Axial monumentality and a desire to create intimate street settings and a varied urban structure characterize this plan, which is geared to a population of ca. 170,000. Furthest south are fashionable residential districts with villas. Areas with blocks of flats were intended for the middle and working classes. It was proposed that the northern districts should be built with villas as well as terraces and small houses for workers. Industrial area is located to the north-west. Only certain parts of the area furthest south were realized according to the plan. *Source:* The plan exists in book form, see Saarinen (1915).

small house estates for the working class, and fashionable residential areas furthest to the south along the shore. These last three all reveal an unmistakable debt to Unwin. Once again the areas of flats are directly influenced by the Sitte school, with their organic street network and concentration of public buildings in varied but always monumental public places. The street vistas have been carefully organized so that almost every one is closed by some architectural feature: a square, a public building, a tower, or an interesting gable-end.

In the 2.5 × 5.0 metre model which has been preserved, more than forty monumental towers give to the urban silhouette a Sitte-inspired painterly quality, while also underscoring the varying level of the terrain. From the Helsinki centre Saarinen has taken the insistence on a common maximum cornice height (23 m). In this way the carefully organized vertical accents add a sensitively-balanced touch to the urban fabric. The monumental axial perspectives – a counterweight to the organic block structure – have obvious Wagnerian overtones, and the impressive business boulevards could have been taken straight from Haussmann's Paris. This resemblance is reinforced by two star-shaped places, one open and one closed. The design of the northern part of the suburb reveals an obvious structural link with Howard's concept of the garden city (Mikkola, 1984a).

Of this plan for Munkkiniemi-Haaga only fragments were ever realized. Nonetheless it came to represent a shining example to the town planners of the 1920s, and the actual process of planning at Saarinen's studio included an element of urbanistic training. O.-I. Meurman, a member of the team and later professor at the Institute of Technology, has pointed out that Finnish town planners did not break free of Saarinen's planning principles until after the Second World War (R. Nikula, 1981).

The Munkkiniemi-Haaga plan suggested something of a total plan for the whole Helsinki region. But Saarinen and the private company which he represented did not suggest any major changes for Helsinki itself. Also, his scheme was criticized for its unilateral concern with the north-west in plans for extending Helsinki. But Saarinen was not uninterested in studying the whole urban organism on a grand scale. Immediately after Finland's independence and during the bloody civil war of 1918, Saarinen and Einar Sjöström together with Jung, who had now left his job as town planner in Helsinki, published a general plan for the whole capital-city region (figure 3.10). The plan was entitled 'Pro-Helsingfors', and it was financed by a businessman who intended to donate it to the city of Helsinki on his own sixtieth birthday. It provides a vision of a future Greater Helsinki and in character represents a development of Howard's garden city model adapted to the existing urban structure and the conditions of land ownership.

The plan suggested that, to the old inner city, a new business centre should be added, round a new railway terminal 3 km north of the original city centre. A monumental 'King's Avenue' lined with residential and business-blocks, and with a transverse axis of public buildings (the administrative centre of independent Finland) was proposed, to bind the old and new cities together, and the idea was that this compact urban structure should expand both north-east and north-west. Further out from the centre, smaller suburbs with 10,000–12,500 inhabitants are woven into a network of satellite towns, each one round its own station and centre. These are connected by a traffic system based on railway, tramway and suburban lines. It has been claimed that Saarinen's ideas recall the neighbourhood ideology of the 1930s, with small independent units in which the school was the module (Meurman, 1969). With his bold idea of moving the railway station, the administrative centre and even the university towards the north, Saarinen has succeeded in creating a radically new urban structure. The suggestion was that the earlier semi-circular town should

Figure 3.10. Greater Helsinki, town plan proposed by Eliel Saarinen and Bertel Jung 1918.
Vision of an administrative, commercial and industrial centre for Finland. Intended for a population of ca. 0.7 million, in a series of satellite towns in a semicircle round the old city and connected by railway and tramlines. Planted areas form corridors linking the different parts of the town together and continuing all the way to the centre. The plan made no immediate impact on urban development in the Helsinki region. *Source:* The plan is published with a description in Jung (1918).

be developed concentrically, focusing on the new commercial centre of Pasila (Fredriksberg). This meant a radical alteration in the position of the Munkkiniemi-Haaga area; it would now be as close to the city centre as the old city would be.

However, the gap between vision and resources was a big one. The young capital city remained locked within its boundaries. Helsinki could not realize the plan. The private landown-ing companies, governed by the profit motive, were dependent on the ups and downs of the building cycle. The only way in which Helsinki could step in and impose any kind of planned development would be by acquiring the land. But it was not for sale. Saarinen's brilliant design and grand vision were at one and the same time necessary and impossible. In 1924 the architect moved to the United States for good.

THE 1920s – THE EMERGENCE OF PUBLIC PLANNING

It was the uncontrolled development around Helsinki, Tampere, Turku and Viipuri which in 1919 triggered the preparation of a new Town Planning Act framed in 1931 that came into force in 1932. John Uggla, the lawyer who drew up the Act, had previously assisted Saarinen on technical points of law in the Munkkiniemi-Haaga plan. He was in touch with Swedish conditions and was familiar with the general architectural debate about the physical and functional qualities of towns. He made a careful study of the Swedish Town Planning Act of 1907 and the work that preceded it (see pp. 179–180). 'We must assume that building developments in future will to no small extent take place on privately owned land; and this inaugurates a new and important phase in the history of Finnish urban development'. Thus was the new law motivated.

The main purpose of the Town Planning Act was to regulate the economic relations between the private landowner and the community. Further, a new instrument of control was introduced in the shape of town-planning regulations. Until then, apart from the definition of plot boundaries in the town-plan map, local building ordinances had provided the only opportunity for controlling developments. This technical innovation was copied direct from Swedish law. The idea was to promote 'a good standard type of building'.

By the time the Act came into operation after more than a decade of preparatory work, the problems of the working-class suburbs were worse than ever. Public services had been neglected, traffic conditions were awful, the water supply and sewers were badly organized or left entirely to the inventiveness of the individual inhabitants. The property companies were almost bankrupt. Helsinki bought up the companies one by one, thus acquiring the landowner's right to intervene in the development of

areas in its neighbouring municipalities. But there was no urban planning as such in these areas until 1946, when the suburbs were incorporated into the city of Helsinki.

Since the legislative deliberations took place in the capital city in close collaboration with the architects there, it is not surprising that Helsinki's experiments and experiences were reflected in the Act. A particular case in point was the use of façade patterns. This system had been initiated as early as 1913, when the Helsinki town-planning architect launched a scheme whereby builders buying land from the town were obliged to adopt façade designs, determined as a result of public architecture competitions. At the beginning of the 1920s the baroque façades of seventeenth-century Paris, Nancy and Potsdam were quoted as models for this procedure. Göteborg was also mentioned particularly as a suitable model in Sweden. Brunila's declaration that 'artistic individualism must make way for the overall effect', shows how the individualistic attitudes of the turn of the century were having to yield to the grand and the unified (R. Nikula, 1981). 'It will be the chief task of the immediate future to seek once again to achieve such unity' Strengell wrote in his popular and widely read book *Staden som Konstverk* (The Town as a Work of Art, 1922), which he describes as a reply to A. E. Brinckmann's work, and particularly to *Platz und Monument*, (1912). After 1923, following Meurman's experiment with façade systems in his plan for Riihimäki, the construction of pattern designs became part of the praxis in Helsinki. These contributed to the remarkably uniform urban scene in Vallila (Vallgård) and Töölö, where a Jugend plan in the spirit of Sitte was thus realized thirty years later with buildings in neo-classicist or modern style.

During the 1920s house architecture was widely influenced by the style known as Nordic classicism. But classicism had surprisingly little impact on town planning. Perhaps Saarinen's legacy was too dominating for a new current to get a foothold. However, the architectural profession did establish a firm grip on town-planning activities, while the central state authority, the Public Building Board, remained passive. Viipuri, Turku and Tampere all acquired municipal town-planning architects.

During the 1920s the system of competitions became established as the chief forum for the debate on urban planning. The free-standing building was launched in the town-planning competition in Tampere (1922), where Hilding Ekelund skilfully varied closed blocks with par-allel lamella housing. A new and airy character has been introduced, and a new restraint im-bues the classicist grandeur. The proposal was awarded the third prize, losing to more tradi-tional suggestions reminiscent of Saarinen's approach (Salokorpi, 1984).

The most important planning task from the national point of view – the redevelopment of Helsinki centre – led to a competition in 1924. Saarinen's grand-scale conception was now studied in detail. Oiva Kallio won, with a vision of a great city with splendid buildings,

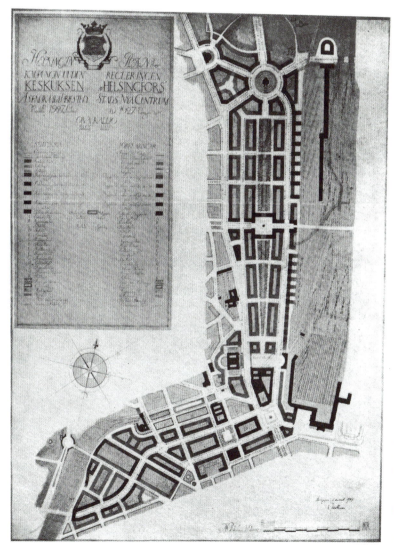

Figure 3.11. Helsinki centre, plan proposed by Oiva Kallio 1927.
This plan bears witness to the trends towards monumentalism in 1920s classicism. Efficient land use does not allow for green corri-dors running out to the edge of town. Strategically located tower blocks, over 50 m high, provide accents in the townscape. *Source*: Helsinki City Planning Office.

monumental places and grand vistas (figure 3.11). The big-city image was reinforced by perspective drawings with aeroplanes and cars sweeping by (figure 3.12). The monumental axiality in the proposal developed in 1927 brought the four main places envisaged together to form an architectural whole dedicated to strict symmetry and monumentality. Saarinen's legacy can be seen in the application of vertical themes. The tall buildings (over 50 metres high in the middle of the central axis) are intended to provide a focal point for the main western artery into the city. Five other equally tall tower blocks are placed as visual points in the background or at the entrance to the most important squares. In Helsinki, where the height of the buildings was traditionally more modest, the effect of all this would have been powerful. The Haussmann-inspired monumentality and linearity of the streets also stems from Saarinen's ideas. Strengell's influence is evident in the rhythmical variation-in-unity which was his aim for the aesthetic quality of the urban image, and in the skilful design of the squares.

In the same competition Ekelund, who was later to be city architect of Helsinki, produced a more refined and varied monumentalism, in which free-standing lamella houses are cunningly used to emphasize the monumental scale of the buildings in Finland's young capital. Water is included in various contexts to offset the closed character of the buildings. His proposal was not awarded a prize, but its perspective drawings reveal classical visions of a great metropolis which are unique in the Nordic countries and represent a high point in the classicist urban planning era in Finland (Paavilainen, 1983).

As well as these exercises in intensive monumentalization, efforts were also under way to tackle the intolerable housing situation of the working-class population. This had been aggravated by the economic decline during the First World War, and the dramatic revolt that ended in a bloody civil war in 1917–18. Ten years earlier the Association for Public Building Operations had been established on the Scandinavian model, providing fertile soil for social, sanitary and architectural reforms. Ambitious

Figure 3.12. Illustration to Oiva Kallio's 1927 plan.
This vision of pulsating life in the densely built business centre was drawn by Elsi Borg. *Source*: Museum of Finnish Architecture, Helsinki.

housing reform congresses were arranged by the Association, and the idea of garden suburbs for workers was discussed. In Helsinki demands for healthy working-class suburbs of good environmental quality were given shape in Käpylä (Kottby).

The district was planned in collaboration with the most active of the town planners, Brunila and Meurman, together with prominent classicists such as Martti Välikangas and Akseli Toivonen. Although the district is called a garden city, it broke with Howard's principles: there are no workplaces, and the community is

too small to support its own services (figure 3.13). All the same, Käpylä was to become a synthesis of the major environmental impulses of the 1920s. Italian-inspired classicism is evident in the low roof pitches, the balusters, festoons, pilaster strips, arcades and the almost abstract window caps. A sort of aesthetic minimalism originating from Tessenow has generated an almost ascetic morphological restraint, a striving for intimacy, light and clarity. The international trend towards unity in the urban scene as advocated by Paul Wolf is evident in the straight rows of free-standing and indi-

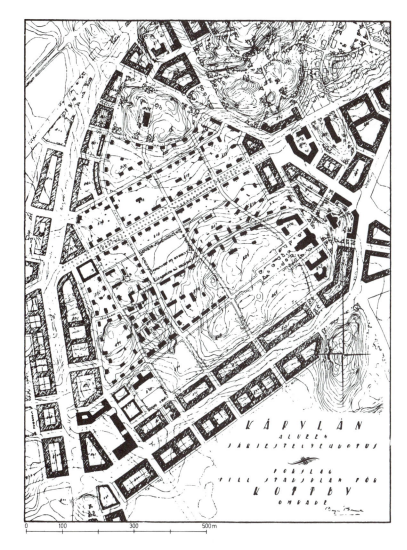

Figure 3.13. Käpylä, town plan for a working-class suburb north of Helsinki by Birger Brunila and Otto-I. Meurman, 1920.
Blocks consisting of detached four-family wooden houses are grouped round common facilities in the middle of each block. The area is separated from the surrounding major roads by blocks of flats. The wooden houses were built between 1920 and 1925.
Source: Helsingfors stads historia, V, 1, 1964.

vidually treated buildings along the streets, while the national legacy appears in the wooden building material and in the grouping of houses round a common courtyard with separate entrances for each dwelling. In the same way a hundred years earlier the international neo-classical style had generated a national version in the wooden architecture of the 'Empire' towns.

It is worth noting that the *storgårdskomplex* – whole blocks built in the same style round a common courtyard – which were so common in Berlin, Amsterdam, Vienna, Copenhagen, Oslo and Stockholm (cf. pp. 23 and 207, and Linn, 1974) remained rare in Finland.

THE 1930s: FUNCTIONALISM AND THE 'FOREST TOWN'

It may at first seem surprising that modernism, as manifest for example in CIAM's meetings, made so slight an impact on planning during the 1930s, although there were two brilliant and internationally receptive advocates of modernism in Finland, namely Alvar Aalto and P. E. Blomstedt. Added to which, ever since the beginning of the century the planning debate had turned mainly on aesthetic issues, sometimes verging on élitist preciosity. In other words the country should have been highly receptive to the pure, intellectual aesthetics of modernism.

But the very well-spring of functionalist town-planning principles, the big city and its sanitary problems, was lacking in Finland. The ultra-conservative German-oriented political climate with its anti-Nordic tendencies provided an increasingly poor sounding-board for a social approach to town planning (Salokorpi, 1984). And the absence of functionalist planning is also partly explained by the fact that the main function of town planning was to regulate the uncontrolled growth of the almost entirely wooden shanty towns round many towns and station communities.

The innovator, and at the same time the

exception, in Finnish town planning was Aalto. After producing competition projects in outline for Norrmalm in Stockholm in 1933 in the international manner, he achieved his breakthrough as a town planner with the plans for the cellulose factory and workers' housing at Sunila in the middle of the decade (figure 3.14). The plan has been called the first Finnish forest town, and it contains many of the features which were to

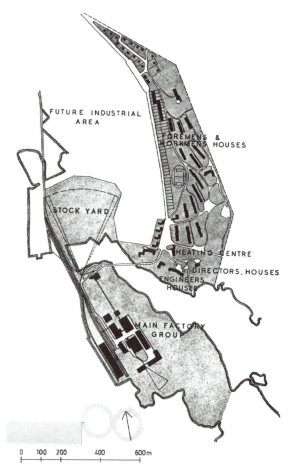

Figure 3.14. Sunila sulphate cellulose mill immediately north-west of Kotka on the south coast. Town plan by Alvar Aalto 1936.

The factory on its island is segregated from the residential area, where lamella houses are located in groups on sandy ground dotted with rocks and pines. Aalto also designed the houses, which were built between 1937 and the mid-1950s. *Source:* Wickberg (1959).

become characteristic of Aalto's town plans (Mikkola, 1980).

The factory with its dynamic profile is at the core of the plan. It is designed as a series of uniform rectangular blocks. The factory's rectangular design contrasts with the houses, located informally and rhythmically in the surrounding terrain. The social commitment which is an important ingredient in functionalism is evident in Aalto's striving for equality: the overall concept here is that everyone regardless of rank should have a good house and equal access to nature, although in social terms the community reflects a traditionally hierarchic system. The managers' detached villas, the engineers' and foremen's terrace houses, and the workers' multi-storey buildings and owner-occupied homes form an organic whole, consisting of houses individually and sensitively adapted to the nature of the terrain. Pines and rocks have been left as they were between the houses. Many writers have emphasized the biological conception that dominates this area. Leonardo Mosso, for example, describes the architectural structure as 'free in the same way that an organic and infinitely complex growth process is free, or as hundreds of logs are free as they float down the river' (Mosso, 1967). Certainly the visual impression created by the town plan is reminiscent of actual elements in the production of cellulose: the houses, for instance, can be seen as the logs, floating towards the factory buildings. The radical functionalists' persistent emphasis on the international impulse in cultural development has also left its mark on Sunila in the pure clear colours of the dwelling-houses, which was the contribution of Aalto's friend Fernand Léger (Lindberg, 1978).

Among the few functionalist town plans to be found in Finland mention should be made of the plan for the Olympic Village in Helsinki by Ekelund and Välikangas, and which was built during 1939–40 (figure 3.15). This was the first suburban district in the country to have lamella housing. The open type of building subtly adapted to the contours of the terrain reflects a fundamentally humanistic approach to the design of a residential area. Further, the architecture also marks a return in a simplified form to the ideals of the previous decade.

With these two plans Finland had acquired a national variant of the German Siedlung principles. Both Sunila and the Olympic Village exemplify new planning ideals which were also beginning to appear in the other Nordic countries, and which were to be generally applied over the following decade (Helander, 1983). The Finnish element can be seen in the close relationship between buildings and landscape, and the reciprocal relationship between house planning and town planning. The establishment in 1940 of a chair in 'town-planning theory' at the Institute of Technology reflected the view of town planning as an integral part of the architectural discipline. There have never been separate town-planning programmes at the first academic level in Finland, which perhaps explains the close connection there between town planning and house design.

RENEWAL AND ANGLO-AMERICAN INFLUENCE

The post-war years became a period of national reconstruction and cultural reorientation. Finland's former political and cultural ally, Germany, had been defeated. The Soviet Union, regarded by the conservative parties and the social democrats alike as the arch-enemy, had not only conquered Finland but had also destroyed for ever the great national dream of annexing Carelia and the vision of a greater Finland. The formerly proscribed communist party and a broad leftist alliance enjoyed considerable success in the first political election of the peace. Collaboration and peaceful co-existence with the Soviet Union was the only politically feasible path to follow for the redevelopment of the country and of a Western-type democracy. National renewal meant a clear

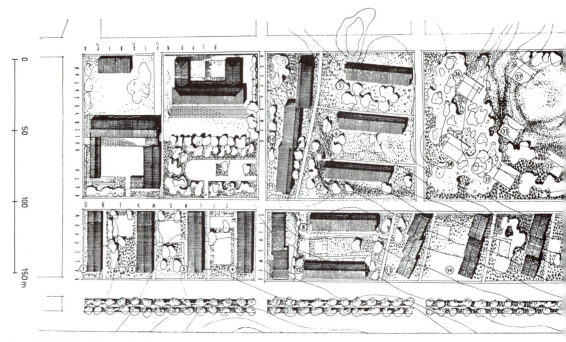

Figure 3.15. The Olympic Village in Käpylä, Helsinki. Town plan by Hilding Ekelund and Martti Välikangas, 1938. The area was built in 1939–40 for the 1940 Olympic Games which were cancelled. *Source:* Wickberg (1959).

cultural shift towards the Anglo-Saxon world. Lewis Mumford's *The Culture of Cities* was published in Finnish in 1946, and it also contained Sir Patrick Abercrombie's plan for Greater London and the general plan for the London County Council produced in collaboration with J. H. Forshaw (Mikkola, 1972). The English neighbourhood-unit concept, which was known as the 'residential neighbourhood theory', became known more widely among Finnish architects when, in 1947, Meurman published his Stübben-inspired *Asemakaavaoppi* (Town Planning Theory).

In 1939 only 20 per cent of the population lived in towns or boroughs. Of these barely 1 million people, one-third were to be found in Helsinki. Even during the 1940s, the post-war reconstruction programme did not lead to extensive urbanization. The men returning from the front, and the populations of the ceded territories amounting to 425,000 people, often settled in the rural areas in small village-like communities. The government resettlement authorities effected a land reform, creating many new small farms and intervening in the private ownership arrangements of the countryside. Areas with simple wooden buildings were also erected around many towns (resettlement areas). Traditional wooden building techniques in an extremely standardized form offered a method of solving the acute housing shortage in both rural areas and towns. Sweden donated about 2,000 industrially produced small houses designed by Finnish architects. Building in the rural areas continued to be free until 1949, after which building plans and building permits were also required for building outside the boundaries of towns and boroughs. But no town plans were required for these areas, and a second generation of scattered small-house districts thus grew up at random round the towns.

Aalto's importance in designing the strategy for the post-war renewal programme and in maintaining a strong social and humanistic

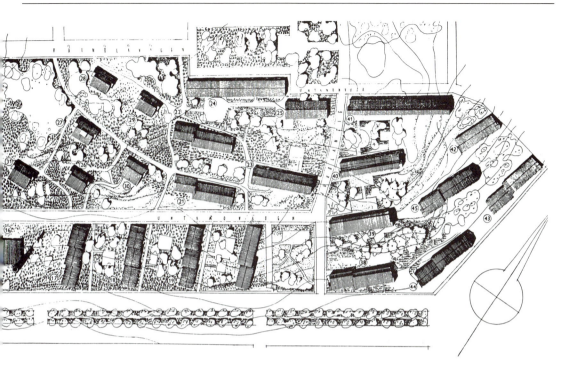

commitment to developing the architectural basis for industrial mass production, is often cited. He was the driving-force behind the re-development bureau at the Institute of Finnish Architects, which was later to be known as the Standardization Institute (Helamaa, 1983). Aalto recognized that redevelopment could not be effected simply by a rapid extension of the towns. His 1941 manifesto was headed 'Build-ing in the Rural Areas' and its subheading was 'The most vital issue in our redevelopment operations and, in a longer perspective, in our country's building culture as a whole and thus our internal social balance' (Aalto, 1941b). In the United States he had worked for the idea of *The American Town in Finland*, a model for urbanization. Together with the Disaster De-partment of the American Red Cross at MIT he had developed the notion of the 'Embryo Shel-ter' as the basic unit for continual extension. The focus was on housing for rural districts.

Under Aalto's chairmanship (1942–58) the Institute of Finnish Architects' redevelopment bureau also produced a model plan for the redevelopment of Rovaniemi, which was burnt down by the Germans as they withdrew. This was known as the 'Antler Plan' of 1944–1945. The plan, which retained a gridiron pattern in its central area, consists otherwise of apparently informally arranged building lots round the five main arteries (or branches of the antlers) which converge at the centre. All the public buildings were linked to these arteries. The importance of this central place as a traffic junction could not have been more clearly emphasized. The resi-dential areas were 'clustered like crystals' in the sections between the arteries. It was expressly stated that the plan should allow for flexibility to later needs, but 'the community need not for this reason remain either now or in the near future a formless surrogate for a more grandiose tomorrow' (Salokorpi, 1984).

The first regional plan in Finland, the area plan for the Kokemäki (Kumo) valley (1942–43), drawn up by Aalto and inspired and financed by an industrialist, was also Anglo-

American in its approach. Aalto's activities at MIT and the influence of Mumford's book lie behind this plan, which also has affinities with Henry Wright's regional plan for New York. Other regional studies such as the Imatra master plan at the end of the 1940s (figure 3.16) were also privately financed, in this case by the large forestry corporation Enso Gutzeit. A region of over 300 km² in Imatra was to be given a uniform dynamic form, around three residential centres. Aalto himself speaks of 'cells' when he refers to the flexible allotment of land for the residential areas, where different types and sizes of housing were freely combined (Rautsi, 1984).

Aalto's most detailed regional plan was the 'General Plan for Lappland' of 1950–55 (figure 3.17). The redevelopment of the landscape which had been almost totally burnt by the Germans, was discussed in this experimental plan; particularly important was the analysis of the special character of the northern landscape, natural and cultural. Aalto provided here a model for regional planning of a type he had been calling for as early as 1941. At that time, in his article 'Building in the Rural Areas', he predicted the urbanization process which would spread not only in the population centres but also in the countryside. 'It is quite obvious that a completely new and ramified societal level is emerging in Finland, higher than the level embraced by the urban concept. It will consist of a combination of industrial, agrarian, communications and cultural activities distributed over extensive areas.'

Aalto's activities as the founder of Finland's regional planning system took place independently of the kind of planning based on private initiative and supported by the Institute of Finnish Architects, which ultimately led to the institutionalization of the system. The Central Association for Regional Planning (*Seutusuunnittelun Keskusliitto*) was founded in 1956. In 1958 the regional plan was established as an official planning tool, and it assumed legal form

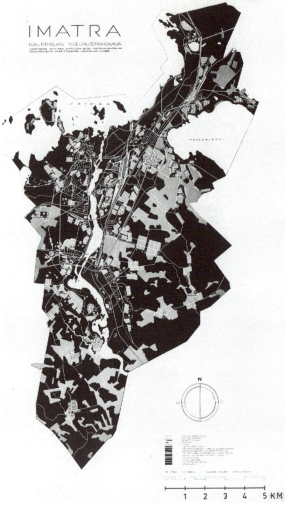

Figure 3.16. Imatra general plan by Alvar Aalto, 1952. In the plan for this heavily industrialized municipality of ca. 300 m² land was earmarked for a railway, a rapid transit road, streets, power lines, public buildings, a sports and recreation ground, a business centre, high-rise houses, owner-occupied homes, gardens and allotments, parks, plantations, industry, small industries, a cemetery. The area was intended for a population of 100,000 divided between densely-built rural villages and seven communities with houses up to three storeys high. The main centre was to be near the bridge about 3 km south of the mouth of the river. The plan made little impact on actual developments. *Source*: Museum of Finnish Architecture, Helsinki.

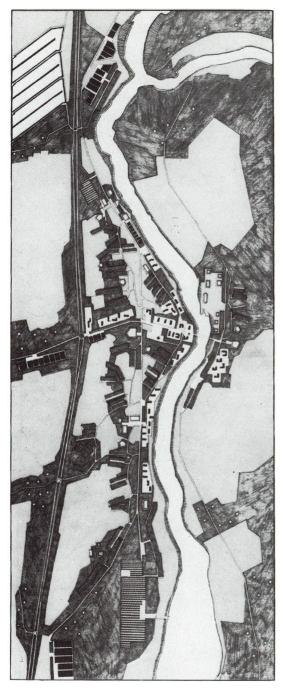

Figure 3.17. Pelkosenniemi, Lapland, illustration to the general plan by Alvar Aalto, 1955.
The former scattered building pattern was to be concentrated into a few densely built villages, with some land reserved for industry. The new regional highway was to be combined with existing roads for local traffic. The plan is more in the nature of a theoretical and experimental study, and is one of the plans which together are known as 'the General Plan for Lappland'. It was never realized. *Source*: The architectural firm of Alvar Aalto & Co, Helsinki. (Scale 1:2500)

protect agricultural and outdoor recreation areas. Thus Aalto's active guiding plan underwent a long metamorphosis, ending up as a passive plan for safeguarding the arable land, the woods and the shores which were still unbuilt by the 1980s. Regional planning never caught up with the control of urbanization; instead it became a way of checking up on land-use development.

Another good example of the strength of the Anglo-Saxon influence is provided by Tapiola (Hagalund), which is described as a garden city, but which is really more of a New Town on British lines. This 'daughter town' of Helsinki, as Tapiola was often called during the 1950s, is dominated by multi-storey houses and it is the result of a private initiative. A citizens' organization with both conservative and social democratic affiliations was formed as land was acquired by the public utility company Population Association (*Väestöliitto*/Finnish Population and Family Welfare Federation) under its director, the lawyer Heikki von Hertzen. The company arranged for the planning of this former country estate, amounting to 230 hectares, and building began in 1951. The main idea was to create an agreeable high-quality architecture in close proximity with nature, as well as to prove that good residential areas could be produced under private auspices on a public-utility basis. Von Hertzen's pamphlet *Koti vaiko kasarmi lapsillemme* (Homes or Barracks for Our Children, 1946) provides a good description of the ideals that inspired this project.

in 1968 as a result of a change in the law. Thirty years after Aalto's initiative, the Finnish regions had acquired their first subplans, not mainly in order to control urbanization but to

The record-quick building of the town during

the 1950s owed more, architecturally speaking, to ideas about a new Finnish type of close-to-nature urban living than to any town plan. Meurman had, in 1946, produced a layout housing plan for one-family homes which simply defined the main lines of the street network and the rough position of the centre. But in the actual process of planning, the leading architects who had been invited to take part were given a relatively free hand in designing and locating houses in their own particular sections. A free way of working without a town plan seemed to be the natural solution. An overall urban-planning concept would have made it difficult to consider the natural landscape to the extent required by the original idea. The urban structure that gradually emerged from the 'unplanned' planning of these collaborative architectural efforts was divided into several neighbourhood units, one to the east,

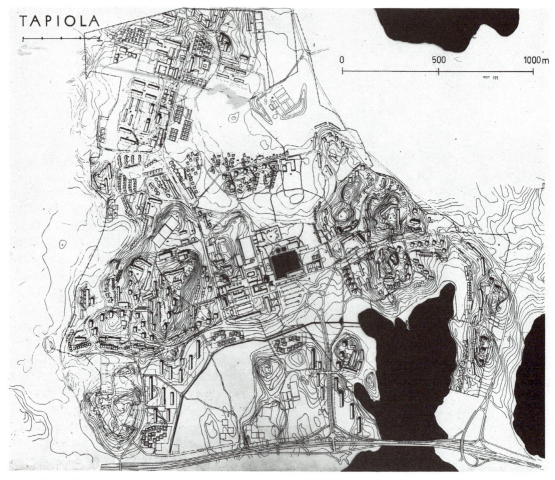

Figure 3.18. Tapiola garden city, Espoo (Esbo), begun in 1951.
The plan is divided into a centre and neighbourhood units – east, west and north – and was the result of close collaboration with the architects who designed the houses. The traffic network with its central streets derives from a 1945 plan for a villa district. The dwelling-houses are arranged informally, in contrast to the rectangular structure of the centre. The northern neighbourhood unit was added in 1958 and marks a return to a more formal town plan.
Source: Museum of Finnish Architecture, Helsinki.

one to the west and later also a northern neighbourhood unit. The final shape was largely the result of collaboration between the architects and the enthusiastic idealist and organizer, von Hertzen (figure 3.18).

Lamella houses, point blocks and terrace houses were arranged informally in the forest. Open areas were retained, offering a counterpoint to the wooded landscape. The lamella houses break off as the terrain requires. To balance this freedom, we have the commercial and business centre with its closed rectangular structure, its focus on the central tower, and the broad and almost square reflection in the water. Structurally, the pattern derives from Sunila, and there is also a striking affiliation with Aalto's town plan for the Institute of Technology in Otaniemi (Otnäs), the result of a competition in 1949. The rhythmical arrangement of the buildings around a central unit here, and the broad stretches of green in front of the centre of the complex, stem from the same underlying principle as Tapiola.

The municipality on whose land Tapiola was built had little opportunity to influence the design of the town. The townscape was economically, politically and municipally as independent as the suburbs round Helsinki at the beginning of the century. The statutory rules of urban planning had not reached Tapiola. On the other hand, government financing did reach Tapiola, by way of the national social home grants system for towns which had been established in 1949. We should note that before this date only the rural areas had enjoyed a system of this kind.

THE MASSIVE URBANIZATION OF THE 1960s

Within a short time the economic structure of Finland had changed on a scale unmatched, in relative terms, in the history of the Western industrial countries (Perälä, 1983). The need to pay heavy war reparations led to the creation of a new and expanding manufacturing industry. An increasingly rapid integration into the international trade and production network and the development of highway and air traffic – late, but rapid when it came – gave a powerful impetus to urbanization. The state also made an important contribution by providing aid for home-building and the development of public services. Administrative changes, such as municipal mergers and the addition of new areas to many old towns, also helped to promote rapid urbanization.

Revision of the 1931 Town-Planning Act had started in 1944. No radical change was envisaged in the earlier Act, in which land-owning interests were provided for to a greater extent than the general interests of the community. The idea was rather to get control over building activities in the small rural development centres and to introduce rules for overall regional and master plans and to give them legal status.

When the new building law came into operation in 1959, the biggest change lay in the fact that for the first time building and land-use planning were now regulated by a single law. The government was given little chance of intervening actively in land-use policy. The right to acquire private land was granted only for municipal utilities and for the government's or the municipality's own buildings. But the municipality did acquire a monopoly on planning. No-one other than the municipality was allowed to put forward plans for approval by the government within its area. The government's approving agency, the Ministry of the Interior, was indirectly granted wide-ranging powers in that it could refuse to approve plans and, on certain conditions, could call for town plans for areas in the municipality which it had itself defined. The Public Building Board lost its former influence on planning policy. In practice, regional and master plans had no direct legal significance in determining land use, and not until 1968 did the general plan become obligatory as the form for planning in Finnish towns.

The restricted legal force of land-use planning as an instrument of control in the new building law might perhaps be explained as a reaction against the heavy state intervention which had been necessary just after the war, in order to provide land and houses for weary war veterans and the inhabitants of territories ceded to the Soviet Union.

Another factor also made planning controls at the municipal level a ticklish business. This was the absence of any regional administration. At the beginning of the 1960s the country had 549 municipalities and a population of 4.4 million, so it was obvious that many municipalities were forced to compete with one another for the two basic factors of growth, people and business enterprise. The municipalities were not geared to mutual collaboration on regional plans. This often led to uncontrolled rivalry between municipalities, which produced inflated plans and tendentiously optimistic development forecasts.

The municipal mergers were to be an important government tool for creating larger planning units based on the old towns. Further, the government's policy of investment in housing production, public building, communications and state-financed industry was a major factor in creating a network of growth centres throughout the country. Another instrument available to the central government authorities lay in the granting of town or borough status to municipalities. Between 1905 and 1960 no municipality or borough had been granted town status, but between 1960 and 1976 forty-nine municipalities achieved this status, thus increasing the number of towns from thirty-five to eighty-four. After that a standard designation was introduced, which abolished the differences between town, borough and rural district.

Under these circumstances it was obvious that active policies for land use and planning also required ownership of the land. The old towns had land at their disposal within their own borders, albeit to a greatly varying extent. The new towns generally had no land. During the 1950s private land outside the city centres was therefore once again the object of speculation. Local large-scale builders had appeared just before the war in the Helsinki region, in the shape of housing companies geared to the production of social housing. In their wake came the private commercial builders, often with affiliations in the building industry. Massive investment in housing helped to accumulate capital in the building sector, which in turn made it possible to purchase large tracts of land, particularly in the region of the capital city but also within the housing and labour-market areas of the medium-sized towns. Private capital was attracted by tax subsidies to housing production.

Planning capacity and the technical knowledge needed for realizing large-scale developments were available in the old towns, but not in the most expansive areas round the towns. Under these circumstances the initiative for planning and building houses as well as schools, nursery schools, roads, water mains, and sewers slipped into the hands of the private building companies and land-owning interests. Area building contracts then became the praxis, when it came to regulating the arrangements between these companies and the municipalities. The municipalities undertook to prepare the legally binding town plans with the specifically agreed amount of building rights, while the builder once again undertook the planning and realization of the overall area and in many cases even the financing of items which according to the Building Act should have been the municipality's obligation. The Helsinki rural district alone made area building agreements for eight areas with building rights amounting to 2,250,000 m^2 between 1968 and 1970, which created a capacity for increasing the population from 60,000 to 150,000 (Saarinen et al., 1973).

It is obvious that under such circumstances the form of the communities in the growth centres would be steered by land-ownership conditions rather than by any considerations of planning. The community structure was so fragmented by the building activities of the 1960s, that subsequent overall land-use planning was seen as a way of 'filling in' and 'making whole'.

The physical form of area development during the 1960s was firmly entrenched in the legacy of Sunila, Olympic Village and Tapiola. The idea was to develop a forest town in close proximity with nature, interacting with the conditions which the terrain and the increasingly industrialized production methods allowed.

Reima Pietilä has formulated the goals for the Finnish forest town most clearly. In his 1960 exhibition 'Morphology – Urbanism' the criteria for a good plan were defined in the 'Finnish Master Plan 1960' in aphoristic form, published in *Arkkitehti* 1960:

- A good plan is a work of art.
- A good plan is plastically structural, plastically expressive and visual: it is architectural.
- A good plan takes its form from the shape of the landscape, it is a way of exploiting the morphological resources of nature.
- A good plan remains flexible *vis-à-vis* the changes that accompany development; the striving for durability should be combined with foreseen changes.

Pietilä's description of the attributes of the forest towns are intentionally clothed in aesthetic garb, with a touch of the mysticism that attends a romantic view of nature. No attention is paid to the social content of the town plan or the town. Pietilä's criticism of suburban building is based exclusively on aesthetic values on a macro-scale. The central relationship is that between buildings and landscape, lake and forest. Pietilä's reduction of urban life to the individual relationship between man, building and nature is understandable, in view of the social background to urbanization. The net immigration into population centres, which

reached an annual level of 1.7 per cent during the 1960s, consisted of people from sparsely populated areas where the cultural links with forests, lakes and fields were stronger than the links with the social community.

Pihlajamäki (Rönnbacka) in Helsinki exemplifies an intentionally sculptural design for a 'forest town'. The plan was drawn up in 1960 by Professor Olli Kivinen, a pupil of Meurman's (figure 3.19). Its basic architectural idea consists of the interaction between unusually long lamella houses, curving where the contours of the terrain so require, and vigorously vertical point blocks. The area is divided into two equally large sections by a canyon, in which the main traffic artery has been located. Each half has two separate 'residential cells', and each of these has its own food shop and day nursery. The cells are linked by a primary school, which they share. The high-rise blocks have been located at the highest points so that in the landscape the suburb gives the impression of a uniform, white city-wall embracing these tall buildings that recall mediaeval towers. The architectural design of the houses – the linear façades of the lamella houses and the vertical lines of the point blocks – reinforce the effect that was called for in the plan. The town-plan concept provided the basis for a special public housing design competition, which in turn led to a revision of the plan. Functionally speaking this is a typical example of the large-scale suburban projects of that time. The school, the day nursery and the shopping centre are the only functions represented apart from dwelling-houses. The area was the first suburban project based entirely on prefabricated units. The technical knowhow was provided by Sweden, whose example was of fundamental importance to the whole urbanization process. To a great extent both planning methods and size norms were borrowed intact from Sweden. As Jere Maula has put it, Finland followed Sweden as the carriages follow the engine.

In many other plans for Helsinki's suburban

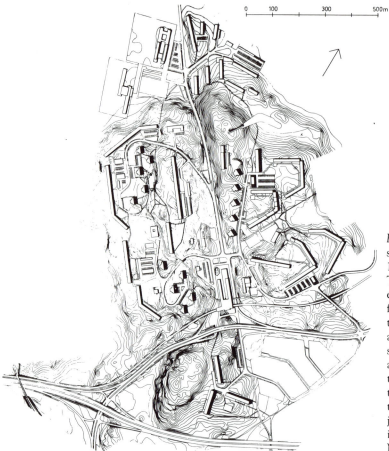

Figure 3.19. Pihlajamäki, Helsinki, town plan by Olli Kivinen, 1960.
This suburb, divided into two equal sections, exemplifies the first phase of massive urbanization. The overall design of the area on its hill is large-scale and sculptural. The only buildings apart from dwelling-houses are the business centre to the south, the school to the north, one or two day nurseries, and the ski-jump. The area was built according to the plan. *Source: Arkkitehti,* Nos. 10–11, 1964.

area, such as Lehtisaari (Lövö, 1960) and Laajasalo (Degerö, 1965), Kivinen has given proof of different versions of a scenic and sculptural approach, whereby new units are shaped firmly and uniformly in symbiosis with the topography. The immediate environment affecting pedestrians in the area was not dealt with in the plans. The space between the houses was regarded as a non-essential element in the residential setting. The paramount criterion of a good living environment was the view from the individual homes over the wood or out into nature.

THE NEW GRIDIRON PLAN AND THE COMPACT TOWN

Around the middle of the 1960s criticism of the 'forest towns' began to be heard among young architects in the capital. The main target of attack was the 'shapelessness' of these towns and the 'anti-urban romanticism' of the post-war years. Tapiola was frequently in the line of fire. A return to a stricter urban pattern, an emphasis on rectangularity and aesthetic values was called for. The informally located houses were replaced by regular blocks and street systems in which residential roads, feeder roads and pedestrian precincts are set at right angles to one another. Pentti Ahola, who was responsible for a massive planning effort during the 1960s, had indicated the way things would go in a competition entry in 1958, with his plans for the northern neighbourhood at Tapiola. The houses are still arranged fairly irregularly in relation to one another, but the street network is already right-angled (Salokorpi, 1984).

When Bengt Lundsten won the competition for the residential area of Haukkala outside Jyväskylä in 1965, the new gridiron plan achieved its definitive breakthrough (figure 3.20). The houses were built round a common courtyard, while the pedestrian space was to regain the strict form of the old Finnish wooden towns with their detached houses along the

streets linked together by a wooden fence. The two-storey houses with their wooden cladding reveal a certain affinity with traditional urban wooden building. The system is clearly additive: how many blocks there are depends on the extent of the programme. Block is added to block, and they are all linked together by absolutely straight central pedestrian streets. Traffic is fed in from an outer distributor road. Functionally, the area is provided with central and local services. With good reason, this type of plan has been called the new Finnish gridiron plan. Although the new block pattern resembles the plans of the old towns, there is no evidence that the chosen form was influenced by

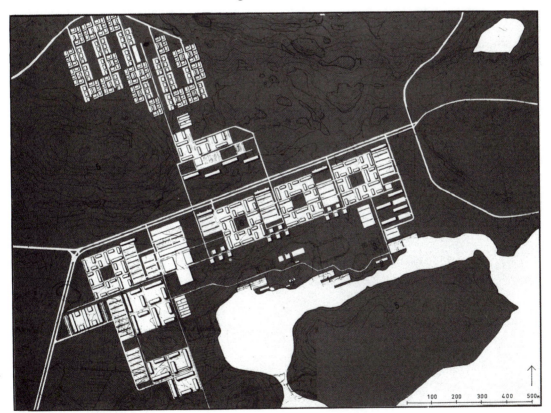

Figure 3.20. Haukkala (Kortepohja), Jyväskylä, town plan and winning competition entry by Bengt Lundsten, 1964. Compare the arrangement of the houses here with their prototypes in the 1827 Turku plan (figure 3.2) or the courtyards with the fire squares in the 1879 Nurmes plan (figure 3.4). The Haukkala plan consists mainly of two or three-storey lamella housing, however, and it became a model in its turn for many other plans over the next ten years. The area was built according to the plan, and was extended later. *Source*: The architectural firm of Bengt Lundsten, Helsinki.

an interest in these towns or by any study of their environmental qualities. On the contrary, the block pattern recalls the form that Olli Kivinen, above all, adopted in his projects for the total clearance of old towns (see below, p. 100). His proposals for the demolition and rebuilding of Kemi on flat ground in 1962 (figure 3.21) contain the same block pattern and the same disposition of the blocks as the Haukkala plan on sloping ground, for instance, or the Olari (Olars) plan for building on a ridge (figure 3.22). This shows how a planning principle became a rule applied regardless of topography or the nature of the building project.

Perhaps the most important reason for the renaissance of the gridiron plan was nonetheless an admiration for the traditional Japanese architecture which had been widespread among young architects since the beginning of the 1960s, and the enthusiasm aroused by the architecture of Mies van der Rohe. Aulis Blomstedt explained in *Arkkitehti*, 1961 the reason for this enthusiasm: 'Mies is perhaps the only master of his generation who has intentionally turned his back on the kingdom of the romantic. On the architectural map we find him at the intersection of the main lines of development. Its coordinates are the classical tradition and the new technology'. This view was typical of the architectural stance which became known as 'Miesism' or constructivism, and whose antipole was exemplified by the two individualists Aalto and Pietilä.

Further, the influence of the international debate also triggered off the renaissance of the gridiron plan. Albertslund Syd near Copenhagen by Peter Bredsdorff, Knud Svensson and Ole Nörgaard, for instance, was published in *Arkkitehti* in 1963 and duly studied. The straight pedestrian streets which became the distinguishing feature of so many plans presumably stemmed from the example of Albertslund Syd. Serge Chermayeff's narrow house type, introduced in the book *Community and Privacy*, which he wrote together with Christopher Alexander in 1963, was admired by young architects. The book was reviewed in the national architectural journal in 1967, while Chermayeff's own house had been presented in the same journal the year before. The major project for Järvafältet in Stockholm with a plan by EELT (1966) resurfaces in Aarno

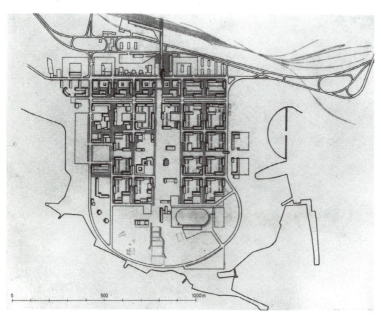

Figure 3.21. Kemi, proposed town plan for the redevelopment of the predominantly wooden town; Olli Kivinen's winning competition entry 1962.

The 1860s disposition of the blocks has been partly retained, but it is proposed that the existing wooden houses be demolished to make way for three-storey lamella blocks. Traffic is consistently segregated. The plan made a certain impact on the development of Kemi. *Source:* Sammalkorpi (1963).

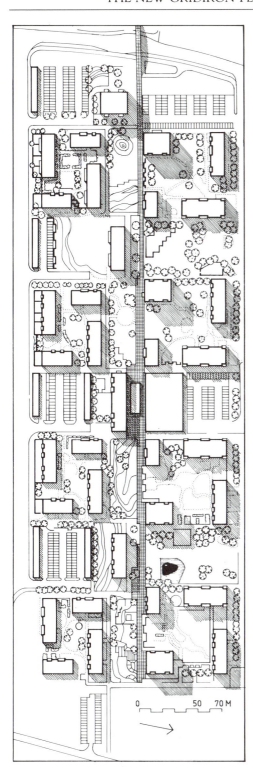

Figure 3.22. Olari, plan made at the end of the 1960s by the Espoo town planning office in collaboration with the Järvinen-Valjakka firm of architects, which produced the designs for the houses. The pedestrian street runs along the flat ridge. The blocks of flats range from three to nine storeys and the area is intended for a maximum population of 2,270. The semi-closed blocks came to be known as the 'windmill' model. The area was built 1969–73 and was later extended. The illustration has been redrawn by the author. *Source: Finland bygger,* **5** (Helsinki: Museum of Finnish Architecture, 1966).

Ruusuvouri's winning entry for the satellite town of Hervanta near Tampere in 1968, built to house a population of 50,000.

The massive investment in new urban units at the end of the 1960s came at a time when criticism of the urbanistically and functionally one-sided design of many suburbs and the 'anti-urban' forest towns was acquiring cultural and social overtones. Young civil engineers, architects, authors and film-makers accounted for the substance of a debate which only now began to spread outside the architectural profession. This cultural criticism drew its strength from a desire for the European type of urban space with its traditional streets, its comprehensible block structure and its public spaces with public functions. Prefabrication technology was obviously accepted and seen as a rational alternative to the craft type of production in the forest towns. The need to cope with a combination of public transport and private motor-cars was regarded as a challenge. Cultural radicalism and a kind of techno-romantic rationalism coloured political attitudes. 'Industrial form is or should be entirely logical. At its best, form follows the function of the product, the material used and the requirements of the production method. The beauty born of these sources is more universal than traditional beauty springing from aesthetic values'. Thus ran the younger generation's technocratic manifesto at the close of the 1960s, as formulated by Reijo Jallinoja in *Rakennustekniikka,* 1968.

The social critics recognized the need for a more varied pattern of human contact and social integration. Both new and old service facilities such as swimming pools, libraries, cinemas and inns were seen as elements promoting this social process. 'The contact city = the compact city' was a popular slogan coined at the time. There was great faith in the efficacy of the central pedestrian precinct. 'A compact milieu permits a high happenings-intensity = a high experience-intensity. Human movement in the town should be a happening' (Murole, 1967). The Swedish exhibition *Hej Stad* (Hello City!) was put on in 1966 amidst much publicity, and in Finland the young cineaste Risto Jarva produced two films which argued convincingly for the traditional urban environment and a renewal of urban life.

The gridiron plan was so consistently adopted during the late 1960s, that we can speak of a new era of classical and constructivist trends in urban planning. The basic rectangular pattern of repeated blocks is matched by the design of the façades with their line-screen effect. Alternating horizontal and vertical elements strongly suggest the actual construction of the houses. The 1966 plans for Koivuhaka in Kokkola by Risto Kauria and Risto Turtola, and the multistorey housing scheme for Olari in Espoo by Simo Järvinen and Eero Valjakka in 1969, represented stages in a lengthy development process which was to continue throughout the 1970s.

Design gradually became less prominent in urban planning. Flexibility and universality came to be the key requirements at the level of the district, the block and the individual building. Traffic and building-technology considerations, together with a general desire to create opportunities for a rich urban life rather than to give form to the urban setting, constituted the substance of the town planners' goals well into the 1970s. The ties with the pioneers of functionalism in Finland were broken. Aalto was looked upon as a formalistic aesthete, and sub-

jected to cynical criticism by some and totally ignored by others.

This technocratic period of constructivism in Finnish urban planning resulted in a whole series of schematic structural models, which were to open the way for a new form of urban living in the country. The gridiron plan with an open or half-closed building form was the chosen mode for many plans produced by entrepreneurs in collaboration with municipal authorities for land bought up by builders. The schematic nature of the plans was also a result of tight time schedules. In the growth centres of southern Finland it was necessary to build quickly to allow for the structural reorientation which was taking place in the country towards manufacturing and service industries. Moreover many leading politicians felt that the shortage of houses in Finland's growth centres, in combination with attractive conditions on the Swedish labour market, lay behind the population drain which led in 1969 and 1970 to net emigration amounting to 80,000 people. The political desire to check the flow of manpower out of the country tended to promote both planning and building (Peltonen, A., 1982).

In the Koivukylä (Björkby) plan for the rural district of Helsinki, where the two major area contractors HAKA and SATO were to build a new suburban area, the timetable presupposed a building start eighteen months after the initiation of area planning. The plans for this new community for 20,000 people and 4,500 workplaces included a comprehensive theoretical section, in which seven models were analysed with the help of ADP (figure 3.23). This study was published in 1968 and it set the norm for the technocratic and rationalistic planning of suburbs, in which the emphasis was on development programmes which would be economically efficient from the point of view of both the builders and the municipality. It showed how it was possible to maximize the volume of building and minimize the statutory costs of the municipalities.

Figure 3.23. Koivukylä, Vantaa (Vanda), layout plan, 1968.
This plan was known as 'alternative 2 B^{IX}' and it assumed that an area of 1,000 hectares would be successively extended between 1969 and 2000 and would ultimately cater for a population of 30,000. It was proposed to locate the 8,000 workplaces in the area east of the motorway and the business centre close to Finland's main railway line. The area has been built according to the plan but it is clear that its dimensions will be scaled down. *Source: Koivukylä I. Kaavarungon perusselvitykset* (Helsinki: Helsingin maalaiskunnan julkaisu, 1968).

New building in Finland was dominated by suburban complexes of this kind right up to the 1980s. They came to be just as isolated from the rest of the country's urban structure as ever their criticized predecessors, the forest towns, had been. The dense population did not bring about the richly varied urban life which had been hoped for; in fact the quality of the urban scene was generally much worse than in the forest towns. Further, the intended building time was prolonged, partly because the plans were over large and partly because many areas within the individual municipalities were being developed simultaneously. The uncontrolled rivalry between municipalities and between builders contributed to this unfortunate development. Although there had been intensive debate ever since the 1960s on the subject of an intermediate administration between the municipality and the state, no organization had yet appeared which could control the location and programming of urban expansion.

CLEARANCE OPERATIONS: A BREAK WITH A UNIFORM URBAN TRADITION

In the Finnish towns, new dwellings had been largely built in suburban areas. The central areas did not offer much opportunity for large-scale new construction. Over the years the towns had been transferring building land into private hands plot by plot. The age of the houses in one and the same area could vary very much, but even at the beginning of the 1960s most existing urban building consisted of wooden houses. Even large towns, such as Tampere and Turku, possessed extensive wooden housing zones in the old gridiron areas in the city centre. The uniform wooden character had been retained in Finnish towns, although building rights for buildings in brick or concrete represented a much greater area in terms of actual floor space than the existing wooden buildings. Up to 1959 building rights were mainly regulated by the local building ordinances, which embodied the hundred-year-old ambition to build in stone.

Not until the beginning of the 1960s, after the era of post-war reconstruction, did it become economically possible to tackle the redevelopment of the wooden towns. Ideologically there was no obstacle to a policy of total clearance, i.e. demolition and rebuilding. People had never seen any particular value in the ordinary wooden town. At the beginning of the century the rare wooden-house districts with irregular plans had been admired, but people had no time for the absolutely straight Empire-style streets with their air of dreariness. Although the functionalists had recognized the value of the sparser building mode, they wanted open lamella housing instead of wooden houses. And property-owners, aware of the favourable rights connected with rebuilding, had neglected to maintain and re-equip these houses for so long that now only one alternative remained: the wooden districts had to be demolished and replaced by lamella or tower blocks (Helander and Sundman, 1972).

It was Kivinen who, in a thesis presented at the Helsinki Institute of Technology in 1960, had launched the redevelopment model with free-standing lamella houses and parking places between the houses. Houses set back slightly from the block boundaries would allow for broader streets where required. Space was also provided for planted areas or 'low-rise' business premises in front of the houses or at the short ends of the buildings at right angles to the street. A common feature of all clearance schemes during the 1960s was that closed, low-rise building round an open space was rejected.

Thus, paradoxically, the functionalist's town-planning ideals received their clearest expression in Finland thirty years after they had been formulated, in a context which had originally accorded well with the functionalists' own criteria in urban-planning terms.

Between 1960 and 1965, ten competitions were arranged, to produce plans for the total clearance of the wooden houses in the old towns. In addition extensive consultations were held to discuss town or plans, and this opened the way for redevelopment schemes (figure 3.21). By the beginning of the 1970s a large proportion of the country's wooden-house districts had been included in plans involving total clearance – a policy in which the social aspects received little attention.

As a result of this massive planning campaign plenty of opportunities for building became available within the old gridiron areas. As suburban areas outside the towns were also being planned at this time it was already obvious by the beginning of the 1970s that the supply of building land in medium-sized and small towns had far out-stripped the demand. Since town plans generally had to stick to existing property boundaries as most plots were privately owned, and since society lacked any instrument for compelling sale, building was dependent in each case on the willingness of landowners to sell to the builders. Only in larger towns was it possible to redevelop the city centre, replacing wooden houses with dwellings and commercial buildings on a plot-by-plot basis. During the 1970s the situation in the smaller towns became untenable. Renewal progressed very slowly. Instead multi-storey buildings were put up at random in an 'ocean of wooden housing', as Aalto had once called the wooden towns in the 1940s. Whole districts fell into decay, while people hoped for the quick profits from rising land values.

Quite early in the 1960s Nils Erik Wickberg, professor in architectural history, had pointed out the dangers of an indiscriminate urban redevelopment programme in Helsinki. In a series of papers he energetically condemned the threat to an already weak urban building tradition. Towards the end of the 1960s the Institute of Technology began to provide a forum for general social criticism and opposition to current architectural ideals and for a recognition of the values embodied in the regular layout of the wooden towns, which gradually generated a call for a more conservationist approach to redevelopment. The art historian Henrik Lilius wrote several articles pointing out the historical and aesthetic quality of these towns and demanding plans allowing for their retention. The 'Nordic Wooden Town' project of 1970–74 with its long series of reports presented in popular form also helped to direct the attention of a wider public towards the qualities inherent in the Finnish wooden town and the negative environmental effects of one-sided planning.

Several excellent Danish examples of dense low-rise buildings during the 1960s and early 1970s had a decisive impact on the change in opinion in Finland. It was partly due to this that the smaller house came to be seen as a new way of achieving a more individual type of dwelling than the multistorey house could provide. At the same time it opened people's eyes to the qualities of existing districts. When the important RAKEVA competition for the development of suitable types of small house was judged in 1966, it was claimed that the tra-

ditional Finnish town with its wooden houses and with semi-enclosed courtyards provided an agreeable and harmonious urban setting. The renaissance of the gridiron plan, which we have already mentioned, also contributed to this change of opinion, as the wooden towns were of course built on chequerboard lines.

Even at the beginning of the 1970s the environmental debate was still a question of cultural policy; historical aspects of the environment were the chief concern. Later than the other Nordic countries, Finland then began to adopt a more obviously socio-political approach to the question of the historical environment and to introduce social, economic and political arguments into the debate. Although late, this approach quickly made a great impact, as it generated local demonstrations in favour of the maintenance and repair of existing environments, first of all – in 1969 – in Kumpula (Gumtäkt) and Käpylä in Helsinki. Demonstrations of this kind had never occurred before. The new political interest in the environment was further encouraged by some pamphlets which were widely read during 1970 (Helander and Sundman, 1970).

By the beginning of the 1980s the evolution of the Finnish wooden town with its predominantly Empire style and its gridiron plan had come to an end. It had either vanished under new buildings or become hopelessly fragmented and replaced by three- to seven-storey lamella houses in line with the thinking that prevailed in the late 1960s. A whole form of urban culture had disappeared and was now to be glimpsed only in fragments or as specially protected districts in the centre of about ten towns.

The revised plan for Käpylä in Helsinki initiated a long series of schemes for a more conservationist approach to rehabilitation and for the alleviation of mistakes that had already been made in the individual wooden districts. The move towards a radical programme of rehabilitation and modernization was supported by the attitude of the central authorities, the

Housing Board with its substantial credit resources and the Building and Planning Department at the Ministry of the Interior which from the middle of the decade began to work energetically for a conservationist line.

Working-class districts with wooden housing from the early days of industrialization or from the beginning of the present century have been wholly or partly redeveloped according to revised town plans: in Helsinki this applies to Vallila and the '100-mark homes' as well as to Käpylä; in Turku to Port Arthur; in Tampere to Pispala; and in Pietarsaari (Jakobstad) to Poh-

joisnummi (Norrskata). In many small towns, particularly along the coast of the Gulf of Bothnia and the Gulf of Finland, conservationist plans have been applied to whole districts (figure 3.24). But the lamella and tower blocks of the 1960s and 1970s strike a disharmonious note on the skyline and along the streets.

CITY CENTRE RENEWAL IN HELSINKI

The renewal of Finland's medium-sized towns on a basis of existing gridiron plans rendered separate regulations for the town centres un-

Figure 3.24. Rauma, illustration of the plan for the conservation of the old urban core of Rauma on the Gulf of Bothnia.
The old houses which have survived all fires since 1682 are retained; some buildings have been added in accordance with strict directives. The area includes about 200 business premises and workshops as well as just under 600 dwelling units. The plan was completed in 1980 and is being realized in stages. *Source: Vanha Rauma* (Helsinki: Kaupunkimaisten yhdyskuntien kehittämiskampanja, julkaisu 2, 1982).

necessary. Differentiation in the traffic network and new motorway-type arteries through the centres or close to them could cope to a great extent with the growing volume of private motor traffic. The bleak squares criticized by Sonck sixty years earlier allowed sufficient space for banks, insurance companies and department stores. In Helsinki's city centre, however, one big problem remained unsolved. Saarinen's plans had presupposed a radical shift in the central focus towards the north, filling in the central Töölö bay. Later, during the 1930s, this proposal was violently criticized by P. E. Blomstedt. And another problem was the need to cope effectively with the private cars in the centre, where there is – for the Nordic countries – an unusually heavy concentration of public administration buildings and company head offices.

Commissioned by the government, Aalto produced grandiose plans for the centre in 1961–1964 (figure 3.25). The idea was to create a monumental centre for modern post-war Finland, corresponding to Senate Square, centre of the old class society of autonomous Finland. Aalto not only retained the Töölö bay, but emphasized its importance by letting a row of white palaces of culture and science cast their reflections on its waters. A series of monumental radiating squares was to link the different elements and orientations in the civic structure. The overall concept is based on a contrast between the great flat terrace-square composition with its solid backdrop and the open mirror of the water with its border of free-standing palaces.

The plan treats the centre as the cultural and political assembly point for the townspeople, as the terminus of railway and buses, and the convergence of numerous traffic arteries all connected to great underground carparks. The centre, developed in detail in a 1:200 model, is treated as a plastic whole viewed from the driver's seat. The motorway into the centre is carried over the railway in order to offer an

Figure 3.25. Helsinki centre, plan for redevelopment by Alvar Aalto 1961, 1964.

The fanshaped civic square and the palaces of culture reflected in the water were to embody the new character of the centre. The commercial buildings at the bottom of the plan were intended to form a backdrop to the vista opening from the proposed new motorway to the centre. Only one building was built according to the plan (Finlandia Hall, by Aalto). *Souce:* Aalto (1965).

all-embracing view of the centre itself and the outlook towards the eastern and western sections of the urban peninsula. The town was to be perceived by drivers and bus travellers as an integrated unit. Criticism of this plan turned on the concentration of cultural institutions, the position in the town of individual private car traffic, and the buildings in the parks. The result was that the plans were shelved.

As more companies established themselves all over the inner city and the centralized state authorities expanded within the same area, there was an increasing imbalance between workplaces and inhabitants in the capital. As early as 1953 and despite extensive new housing production, the number of inhabitants in the inner city began to fall. As the decline accelerated until it reached an annual rate of about 5,000 by the mid-1960s, and the number of workplaces rose at the same time by about 5,000 a year, it was decided that a master plan should be drawn up to regulate the functional changes in the town, to promote residence there, to support a concentration of commercial life and administration to the city area, and to curb the demolition of existing buildings. Following the example of Stockholm's zone plans (Zone Plan 1962 and the preparations for Zone Plan 1970), a plan for the inner city was published in 1973 and accepted by the town in 1976. To a great extent the plan resembles in its methodology and design not only the Stockholm plan but even Oslo's *Soneplan*, which was also published in 1973. But conservation and clearance considerations based on the utilization of existing buildings play a more prominent role in Helsinki than in the capital cities of its Scandinavian neighbours.

LEGISLATION THAT CAME TO NOUGHT

As we have seen a new Building Act came into operation in 1959. The most important change was that dense building could only be erected in accordance with approved town plans, on the lines already laid down in Swedish building law.

More scattered building, on the other hand, remained free and could still be undertaken with very few restrictions. As a result of the mandatory town plans, an extensive system evolved for getting round the regulations by way of a series of individual dispensations, presented by the municipalities and approved by the state planning authority. In 1968 the Act was completed in order to provide a basis for physical planning at the regional and master plan level. The Building Act had created a planning system, with the emphasis on detailed planning. The weak position of regional and master planning as a control instrument was to give rise to further legislative activity ten years after the Act came into operation.

The reform in the law which was sketched out in the mid-1970s was mainly concerned with regulating land use in sparsely built areas. The uncontrolled and unsystematic extension of densely populated areas was seen as another reason for revising current legislation. The role of regional and master planning as a political means of controlling land use within the municipalities was also to be developed along Danish lines.

Most importantly, the municipality was to have greater powers for acquiring planning land that had been left unbuilt and which was needed for expansion plans, at a price motivated by its actual use. A planning fee was also suggested, which would give the community 80 per cent of the increased land value in cases of building on private land. The reform proposals were inspired by a desire to use physical planning as part of the general effort to create a welfare society adapted to the material, social and cultural needs of the population. A further explicit goal was to strengthen democracy in every aspect of social life (Heino, 1984).

In view of the way social developments have moved during the late 1970s and the 1980s, it does not seem likely that the reforms will be realized to the extent originally envisaged. Both building and urbanization slowed down towards the end of the 1970s. An increasing number of towns registered declining population figures. Conservative trends and a stronger non-socialist majority followed a short period of domination by the left in parliament between 1966 and 1970. A total reform of the Building Act has thus been replaced by detailed reforms to take care of the most urgent needs.

It has been a recurrent feature of Finnish building legislation that social developments inspire reforms which are carried out only when the needs have already changed, and that planning law has been late to develop both in comparison with the other Scandinavian countries and in relation to actual needs.

THE REACTION AGAINST INDISCRIMINATE MASS PRODUCTION

It was obvious quite early on that it would be difficult to achieve urbanization by concentrat-ing on multi-storey dwellings. This type of hous-ing had no tradition in the country outside Helsinki and the old town centres. In 1960 only 5 per cent of all residential housing in towns and boroughs consisted of multi-storey buildings in concrete or brick. The demand for more small houses began in the mid-1960s and has in-creased since the environmental and social problems of recent suburban high-rise areas have become obvious. The gridiron plan pro-vided the solution here too. The rapid develop-ment of DIY and of industrially produced small houses, and a growing range of house types, obliged municipalities to produce broad plans regulating the location of the buildings on the plots, the material of the façades, and the shape of the roofs. Everything else was regulated by the market. Although the propaganda of the Housing Board and the well-attended, annual housing fairs have had an important impact on the development of small-house types, the plans

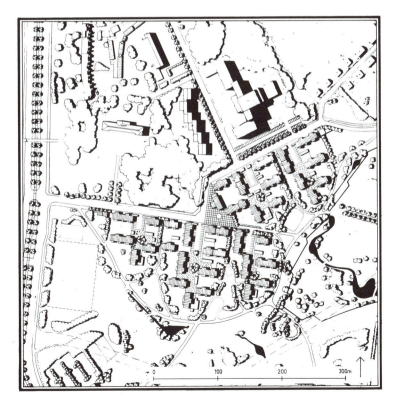

Figure 3.26. Sofianlehto, Helsinki, 1985 plan for a social housing estate. Architect Reijo Jallinoja.

The three-storey narrow blocks are arranged in five groups with a total of 258 flats. Each group has its own entrance courtyard behind the parking area. *Source*: Helsinki City Planning Office.

for areas of this kind have often represented schematic or ill-prepared solutions.

In many areas where planning is more environmentally aware, a Danish influence is clearly visible. For instance, Jørn Utzon's atrium house arrangements have inspired Ahola's groups of small houses in Tapiola. This undercurrent of Danish influence has appeared frequently since the 1960s, right up to Jallinoja's 1985 plan for Sofianlehto (Sofielund) (figure 3.26), which shows a striking resemblance to the Tinggården near Køge by 'Vandkunsten'.

Particularly in the Helsinki region many serious attempts were made at the beginning of the 1980s to combine a programme of social housing with a high standard of architecture.

In 1977 in Suutarila (Skomakarböle), the architectural firm Gullichsen, Kairamo and Vormala combined a desire to create a compact village-like setting with brick houses reminiscent in some respects of traditional English homes. In 1978 the same firm designed a modernistic variant of the small traditional Finnish family house in a closed rectangular block plan in Konala (Kånala). For Leppävaara (Alberga) in Espoo, the firm of Nurmela, Raimoranta and Tasa produced a social housing estate in which one- or two-storey white painted houses, the exploitation of the nature of the terrain, and the adoption of large courtyards have produced a special local character (figure 3.27). Among the small areas of social low-rise housing built to-

Figure 3.27. Leppäsilta social housing estate in Leppävaara, Espoo. Plan, 1981 and buildings, 1982–83 by the architectural firm of Nurmela-Raimoranta-Tasa.

The plan reveals an ambition to draw on the traditional Finnish urban model with small houses round planted courtyards. In the middle of each of the three courtyards another house has been built. The illustration has been redrawn by the author. *Source*: The architectural firm of Nurmela-Raimoranta-Tasa, Helsinki.

wards the end of the 1970s Erik Adlercreutz's plans in Pukinmäki (Bocksbacka) should be mentioned.

What these neighbourhoods, where the borderline between house planning and town planning is indistinct, have in common – and what is therefore perhaps typical – is their roots in the modernistic tradition. The absence of romantic details, the emphasis on a dominant but varied structural idea, and the close contact with the ground and with nature are signs of this tradition. This is well illustrated in Juha Leiviskä's little study for Kannelmäki (Gamlas) in the mid-1970s (figure 3.28). But constructivist principles were also being followed up. As early as the mid-1960s when the industrial production of small houses was on the increase, the most architecturally interesting solutions were

Figure 3.28. Kannelmäki, Helsinki, outline plan for a small residential area by Juha Leiviskä, 1974.
The plan reveals a new ambition to combine buildings and nature into an integrated whole. The main features of the plan were realized, but the buildings were heavy and uninteresting. The author of the plan was not responsible for the building design in this case. *Source:* The architectural firm of Vilhelm Helander, Juha Leiviskä, arkkitehdit SAFA, Helsinki.

steeped in the forms of constructivism as inspired by Mies van der Rohe and Japanese
architecture. This line was then pursued, by
among others, Erkki Kairamo, who as recently
as 1982 in the private and prosperous westend
district of Espoo succeeded in renewing the
constructivist ideal of the 1960s in a convincingly restrained whole, in which the power
of pioneering modernism can be felt (figure
3.29). The area bears witness to the vigour and
renewal potential of this Finnish architectural
ideology.

The same attachment to modernistic tradition can be seen in the new dense areas of
multi-storey housing where opposition to the
more acute manifestations of urbanization took
shape. In 1966 Aalto produced an organic forest
town plan for Kivenlahti (Stensvik) on hilly
ground by the sea in Espoo. Seven separate
fingerlike groups of houses were located along
the ridges towards the sea. They start from a
distributor road along which various services
were to be located. Between the fingers green
areas following the valleys continued into the
residential parts. This plan was used for defining
the building rights within the privately owned
area. Four years later the Espoo town-planning
office produced a new project for part of the

area included in Aalto's plan (figure 3.30). This
time large individually designed blocks were
suggested, with a great variety in the building
types. The structure was rectangular but was
sensitively adapted to the topography. Clear
accents in the urban space were provided by the
linear grouping of tall buildings. Terraced
houses in an amphitheatre-like formation combined with a single tall tower block at the
water's edge provided a sharp visual focus for
the whole area. The desire to adapt to the
specific landscape and the sculptural handling of
this plan separate it from the generalized urban
structures of the constructivists. The area took
over fifteen years to complete, but the finished
product accords well with the original
intentions.

The historicizing trends in architecture and
urban planning to be found in many other
countries did not gain a foothold in Finland.
The residential area of Katajanokka in Helsinki, which replaced a shipyard and a marine
base dating from the early days of industrialization, lies next to a dense big-city district built
during the Art Nouveau period. The 1976 plan
by Vilhelm Helander, Pekka Pakkala and
Mikael Sundman represents the first major
municipal investment in new homes in the city

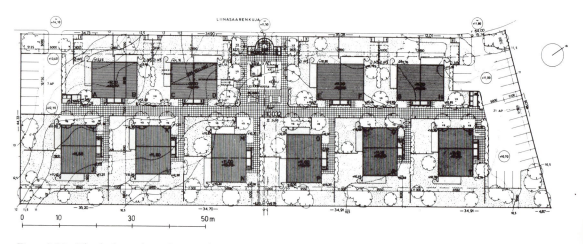

Figure 3.29. This little residential area with ten houses built to a high standard in prosperous area of Westend, Espoo is
by Erkki Kairamo. Plan 1980–81, built 1981–82. *Source: Arkkitehti,* 1982.

area, in accordance with the goals of the master plan referred to above (figure 3.31). The foremost goal, apart from creating a socially varied environment, was to combine new architecture with old as well as to adapt the new architecture to the particular location close to the open sea and to the townscape of the south harbour.

The rejection of historicism was clearly expressed in the presentation of this area in the catalogue for the Sixth Finnish Building Exhibition in 1981: 'The point of departure here is not a repetition of historical forms or the structure of earlier building. The town-planning principles stem solely from the specific requirements of the site and the particular opportunities that it provides.' The plan involved a revival of the brick-building tradition, albeit

over a core of concrete components, while the closed block and the square were also revived in a new guise. Buildings were added to those already existing, partly conceived by C. L. Engel in the neo-classical style of the early nineteenth century, and were made to function as an imposing complex worthy of the foreign service. More recent industrial buildings were now used for public services. There is a certain tension built into the plan between the enlarged neo-classical centralizing core and the asymmetry of the closed residential blocks.

The resulting environment contains many traditional urban elements, such as an enclosed square surrounded by arcades at ground level, visual foci in the street vistas, views towards notable buildings, retaining walls of granite,

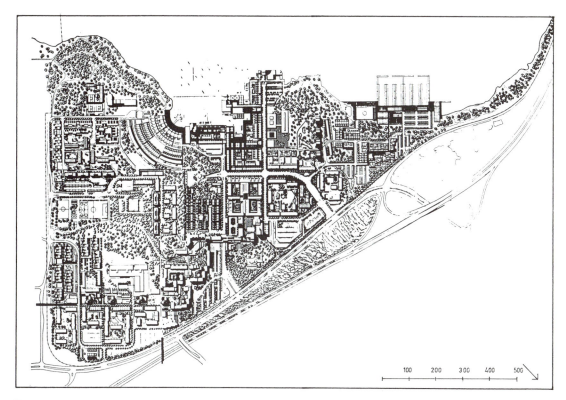

Figure 3.30. Kivenlahti, Espoo, plan made in 1970 and built in 1970–71 for the privately owned (public utilities) housing company which also owned the land.
The abundance of green areas and vegetation, the arrangement in large blocks, and the overall sculptural design give this plan its special character. *Source: Finland bygger,* 5, (Helsinki: Museum of Finnish Architecture, 1976).

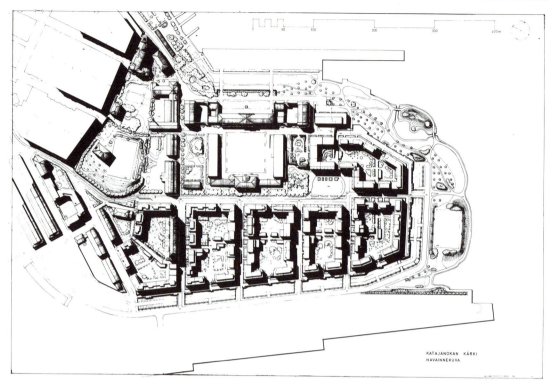

Figure 3.31. Katajanokka, Helsinki, plan for a new residential area including civic offices. Plan 1976 by Helander, Pakkala, Sundman. Built 1978–87.
The area, for about 3,000 inhabitants and 800 workplaces, is in central Helsinki. The buildings in hatched lines, either retained or rebuilt in replica, belonged to the former marine base and shipyard on this site. Commercial services are located behind the arcades in the square to the right. *Source*: Helsinki City Planning Office.

and public spaces paved with unhewn stone. Katajanokka injected an element of social policy into his approach, with a view to keeping prices down and allowing for a socially varied population structure, as well as guaranteeing a high environmental standard. According to this system (known as HITAS) the town, as the landowner, incorporates rules in the leasehold contracts regulating the form of financing and the selling price, as well as imposing obedience to the environmental directives proposed by the town-planning authorities. Of the 1,300 dwellings in the area just under half are privately financed and owned by private shareholders, who generally live in the appartments. However, as a shareholder in these companies the

municipality has first option at a fixed price in case of sale, which gives them a means of controlling prices. The rest of the dwellings consist of social housing with restricted rents or selling prices.

The HITAS system quickly became generally accepted and is applied to all projects in which Helsinki is a considerable landowner. Both in the 1979 plan for Western Pasila (Böle) with 6,000 inhabitants (figure 3.32) and successive plans between 1973 and 1985 for the suburb of Malminkartano (Malmgård) with 9,000 inhabitants, the reaction against the mechanical gridiron plans reveals itself as a new expressiveness in the design of the plan combined with districts which recall completely 'uncontrolled'

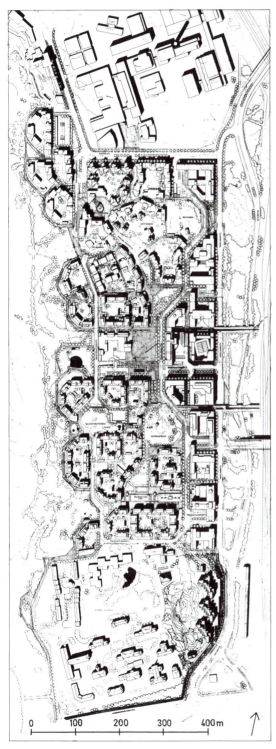

Figure 3.32. Pasila represents an attempt to combine residential and city functions with a view to relieving the pressure on office space in the centre of Helsinki.

The area, immediately north of the centre, was planned in two phases: the gridiron plan in the eastern half 1971 and the western half 1979. It exemplifies the kind of densely-built solutions which will be appearing in medium-sized towns and in the capital city region well into the 1990s. Western Pasila is intended for 6,500 inhabitants (2,200 dwelling units) and has 5,200 workplaces. To save space, parking is concentrated in underground areas beneath the central pedestrian precinct, at the junction between the workplaces and the dwelling units. These last face towards the central park to the west. *Source*: Helsinki City Planning Office.

building patterns. However, in Pasila these districts are actually structured by three monumental squares and in Malminkartano by pedestrian streets proceeding in a continuous rhythm and lined with multi-storey houses. The basic functional idea in both areas is to combine workplaces and dwellings in neighbourhood units. Brick is used throughout, as required in the plan.

During the 1980s a 'regionalistic' architectural current has appeared, associated with the Oulu school of architecture. Its idiom, putatively based on the local northern tradition, has been discussed and criticized particularly by the architects attached to the modernistic tradition with its ties to the capital city, who have waxed ironical over this 'artificial return to the vernacular tradition' and the 'formal imitations of historical styles'. The most eminent member of the humanistic architectural tradition besides Aalto, the historian Wickberg put his criticism into words in 1984: 'To seek a cure for schematism in so-called post-modernistic cosmetics cannot provide a valid solution. Columns, arches, mouldings, such as to our astonishment we see being used in certain new buildings out in the world, are not more than bits of cheese in a mousetrap.'

However, no regionalistic urban planning school has been established in Finland. In many instances individual buildings with historicizing and sometimes shocking forms have been incorporated into existing structures. But no planning proposals have been made, and it is doubtful whether an architectural idea which is so deliberately aesthetic and lacking in societal significance is capable of providing valid grounds for urban development.

The town-planning tradition in Finland is not strong. Architecture has made a deeper and more significant impact on the cultural history of the country. The development of urbanism started late but was then rapid, and over the last century it has generated a built environment in which integrated conceptions of excellence and originality are rare. Finland has received impulses from Scandinavia and continental Europe, which have been fused into national and often unassuming forms. To a greater extent than other countries Finland has made use of competitions, which have not infrequently resulted in interesting projects. Many plans which have led to outstanding environments have come into being under private auspices or on private initiatives. However, the fact that the public planning system has not been developed to the same extent as in the other Nordic countries and that private initiative has had more scope, has not generally ensured a balance in societal developments. At the same time the negative effects on the built environment are all too obvious.

ANNOTATED BIBLIOGRAPHY

Aalto, Alvar (1941a) Europas återuppbyggande aktualiserar det viktigaste problemet i vår tid. *Arkitekten*, No. 5.

Aalto, Alvar (1941b) Landsbygdens byggandsfråga. *Arkitekten*, No. 8.

Aalto, Alvar (1965) Helsingin keskustasuunnitelma, *Arkkitehti*, No. 3.

Åström, Sven-Erik (1956) Stadssamhället i brytningsskedet, in *Helsingfors stads historia*, IV 2. Helsingfors.

Åström, Sven-Erik (1957) *Samhällsplanering och regions-bildning i kejsartidens Helsingfors*. Helsingfors.

Brinckmann, Albrecht Erich (1912) *Platz und Monument*. Berlin.

Brunila, Birger and af Schultén, Marius (1955) Stadsplan och byggnadskonst 1875–1918, in *Helsingfors stads historia IV 1*. Helsingfors.

Byggnadsvårdskommitténs betänkade (1974), Helsinki: Komiteanmietintö 1974:80.
This government committee report demonstrates a new approach among other things to the town-planning principles for Finland's wooden towns. It is recommended that conservation should be an integral part of housing policy (government grants) and of land use planning (requirements regarding the maintenance and protection of existing environments and buildings).

Chermayeff, Serge and Alexander, Christopher (1963) *Community and Privacy. Toward a New Architecture and Humanism*. New York: Doubleday.

Gardberg, Carl Jacob (1981) Kaupunkilaitos keskiajala ja uuden ajan alussa, in Tommila, Päiviö (ed.) *Suomen kaupunkilaitoksen historia*, Vol 1. Vantaa: Suomen Kaupunkiliitto.
See comment under Jutikkala.

Gyldén, Claës Wilhelm (1845) *Historiska och statistiska anteckningar om städerna i Finland*. Helsingfors. Wasenius ska boktryckeriet.
A short systematic statistical survey of Finnish towns at the beginning of the 1840s. The book accompanies a set of plates with planimetric maps of all towns according to current or currently evolving town plans.

Hallman, Per (1900) Några ord om stadsplaner. *Ateneum*, No. 1, Helsingfors.

Harvia, Yrjö (1936) *Helsingfors inkorporeringsfråga, huvudbetänkande och specialutredningar*. Helsingfors: Helsingfors stads statistiska byrå.

Heino, Veikko (1984) Periaatemietinnöstä rakennuslakiluonnokseen; mitä jäi matkalle? *Yhteiskuntasuunnittelu*, No. 3.

Helamaa, Erkki (1983) *40-talet, korsurnas och återuppbyggandets årtionde*. Helsingfors: Finlands arkitekturmuseum.

Helander, Vilhelm (1972) *Saneeraus suomalaisessa kaupungissa II*. Espoo: Helsingin teknillinen korkeakoulu, arkkitehtuurin historian laitos, 6.

Helander, Vilhelm (1983) Arkkitehtuuri in *Suomen kultuurihistoria*, No. 3. Helsinki: Otava.

Helander, Vilhelm and Sundman, Mikael (1970)

Vems är Helsingfors? Helsingfors: Holger Schildts förlag.

Helander, Vilhelm and Sundman, Mikael (1972) *Saneeraus suomalaisessa kaupungissa.* Helsinki: Asuntohallituksen tukimus- ja suunnittelutoimiston sarja A:5.
This publication and Helander (1972) contain a penetrating analysis of the complex motives – theoretical, economic and, in planning terms, technological – for the destruction of the Finnish wooden towns during the 1960s and 1970s.

Jallinoja, Reijo (1968) Teollistuva yhteiskunta ja teollinen rakennustuotanto. *Rakennustekniikka,* No. 3.

Jung, Bertel (1901) Ett problem, *Ateneum.*

Jung, Bertel (1918) *Pro Helsingfors. Ett förslag till stadsplan för Stor-Helsingfors utarbetat av Eliel Saarinen m.fl.* Helsingfors.

Jutikkala, Eino (1983) Urbanisoituminen in Tommila, Päiviö (ed.) *Suomen kaupunkilaitoksen historia,* Vol. 2. Vantaa: Suomen Kaupunkiliitto.
The Union of Finnish Towns has published a work in three volumes on the development of the urban system in Finland from the Middle Ages to the 1980s. The various contributions take note of both economic and social history and also of the history of planning. The period from 1856 to 1917 (Volume 2) is described in a series of comprehensive summaries of the formal development of town planning by Henrik Lilius and Riitta Nikula. These are accompanied by descriptions of the typology and architectural development of the buildings by Henrik Lilius and Ritva Wäre. In the volume on the period 1918 to ca 1980, the planning history of urban development is described in a comprehensive essay by Asko Salokorpi, but without any discussion of the evolution of building types.

Kaavoitus- ja rakennusasiain neuvottelukunta (1975) *Rakennuslainsäädännön uudistaminen.* Helsinki: Komiteanmietintö 1974:44.
This government committee report reflects a well-developed social approach combined with the demand for an effective response to the requirements of massive urbanization, which was to be guided by conditions for the public good within the system of municipal autonomy.

Kivinen, Olli (1960) *Kaupunkiemme keskusalueiden rakennusoikeudesta, sen kehityksestä ja mitoituksesta.* Helsinki.
In his dissertation Kivinen showed how building rights in the Finnish towns, following Central European examples, had been on too generous a scale for Finnish conditions. At the same time the dissertation fashioned the model for the demolition and rebuilding of Finnish towns in the period of the most rapid urbanization during the 1960s.

Kuosmanen, Merja (1972) *Työväen asuntokysymys Helsingissä 1880–1930.* Espoo: Helsingin teknillinen korkeakoulu, arkkitehtuurin historian laitos 5.

Lagberedningens förslag till stadsplanelagstiftning samt allmän byggnadsstadga jämte motiv (1924). Helsingfors: Lagberedningens publikationer No. 2.
The lawyer John Uggla, who advised Eliel Saarinen (cf. below) on the legal aspects of planning and building in Munksnäs-Haaga, wrote the preparatory study to the subsequent Town Planning Act. His report provides a good account of the problems in growth areas as the towns' own land holdings began to run out. The international review of urban planning and building legislation makes it easier to understand the special nature of the Finnish legislation.

Lento, Reino (1951) *Maassamuutto ja siihen vaikuttaneet tekijät Suomessa 1878–1939.* Helsinki.

Lilius, Henrik (1981) Kaupunkirakentaminen 1617–1856, in Tommila Päiviö, (ed.) *Suomen kaupunkilaitoksen historia,* 1. Vantaa: Suomen Kaupunkiliitto.
See comment under Jutikkala

Lilius, Henrik (1983) Kaupunkirakentaminen 1856–1917, in Tommila Päiviö, (ed.) *Suomen kaupunkilaitoksen historia,* Vol. 2. Vantaa: Suomen Kaupunkiliitto.
See comment under Jutikkala

Lilius, Henrik (1985) *The Finnish wooden town.* Rungsted Kyst: Anders Nyborg.

Lindahl, Göran (1974) *Mönsterstäder.* Stockholm: Sveriges arkitekturmuseum.

Lindberg, Bo (1978) Den nya arkitekturen, in Sixten, Ringbom, (ed.), *Konsten i Finland, från medeltid till nutid.* Helsingfors: Holger Schildts förlag.

Linn, Björn (1974) *Storgårdskvarteret.* Uddevalla: Statens institut för byggnadsforskning.

Lundsten, Bengt (1967) Jyväskylän Kortepohjan asuntoalue, *Arkkitehti,* Nos 3–4.

Maisala, Pertti (ed.) (1968) *Koivukylä 1, kaavarunkotyön perusselvitykset.* Helsinki: Helsingin maalaiskunnan julkaisut.
A typical planning document which presents goals, planning hypotheses and planning methods for large new suburban areas in the capital city region during the period 1970–1980.

Maula, Jere (1978) Suomalaisen yhdyskuntasuunnittelun 60 vuotta. *Arkkitehti*, No. 3.

Meurman, Otto-I. (1969) Drag i Helsingfors stadsplanehistoria in Olof Stenius, *Helsingfors stadsplanehistoriska atlas*. Helsingfors: Stiftelsen Pro Helsingfors.

Mikkola, Kirmo (1967) Kaupunkisuunnittelun tilanne. *Arkkitehti*, Nos 3–4.

Mikkola, Kirmo (1972) *Metsäkaupungin synty*. Espoo: Helsingin teknillinen korkeakoulu, yhdyskuntasuunnittelun laitos, arkkitehtuurin historian laitos.

This Licentiate dissertation from the Department of Architecture at the Helsinki University of Technology discusses the development of the ideas behind functionalist town planning and reveals major differences between the planning ideologies of the earlier and later functionalists. At the same time the dissertation demonstrates the primary importance to planning of the strong aesthetic element in functionalist goals.

Mikkola, Kirmo (1979) *Funkis. Modernismens intåg i Finland*. Helsinki: Helsingfors festspel.

Mikkola, Kirmo (1980) Alvar Aalto and Town Planning in Mikkola, Kirmo, (ed.) *Genius Loci: In Commemoration of the 90th Birthday of Otto-I. Meurman, 4.6.1980*. Helsinki: Rakennuskirja.

Mikkola, Kirmo (1981) Konstruktivismi – rakentava ajatus, in Levanto, Marjatta (ed.), *Muoto ja rakenne. Konstruktivismi Suomen modernissa arkkitehtuurissa, kuvataiteessa ja taideteollisuudessa*. Helsinki: Ateneumin taidemuseo.

Mikkola, Kirmo (1984a) *Eliel Saarinen aikansa kaupunkisuunnittelunäkemyksen tulkkina – Suomen aika*. Espoo: Helsingin teknillinen korkeakoulu, yhdyskuntasuunnittelun jatkokoulutuskeskus.

Mikkola, Kirmo (1984b) The roots of Eliel Saarinens town plans, in *Saarinen in Finland*. Helsinki: Museum of Finnish Architecture.

Mosso, Leonardo (1967) *Alvar Aalto. Teokset 1918–1967*. Milano–Helsinki: Otava.

Murole, Pentti (1967) Ihmisen kulkemisen suunnittelusta. *Arkkitehti*.

Nikula, Oscar (1981) Kaupunkilaitos 1721–1875, in Tommila, Päiviö (ed.), *Suomen kaupunkilaitoksen historia*, Vol. 1. Vantaa: Suomen Kaupunkiliitto.
See comment under Jutikkala

Nikula, Riitta (1981) *Yhtenäinen kaupunkikuva 1900–1930*. Helsinki: Bidrag till kännedom om Finlands-natur och folk, utgivna av finska vetenskapssocieteten, H. 127.
This is the standard work on the theory and practice

underlying the classicizing town planning of the 1920s in Finland, with a broad discussion of the relationship between Finnish planning and Nordic and Central European theory-development around the beginning of the century.

Nikula, Riitta (1983) Kaupunkirakentaminen. Asemakaavoitus n. 1900–1920, in Tommila, Päiviö (ed.), *Suomen kaupunkilaitoksen historia*, Vol. 2. Vantaa: Suomen Kaupunkiliitto.
See comment under Jutikkala

Nordberg, Lauri (1979) *Översikt och jämförande analys av planeringslagstiftningen i den nordiska länderna*. Stockholm: Nordiska institutet för samhällsplanering R 1979:2.

Paavilainen, Simo (1982) Nordic Classicism in Finland, in *Nordic Classicism 1910–1930*. Helsinki: Museum of Finnish Architecture.

Paavilainen, Simo (1983) Hilding Ekelund ja pohjoismainen klassismi. *Arkkitehti*, No. 8.

Palenius, Pentti (ed.) (1970) *BES. Tutkimus avoimen elementtijärjestelmän kehittämiseksi*. Lahti: Suomen Betoniteollisuuden keskusjärjestö r.y.

Peltonen, Arvo (1982) *Suomen kaupunkijärjestelmän kasvu 1815–1970*. Helsinki: Bidrag till kännedom om Finlands natur och folk, utgivna av finska vetenskapssocieteten, H. 128.
This dissertation in urban geography quantifies urban growth during the period 1815–1970 and establishes the relation between industrial expansion in the country as a whole and growth in the size of the urban population. The author also describes how industrialization affects the quantitative relationship between different large towns. He shows that the successive concentration of the population towards the south is not matched by a polarization of growth in favour of the big towns at the expense of the smaller ones.

Peltonen, Vesa (1983) *Piirteitä eräiden Helsingin huvilakaupunkien syntymisestä*. Espoo: Helsingin teknillinen korkeakoulu, arkkitehtuurin historian laitos.

Perälä, Tauno (1983) Kaupunkien aluepolitiikka ja esikaupunkiliitokset 1875–1918, in Tommila, Päiviö (ed.) *Suomen kaupunkilaitoksen historia*, Vol. 2. Vantaa: Suomen Kaupunkiliitto.
See comment under Jutikkala

Ranta, Raimo (1981) Suurvalta-ajan kaupunkilaitos, in Tommila, Päiviö (ed.) *Suomen kaupunkilaitoksen historia*, Vol. 1, Vantaa: Suomen Kaupunkiliitto.
See comments under Jutikkala

Rautsi, Jussi (1984) *Alvar Aalton toteutumattomat alue ja kaupunkisuunnitelmat*. Helsinki: Helsinki University.

Saarinen, Eliel (1915) *Munksnäs-Haga och Stor-Helsingfors. Stadsplansstudier och förslag.* Helsingfors: Ab M. G. Stenius.

Saarinen, Riitta, Mattila, Markku and Salminen, Martti (1973) Aluerakentaminen Vantaalla. *Yhteiskuntasuunnittelu*, Nos 2–3.

Salokorpi, Asko (1984) Kaupunkirakentaminen in *Suomen kaupunkilaitoksen historia*, Vol. 3, itsenäisyyden aika. Vantaa: Suomen kaupunkiliitto. See comment under Jutikkala.

Sammalkorpi, Risto (1963) Kaksi asemakaavakilpailua. *Yhdyskuntasuunnittelu*, No. 1.

Sonck, Lars (1898) Modern vandalism: Helsingfors stadsplan. *Finsk tidskrift*, No. 44.

Sonck, Lars (1901) Våra småstäders gestaltning. *Ateneum*, Nos 10–11.

Strengell, Gustaf (1922) *Staden som konstverk.* Helsingfors: Albert Bonniers förlag.

Wickberg, Nils Erik (1959) *Finnish Architecture.* Helsinki: Octava.

Wickberg, Nils Erik (1973) *Carl Ludvig Engel.* Helsinki: City of Helsinki.

Wickberg, Nils Erik (1983) Strödda reflexioner om arkitektur och historia. *Arkkitehti*, No. 1.

4

URBAN PLANNING IN NORWAY

Erik Lorange and Jan Eivind Myhre[1]

THE PRE-INDUSTRIAL TOWN

The earliest towns in Norway grew from tiny local centres in certain regions where the natural conditions were especially favourable, offering various means of subsistence. Pasture for cattle, fertile soil for agriculture and access to fishing in rivers and sea, were basic. Important were also nearby supplies of game, timber, metal, etc. The first dense settlements came into being where valleys met fjords, and there were natural sheltered harbours.

Settlements in such locations gradually became numerous enough, and the surplus of products sufficiently large, for an organized exchange of commodities to develop. This again stimulated sea transport and shipbuilding. Power began to be concentrated, first in the hands of regional chieftains and later (about 900 AD) at a national level. Both encouraged urban growth. When Christianity had become established (after 1030), the first churches and monasteries appeared in and around the towns.

Tunsberg (Tønsberg) claims to be the oldest town in Norway, dating from before 900 AD. According to the *Sagas of the Norwegian Kings* by Snorre Sturlason, four other towns of importance were founded by kings: Trondheim in 997, Borg (Sarpsborg) in 1016, Oslo in 1048,

and Bjørgvin (Bergen) in 1070 (see figure 4.1). These statements should hardly be taken literally. But the towns mentioned did alternate as the capitals for the kings during this period when they and their armed men had to change abode in order to maintain the royal sway.

The coastal towns of Stavanger, Borgund and Skien also came into being in the twelfth and thirteenth centuries, together with Hamar, on the shore of Lake Mjøsa. As a rule, the principal towns were defended by royal castles which over the years were extended and reinforced. Tunsberg had its Slottsfjell (now in ruins), Bergen had both Bergenhus castle and Sverresborg, Trondheim also had a Sverresborg, while Oslo got its Akershus castle around 1300. Churches, dedicated to local and other popular saints, rose in the towns, while monasteries belonging to the various religious orders were built on the outskirts. In the towns, the principal churches were given conspicuous locations, on high ground or protruding headlands. Bergen, the thirteenth-century capital of King Haakon IV Haakonson, had its cathedral near the king's castle, eight other churches, three monasteries and a number of chapels. Oslo had its St. Hallvard's Cathedral near the bishop's castle and six parish churches, three monasteries and a fourth on Hovedøya island nearby. It was not until 1294 that Oslo became the official capital of Norway. The greatest ecclesiastical building in the country was the Nidaros Cathedral in

1. Jan Eivind Myhre has written the section, 'The urbanization of Norway 1850–1980', Erik Lorange the rest of the chapter.

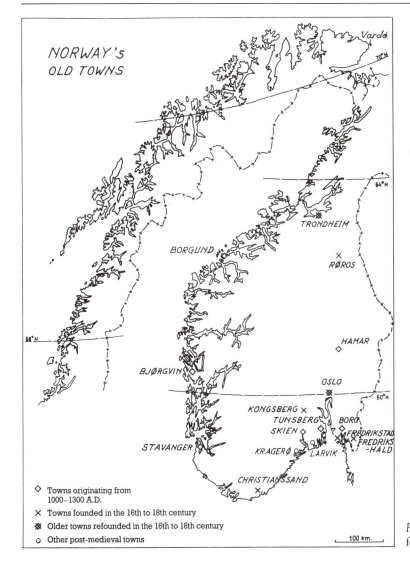

Figure 4.1. Norwegian towns founded before 1700.

Within the map:

NORWAY's
OLD TOWNS

Vardø

Trondheim

Borgund

Røros

Hamar

Bjørgvin

Oslo

Kongsberg

Tunsberg

Skien

Borg

Fredrikstad

Fredriks-Hald

Stavanger

Kragerø

Larvik

Christiansand

◇ Towns originating from 1000–1300 A.D.
× Towns founded in the 16th to 18th century
✳ Older towns refounded in the 16th to 18th century
○ Other post-medieval towns

100 km.

Trondheim. Containing the shrine of St. Olav, this was the see of the archbishop of Norway and an object of pilgrimage for the whole of Scandinavia.

The layout of the Norwegian mediaeval towns followed certain common planning principles. Easy access to the sea and port facilities was fundamental. Behind the wharfs there were densely built-up areas with premises for stores, shops, offices and dwellings. The building units, as can still be seen in Bergen at the Bryggen (see figure 4.2), could extend back and uphill for 100 metres, with additional storehouses, outhouses, stables, cattle sheds and barns. At the upper end there would be herb gardens and access to a common back street. The streets were mostly narrow and winding, following the contours of the terrain. Somewhat wider streets led to the few open spaces and to the churches, which were generally surrounded by burial grounds. Only churches and a few secular buildings of importance were built of stone. For the rest, the

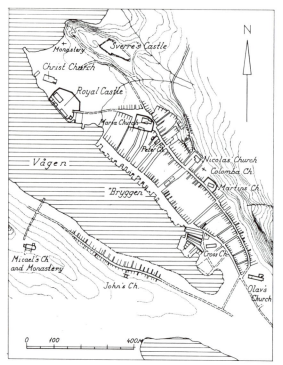

Figure 4.2. Bjørgvin (Bergen) around 1300.
Redrawn after map by Gerhard Fischer.

houses were wooden. King Magnus Lagabøte's Town Act of 1276 laid down the duties and rights of the townsmen. It also contained regulations on buildings, street widths, measures against fire, etc. The Act applied primarily to Bergen, which at the time was the greatest town in the country.

The Norwegian Kingdom was coming to an end. In 1349 the Black Death had greatly weakened the country by reducing the population to less than half its previous size. The towns stagnated, and so did life in the sparsely populated countryside. From 1380 onwards Norway came under the rule of the Danish kings. More than two hundred years were to pass before there was further progress in urban development. The first foundation of a new town took place in 1567, when the Danish-Norwegian King Frederik II founded Fredrikstad, near the

mouth of the Glomma, Norway's longest river. Strategic and commercial considerations lay behind this decision. The new town, located on a flat river bank, was laid out in keeping with the latest town planning principles of the time. A regular but oblique grid system of streets divided the town into blocks of different sizes (see figure 4.3). A small formal square was laid out at the intersection of the two main streets. In the mid-seventeenth century the town was provided with fortifications: star-shaped salients, bastions and moats. By about 1700 Fredrikstad was the strongest fortress in Norway.

In 1624 King Christian IV, the great founder of towns and palaces, commanded that the old town of Oslo, recently devastated by fire, should be rebuilt on a new site and provided with a modern town plan. The new town of Christiania (called Kristiania from 1877 onwards) was laid out below the bastions of Akershus Castle. This was supposed to give both town and castle better conditions for defence, should the enemy (i.e. the Swedes) attack. The town plan (figure 4.4) is reminiscent of seventeenth-century Dutch towns. The right-angled street pattern contained blocks of very different sizes. The market-place was located near the highest part, about 10 m above sea level. Here a church and the town hall were built. From the main town gate in the north, the Kongens gate (King's Street) led south towards the entrance to the castle. It was prescribed that all houses should be built of brick. This was unusual in Norway at the time, and represented no small economic burden. It was originally intended that the town should be fortified on the land side with walls and moats. These were never fully completed, however, and after a severe fire in 1686 it was decided to do without them. The church, which was also badly damaged, was not allowed to be rebuilt on its old site for military reasons. Instead a new church (the present Oslo Domkirke) was erected outside the town walls to the north. In front of it a new market-place, the Stortorvet, was laid out.

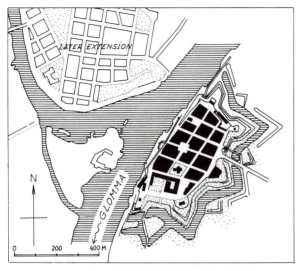

Figure 4.3. Fredrikstad, founded by King Fredrik II in 1567.
Redrawn from Krums oppmåling.

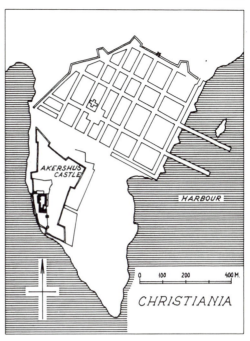

Figure 4.4. Christiania, founded by King Christian IV in 1624.
Redrawing of original plan structure.

Christian IV also founded the mining towns of Kongsberg in 1624, and Røros in 1644. Kongsberg, the 'Silver Town' had more than 8,000 inhabitants in 1770, and was consequently the next largest town after Bergen. Its old town plan was an adaptation of a grid system, not too strictly followed. Røros was situated in a mountain valley, 700 m above sea level. Exposed to a severe climate, a very distinctive type of urban community evolved here. The town grew up on both sides of a small river, in a somewhat 'organic' way. (With its well-preserved and tightly packed wooden buildings, Røros was chosen as one of Norway's three pilot projects for Architectural Heritage Year, 1975.)

In his old age Christian IV also founded the town of Christiansand (1641) on the south coast (from the nineteenth century onwards called Kristiansand). Again strategic considerations were decisive. On a flat plain at the mouth of the River Otra, the town was laid out on an almost quadratic plan (see figure 4.25). It consisted of nine by six rectangular blocks, all the same size and all framed by straight streets, 15 m broad. The new town was amply provided with royal privileges in order to encourage growth, but even so more than a hundred years passed before the relatively large designated urban area was built up with one- and two-storey wooden houses.

In 1665, as a move in the recurring warfare against the Swedes, Frederik III established the border town of Fredrikshald (Halden) beneath a strong hill fort, the Fredriksten. As was the fashion of the times, the town was laid out on a grid pattern of moderate extent.

Trondheim represented the most interesting town plan of this period. After suffering great war damage in 1681, this old city was rebuilt on a new grandiose plan, designed by General C. Cicignon, in the service of the king (see figure 4.5). Disregarding the mediaeval street pattern, he arranged the town on 'modern' baroque lines. From the old cathedral a broad axis (35–40 m), Munkegaten, was oriented towards the small fortified island of Munkholmen one mile

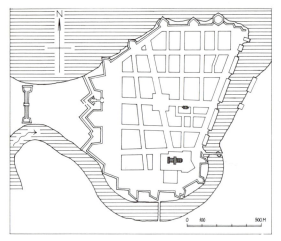

Figure 4.5. Trondheim.
Redrawing of the original town plan of 1681 by General C. Cicignon.

out in the fjord. This axis was crossed by another east-west axis, King's Street. The crossing was marked by a central square, whose quadratic form cut into the adjacent blocks. The town plan is remarkable for its exceptionally broad streets and its functional adaptation to the site. Thus, along the river bank a broad tree-lined street was built on two levels, to give access to the low-lying rows of gabled warehouses. The fortification of Trondheim was limited to the land side in the west, but a castle, Kristiansten, was built on high ground to the east of the town proper. Brick building was never prescribed for Trondheim. In the eighteenth century some of Norway's greatest and finest wooden buildings were erected along the main streets of the town.

For a long period (1343–1560) Bergen had been an important Hansa town. It had continued to grow on the narrow strips of land below the steep mountains and round Vågen, the harbour bay. The mediaeval town pattern consisted of rows of wharfs (*brygger*) with tightly packed gabled wooden houses on the inside, and a system of narrow winding streets following the contours of the terrain. Like all

wooden towns, Bergen was frequently exposed to fire. Some fires were disastrous, like the one in 1582 when 2,500 houses burnt down.

Each town fire led to renewed demands for new fire-breaks or openings in the urban fabric, *almenninger* as they were called. These open strips or streets have been a characteristic feature of the town plan of Bergen ever since Hanseatic times. As a rule the openings cut through the densely built-up area, straight from the harbour and up into the hills, often providing fine views over Vågen from the upper parts of the town behind (see figure 4.15).

From the second half of the sixteenth century onwards a number of small densely built places grew up along the Norwegian coast. Many of them obtained the right to function as market towns during the seventeenth and eighteenth centuries. On the south coast the economic basis for these towns was the export of timber to continental Europe and to Britain, together with shipbuilding, fishing, trade and industry. Examples of such towns were Drammen, Moss, Larvik, Kragerø, Risør, Arendal and Mandal. On the west and north coast fishing and the export of fish provided the main basis for urban growth. Examples here were Molde, Ålesund, Kristiansund, Tromsø, Hammerfest and Vardø.

In each case the physical structure, form and appearance of these towns was determined primarily by the natural features of the site. Favourable harbour conditions were vital. (The slight tides represented no problem.) Strong ties with the hinterland and access to resources there were also important. The ground inside the harbour basin was sometimes steep and difficult to build on, as in Kragerø (figure 4.6) and Arendal (figure 4.10), but the problems were overcome by the careful and flexible arrangement of the houses, landing-stages, stone walls, gardens, flights of steps, footpaths and streets. Thorough and detailed planning, strict attention to the economic facts and cooperation were essential conditions.

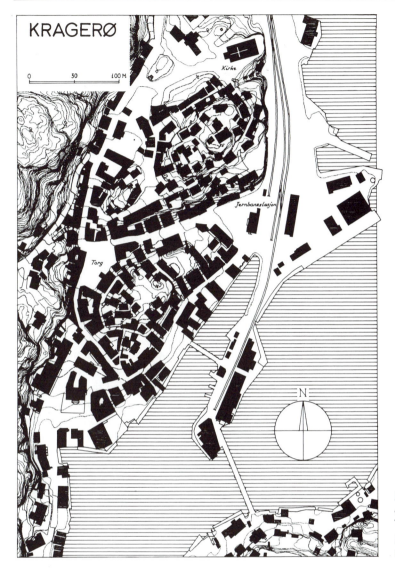

Figure 4.6. Kragerø. Map of the central area from 1965.
The town is an example of organic growth towns from the seventeenth century.

The building density was sometimes fairly high, involving the danger of fire. Most buildings were wooden with one or two storeys, often of standardized dimensions and with the same type of roofs, façade details and colours. Older surviving parts of these towns are often very picturesque and charming. As we shall see, however, these unique examples of old townscapes were greatly disparaged in the nineteenth and twentieth centuries. They were often subjected to radical redevelopment, especially after fires, but also in recent times in an effort to improve traffic conditions, to provide parking space, and in order to reserve central sites for commercial and administrative building.

THE URBANIZATION OF NORWAY
1850–1980

General Remarks

We shall start our survey of the process of urbanization in modern Norway around the year 1850. Several factors justify the choice of this date as our starting point. The first is purely statistical. Urbanization increased rapidly after 1845 (year of census), both in terms of the total urban population and the ratio of the share of the population of urban places in the country's total population. In the generation preceding 1845, only two towns had grown at a considerably faster rate than the rural population: Kristiania, due to its new status as Norway's capital, and Stavanger, because of the rich herring fisheries that were established immediately after the turn of the century.

The causes of this urban upswing will be discussed below. The contemporary concept of 'urban' or 'town' had no direct connection with the increasing speed of urbanization, and only a loose connection with its causes. But the changing urban concept is a reason in itself for regarding 1850 as an important chronological dividing line.

In the years around the middle of the century the authorities showed definite signs of abandoning the older static view of what a town was. As an example, they began to recognize that suburbs were an expression of urban growth, and a problem to be dealt with, for example by incorporating them into the town.

Norwegian settlements were given formal status as towns by giving them the rights of a *kjøpstad* (literally 'buying place') or a *ladested* ('loading place'). The towns were meant to be places of commerce, above all for foreign trade. Almost all Norwegian towns older than 1827 were based on the export of timber, fish or metal.

Between 1839 and the 1850s, a wave of incorporations took place on the Norwegian urban scene. In the period 1839–1848 fourteen towns were granted *kjøpstad* or *ladested* rights, as opposed to ten in the four preceding decades. The new incorporations, however, were different from earlier ones. The new towns were part of a large-scale attempt to expedite Norway's economic modernization by developing its infrastructure. They were meant to be distribution and production centres for different areas, helping to develop the rural hinterland. It is notable that six of the towns were located in the interior. If we except the special case of Kongsberg, the silver-mining town, the six were the first inland towns in Norway. Two of them, Hamar and Sarpsborg, had been small urban places during the Middle Ages, but returned to rural status long before the nineteenth century.

Among other measures taken by the liberal government around the middle of the century to foster economic growth, were the improvement of roads, the building of railways, the establishment of a stable currency, and the abolition of former restrictions on trade and production. All served to develop communications and economic relations, which were of the utmost importance to the growth of towns and cities.

In 1845, the official statistics publicized for the first time a list of unincorporated urban places (areas), including suburbs, fishing hamlets, iron works, copper works, larger saw-mills or other proto-industrial activities, and a host of other settlements with a variety of descriptions, like 'ferry-place' (*sundsted*), 'trading place' (*handelssted*), or 'shore-place' (*strandsted*). Many of these settlements were really the beginnings of small central places, built around country stores, places for change of transport, and seasonal markets. Their population ranged from a couple of thousand down to nineteen. The last figure is not as ridiculous as it may sound. Lacking the phenomenon of the continental agricultural village, almost any cluster of people amounting to more than, say, fifty or a hundred persons, could be considered an urban, or at least semi-urban phenomenon. These clusters contained few, if any, people employed in agriculture. Contemporary settlement statistics in Norway employ a lower limit of 200 inhabitants for a densely built-up area to be labelled urban (*tettsted*). This definition is used in the figures below, although one might argue that the limit ought to change with time, following the changing economic and social conditions. However, such a procedure would have made little difference to the trends in the figures below.

Although the idea of cities as central places (the term is a later invention) was a major novelty of the mid-nineteenth century, the idea of towns as centres of production also gained ground, although it received little attention at the time. In a few cases productive activities (most often still proto-industrial) were submitted as an argument in favour of incorporation, not always successfully.

We have dwelt on these features from around the mid-nineteenth century to illustrate an important feature of Norwegian urbanization: the tension between the 'general' function of the towns as servants and masters of the surrounding areas on the one hand, and their 'specific' roles which tied them to physical locations –

waterfalls, iron ore deposits or break-of-bulk points.

In a limited sense, the pre-1850 towns represented both. They were often to be found at the estuaries of rivers running through forested districts, and they formally partitioned the rural areas between them for purposes of internal trade. Both the type and the scale of late nineteenth-century production and inland commerce, however, different markedly from that of the early nineteenth century.

Norwegian urbanization from 1850 to 1980 may be divided into three phases, according to the speed of the process (the most important factor), the causes of urban growth, the development of town and city structure, and the socio-political consequences of urbanization. The phases are: (1) 1850–1920; (2) 1920–1945; (3) 1945–1980. The dates are approximations. Figures 4.7 and 4.8 give an impression of the speed and level of Norwegian urbanization, 1845–1980.

The First Phases of Industrialization, 1850–1920

Although there was rapid urbanization in every decade of this period, indeed the most intense in

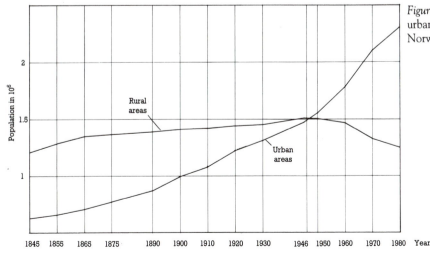

Figure 4.7. Population in urban and rural areas in Norway, 1845–1980.

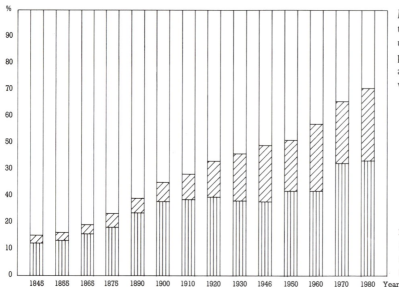

Figure 4.8. The relative distribution of incorporated urban population, unincorporated urban population, and rural population in Norway, 1845–1980.

Key
☐ Rural population
▨ Unincorporated urban population
▥ Incorporated urban population

Norwegian history, a division into three shorter periods is advisable. This is because the forces at work behind the urbanization process varied from one period to another. The approximate dates separating these sub-periods are 1865 and 1900.

Apart from an almost uninterruptedly fast urban growth, two features characterize the period as a whole. First, there is the rise of the towns as central places. The increasing interchange of goods, services, information, and people between rural and urban areas was highly conducive to making towns and cities grow. Smaller or larger urban places appeared within reasonable reach of most of the rural population, which was swiftly moving away from a subsistence economy, and therefore needed places to sell or buy. Norway's central place par excellence was Kristiania (Oslo), whose share of the urban population increased from 17 per cent in 1845 to 32 per cent by the turn of the century.

The second feature is industrialization, in a broad sense of the term. The whole society was to an increasing degree based on industrial products, buildings, tools, and means of communication. This had important consequences for the relations between town and country mentioned above, and therefore for urban growth. This kind of industrialization advanced fairly steadily throughout the period.

Industrialization, defined as the activity pursued in factories, had a more ambiguous influence on the urbanization process, since the growth of the urban population and the growth of the number of industrial workers were not well synchronized. The Norwegian factory system showed an uneven development in the seventy-five years from 1845 to 1920. During the first two decades industrialization took place mainly in or near the larger towns. It was comprised of the manufacturing of textiles, metal products, and beer, tobacco and foodstuffs. The second period, from the 1860s, witnessed the rise of the multifarious Norwegian wood-processing industries, often located in small urban places or in the countryside. In the latter case, the factories often became the basis of small urban places. This was also the case with the power-consuming electrotechnical and electrometallurgic industries that were established during the first decades of the twentieth century in locations where water power was abundant, above all in the western fjords.

In some cases the industrial places developed central functions as well, particularly if the railway happened to pass through. The railway was a strong urban developer during this epoch, especially in the last two periods. The combined effect of industry and railways on the making of new urban places is shown by the following figures. In 1845 there were eighty-seven urban places in Norway having more than 200 inhabitants. By 1865, the figure had only risen to 117, although the urban population had increased by 64 per cent. In 1900, however, there were 213 urban places, and in 1920, as many as 347.

The decades between 1850 and 1880 represented the golden age of Norwegian shipping. To the Skagerak coast (Agder) in particular, the white sails brought prosperity and fast urban growth. The towns of Agder coped badly with the ensuing transition from sail to steam, and went into a long period of stagnation from around 1890. Other towns and cities, such as Kristiania, Bergen, Tønsberg, and Haugesund, adopted the new technology quite quickly, and owed much of their twentieth-century growth to shipping and foreign trade.

The three periods also had demographic characteristics that separated them from each other. Until about 1900 a high birth rate combined with a low and falling death rate, caused a high natural population increase in Norwegian towns and cities. The death rate in particular was extraordinarily low, even in the largest urban areas, such as Kristiania. Natural increase in population remained annually at between 10.4 and 16.2 per cent between 1845 and 1900 (for incorporated towns only), and for Kristiania at between 5.5 and 19.5 per cent. Natural growth accounted for more than half the growth in urban population in every decade from 1845 to 1900, even when new incorporations and territorial annexations by the towns are included.

Another reason for the modest relative contribution of net in-migration to urban population growth, was the massive overseas emigration, only surpassed by that of Ireland. More than 200,000 urban citizens left for America during the period 1866–1920, i.e. more people than the whole incorporated population in 1855.

Until 1855, however, emigration was modest. The net in-migration from rural to urban areas was smaller in the two decades between 1845 and 1865 than it became later. Mass overseas emigration from the countryside had not yet begun. That is why the rural districts showed strong population growth during the two decades, the only example of this from 1845 to the present. After 1865, most of the rural population surplus was swallowed by the towns or by America. After 1900, this influx was needed more than before by the towns, because the birth rate dropped. During the period we are dealing with here, however, the towns came nowhere near a birth deficit.

The structure of the Norwegian towns and cities underwent important changes during the seventy years from 1850 to 1920. The changes were most noticeable in the larger urban areas. In 1850 practically all urban houses in Norway were made of wood. The central districts of Kristiania (Oslo) were the only important exception. While the smaller towns remained wooden, in the larger ones considerable numbers of brick buildings were constructed, mainly apartment houses. By 1920, the percentage of stone buildings in Kristiania was 73 per cent, in Ålesund (which was completely destroyed by fire in 1904) 44 per cent, in Bergen 28 per cent, in Kristiansand 23 per cent, and in Trondheim 22 per cent.

Another new trait became particularly visible after the turn of the century: the close, compact shape of the nineteenth-century town was destroyed. Villa suburbs, mainly middle class and located quite far away from the town centres, were made possible by the development of suburban communication links. Again, this was most noticeable in the larger urban centres.

This tendency was accompanied by the emptying of the city centre as a residential area. Commercial activities began to dominate the central parts, forcing the inhabitants out. The wealthy and their servants moved to new fashionable villa suburbs, the less well-to-do to more modest neighbourhoods, in some cases to tenement housing. The bigger the town, the clearer was this pattern. In general there was an increasing tendency for physical distance to reflect social distance.

Economic Crisis and Slow Urbanization, 1920–1945

As figure 4.7 shows, the two intercensus periods 1920–30 and 1930–46 show the slowest urban growth over the course of the whole 1845–1980 period. In the 1930s and during the Second World War the sluggish urban growth was accompanied by the strongest rural growth since 1855–65.

The key factor in explaining the tentative urban growth and the slow urbanization, is the inter-war international economic crisis. America no longer acted as a safety valve for population surplus. The bad times hit the countryside as well as the towns and cities. There was, however, a fundamental difference between the two in their capacity to respond to the crisis (or crises, as there were more than one).

Norwegian agriculture in the 1920s and 1930s was still fairly labour-intensive, the individual farm grew a variety of crops, and most of the food was still consumed locally. Around 1930, the trade in agricultural products became better organized to the benefit of the producers. All this made the rural districts quite elastic with respect to the capacity to support a large population. The authorities saw this clearly and encouraged the reclaiming of new land and the establishment of more farms.

In the urban areas unemployment was widespread. Fertility sank to a very low level in both town and country, but the natural growth was weaker in urban than in rural areas. Nevertheless, the urban population of Norway increased by 35 per cent between 1920 and 1946, and its share of the country's total population rose from 43 to 49 per cent. Thus the urbanizing forces must, all in all, have remained fairly strong during these twenty-six years.

The industrialization of Norway continued in spite of the crises. The manufacturing and building industries increased their share of the gainfully employed population from 29 to 32.5 per cent during the period, an increase that mainly benefited urban areas.

Other 'urban' occupations that became relatively more important in the inter-war years, were communications (excluding sea transport), public administration, and private service activities (domestic servants excluded). Their proportion increased from 9.5 to 15 per cent. Business activities, too, became relatively more important.

This all points to the fact that towns and cities continued to grow as *central places*. It happened at all levels in the urban hierarchy, from the tiny towns of 200 inhabitants to the major cities. Several new urban places appeared to fill in the pattern of central places.

At the top of the hierarchy was Oslo, with a population of 330,000 in 1920 and 465,000 in 1946 (suburbs included). From a modest position as the country's second town in 1800 (population about 10,000), it rose to a pre-eminent position among Norwegian urban places at the turn of the century (population about 250,000). Up to the 1860s the town's role as Norway's capital was the most important factor behind its amazing growth. Through its uniquely central location and the virtual monopoly it had on important public and financial institutions, Oslo continued to grow of its own momentum, even during times of economic hardship.

The First World War saw a breakthrough for public involvement in economic and social affairs. The public share of the Gross National Product increased from 7.4 per cent in 1915 to 24.7 per cent in 1946. This meant more public employees, who were mainly city- and town-dwellers. It also meant, however, that municipal authorities increased their responsibility for urban services, including housing. This led to a more planned urban structure, particularly near the town centre, and inside the boundaries. Suburban villa growth, both inside and outside the limits of the towns and cities, continued to spread rather uninhibitedly. In 1946 almost 700,000 people, or 21 per cent of Norway's population, lived in unincorporated urban areas: suburbs or towns that had not been given official status as *kjøpstad* or *ladested*. From the environs around the larger towns and cities, an increasing number of commuters made their daily journeys to work in the urban centre. Oslo received 70,000 commuters daily in 1930.

From Fast to Slow Urbanization, 1945–1980

Immediately after the Second World War the process of urbanization gained momentum. The years between 1945 and 1950 marked a turning-point in two respects: for the first time in history there were more urban than rural people in Norway, and for the first time in about 130 years, the rural population declined.

The growth rate of the urban population between 1946 and 1970 almost approached that of the period 1845–1900, but since the rural population after the war declined fast, as opposed to the situation in the nineteenth century, the process of urbanization was perhaps even swifter in the latter period (depending on how we measure it).

The period was one of continued industrial growth. Manufacturing employees increased their percentage of the gainfully employed population from 32.5 to 37.5 per cent between 1946 and 1970. There was also a considerable relative increase in the tertiary sector. The changes in the occupational structure were partly the result of a deliberate official economic policy, carried out to strengthen economic growth by transferring people from low productive to high productive activities. An exodus from agriculture, forestry and fishing was the result. Their share of the workforce dropped from 30 per cent to 12 per cent during these twenty-four years.

The beneficiaries were the economic activities that settled for little space, looked for central locations, and required proximity to a host of other activities. Towns, and especially bigger towns and cities, offered the most advantages. In the 1970s, however, the largest urban places became the least advantageous in some respects: lack of space, inadequate housing, traffic congestion, and high land values.

From around 1970 the urbanization process slowed down, both in rural depopulation and urban growth (figures 4.7 and 4.8). This Norwegian version of the international urban 'turn-around trend' was not evenly distributed throughout the urban system. Two types of urban places in particular showed stagnation or even decline in their population during the 1970s.

First, there were the cities and towns with manufacturing or fishing as their main economic base. In many cases these were the same urban places that grew exceptionally fast during the first couple of decades after World War II. The economic crisis hit some of the Norwegian manufacturing industries hard from around 1974 onwards. Employment in the manufacturing and building industries dropped from 37.5 per cent to 29.5 per cent between 1970 and 1980.

Norwegian manufacturing towns may be divided into two types, which fared differently in the 1970s. Some, usually the larger ones, had a broad industrial base with a variety of industries and firms. They managed fairly well. The other type, the so-called 'single-industry places' were in many cases in severe difficulties. Quite a few of them were small towns in the western fjords or in northern Norway, which based their existence on power-consuming plants whose products were in less demand on the international market than they had been. In the north many small towns had been based on the fisheries, which in the 1970s experienced a resource shortage.

The other type of urban place that fared badly after 1970 were the largest towns and cities. The eight or nine 'city regions' (cities exceeding 50,000 inhabitants including their main commuting municipalities) grew particularly fast in the 1950s and 1960s. Around 1960 three-quarters of Norway's annual population increase took place in these city regions. This process of regional concentration slowed down in the early 1970s, and in the latter half of the decade the city regions actually grew more slowly than the country at large. Norway therefore experienced a regional *de*concentration.

The small and medium-sized central places, however, grew faster than ever in the 1970s. The Norwegian central place pattern in 1970 still had 'underdeveloped' urban places and empty areas that waited to be filled. Public service increased considerably in the 1970s, irrespective of the economic crisis, which actually hit Norway very late in the decade. The larger central places experienced a marked increase in public employees in nearly all domains of public service.

In the 1960s the threat of a highly unbalanced regional development led the government to encourage economic development in a number of small urban centres (*vekstsentra* – 'growth centres'). The programme had some success in helping to develop peripheral areas and in relieving the pressure on some of the larger urban areas. The smaller, local centres benefited especially from a strong increase in public health, social services, and the centralization of schools.

The new urban areas of the years after World War II were space-demanding. Whereas every inhabitant in Kristiania (Oslo) had on an aver-

age 50 m^2 at his disposal in the 1880s, his descendants in 1970 had 250 m^2 (both calculated for the built-up area). There were now more rooms per person in the apartment houses near the centre. In addition the extensive areas of villas and semi-detached houses consumed a good deal of space. The satellite towns (*drabantbyer*) around the larger towns and cities had many tall buildings, but with plenty of space between.

The physical dividing-line between urban and rural became increasingly difficult to draw in the 1960s and 1970s. The older urban definition, based on a certain density of settlement and a minimum population, proved inadequate for the 1970s. The concepts of 'hidden urbanization' and 'dispersed urbanization' were introduced (Hansen, 1975). The first described a situation in which houses in the countryside changed function, so that they now housed commuters. The second denoted *new* buildings that housed commuters but were located in a dispersed settlement falling outside the urban definition.

Recent literature speaks of the 'city regions', in other words a central city and its surrounding suburban municipalities, i.e. those that have a certain proportion of commuters (Myklebost, 1979). Another recent expression is 'commuting region', designed to encompass small towns as well. The commuting region consists of a central small town, incorporated or not, with at least 2,000 inhabitants (topographically defined), plus the adjoining census districts (the smallest geographical units of the censuses) with a certain proportion of commuters.

The distinction between urban and rural areas was also blurred by another tendency: 'urban' and 'rural' were becoming more and more difficult to separate on a basis of occupational information. In 1980 the genuine rural occupations, agriculture and forestry, accounted for 8 per cent of the gainfully employed population, while the rural population constituted around 30 per cent of the country's total population. Even in the most rural areas secondary or tertiary occupations were more numerous than primary ones.

THE PROGRESS OF TOWN PLANNING IN NORWAY

1845–1920: Legal Provisions and Influences from Abroad

Considerations of health and access and the danger of fire were the factors that provoked legal provisions for the physical design and appearance of Norwegian towns. The first real building legislation was introduced in the capital, Kristiania, in 1827. A few years later Bergen and Trondheim followed suit. Local self-government was granted to all Norwegian municipalities from 1837, and in 1845 the national assembly or *Storting* passed a Building Act to take effect in all other towns.

The Act ordered the establishment of a building commission and a planning commission. The latter, which consisted of four officials and two elected politicians, was made responsible for the preparation of town plans to be submitted for sanction by the king. The planning regulations in the Act were rigid and based on a blind faith in the blessings of the grid system. All streets were to be straight and at least 12.5 m wide. No blocks were to exceed 4,000 m² in size. Certain elementary zoning rules had to be followed. With the exception of Kristiania, the traditional wooden houses were still allowed in

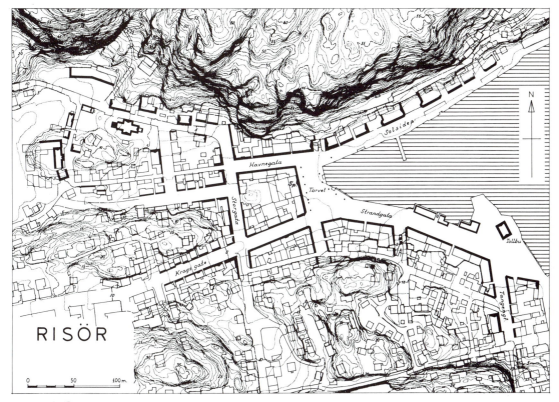

Figure 4.9. Risør.
Map drawn by the author, based on official map. Contour intervals 1 m. Risør is a charming wooden town from the seventeenth century, replanned and rebuilt after a fire in 1861.

the towns, but only up to two storeys. Restrictions were imposed on the height and pitch of the roofs, on street corners (which had to be cut diagonally), on the distance between neighbouring buildings and on construction methods. Aesthetic considerations played a certain part, as well as the purely functional.

The Act had immediate consequences for the physical conversion of many old towns and town centres. For all new foundations it was decisive. Fires that subsequently hit a number of towns (Levanger in 1846, Risør in 1861, Arendal in 1863 and Drammen in 1866, etc.) led to the radical replanning of the old 'self-grown' central districts. With varying success new grid plans were imposed, often without any consideration for difficult terrain, prevailing winds, sunlight, old building traditions, or regional distinctions.

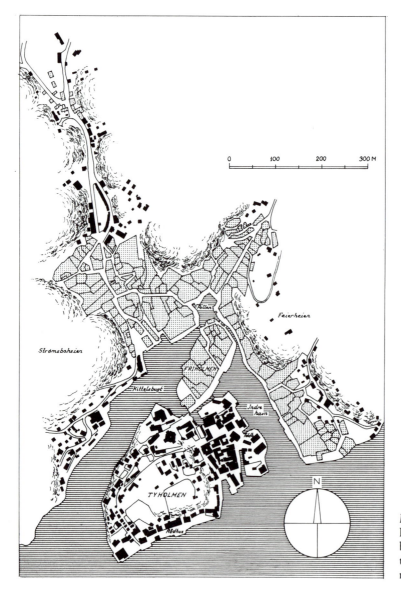

Figure 4.10. Arendal.
Left: town fires 1863–68. The burned areas are dotted. Right: the new town plan of 1868. The maps are adapted by the author.

Nevertheless, an old wooden town like Risør on the south coast (figure 4.9) is an example of quite a successful plan, thanks to a skilful planner, Lieutenant Birger Hielm (also responsible for the plan for Arendal [figure 4.10]). In Risør, despite the letter of the law, he obviously strove to fit the town plan into the landscape.

Towns that were founded during this period or were granted market town status, such as Hamar 1848, Hønefoss 1851, Haugesund 1854, Gjøvik 1861 and Bodø 1860, were all given modern grid plans. The town plan of Gjøvik (figure 4.11) shows a not very successful compromise between three different grid systems and an obstinate terrain (contour intervals 5 m). The town plan of Haugesund (figure 4.12) shows a consistent use of a standardized grid system.

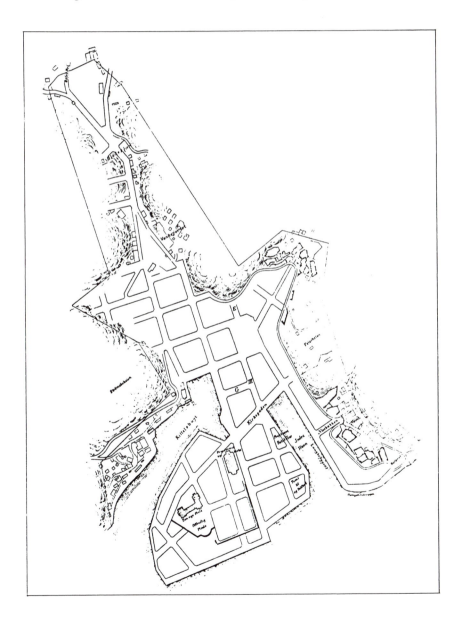

Figure 4.11. Gjøvik.
Redrawn simplification of an official map. The town plan is from 1861. Contour intervals 5 m.

Models for the Norwegian town plans can be found in many contemporary plans for Swedish, Finnish and to some extent Danish towns. While most of these towns were located on relatively flat ground, the Norwegian town sites were often quite hilly. Thus, it was often difficult or impossible to build straight streets as demanded because of the shape of the terrain. If built they often became too steep for vehicles. It could also be necessary to shift huge amounts of stone or rock in order to achieve the desired street grid.

Towards the end of the nineteenth century industrial development led to rapid urban growth in the bigger towns. The population of Kristiania increased from 47,000 to 227,000 between 1860 and 1900. The shortage of housing for the new worker population became overwhelming, and building was urgently needed. When the town was founded in 1624, brick building was compulsory within the planned area. This was such an expensive way of building at that time, that only the well-to-do could afford it. People of humble means were left to put up their small, timbered houses *outside* the

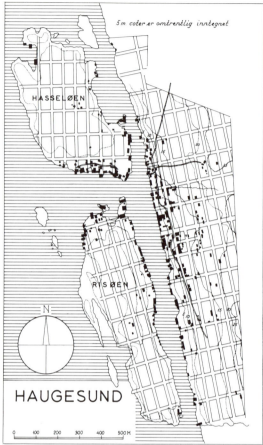

Figure 4.12. Haugesund.
Redrawing of the 1856 town plan, with the already existing buildings in black. Contour intervals 5 ms.

town proper, in 'self-grown' suburbs, on hills and unproductive land. As time went by these suburban residential areas became so populous that by the end of the eighteenth century more people lived in them than in the town itself. Gradually, however, various factors such as urban expansion, new legislation, fires, and calls for a more intense use of the urban area, led to the introduction of the continental tenement house. Before long this was to change the overall exploitation ratio and the total appearance of the city.

The first major alterations occurred in connection with the planning of the fine new main axis, Karl Johan Street, named after the first Swedish-Norwegian king. This street, laid out about 1840, connected the new Royal Palace, which was completed in 1848 on its conspicuous site at the top of a beautiful rounded hill, with the older parts of the town. The street ran past the new university buildings, completed in 1852, to the new building for the *Storting* which was completed in 1866. The town plan was worked out as early as 1838 by H. D. F. Lin-

stow, the same architect who had designed the Royal Palace. Figure 4.13 shows the central part of Kristiania at the end of the nineteenth century, when the grand central park axis on the south side of Karl Johan Street had also been realized.

Along the new streets three-storey houses for the well-to-do were built. This led to a general introduction of three- and four-storey brick buildings in the town centre, often with shops

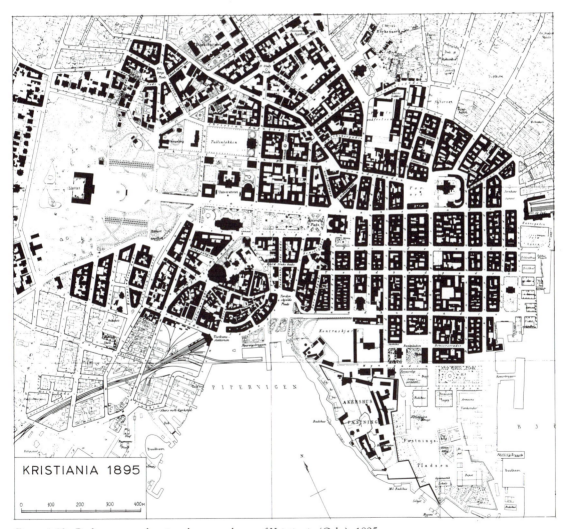

Figure 4.13. Redrawn map showing the central part of Kristiania (Oslo), 1895.
To the right: Akershus Castle and the 1624 grid plan. To the left: The Royal Palace with the Karl Johan Street and the park axis in the centre.

on the ground floor and offices higher up. The breakthrough for the three- and four-storey pure tenement houses, assembled in rectangular densely built blocks, occurred about 1870. From then until the turn of the century numerous big tenement blocks were planned and erected by landowners, contractors and speculators. During this period the new town plans for Kristiania were undoubtedly influenced by Lindhagen's city plan of 1866 for Stockholm. The tenement houses themselves had evident prototypes in Germany. This 'Berliner architecture' was often imported by young architects and civil engineers, recently graduated from German Technische Hochschulen and universities.

The largest of the new residential districts was Grünerløkka (figure 4.19), a densely built working-class area on the east side of the city. When completed it comprised 6,600 units, mainly flats with one or two rooms and a kitchen, in buildings of three, four and sometimes five storeys. During the last half of the nineteenth century about 35–40,000 dwellings were put up in the rapidly growing capital in similar densely built tenement areas. These are the same residential districts that are undergoing a very necessary but difficult process of renewal today.

It is interesting to note that during these same years, 1860–80, a new housing estate, Homannsbyen, with eighty handsome plastered brick villas for upper-class families, was laid out and built in an area west of the Royal Palace Park.

Bergen, surrounded by steep mountains, was always short of land suitable for building. During this period of rapid growth the town was therefore obliged to introduce the same type of brick tenement houses as those in Kristiania. In other Norwegian towns most of the building was in the form of individual wooden houses. Within the framework of rigid grid street plans, houses of one and a half or two storeys were evenly distributed, each located in the middle of its own lot.

An important and positive step forward in town planning was the introduction of public parks in the new urban schemes. Following international models, many of the parks were given a formal and often geometrical design, while others had a more natural style. The largest and most elaborate parks appeared in Kristiania and Bergen, but most other towns also had parks, both for recreational and for more ceremonial purposes. Quite often small steep hills that were difficult or too expensive to develop for housing, were used for parks instead. In Kristiania a most successful public park of this type was St. Hanshaugen, which is well known for its beautiful view over the city.

A new building Act was passed in 1896. This applied to all towns in the country, except the three largest which were already covered by their own special stricter legislation. According to the new Act, towns were now entitled to prepare plans for a 200 m broad belt of land *outside* the town border as well, in order to keep some control over urban expansion into the neighbouring rural districts. The requirement regarding straight streets and rectangular blocks of restricted size was retained. The planning of public squares for various purposes was recommended. The restrictions on wooden buildings were tightened up. The base of such houses was not to exceed 300 m², and they had to be separated from neighbouring houses either by fireproof walls or by a distance of at least 5 m. The houses did not necessarily have to be placed directly fronting the street. A recession of 5 m at most was acceptable in residential districts. In practice these various regulations stimulated an open type of plan, with detached houses. Beyond the older quarters, such new housing areas were now growing rapidly in the larger towns.

The worst threat to the wooden towns came from the frequent fires. They seemed to come like a bolt from the blue, and could be devastating. During a western gale in 1892, Kristiansand suffered a disastrous fire. One-third of the houses in the town were burnt down, and 4,000 people lost their homes. In January 1904 Ålesund, another coastal town, was razed to the ground by a terrible fire that could not be extinguished. 12,000 people lost their homes in this densely built wooden town. In 1904, frightened by these experiences, the *Storting* passed a new bill on the 'prohibition against erecting wooden buildings in towns in this country'. Most people regarded the compulsory use of brick (or concrete) for all building far too drastic. The cost threatened to become prohibitive, and since additions and major repairs to existing wooden houses were forbidden, it was all too likely that many attractive wooden townships would fall into disrepair. Over the next few years a number of exemptions from the law were granted, but seldom in the central parts of the towns. In practice 'brick compulsion' was enforced within the central boundaries, while most new housing – detached wooden houses – went up in the residential areas on the outskirts.

After the fire of 1904, Ålesund was rebuilt in brick and stone, on the basis of a new town plan. This town is special in many ways. The densely built-up area stretches over a series of hilly and quite steep islands. In places the buildings seem barely to be hanging on. Under such circumstances it was not easy to effect a regular street grid, as the law more or less prescribed. Figure 4.14 shows the developed parts of Ålesund in 1929. We can see many compromise solutions in the grid system, as well as examples of straight streets that have become precipitous at their upper or lower ends.

The town was rebuilt over a period of a few

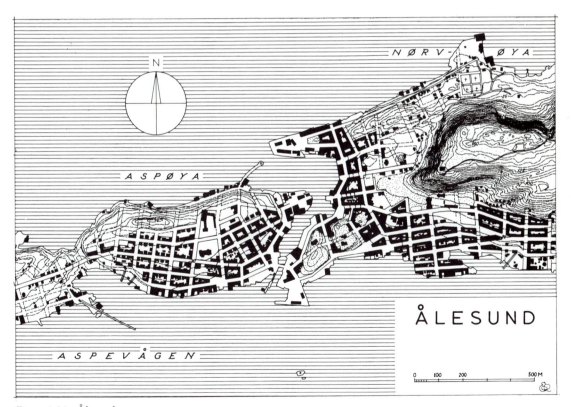

Figure 4.14. Ålesund.
Redrawing of A. Gjortz map of 1929. Contour intervals 5 m. The town is situated on a series of islands. After a devastating fire in 1904 the town was rebuilt on the basis of a new plan.

years, just when the Art Nouveau style was fashionable with Norwegian architects. The lively and varied façades, the often oblique, steep and disconnected streets with frequent glimpses down to the harbour and the sea, all serve to make Ålesund an unusual and exciting urban experience.

When Norway decided in 1905 to terminate the union with Sweden, certain national trends had begun to appear in Norwegian architecture and gradually also in town planning. The prescript that all Norwegian towns should be planned according to standardized grid systems became the target of growing criticism. The main objections were on aesthetic grounds or based on landscape considerations, but there were also strong technical and economic arguments.

The change in ideas was clearly attributable to new European trends around the turn of the century. The many negative aspects of industrial and urban development had become obvious: overcrowded cities, continuous expansion, schematic town plans lacking any character, and a universal absence of social and environmental qualities in the urban scene.

The Viennese architect Camillo Sitte, the pioneer of the garden city Ebenezer Howard, and the town-planner ecologist Patrick Geddes, each in their way came to influence urban development in the new century. Howard's and Sitte's ideas were reflected in the town plans of Raymond Unwin and Barry Parker for Letchworth and Hampstead Garden Suburb. In Germany, too, interesting new models appeared in

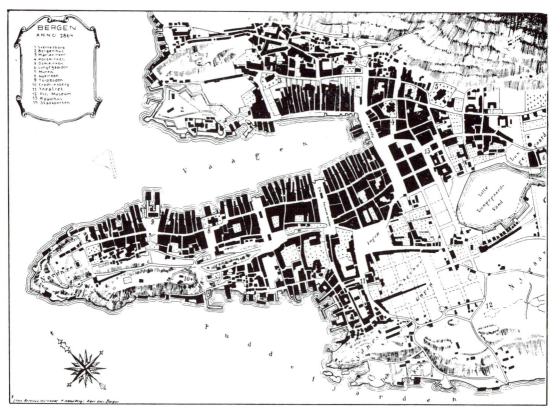

Figure 4.15. Bergen.
Military map from 1864. Notice the characteristic fire-breaks or *almenninger*.

the works of architects such as Karl Henrici. Norwegian architects, civil engineers and medical practitioners returned from study tours abroad, inspired by the new ideas they had found there, particularly in Britain. Over these years a town-planning profession was gradually evolving in Norway, recruited from the growing numbers of architects and civil engineers.

In the period that followed, several important town planning competitions were held in Norway, often on a Nordic basis. The competitions provided favourable opportunities for launching the new ideas. At first Swedish planners often carried off the top awards, but gradually Norwegian architects and civil engineers began to assert themselves. One of the leading planners was Sverre Pedersen (1882–1971), architect in Trondheim. In 1920 he became the first professor of architecture and town planning at the Norwegian Institute of Technology in Trondheim. Other outstanding names during this period were Harald Hals (1876–1959),

T. *Torgalmenningen*
O. *Ole Bulls plass*
LL. *Lille Lungegårdsvann*
N. *Den Nationale Scene*
D. *Domkirken*

BERGEN

0   100   200   300   400 M.

Figure 4.16. Bergen. Map of the central part, 1960. The design of the area between the Vågen, the theatre (N) and the lake (LL) was the result of a town planning competition, after the fire in 1916.

architect and chief planner in Oslo from 1926, and Oscar Hoff (1875–1942), architect and a frequent winner in town-planning competitions particularly in Oslo.

A competition typical of the times concerned a central part of Bergen (figure 4.15), which had been devastated by fire in 1916. In many of the best projects, and especially in the winning plan, the layout had a certain monumental character and a three-dimensional quality, which consciously exploited the terrain and the possibilities of the landscape. The main elements of the winning project, by the two Swedish planners Lilienberg and Samuelson, were later realized. To implement the new division of sites according to the new plan, a special Bill of Expropriation was passed. Figure 4.16 shows the competition area as part of present-day Bergen. The Torgalmenningen (T) – the main square – was designed carefully and in detail. Firmly framed frontages, partly colonnaded,

with views towards the surrounding mountains, and with easy connections to Vågen harbour and Lille Lungegårds lake, it provided a worthy and appropriate background for public events and ceremonies in Bergen.

Another Nordic competition that should be mentioned, concerned a new suburb to Kristiania, Ullevål Hageby or garden city. The winning project, by Oscar Hoff, aptly adjusted to the contours of the terrain and was obviously inspired by garden city ideas in Britain and on the Continent. The plan was realized by the municipality between 1916 and 1921. With houses for about 5,000 people, it was regarded as a grand social housing project, mainly comprising terraced and semi-detached brick houses. Figure 4.17 shows part of the garden suburb with its local centre, Damplassen, as it is today.

The introduction of the garden city idea coincided with other strong social currents in the

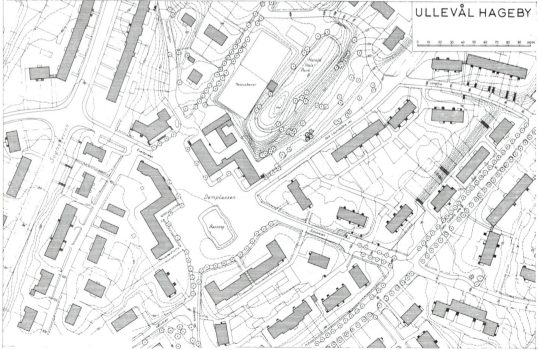

Figure 4.17. Ullevål, Oslo.
Central part of a garden suburb built 1916–21, as a municipal housing project. Copy of the actual map.

early years of the century. They led among other things to the foundation of a Norwegian Association for Housing Reform in 1913 and a National Association for Town Planning in 1919. Housing and planning in Norway received substantial encouragement from the activities of these associations. They organized lectures and open discussion meetings, excursions abroad and publications. There was a broader awareness of town planning in professional and political circles, which gradually influenced practical policy at both the state and the municipal levels. (The two bodies have now merged and are associated with the International Federation for Housing and Planning.)

After the presentation in 1912 (by the chief planner of Kristiania, Hjalmar Torp) of a new town plan, a distinct shift in urban design became noticeable. Attempts were made to get away from the usual dense type of tenement block, just at the same time as a new social housing policy was launched in the capital. An example of the new trend was the municipal housing scheme in Sagene, designed by the architect Kristian Rivertz. Here for the first time three-storey tenement houses were grouped in parallel rows, oriented north-south, with green spaces between. An incipient functionalism was evident in the concern for sunlight and green surroundings. Another social housing project with unquestionable environmental qualities is the Torshov residential district, built by the municipality between 1917 and 1925. Well-planned outdoor spaces in streets and courts were organized in association with a fine public park. A section of the area as it is today is illustrated in figure 4.18.

It was not until later that Patrick Geddes' ideas and methods, on regional coherence and analyses, on ecology and comprehensive plan-

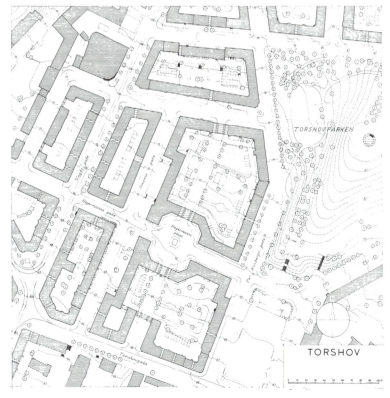

TORSHOV

Figure 4.18. Torshov, Oslo. Municipal housing estate, built 1917–25. The blocks of flats are in three storeys. Actual map.

ning, were to influence Norwegian planners. But some aspects of development at this time had a certain affinity with Geddes' thinking. The utilization of Norway's vast hydroelectric resources – the production of 'white coal' – began to accelerate from 1905 onwards. This phase of development clearly had 'regional' aspects that were of increasing importance to the remote parts of this extensive but sparsely populated country.

In order to exploit the power resources and the industrial potential of the peripheral areas, new small industrial centres and small towns were founded. The establishment of Norsk Hydro (Norwegian Hydroelectric Nitrogen Company Ltd, a pioneer industrial firm, established 1905) in Rjukan and Notodden gave rise to the creation of two new towns (1908–20). Other small urban communities sprang up on the west coast, for instance at Odda, Sauda and Høyanger. The planning and realization of these small urban centres represented a challenge of a special kind. The places were remote and lacking in communications and technical and social services; the terrain was also often extremely difficult. Thanks to the achievements of a few young civil engineers and architects, these centres were given interesting town plans and an architectural unity in keeping with the stylistic language of the period. Only fairly recently have the original and distinctive features of these places been fully appreciated. At the same time, however, they are now threatened by plans for rationalization, redevelopment and general change, which may well jeopardize many of the original environmental qualities.

1920–1940: Modernization of the Planning Remedies

The need for reforms in town-planning legislation had now become evident. In the bigger towns the planners were abandoning the rigid schematic recipes provided by the old law. Thus in many respects the new Building Act of 1924, which had been in preparation for ten years,

only confirmed a practice that had already begun.

The new Act applied to the towns (boroughs), but could be extended to apply to rural districts as well. This had a special relevance for municipalities around the larger towns, where suburban development was taking place. The Act prescribed that each municipality should appoint a local Building Board to apply the law. The composition of the Board was more democratic than in the previous Building Commissions. Half the members were to be politically elected, while the other half were still to be officials. Not until the Building Act of 1965 was it decided that *all* members of the Board should be politically elected. The Board had two responsibilities:

1. to see that new town plans were prepared and obsolete plans revised;
2. to approve of building projects submitted.

In the more populous towns specific Planning Boards took over the first of these tasks.

The previous rigid provisions regarding the shape of the town plans were abandoned. Now attention was to be focused on 'the situation and development of the neighbourhood' and the need 'for housing, traffic, fire safety, health measures and sewage discharge'. As to the buildings, they 'should be arranged in an architecturally attractive way, and in such a manner that new and old buildings could be harmoniously adjusted to each other'. Explicitly, the nature of the terrain should always be taken into account, as should street gradients and local requirements for recreation and play areas. The minimum width for main streets was to be 15 metres. It was recommended that building height should be limited to two storeys. Only in the commercial centres of the bigger towns could more than three storeys be accepted.

Building in brick (or concrete) was still compulsory in the central parts of the towns, and the restrictions on wooden houses as regards area, height and distance to the boundaries of neighbouring plots were tightened up. Here it should be remembered that detached one-family wooden houses still constituted the majority of new houses in Norwegian towns (more than 80 per cent). The law demanded that all buildings should satisfy reasonable aesthetic standards, although no directives on definite aesthetic specifications were given either for buildings or in connection with town planning.

For the implementation of approved plans, local authorities were granted the right to expropriate private property for certain new uses, and to claim reimbursement for public expenditure on infrastructure which benefited private owners.

The Act was primarily a tool for controlling the physical growth of towns and for shaping all *new* development. There were no provisions whatsoever for the rehabilitation of old buildings, or remedies for solving the problems of preserving buildings, streets or other existing environmental values. This may explain why so many distinctive and interesting old buildings and street fronts were ruthlessly demolished and replaced by new buildings during the period which followed.

The law emphasized the many *functional* aspects that should be considered in the new town plans. Not only should the street pattern be indicated in detail together with the division of the areas into separate building plots. The basis had now also been given for the overall physical planning of the towns which was to determine their future appearance and function: expansive urban patterns, road systems and zoning, with the emphasis on the division between residential and industrial areas, and between commercial and other kinds of development.

The main tool in this planning process was the layout plan (*reguleringsplan*). In these plans the size, form and character of the buildings were specified in considerable detail. Layout plans were in fact obligatory for the whole of the urban area. Most of those produced between the wars concerned new residential areas for detached houses on the periphery of the towns. For the most part, they took into account variations in the terrain, orientation, sun, view, garden possibilities, vegetation, etc. Playgrounds were sometimes included.

Sverre Pedersen, the professor of town planning mentioned above, played a leading role during this period. He advocated architectural composition in his plans and utilized the form of the landscape to give character to the towns, often by introducing axial effects. As the winner of many town-planning competitions, and through his numerous consultant jobs in the 1920s, and 1930s, he left his mark both on his home town of Trondheim and on several other towns (Tromsø, Narvik, Svolvær, Hamar, Hønefoss etc.).

Oslo (the old name, Oslo, was restored in 1925) and its suburbs continued to grow in the new century. The total population of the municipalities of Oslo, Aker and Baerum rose from 265,000 in 1900 to 370,000 in 1930. The open type of development led to a great increase in land utilization for urban growth. In 1929 Harald Hals, chief planner of Oslo, presented an important new master plan proposal for the capital. It appeared in the form of a book, *From Christiania to Greater Oslo* (Hals, 1929), amply illustrated with maps and drawings. By Norwegian standards this was an exceptional work. For the first time a comprehensive town-planning scheme was published in this way; moreover it was supported by historical elucidation, topographical and climatic descriptions, demographic studies and studies of social and economic development, of transportation and traffic conditions, etc. In this book, Hals also presented contemporary town-planning ideas: Ebenezer Howard's garden cities, German star-shaped town patterns and Le Corbusier's high-rise city of 1922 (Paris). He also referred to British, American and Swedish examples of regional planning in metropolitan areas. Hals does not mention Patrick Geddes by name, yet his work shows clearly the influence of the ideas and methods of this planning pioneer.

As a result of the book an inter-municipal planning committee was appointed, which presented the first regional plan proposal for the Oslo area in 1934. Although this plan never acquired any legal basis, it had considerable impact on the subsequent development of Oslo – particularly on the organization of the transport system, including the suburban railroads.

Around 1930 a big clearance and redevelopment process had begun in central Oslo, in connection with the erection of the new city hall in Piperviken. Most of the plan was realized before the war. After 1950 the neighbouring district of Vestre Vika was totally redeveloped (see figures 4.13 and 4.27).

The international crisis at the beginning of the 1930s meant, in Norway as elsewhere, that the production of houses nearly ceased. The crisis aggravated the economic and social problems of the country, and made for a radicalization of political development. The Labour Party, which came into power in 1935, stepped up national and municipal engagement in housing policy. Following a Swedish model, co-operative housing production was organized in Oslo in 1929 (OBOS, Oslo Bolig og Sparelag). The first housing projects launched by the co-operative organization were clearly stamped by the new functionalistic principles. This new trend in architecture and planning had been introduced effectively into the Nordic countries by the famous Stockholm exhibition in 1930. The changes, both social and architectural, took place over a comparatively short period, although not without intense debate. An interesting element here was a new socialistic periodical, *Plan*, edited by a group of young radical architects. They attacked both professional and political attitudes, which stood in the way of a new scientific approach. They advocated the use of functional analysis, sober objectivity and social responsibility. All 'geometrical romanticism' was rejected. The periodical ceased in 1936. By this time an obvious change of attitudes in housing and planning had occurred, with clear parallels in contemporary developments in the other Nordic countries.

The traditional closed block structure in the densely built-up areas was strongly condemned. Instead lamella housing was launched. The principle was that blocks of flats should be orientated north-south in parallel rows, in order to obtain the best possible sun and light conditions. Broad openings between the blocks of flats should be reserved for recreational purposes, and provided with trees and playgrounds. As a rule the blocks rose to three or four storeys, but were sometimes considerably higher. Certain concessions were made to meet the growing problem of traffic. Thus, for the first time, the segregation of the main traffic arteries was proposed.

During this last decade before the war only a few projects were carried out in accordance with the new planning principles, and then mainly in the three biggest cities – Oslo, Bergen and Trondheim. Within this short period, however, a stream of new proposals and vigorous ideas were brought forward, many of them in connection with town planning competitions (Vestre Vika, Oslo and the Blindern division of Oslo University), or as idealistic and theoretical projects presented in papers and periodicals. An extreme but in many ways typical project from this period was a slum clearance and redevelopment scheme in 1936 for the old working-class district of Grünerløkka in Oslo (figure 4.19). This proposal was fortunately never realized. Today we may wonder at its author's consistent pursuit of a single planning principle. Also conspicuous is the professional self-confidence which expected to be able to carry out a clearance and rebuilding process on this scale (20,000 inhabitants) at one stroke.

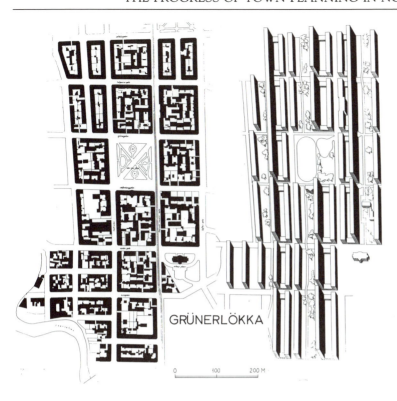

GRÜNERLÖKKA

0   100   200 M

Figure 4.19. Grünerløkka, Oslo. To the left: redrawn map from 1935, showing the densely built-up tenement blocks from 1860–85. To the right: redrawn plan proposal from 1936 for a total redevelopment. The plan was never carried out.

1940–1965: Reconstruction and New Challenges

The German assault on Norway in the spring of 1940 resulted in severe war damage. Central parts of the towns of Molde, Kristiansund, Steinkjer, Namsos, Bodø and Narvik, plus fifteen other smaller but important places (Voss, Åndalsnes, Elverum etc.) were destroyed by explosives and incendiary bombs. In June 1940 a special planning office at the state level was established to prepare new town plans for the reconstruction of these places. This new office, Brente Steders Regulering (BSR), was headed by Sverre Pedersen. The work was pushed ahead, partly under pressure from the German authorities who also demanded to be consulted and wanted to give their advice.

No general survey or comprehensive analysis was made nor any special forecast of future needs and functions. The primary task was to produce layout plans for the town centres, and

to prepare for speedy reconstruction. The new plans for the destroyed towns were not unaffected by the new ideas on urban planning. Nevertheless, in the main they were given a somewhat 'neo-classical' character. The street patterns were generally orthogonal, often as a continuation of the old streets from the nineteenth century. These would then be widened and straightened according to the new plans. Some of the more important streets were given a particularly grand design: broad, tree-lined and furnished with some interesting focus such as a new church, a town hall, a fire station, etc, or an effort was made to enhance existing landmarks and views, for instance of distant mountains. There was rarely any differentiation of traffic.

Centrally located new housing blocks were arranged in straight and often monotonous rows of uniform height, seldom more than three storeys. Symmetrical effects were often proposed, even in residential districts. In the layout

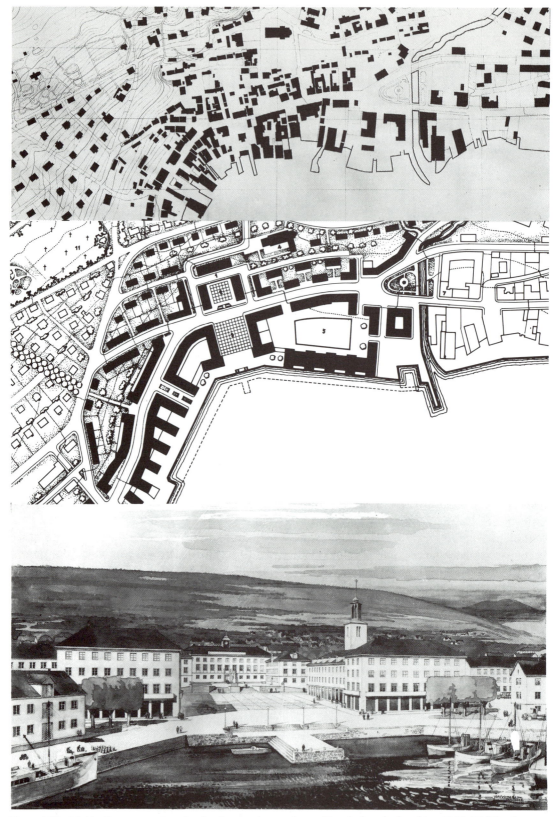

Figure 4.20. Molde. Reconstruction plan for the war-damaged area. Top: before the bombing 1940. Middle: the new town plan by BSR 1942. Bottom: perspective drawing of the main square as proposed, by Jacob Hanssen, 1942.

of the squares, and where streets were widened, a symmetrical approach to the location and dimensioning of buildings was frequently adopted. In many cases long unbroken street façades were designed by well-known and specially commissioned architects. These designs were to serve as a guide for the local building boards in deciding such details as the height and form of cornices, the pitch of roofs and various common architectural details. In spite of a certain uniformity in most of the plans, the towns nevertheless retained their own individual character, first and foremost thanks to differences in terrain and the surrounding landscape.

The plans for the relatively level town centres of Bodø and Namsos turned out to be rather schematic and ordinary. More successful were the plans for the centres of Molde and Kristiansund on the west coast (figures 4.20 and 4.21).

After the war many of the BSR town plans were the subject of a good deal of criticism from architects and planners, although not always deservedly. A few interesting proposals for more vivid and subtle architectural solutions in some of the town centres were put forward, but

they did not lead to any fundamental changes in the war-time plans. Too many decisions had been taken during the war years, so that few local situations could now be altered. Nonetheless, over the next few years many details in the plans, and numerous single buildings in the centres, assumed rather a different architectural shape than the one originally intended.

In the last stages of the war the Germans applied a scorched-earth policy in the northermost region of Norway. Nearly all buildings, quays, bridges, roads, etc. in the county of Finnmark and the northern part of the county of Troms were blown up, burned, or otherwise destroyed by the Germans as they withdrew from the northern front in Finland during the winter of 1944. The major part of the population of Finnmark was forceably evacuated to other parts of Norway. When peace had been restored in June 1945, the BSR was reorganized and charged with the task of preparing new town plans for these regions too.

This time, collaboration with the local population was happier, and plans could be based more on their expressed needs and wishes. The task was urgent, however, and had

Figure 4.21. Kristiansund. Perspective drawing by Jacob Hanssen of the Kaibakken axis towards the harbour, as proposed in the BSR reconstruction plan, 1941.

to proceed under rather difficult conditions and without adequate maps, etc. The winter in these remote parts of Norway is severe. The natural resources are meagre and the basis of subsistence is vulnerable and one-sided: fishing, fish processing, mining and cattle breeding. The proposed town plan for Hammerfest, the northernmost town in Europe, is shown in figure 4.22. The plan was produced by Bjarne Lous Mohr, architect and later professor of planning.

Many of the young architects working in the war-damaged districts were acquainted with Lewis Mumford's important book, *The Culture of Cities* (1938). They now demanded a broader and more reliable basis for a comprehensive and

long-range planning policy in both urban and rural Norway, with regional analyses and the integration of physical, social and economic planning. In the summer of 1948, and in enthusiastic mood, a one-week planning conference was held in Alta, Finnmark. The main topics discussed were regional planning and the participation of the people. Experiences from the Tennessee Valley (TVA) project in the United States were presented and debated in connection with the current reconstruction task in Finnmark. In the BSR a special division was organized to study and develop theories and methods, to advance modern regional planning in Norway. To the great disappointment of many, this urgent and long-range undertaking,

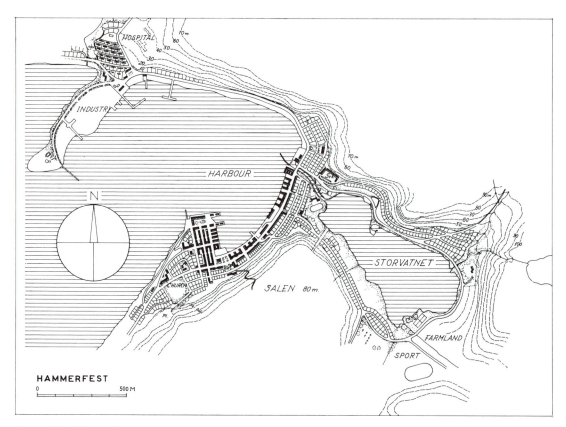

Figure 4.22. Hammerfest.
Redrawing of the new town plan proposal by Bjarne Lous Mohr, 1946. This fishing town of 7,000 inhabitants is situated at nearly 71° north.

together with the other activities of the BSR, was wound up by the government in 1952.

The city of Bergen had also suffered substantial war damage. Nordnes, an old residential district in the city centre, with its picturesque and tightly packed wooden houses covering the southern shore slope of historic Vågen, had been severely hit. In the reconstruction plans an exceptionally high plot ratio was adopted. This, together with changes in the original land use, meant that the south-western part of the Vågen landscape lost most of its earlier character and charm and became a rather dense and monotonous section of the city centre.

After winding up the BSR the government launched a new type of county 'planning' or area analysis (*områdeplanlegging*), which was directed by economists without the cooperation of any physical planners. They made studies of economic life and conditions in every county and discussed the possibilities of providing new jobs in case of unemployment. Because of this one-sided approach, their work did little for the development of a genuinely comprehensive regional planning system. Earlier attempts to achieve a combined physical, economic and social approach to planning at the regional level were abandoned, not to be resumed until 1965 when the new Building Act at last established integrated planning along these lines.

In the meantime the continuing expansion of the major Norwegian cities called increasingly for an intermunicipal and interdisciplinary type of planning. In the 1950s this obvious need led to the formation of *voluntary* regional planning bodies in the urban regions of Oslo, Bergen, Trondheim and Kristiansand, and later in a few other towns as well.

During the war years Norwegian planners had been cut off from normal professional contacts and the inspiration of colleagues in other countries. Their receptivity was therefore at a maximum when all this again became possible. Planners went on study tours and attended international planning conferences, especially those organized by the International Federation for Housing and Planning. As already mentioned, Lewis Mumford's *The Culture of Cities* also inspired Norwegian architects and planners. Patrick Geddes' planning philosophy and analysis methods seemed to be particularly relevant to the Norwegian regions.

The epoch-making Greater London Plan, with its green belt and new towns, was studied with the greatest enthusiasm. The ideas of decentralized development patterns in the great urban regions met with a very sympathetic response in Scandinavia. The new growth pattern of Greater Stockholm, with suburban satellite towns bound together by a comprehensive and rapid mass-transport system, was also regarded as the right fundamental solution for Greater Oslo.

Inspiration also came from British and Dutch reconstruction plans for war-damaged cities. Examples were the plans for central parts of Coventry, London and Rotterdam among others, and the plans for the second generation of new towns in Britain: Harlow, Stevenage, Crawley, etc. The new ideas for organizing separate pedestrian malls and precincts as links in the new traffic plans for large and medium-sized cities were also fascinating. The Lijnbaan in Rotterdam and the new pedestrian precincts of Coventry were of particular interest.

During the war practically all house construction had come to a standstill. Afterwards a great accumulated demand for new homes had to be satisfied as soon as possible. Both private and co-operative house construction had to be encouraged. The financing possibilities were greatly improved at a stroke, when the Norwegian State's Housing Bank was founded in 1946. In the same year a State Directorate for Housing came into operation under the efficient leadership of the architect, Jacob Christie Kielland. Apart from reconstruction work, priority was now given to the task of erecting houses in the major cities.

In 1948 Oslo was merged with the neighbouring municipality of Aker, and the population of the capital rose to 425,000. In 1950 the City Planning Office, under its new leader, the architect Erik Rolfsen, produced a master plan proposal, intended to provide guidelines for the further expected growth of Oslo. This plan was based on a decentralized model, with new residential areas connected to a number of local centres around the old city. Rapid rail transport, radial main arteries and ring roads with bus and tram services were to connect the new urban districts with the old ones. The new 'suburban towns' were to differ in size from 5,000 to 20,000 inhabitants. Besides the necessary social and commercial amenities, the new local centres should also contain industrial working places. Nonetheless most people in the new residential units were expected to have their workplaces in the old commercial centre of Oslo and in old or new planned industrial areas – the

new ones mostly in the Grorud Valley to the east. The master plan, revised and added to in the plan of 1960, became the guiding instrument for the expansion of Oslo in the following decades.

Important elements in the master plan were: an overall park system for the total urban area, and a definition of the extent of the Oslo-marka, the forested and mountainous tract of land to the north and east and south-east of the city. The park system, including all types of recreational areas and forming continuous green paths for walking and skiing was to connect all urban districts and to provide free access to the natural and protected areas in the city surroundings. In all, these green spaces covered some 300 km^2 of the capital's total 450 km^2. The principles of this 1950 plan are shown in figure 4.23. Indirectly the plan also suggests the pattern of planned urban development for a

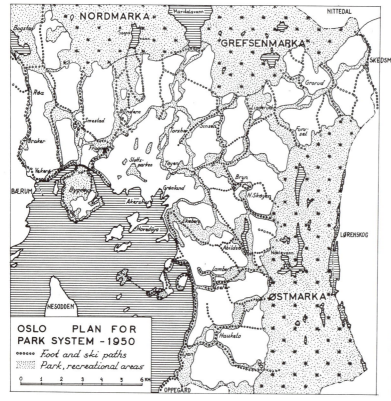

Figure 4.23. Oslo. Proposed plan for a new park system, as part of the master plan from 1950. Redrawn from a municipal publication, 1950.

period of thirty to forty years. The associated communication network is not indicated.

The preparations to start building the first 'suburban towns' began immediately. Lambertseter, to the south-east, originally planned for a population of 10,000, became a pioneer project. This forested, hilly area (ca. 160 m above sea level) was planned by a group of young architects under Frode Rinnan. The proposed plan, shown in figure 4.24, shows the main principles that guided many of the new satellite towns on the outskirts of Oslo between 1950 and 1970. Lambertseter became a semi-self-contained urban unit for 13,000 people, with its own multi-purpose local centre and with residential areas organized in individually designed neighbourhood units, separated by large areas for recreation. Most dwellings were in three- or four-storey blocks of flats. There were also a number of high-rise blocks and some areas of terraced housing.

The planning and building of further 'suburban towns' continued: in the south-east, Bøler-Bogerud for about 13,000 people. Manglerud for 20,000; and Skøyen-Oppsal for 17,000. East of the city, in the Grorud valley, new urban units for a total population of some 50,000 were realized before 1970, mostly on undulating and sloping farm land (Veitvedt, Rødtvedt, Ammerud, Kalbakken, Tveita).

In the valley bottom, large flat areas were marked off for industrial development, with easy rail and road connections. In accordance with the master plans of 1950 and 1960, a new suburban railroad system, branching off in four directions to the east and south, was constructed to connect the central underground system in Oslo East with the new urban districts. The bulk of the new development occurred on old cultivated land, acquired by the municipality and leased to the cooperative building society of OBOS. During this period of rapid development hardly anybody worried about the large amount of rich agricultural land that was being lost to the process of urban

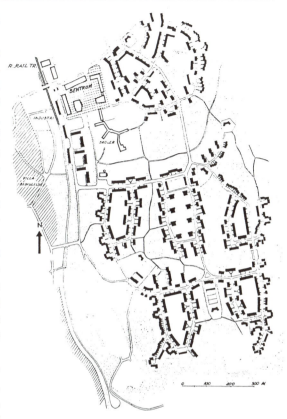

Figure 4.24. Lambertseter, the first 'suburban town' of Oslo. Simplified drawing of the originally proposed plan, 1950. Architects: Rinnan, Tveten and Colbiørnsen. The plan is based upon neighbourhood units separated by recreational areas.

expansion. In a country in which arable land accounts for only 4 per cent of the total area, this attitude rather naturally changed radically in the period that followed.

In the Bergen region an intermunicipal plan for the city and six neighbouring municipalities was put forward in 1957. High mountains, steep terrain and old intricate borders between the municipalities were obstructing a 'natural' urban growth. And yet many examples of residential areas well-adjusted to the rugged and difficult mountainous terrain can be found in and around Bergen. Hardly any arable land was used for this development. In the regional plan a large area known as Fyllingsdalen, south-west of the city, was launched as a major contribution to the urban development of the area. This rather rugged valley region was incorporated into the city in 1955 and has since become a satellite town for some 25,000 people. A long road tunnel completed in 1968 and a large bridge over the Puddefjord now connect the valley to the city. The planning principles for Fyllingsdalen were those that had been widely adopted during the 1960s: neighbourhood units separated by open (forested) land and sur-

rounding the common local centre; here social, cultural and commercial services were provided. The new urban districts of Bergen are favoured by a magnificent natural setting, between high mountains and fjords.

In the Kristiansand region, too, the master plan kept to a decentralized pattern (figure 4.25). The new urban districts were equipped with local centres and new industrial areas nearby. Kristiansand underwent exeptionally rapid expansion after the war. The population (now 62,000) doubled over a period of twenty-five

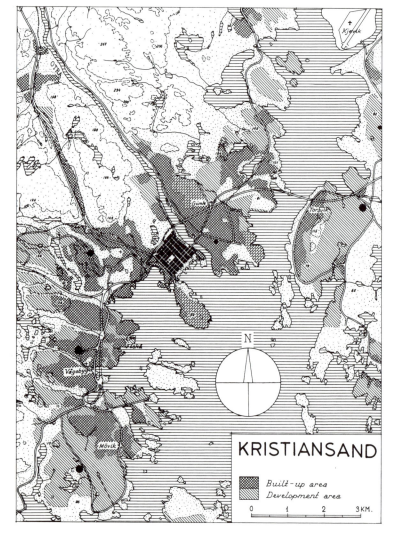

Figure 4.25. Kristiansand (with Christian IV's town in the centre).

Redrawing of the regional plan of 1974. Black circles indicate local centres. In the post-war period this region had the highest increase in population of all urban regions in Norway.

years. The new urban units were built on low but rather rugged mountainous terrain, occupying hardly any cultivated land at all. In the old centre the regular street pattern of the original 1641 town plan was maintained. But numerous old wooden houses were torn down and replaced by new offices and commercial and residential buildings in concrete. Later, however, a change in attitude and amendments to the local by-laws made it possible to save blocks of houses with their characteristic wooden buildings from destruction. Apart from their rare architectural charm, these houses are also of a high residential quality, when in good repair.

The national policy of economic structural rationalization developed during the 1950s and 1960s. In all expanding towns of any size, the central areas were subjected to great changes. The reasons were familiar: central service functions were multiplying, particularly in commerce, banking, insurance and administration, and in both the private and public sectors. Old central residential districts tended to deteriorate as houses disappeared, land use changed, and new activities took over. Often several small neighbouring properties would be joined together, cleared, and redeveloped as multi-storey concrete buildings. Owing to the intensified plot ratios and the unceasing rise in the number of cars, the centres of even medium-sized towns were gradually becoming overloaded with traffic and parking problems. In the 1950s and 1960s, however, the attention of the authorities was mainly focused on the job of providing enough housing, most of it on the outskirts of the towns. The problems of the urban centres were either postponed or tackled piecemeal. Nonetheless, just after the war a few redevelopment plans for city centres were proposed. In 1946 in Stavanger, for instance, the city council approved a new plan for the rebuilding of the old centre, which still bore evidence of its medieval origins (see figure 4.26(a)). The plan presupposed that the narrow and tortuous street pattern north of the twelfth-century

cathedral (Domkirken), must yield to 'more spacious and grandiose planning principles'. The street pattern was to be simplified, opened up and straightened. The central area was to be adapted to a fashionable type of commercial development in four or five storeys. Fortunately only minor parts of the plan were ever carried out. A growing understanding of the particular qualities of this old wooden urban environment gradually took a hand in its fate. Two successive chief planners and architects, Olav Nesse (later chief planner of Bergen) and Per Andersson (later professor at Nordplan, Stockholm) contributed to the preservation of the most valuable parts of the old urban fabric. They also directed a fairly well-balanced redevelopment process in the area to the west and east of the market-place (Torget). Thanks to a number of architectural competitions, these new areas achieved a certain architectural unity, which serves to emphasize the pleasant urban spaces around Vågen and Bredevannet. By saving the northern core from all through traffic, it became possible to retain most of the charm of its narrow winding streets and to reserve them for pedestrians (figure 4.26(b)).

A remarkable achievement worth mentioning is the conservation and rehabilitation over a period of twenty years of 150 old wooden houses in a unique residential district, Stranden, on the west side of the harbour in Stavanger. Einar Hedén is the architect who has been the driving-force behind this project.

In Oslo an important city-planning competition was held in 1947. It concerned Vestre Vika, a central area to the west of the new City Hall. Complete clearance of the old blocks and a comprehensive redevelopment was projected, and this was also the outcome (see figure 4.27). The layout plan finally adopted was based on a rather high plot ratio, in order to facilitate the financing. However, the plan met with considerable opposition: the land use, the traffic solutions, the formal layout and the height of the buildings were all questioned. In a period

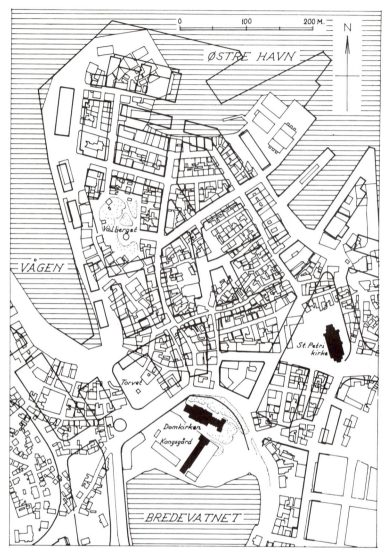

Figure 4.26(a) Stavanger.
The old urban structure of the city with the new town plan of 1946 superimposed. The plan was not carried out. Redrawing of the official plan.

when future traffic problems could not possibly be fully foreseen, no allowance was made for pedestrian malls, for peaceful squares, or for outdoor leisure activities, and very little for any green spaces at all. Alternative proposals were suggested by some architects, but no real changes were made. The financial side of the project had become a dominating factor. Luckily, the plans for Oslo's new concert hall were realized within this area in 1977, but on a site wedged in between office blocks.

In Bergen another planning competition (1955) was held for the central area east of Vågen and north of L. Lungegårdsvann (see figure 4.15 and 4.16). Here the street pattern was of mediaeval origin, and the wooden houses among the oldest in Bergen; two old stone churches were also situated in the area (Domkirken (D) and Korskirken (K)). The prize-winning projects all aimed at virtually total clearance and redevelopment, which was regarded as unavoidable if the main object was to

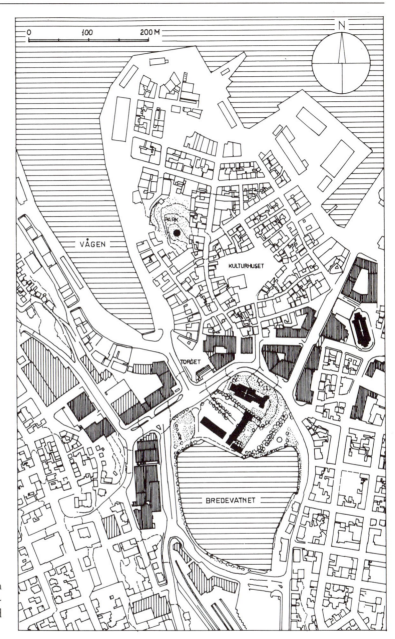

Figure 4.26(b) Stavanger.
Map showing the central area in
1984. Important post-war buildings are hatched. Map composed
by the author.

be achieved: the establishment of much-needed
new traffic arteries.

The proposals were never carried out. The
cost was too high and the whole idea soon
became rather unpopular. Today there is an
active effort to rehabilitate the old buildings in
the area, as well as for other environmental
improvements. The traffic problems, however,
remained unsolved. Hardly any other
Norwegian city centre was encumbered with
such overwhelming traffic difficulties as Bergen,
due to the specific terrain, topography and old

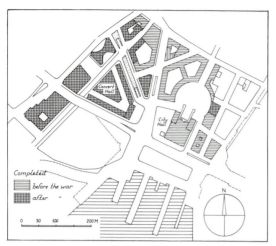

Figure 4.27. Map showing the present state of the Piperviken area in Oslo, with the City Hall, completed 1950, in the central axis. The district was redeveloped 1930–70.

urban structure. They seemed to mock all attempts at reorganizing the central traffic circulation. Only recently has a marked improvement occurred, after the opening of a large-scale bypass road-tunnel, through the mountain north of the centre.

With a view to finding a definitive solution to all Oslo's central transport and traffic problems, a comprehensive transport analysis was carried out in 1963–64, resulting in a vast project for a new urban motor ringroad round the inner city. The plan was typical of the new enthusiastic approach to traffic problems, which had adopted the latest American EDP methods for transport planning. The project was received with the greatest respect – for a while. Gradually, however, this gave way to scepticism and dislike, due mainly to the devastating environmental consequences but also to the astronomical expense. No realistic alternative plans were advanced, which could serve to solve the central traffic problems of the capital effectively. The city authorities for the time being, preferred a more pragmatic approach, first by utilizing the existing street system in a more flexible and efficient way.

A report on Norwegian planning from this period should not omit some mention of the great national effort to exploit the natural resources of the country, while also planning for the development of the weak and remote regions of northern and western Norway. A vital element in this context was the large-scale development of hydroelectric resources. Several new, single-industry communities were built on a basis of this kind of investment, most of them near the coast for the easy sea transport of their raw materials and the electrochemical products. The pre-eminent example was the iron town Mo i Rana. From a small coastal village there grew a modern town of 22,000 inhabitants, according to a town plan produced by the architect Preben Krag. Other new towns or smaller places of this type were Sunndalsøra, Årdal, Husnes and Karmøy in the west, and Mosjøen and Glomfjord in the north. All were developed on the basis of new town plans, generally inspired by garden city ideas and favouring one-family houses.

1965–1989: New Suburbs and Urban Renewal

The economic growth and increasing affluence of these post-war decades was linked to a continual urbanization process. This meant that there was a great need for qualified planners, for more suitable planning tools, and for an updating of the planning legislation. A new Building Act eventually came into force in 1965. It contained ambitious goals. All urban and rural municipalities now became subject to the Act. Of particular importance were the new provisions for regional and master planning. Regional plans were to be prepared for all – two or more – neighbouring municipalities, and a master plan for every municipality. The former type of plan was not obligatory, but in practice most regions embarked on one.

The county commissioner (*fylkesmann*) was made responsible for initiating and controlling these new planning activities. To this end all counties were provided with an administration staff for planning and economic development. In the first ten years the leading actors – economists, architect-planners and civic engineers – were paid by the government. The idea was to try, with the help of the new legislation, to coordinate the physical, economic and social planning process at the regional as well as the local level. At first a great wave of enthusiasm supported these new planning efforts. In the Ministry architect-planner Yngvar Johnsen came to play a leading part in this period.

To relieve the shortage of competent planners, various educational courses were started by, among others, the Ministry of Local Government (now the Ministry of the Environment). An important role was also played by the Nordic Postgraduate Planning Institute, Nordplan, established in 1968 on a mutual Nordic basis. Located in Stockholm, this educational institute admits fifty Nordic planners each year to its interdisciplinary courses. About twelve participants come from Norway.

From 1965 to 1975 regional planning in Norway tended to develop in two different directions. The first was obviously relevant to the physical development of the major urban regions, and to other types of expanding districts. The second applied to regions in the rest of the country, where the characteristic features are large territories with a scattered population, often in decline. Their problems were mainly of an economic and social nature. Both categories were in need of explicit political guidelines at the national level. But the government was unwilling to embark on a major national planning process, as many planners had wished.

Instead *ad hoc* committees were appointed to prepare survey plans for each of the six main parts of the country (*landsdelsplaner*). The committees were made up of politicians and top administrators, whose work required planning expertise of various kinds. These *landsdelsplaner* were prepared between 1965 and 1973. The *Østlandsplan* (for the populous eastern part

of south Norway) was presented first. It included ideas for checking the rapid growth in the central Oslo region, with its ca. 1 million people, by stimulating the development of other regions surrounding the Oslo region, some 75–150 km away.

These ideas met with severe criticism from the rest of the country, and from numerous politicians. They anyway disliked the persistent immigration into the urban centres of this part of the country, which they claimed occurred at the cost of all the other regions, particularly those in western and northern Norway. They demanded a regional policy for the whole country, which would maintain investment and population stability in *all* regions. The plans that later appeared for the other parts of the country more or less confirmed these wishes. The total impression from this comprehensive planning activity thus tended to be rather confusing. It also turned out to be of little consequence.

More important were the 1973 amendments to the Building Act, whereby county planning became obligatory for all nineteen counties. This again proved to weaken the previous regional planning work, by transferring overall planning responsibility to much larger and more complex geographical units. Many of the regional plans in urbanized areas were said to be unnecessary, after a nationwide merging of numerous municipal units. In practice, increasing emphasis was placed on the master planning of the individual municipalities, while important co-operative efforts between neighbouring municipalities often seemed to lag behind.

Intermunicipal planning in the Greater Oslo region had never found a really satisfactory form, although a number of initiatives had been taken over the years, and a great deal of work had been put into it. The dominating role of the city, compared with the other much smaller administrative units, seemed to be one reason for this. In 1970, after six years' work, a liaison committee for the city of Oslo and the county of

Akershus presented a report and a proposal for a comprehensive development plan for the whole region. The professional part of the work had been carried out by the distinguished planning consultants Andersson & Skjånes in Oslo. A major problem discussed in the report concerned the dominating role of the city as the place of work for the bulk of the people in the Greater Oslo region. Commuting had become a serious problem. A dispersion of the workplaces was strongly advised, along with the further spread of the residential areas. Also, the accelerated renewal of the older residential districts in Oslo was recommended, both in order to improve housing standards and to increase the population of the inner city. The proposals were based on the assumption of continuing rapid population growth in the region as a whole. According to a forecast at the time, the population of the 'central region' would have reached 955,000 by 1990, compared to 670,000 in 1965.

A joint council for regional planning in Oslo and Akershus was appointed in 1968; in 1970 it was provided with a planning staff, under the architect–planner Øystein Bergersen. The earlier plan proposals were discussed and adjusted; new conclusions were drawn from changes then in progress, and various new alternative goals for a future regional situation were analysed. The work concluded with a proposal for a new regional framework for the period 1974–1985. In the mid-1970s, some stagnation in population growth was clearly discernible, not only on a national scale, but in the Oslo region as well. Shortly afterwards both the regional planning council and its office were wound up for reasons that are difficult to ascertain. The intermunicipal planning activities were not resumed until a few years ago, after pressure from the government. As we shall see later in this chapter, common infrastructural questions have now become the focus of attention at the regional level.

In the meantime the local authorities in the region have intensified their work on the municipal development plans. Most of the suburban communities around Oslo have sought to keep down population growth and the rate of development, in order to consolidate their economy and their social standard.

As mentioned earlier, the regional and master planning efforts on a nationwide basis had started enthusiastically. But the work dragged on. It seemed as though local politicians did not want to be tied down by obligatory physical and economic long-term plans. They preferred flexible plans, adaptable to changing conditions. It turned out that only the larger urban and rural municipalities managed to complete their master plans within a reasonable time. The others lagged behind. With the years, however, the Ministry let up on its original requirements regarding the content of these plans.

In 1964 Trondheim was merged with its neighbouring municipalities. The enlarged city, whose population was now growing fast, decided to push on the preparation of its master plan. As early as 1967 the new plan was adopted by the city council. (Its authors had been the consultant firm Andersson & Skjånes, ASPLAN.) One of the main proposals in the plan was to establish a new 'grand centre' 10 km south of the city, at Heimdal. It was estimated that the old city centre of Trondheim, the *Midtbyen* laid out by Cicignon in 1681, had insufficient capacity for the expected urban expansion, and must therefore be relieved of the burden. The new Heimdal centre was to serve a surrounding population of about 50,000, or one-third of Trondheim's inhabitants as forecast for 1980. Around the new centre, houses for about 20,000 people were also to be built.

In 1968 Trondheim invited Nordic architects to compete for the town plan of this new town. No first prize was awarded, but two competitors received second prizes: the Danish architectural firm Skaarup & Jespersen in co-operation with the civil engineering firm of Anders Nyvig, and a young Norwegian architect, Sigmund Asmer-vik. These winners were asked to try to co-ordinate their proposals into a single project. This was done, and the combined result was presented in 1971 (figure 4.28).

The area comprised a fairly level plateau of some 5 km², surrounded by forest-covered hills and mountains. In the middle is a marshy hol-low, very difficult to build on. Here a great square landscaped park was envisaged, sur-rounded on its four sides by schools and other social and cultural institutions. The area touches on the motorway from Trondheim on the west side, and further west also on the railway. The new regional centre, with office and commercial functions, was located like a broad ribbon parallel to and east of the motor-way, which was to be built here in a sunken course. Near to these central parts three residential areas were laid out, like a clover leaf.

The development of the Heimdal centre has been much slower than anticipated. Population growth in Trondheim has slackened off, as it has throughout Norway, and the economy of the city has gradually become more strained over the last ten to fifteen years. To some extent

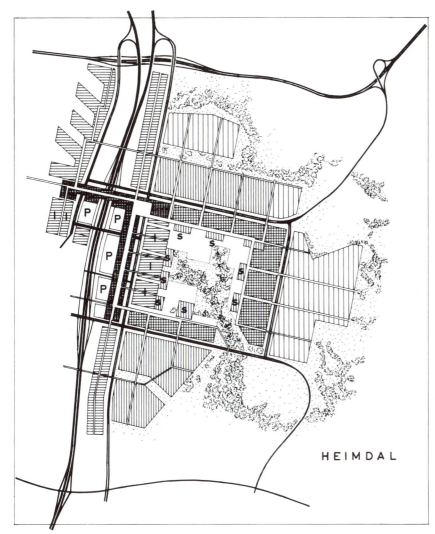

HEIMDAL

Figure 4.28. A sche-matic redrawing of the plan from 1971 for the new Heimdal centre, 10 km south of Trond-heim.
The plan was the result of a Nordic competi-tion. S = schools; I = institutions; P = car parking; dense hatch-ing = commercial areas. (Scale ca. 1:22000)

commercial considerations and profitability seem to have superseded the original strong social and architectural purposes. It remains to be seen what urban qualities will result.

The physical expansion of most of the bigger towns had taken place at the cost of valuable agricultural areas. This was particularly the case in Oslo, Trondheim and Stavanger, situated as they were in the middle of very fertile regions. This unrestricted consumption of agricultural land gradually became the target of criticism. By the end of the 1960s the objections had become so intense that a change in attitude occurred. The idea of taking better care of non-renewable resources, of protecting natural environments and securing the cultural heritage everywhere, now began to receive due recognition even in politics. A Ministry of the Environment was established in 1972, as in most other Western countries. From now on it became an express objective in all land-use planning, to prevent cultivated areas from being used for other purposes.

In 1971, in the Stavanger-Jæren region (with a population of 130,000), the regional planners headed by Unnleiv Bergsgard launched a plan to transfer the expected urban expansion from the cultivated plains around Stavanger and Sandnes to the rugged hills and valleys to the south-east. Similar directives had also been launched in the regional plan for Vestfold county, in order to prevent the expanding coastal towns of Horten, Tønsberg, Sandefjord and Larvik from consuming further agricultural land. A plan was adopted in 1970 for developing a system of 'cluster towns' in the hilly hinterland of the county, but it has not proved to be of lasting interest, since over the last ten to fifteen years the urban population of the county has stopped growing. In the Stavanger region, on the other hand, oil production activities in the North Sea have led to a continual population increase and to an intensification of the urban development problems.

The Building Act of 1965 did not introduce any fundamental changes in the contents or procedure of the *detailed planning*. Regulations for layout plans and building controls were updated, extended and made more flexible. On one point a definite change occurred. The municipal Building and Planning Boards are now to be made up exclusively of politically elected members, rather than as before of officials and elected members equally. The relevant officials are to attend meetings, but without the right to vote.

In order to ease tendencies towards red tape, some modest delegation of decision powers from the state level to the county and sometimes even to the local level was inaugurated during the 1970s. The Planning and Building Act of June 1985 goes further in this direction. This new Act aims at a simplification and coordination of the total planning process, together with an increased emphasis on public information.

Over the last fifteen years or so simplified two-dimensional layout plans (with accompanying regulations) have come to be increasingly used. This type of plan, supposed to be more suitable and flexible if conditions change, certainly has some practical advantages, but it also has obvious drawbacks. Such plans often tend to stress the economic and functional utilization of the areas, while the consideration of three-dimensional landscape and architectural values may well be neglected. This brings us to the new signals in Norwegian town planning, that are clearly related to corresponding tendencies in other countries.

Since the end of the 1960s objections to the monotony, the standardization and the environmental poverty of many new residential areas have been gaining momentum. The dissatisfaction was particularly strong when it came to the *size* of many constructions: high-rise flats, great collections of uniform apartment blocks, parking deserts, supermarkets, etc. Also, many urban redevelopments were criticized for their lack of environmental quality. Social-science researchers had – unexpectedly – revealed many negative sides to life and the environment in some of the larger dormitory towns. At times architects claimed that architectural qualities suffered from the pressure of economic interests. The arguments are well known from the architectural and planning debate in most Western countries over the last ten or more years. Further, many aspects of functionalism that had been dominating since the 1930s began to be called in question. New ideas and new attitudes appeared under different guises during the 1970s. We shall be looking at the practical outcome of these new views below.

In Norway organized town-planning research has been taking place since 1964, when the Norwegian Institute for Urban and Regional Research (NIBR) was founded. Over the years the Institute has been an important factor in the development of the profession, among other things by continually analysing all forms of public planning and their consequences. New approaches to practical planning were also carried out by the Institute, including a new master plan for Tromsø in northern Norway, where the establishment of a new university led to increased urban growth.

Two different tendencies have been noticeable in recent housing and town planning in Norway. One tries to develop the technological and economic possibilities of rationalization, while at the same time retaining the social standard. This trend is represented, among others, by a prominent firm of contractors, Selvaagbygg A/S, which has left its mark on much of the residential building in the Oslo region since the war. In recent years this firm has specialized in building dense groups of blocks in terraces up steep slopes. The blocks are fairly broad with flats of varying size, spacious balconies, and car parks at basement level. Many of these housing estates have become popular, due to a happy combination of high standards and reasonable prices. But they have also been much criticized for their uniformity and harsh domination of the landscape.

The other trend, dominated by architects, is seeking for greater architectural variation, a more human scale of building, better adaptation to the terrain, and – above all – richer urban environmental quality. Some examples are shown here.

Romsås is one of these residential suburbs in the eastern part of Oslo. The site, in places very steep and difficult to develop, called for a costly infrastructure. The realized project, shown in figure 4.29, was completed in 1974 after years of planning and redrafting by the 'Romsås team' (Alex Christiansen and colleagues). The plan is based on an external ringroad system, giving access to separate clusters of apartment blocks, three to eight storeys high. Each cluster or neighbourhood unit has a covered car park, a local shop, a kindergarten and playgrounds. In the inner part of the area, the natural hilly woodland has been marked off for recreation with small hills for ski-jumping and a small lake for bathing. A commercial, cultural and social centre for the 7,500 inhabitants has been skilfully and quite picturesquely adapted to the steep hillside. The centre has a vertical lift connection to the suburban train station, located in a rock tunnel underneath.

In order to recall the fact that most Norwegian housing is still in the form of small wooden houses, detached or terraced, it is worth mentioning the experimental housing area of Selegrend in Bergen, built 1974–76 (see figure 4.30). The architectural firm responsible is Cubus A/S. The housing units are linked together in numerous variations, depending on the terrain conditions, the spatial effects and the wishes and needs of the inhabitants. The participation of the families who were to live in the area was obtained at all phases of planning and implementation, as well as in organizing all the social arrangements. To some extent the plan of Selegrend, on its rugged site recalls some of the old fishing villages on the coast, with their 'organic' town plans.

As an example of a well-adapted and

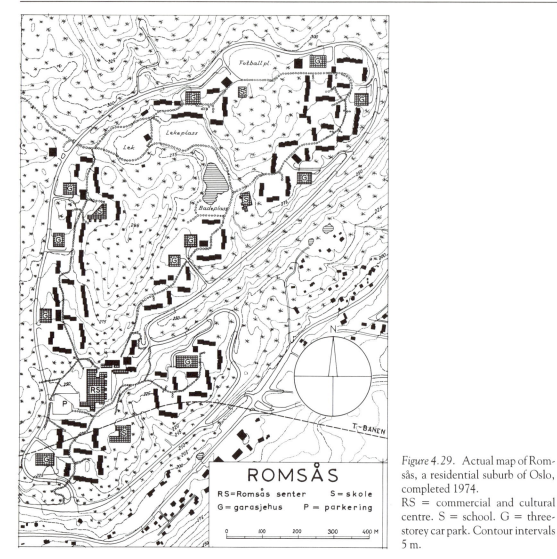

Figure 4.29. Actual map of Romsås, a residential suburb of Oslo, completed 1974.
RS = commercial and cultural centre. S = school. G = three-storey car park. Contour intervals 5 m.

architecturally well-prepared plan in difficult terrain, we can perhaps look at the Hallagerbakken housing estate (completed 1982) in the new 'suburban town' of Holmlia in southern Oslo. The plan is shown in figure 4.31. The architects were Hultberg, Resen, Throne-Holst, Boguslawski, A/S. The rocky site slopes north-west, with a fine view over the Oslo fjord. The plot ratio is relatively high (0.41). The rows of buildings, some three- or four-storey apartment blocks and some terraced houses, have been carefully adapted to the contours of the terrain, and designed to catch maximum sunshine and view. Special care has been taken to obtain a pleasant three-dimensional interplay between the buildings, and to create characteristic street pictures and squares. A covered car park is located on the periphery, which means that the street network can be reserved for pedestrians, except for the transport of house refuse, snow clearing, etc. The natural vegetation has been protected and supplemented.

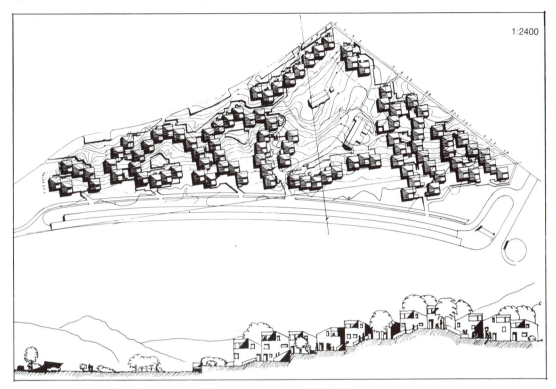

1:2400

Figure 4.30. Selegrend in Bergen, a social housing experiment, 1974–76.
Architects: Cubus a/s. From *Byggekunst.*

The development of *urban renewal* during this latest period deserves brief mention. Almost up to the end of the 1960s the general idea was that renewal of old run-down parts of the urban structure should be effected by means of a process of total clearance and redevelopment. For this purpose a new Act, *Sanerings-loven*, was adopted in the mid-1960s. In the provision of this Act the notion of rehabilitation does not even appear. Typical of the attitudes prevailing at the time is the total clearance and redevelopment of the old residential 'self-grown' area of Enerhaugen in Oslo, a small hill on the east side of Akerselven. Here the characteristic and tightly packed wooden buildings from the first half of the last century, were razed to the ground. A few of the houses were moved to the open-air museum (*Folkemuseet*) at Bygdøy. Instead, a number of fifteen-storey

high-rise blocks and a new Catholic church were erected. Because of the great increase in the number of homes, this project could be realized economically, and its success turned the attention of local authorities to similar old residential quarters in Oslo and elsewhere.

Up to this time the really great challenge of renewal, namely the large collections of cheap tenement blocks from the boom period 1870 –1898 in Oslo, had barely come up. It was obvious that the complete renewal of these dense urban districts would be an extremely expensive operation, which would mean big social and economic problems for thousands of residents.

The policy of total clearance and redevelopment – as it was then being practised – gradually roused ill-will and opposition. From the end of the 1960s students and young architects in Oslo

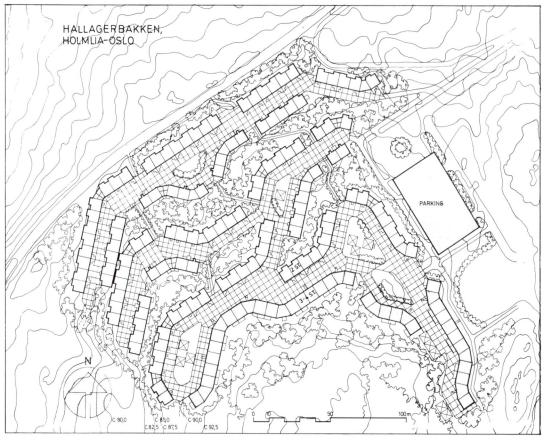

Figure 4.31. Hallagerbakken, a social housing estate at Holmlia, a 'suburban town' in Oslo, completed 1982. Actual map. (Contour intervals 2.5 m)

and Trondheim objected strongly to the plans of the local authorities to clear such old urban parts as Rodeløkka, Vålerenga and Kampen in Oslo, and Rosenborg–Møllenberg in Trondheim. By means of alternative plans they advocated that these old residential areas with their characteristic wooden houses should be protected, renovated and supplied with modern amenities. This opposition received support in many quarters, and particularly from the residents of the old houses.

Nor is there any doubt that the educational activities that accompanied European Architectural Heritage Year in 1975 made an impact on many people's attitudes. Further, a broader understanding also developed among the politicians responsible. It was slowly realized that urban renewal must comprise many more nuances than had hitherto been the case.

In Oslo and Bergen programmes were at last launched for the long-term renewal of the dense tenement blocks from the late nineteenth century (among them Grünerløkka, figure 4.19). Special administrative bodies were established, one connected with the planning authorities and one with the housing authorities. Conflicting attitudes were noticeable, however, between the desire of the former to protect and renovate the old blocks, and the demands of the latter for the provision of as many *new* homes as possible in the old parts of the city by means of large-scale clearance and a high level of land exploitation.

A growing consideration for the needs and wishes of the inhabitants of the old houses has also influenced the urban renewal process. Participation became the slogan that many politicians would like to follow, but which they certainly have found difficult to live up to. A research project, *Inner City Area in Transition* (Oslo, 1982–86), contributed to clarifying the various consequences of the renewal process in practice, such as the fate of the inhabitants and the effects on the environmental and cultural conditions.

Gradually then, and subject to continuous debate, general improvement has taken place in many old urban districts, both in Oslo and other large towns. The process has been led by the local authorities in cooperation with social groupings and private investors. Financial support has been given by the Norwegian State's Housing Bank. Improvement assumed a multiplicity of forms: rehabilitation, rebuilding, new buildings and filling in, clearing of courtyards, planting, face-lifting, the introduction of traffic-free streets and precincts, the furnishing and refurnishing of social and cultural elements. Over the years the *economic* aspect of the renewal policy has become increasingly more difficult. At the end of the 1980s the whole process has threatened to stop from lack of sufficient public financial support.

In 1982 and 1983 two important town planning competitions were held in Oslo. One aimed at a reconstruction and commercialization of the large premises of the old Aker shipyard, centrally situated in Oslo harbour. The other aimed at a long due total redevelopment of the large urban area, Vaterland–Grønland, bordering on the new central railway station.

The common interest and enthusiasm aroused by these two architectural competitions served to inspire other towns to similar initiatives. So in the following years Trondheim, Sandnes, Skien, Haugesund, Drammen and Stavanger in turn launched town planning competitions, aimed at redeveloping centrally situated waterfront areas, that had fallen behind in the urban development. Many interesting planning propositions were awarded prizes in the competitions. As yet, however, only sparse practical results have emerged from the initiatives, due to dwindling economic resources.

In Oslo, however, the 'Aker Brygge' project has, in the main, been carried out, thanks to sufficient private investment. In the newly built area plot ratios are rather high, but due to the excellent location on the western waterside of the Piperviken, near the City Hall, and thanks to a vivid – though dissolved – architecture, the new precinct has become successful and popular. Architects for the town plan are Telje-Torp-Aasen, with detailed plans by Niels Torp.

Greater difficulties met the realization of the winning project of the Vaterland–Grønland competition. The winner was the LPO Architects Office, a team of quite young architects. The plans comprised a new central bus station, large, glazed shopping precincts, a multiplex public hall for ten thousand spectators, and a 35-storey hotel building, besides residential units. Municipal investments in this project have been heavy, the economic outcome seems highly uncertain, and the architectural impression of the whole composition tends to be rather confusing.

At the end of the 1980s the Norwegian economy has suffered a recession. This has involved unemployment and a drastic reduction in building activities and social housing production. The recession has become particularly severe in the northern parts of the country, where, in addition, a fatal ecological crisis in the fisheries has developed during the last five years.

It is difficult, at present, to predict the future trends in Norwegian town planning and town development. It is about time, though, to admit mistakes and omissions in the planning policy of later years and to reconsider the current planning purposes. There has been a marked tendency to prefer concentrating on short-term solutions, and to omit the long-term planning with due respect to ecological considerations. Thus, responsible and binding inter-municipal and regional planning dispositions have been neglected for years in many urban regions. This situation is particularly unhappy in the Oslo region, with a population nearing one million. Here the thirty or forty separate municipalities tend to operate their own 'egoistic' planning policy without any obligatory regional cooperation. Land-use planning, housing policy, location of new commercial centres, etc. are not subjects of deliberation between neighbouring local authorities.

There are bright spots, though. Urgent infrastructural problems have led to the organizing of specific regional structures. During the 1980s a large intermunicipal sewerage system has been organized around the inner part of the Oslo fjord, equipped with advanced cleansing installations. Also, thanks to large state investments and toll road systems, the central road network is now undergoing great improvements. Thus, a new motorway tunnel connection has been completed recently, under the central part of the city. This, it is hoped, will ease the traffic pressure in the city and make urgent environmental improvements possible.

The preparations for a new, highly needed national airport to be built in the Oslo region are also expected to accelerate regional planning activity.

This brief historical presentation shows that urban planning traditions in Norway are on a modest scale, and that professional planning is of recent date. But I have suggested that certain urban environmental qualities of a specific type and interest have existed and to some extent still do exist, in Norway. As everywhere else these qualities are the result of regional and local peculiarities: terrain and climate, resources, industry and economy, transport and trade, cultural traditions and connections, local history and the practice of democracy.

In a historical perspective expansion and growth have always been among the main forces of town planning. Above all it has been a question of constructing new towns or new parts of towns, or urban extension. With such intentions it has always been considered important to follow the latest ideas and models and methods available in other towns and other countries. We must hope that the international exchange of valuable experience of and ideas on town planning will continue. But in the years to come, town planning should be given a stronger and more explicit purpose, namely to maintain, preserve and enhance whatever valuable and unique environments our existing towns and cities may possess. Perhaps we can hope that prudence, consideration, ecological thinking and a respect for inherited cultural values will be given more scope in future town planning than they have received hitherto.

ANNOTATED BIBLIOGRAPHY

(a) Urbanization

The main work of reference on the historical process of urbanization in the Nordic countries is the three-volume report from the Trondheim conference, 1977: Blom, G. A. (ed.) (1977) *Urbaniserings-prosessen i Norden*, 3 volumes. Oslo: Universitetsforlaget. The contributions on Norway are written by Knut Helle and Arnved Nedkvitne (vol. 1 on the Middle Ages), Bjørn Sogner (vol. 2 on the seventeenth and eighteenth centuries), and Jan Eivind Myhre (vol. 3 on the first phase of industrialization ca. 1840–1914). Myhre has also written an overview of Norwegian urbanization since World War I: Myhre, Jan E. (1983) Urbaniseringen i Norge etter første verdenskrig. *Historica IV. Studia Historica Jyväskylänsiae 27*, Jyväskylä: Jyväskylän Yliopisto.

The main contributors to the study of modern urbanization in general have been geographers, in particular Jens Chr. Hansen, Hallstein Myklebost, and Tor Fr. Rasmussen. The main works are: Hansen, Jens Chr. (1965–66) Industriell utvikling og tettstedsvekst. *Norsk Geografisk Tidsskrift*, hefte 6–7, Oslo: Universitetsforlaget, pp. 181–265, which discusses industrial development and the growth of urban places; Hansen, Jens Chr. (1970) *Administrative grenser og tettstedsvekst*. Oslo: Universitetsforlaget, which discusses administrative boundaries and economic growth; Hansen, Jens Chr. (1975) Urbaniseringen av landsbygden, a section on urbanization of the countryside in Fladby, R. and Imsen, S. (eds), *Lokalhistorie fra gard til tettsted*. Oslo: Cappelen, pp. 9–40; Myklebost, Hallstein (1960) *Norges tettbygde steder 1875–1950*. Oslo: Universitetsforlaget, which discusses the urban places of Norway 1875–1950; Myklebost, Hallstein (1979) *Bosetningsutviklingen i Norge 1950–1975*. Oslo: Universitetsforlaget, on population and settlement change in Norway 1950–1975; Torstenson, Joel S., Metcalf, Michael F. and Rasmussen, Tor Fr. (1985) *Urbanization and community building in Norway*. Oslo: Urbana Press; Rasmussen, Tor Fr. (1969) *Byregioner i Norge*. Oslo: Norsk Institutt for By- og Regionforskning, on urban regions in Norway. Rasmussen has also contributed to *NOU*, 1979: 5, Bypolitikk, an official Norwegian report on urban politics.

There are also a number of valuable urban biographies, the most noteworthy for the post-1850 period being those by Knut Mykland and Rolf Danielsen on Trondheim, Egil Ertresvaag, Anders Bjarne Fossen, and Tore Grønlie on Bergen, and Jens Chr. Hansen on Notodden. A five-volume history of Oslo is in preparation. Two volumes were published in 1990: Jan Eivind Myhre (1990) *Hovedstaden Christiania 1814–1900* (Christiania, the Capital) Vol. 3; Kjeldstadli, Knut (1990) *Den delte byen 1900–1948* (The Divided City) Vol. 4. A fifth volume by Edgeir Benum is due to appear in 1993.

A major bibliography is Jan Eivind Myhre (1989) Norway, in C. Engeli and H. Matzerath (eds) *Modern Urban History Research in Europe, USA and Japan*. Oxford: Oxford University Press, pp. 454–62.

A major historiography is Jan Eivind Myhre (1988) Nordic urban history and urban historians in the last decade. *Urban History Yearbook, 1988*. Leicester: Leicester University Press, pp. 65–77.

(b) Town Planning

Andersson, Per (1962) *Stavanger i støpeskjeen. Changed City – Urban Renewal of Stavanger*. Stavanger.
Text in Norwegian and English.

Bergsgard, Unnleiv (1985) Sverre Pedersen, un urbaniste norvégien classique. *Archives d'Architecture Moderne*, no. 29.
An article on the Norwegian town planner professor Sverre Pedersen.

Butenschøn, Peter and Lindheim, Tone (1987) *Det nye Oslo*. Oslo: Dreyers forlag. A presentation of fifty new projects in central Oslo.

Byggekunst
The major Norwegian journal on architecture and planning, with special numbers on, for instance, urban renewal (1972, No. 1), community housing (1979, No. 2) and the replanning of towns destroyed during World War II (1980, No. 5).

Disposisjonsplan for Heimdal. Trondheim: Heimdalskontoret, 1971.
Presentation of the plans for the new suburban centre Heimdal, Trondheim.

Generalplan for Oslo. Oslo: Oslo Reguleringsvesen, 1950.
The official master plan proposal of 1950.

Hagerup, Vegard (1979) *Byplanlovgivning i Norge 1845–1924*. Trondheim: NTH.
An account of planning legislation in Norway 1845–1924.

Hals, Harald (1929) *Fra Christiania til Stor-Oslo*. Oslo: Aschehoug & Co.
A review of contemporary planning principles in the 1920s, followed by the first substantiated master plan proposal for Oslo.

Jensen, Rolf (1981) *Moderne norsk byplanlegging blir til*. Stockholm: Nordplan.
Based on articles in technical periodicals from 1854 to 1930, this book describes the origins of Norwegian town planning.

Lorange, Erik and Nygaard, William (1950) *Fra gjenreising til nyreising*. Oslo: J. G. Tanum Forlag.
A discussion of reconstruction problems and regional planning in war-damaged Finnmark, Norway.

Lorange, Erik (1984) *Byen i landskapet – rommene i byen*. Oslo: Universitetsforlaget.
Analysis of the relations between landscape, town planning and urban space. Examples from Oslo, Bergen, Drammen, Risør and Gjøvik.

Lorange, Erik (1986) Formelle byplaner og selvgrodde byer i Norge, in *Fysisk planlegging*. Ringsaker: Fagbokforlaget.
A discussion of formal town planning and organic growth towns in Norway.

Mumford, Lewis (1938) *The Culture of Cities*. New York: Harcourt Brace.

Nesse, Olav (1983) Bergen – 25 års byutvikling (*Byggekunst*, 1983, No. 6).
With summary in English on twenty-five years of urban development in Bergen.

Oslo – Planning and development. Oslo: Oslo Municipality, 1960.
Text in English and Norwegian. A survey of the geographical and historical background, the development of population and economic activities and the post-war planning and building in Oslo.

Pedersen, Bjørn Sverre (1963) Camillo Sitte og århundreskiftets byplanideal. *Byggekunst*, No. 4.
On Camillo Sitte's influence on Norwegian town planning.

Rolfsen, Erik (1951) Lokalsentre i Oslos ytre område. *Byplan*, No. 16.
Planning proposals for the new local centres in Oslo's 'suburban towns'.

Rolfsen, Erik (1981) Byplan og bolig i Oslo 1906–1981. *Byggekunst*, No. 8.
A review of city planning and housing in Oslo, 1906–1981. English summary.

Stor-Oslo. Forslag til generalplan. Oslo, 1934.
The first inter-municipal plan proposal for the Oslo region, the municipalities Oslo, Aker and Bærum.

Utkast til regionplan for Oslo/Akershus. Oslo: Samarbeidskomiteen for Oslo, 1969.
The regional plan proposal of 1969 for the neighbouring counties of Oslo and Akershus.

5

URBAN PLANNING IN SWEDEN

Thomas Hall

INTRODUCTORY COMMENTS

The idea of surveying the role of planning in the shaping of modern Sweden is an attractive one, but it is also an enterprise beset by problems of definition. To begin with, the concept of 'planning' is extremely capacious, even if we disregard all but its strictly physical aspects. A 'plan' may refer to anything from a whole country to a single property. And it may imply anything from comprehensive guidelines for land use to detailed provisions regarding the appearance of buildings. Moreover, 'planning' can refer to the administrative and political process in which plans are made and approved, as well as to the actual designing of the physical environment, while planning history also includes the ideals obtaining at various times about the functional, social and aesthetic aspects of urban design. In the present survey an attempt has been made to give a general idea of the evolution and implementation of physical planning in Sweden, focusing particularly on the physical layout of the town and discussing both the decision process and questions of form and design.

For most of the twentieth century a basic political goal in Sweden has been to provide all citizens with good housing, and housing production has become an increasingly complex process, administered by a massive bureaucratic apparatus and divers decision-makers, each with their special instruments of control. In a situation of this kind it is not easy to say exactly what 'planning' implies. Moreover, it can be difficult to distinguish between planning as such and the design of buildings, since the overall shape of the planning is often determined by the types of buildings projected. And, in turn, building design is affected by requirements as to dwelling size and type.

Something should also be said about the plan of the chapter and its chronological arrangement. Although the book as a whole concentrates on the period from the mid-nineteenth century to the present day, a brief survey of previous activities appeared justified, particularly since the planning that occurred in Sweden during the seventeenth century was on quite a considerable scale even in European terms. It was also apparent that the period from the mid-nineteenth century up to the First World War formed a coherent unit of its own, while the twentieth century could perhaps have been divided into several sections. Such an arrangement, however, seemed likely to result in excessive fragmentation. One possibility might have been to organize the three periods in roughly the same way, but as the conditions and tasks with which the planning system had to deal were so different at the different times, such uniformity could not be regarded as of paramount importance.

In the following survey examples from Stockholm predominate, particularly in the section

on the twentieth century. This emphasis can be
justified on various grounds; Stockholm, albeit
with some important exceptions, has been the
scene of the best known and most influential
projects and has also been the subject of more
writing than any other Swedish town.

Many of my colleagues have been generous
with suggestions and critical comments which
have greatly helped me in preparing and writing
this chapter. I should like to express my thanks
to Kristina Berglund, Lempi BorgWik, Birgitta
Ericsson, Gärd Folkesdotter, David Goldfield
Arne Granholm, Ingrid Hammarström, Björn
Linn, Lars Nilsson, Ingrid Sjöström, John Sjöström and Lennart Tonell. And I owe a special
dept of gratitude to Gärd Folkesdotter, who has
made many fruitful suggestions and who
allowed me to refer to her doctoral dissertation
which at the time had not yet been published.

URBAN DEVELOPMENT AND PLANNING
BEFORE 1850

Swedish towns, or rather those places which
were so classified before the town was officially
abolished as a legal institution in 1970, can be
roughly divided into three groups: mediaeval
towns (fifty-two, eighteen of which were originally   Danish-Norwegian),   seventeenth-
century towns (twenty-seven, including one
Danish), and twentieth-century towns (forty-
one). In addition there were five sixteenth-
century towns (one of them Danish), one town
dating from the eighteenth century and six from
the nineteenth (see figure 5.1). The seven-

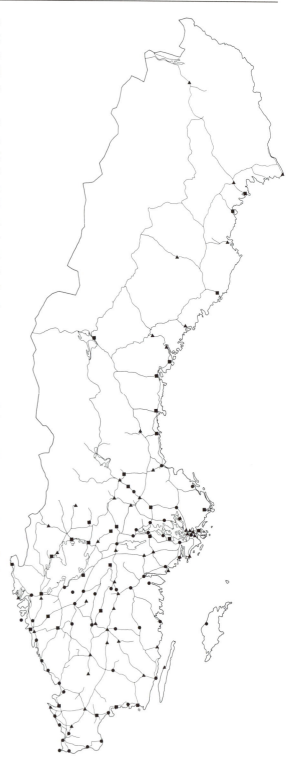

Figure 5.1. The map shows the places which were classified as towns before the town was officially abolished as a
legal institution in 1970, and the railways existing in
1985 (by which time the network had been radically
reduced after many lines had been wholly or partially
closed).
● Mediaeval towns
■ sixteenth- to eighteenth-century towns (generally
new foundations)
▲ nineteenth- to twentieth-century towns

teenth-century towns were generally new foundations planned and realized on the initiative of the central government, while most of the mediaeval and modern towns grew 'spontaneously' on sites favourable to trade and communications.

When did mediaeval Sweden acquire an urban system in the sense that could be applied to continental Europe at the time? There is no clearcut answer to this question. But several of the mediaeval towns certainly started as some sort of meeting place – usually a *thing* or a marketplace – in the twelfth century or even earlier. It seems likely, however, that not until the thirteenth century did their functions and buildings acquire a character such that the designation 'town' becomes appropriate. The reign of Magnus Ladulås (1275–1290) seems to have represented a period of consolidation in Swedish towns, particularly in Stockholm. At least in the Lake Mälar region the expansion of the towns around the beginning of the fourteenth century is closely linked to developments in mining in central Sweden, where what had previously been no more than a peasant enterprise was changing into a genuine export industry, run by professionals. Merchants from Germany, and their descendants, came to occupy leading positions in the most important towns. But it has to be remembered that even towards the end of the Middle Ages, Swedish towns would still rank as little more than villages in any comparison with contemporary continental Europe. Except in Stockholm and Visby the populations were small and most of the buildings were simple wooden houses. Only Stockholm, Visby and Kalmar could boast a city wall of stone.

Sweden's earliest surviving urban code, the *Bjärköarätten* which probably applied in Stockholm towards the end of the thirteenth century, already contained various regulations about buildings; these reappeared in a systematized and extended form in the building code of Magnus Eriksson's Towns Act in the mid-fourteenth

century. Perhaps most interesting in our present context is the stipulation that 'public streets' should have a width of 8 *alnar* (approximately 4.8 metres), 'so that it is possible to drive and ride upon them', since several of the streets in Gamla stan, the mediaeval centre of Stockholm, have just this width. But the building code does not appear to recognize any activities which we could describe as planning. Instead it is concerned with the general legal regulation of certain aspects of building and property ownership.

In many parts of Europe mediaeval town plans have survived fairly intact, and it has thus been possible to use them in the historical analysis of urban planning. This is not the case when it comes to Sweden's provincial towns. Disastrous fires and town-plan redevelopments have made the reconstruction of the original plans a difficult and uncertain business. We must therefore be extremely cautious in drawing any conclusions about mediaeval urban development in Sweden. It seems clear however, that there was no planning of the advanced kind that could be encountered at this time or even earlier in various parts of continental Europe or in England (see Hall, 1978, pp. 122 *et seq.*). But the absence of any prior drawings or marked out plans need not preclude a desire to allow for the topography of a place or to take existing buildings into account.

The first planning task to be documented in the history of Swedish urban development dates from 1473, when six councillors were instructed to stake out plots for Nya Lödöse (later succeeded by Göteborg, within whose present area Nya Lödöse was located). During the sixteenth century there were also a few tentative moves towards planned urban development, but the major wave of planning occurred around the middle of the seventeenth century, when Swedish planning activities were unparalleled in Europe. During the first half of the seventeenth century domestic reforms and military triumphs had promoted Sweden to a leading position in northern Europe. But her towns were few and in almost all cases hardly developed at all. The government of the day, with its sharply mercantile bent, saw the expansion and improvement of the urban network as an important means in acquiring the economic strength that the country needed to meet the new situation. In certain strategically potent areas the towns were also intended to play a significant role as fortresses in Sweden's defence.

Seventeenth-century urban policy (for a more detailed account see Ericsson, 1975) included a variety of measures. Several new towns were founded, particularly along the coast of Norrland, in the mining areas of central Sweden, along the watercourses and roads to the west coast, and in the new counties acquired after 1650. At the same time efforts were made to activate the towns with the help of administrative reforms, by granting trading privileges and donating large tracts of land. These donations were to influence urban development up to our own times (Améen, 1964). Further, it was hoped to modernize the physical layout of the towns by introducing town-plan redevelopments. As one step in this direction maps were made of a great many towns, and new town plans were executed (a great deal of this material has been preserved in various archives; the seminal scholarly analysis is to be found in Eimer, 1961). The new town plans, which were generally drawn up by military engineers or surveyors, usually lacked aesthetic pretensions. They consist of simple right-angled street networks and rectangular blocks laid out with few concessions to or even awareness of topography or existing buildings. This kind of plan is sometimes referred to as the 'Renaissance' type, but the designation is misleading. Any connection with the advanced compositions of the leading, continental theorists is a very slim one. There was fierce opposition to the planning regulations on the part of the populace, and despite ruthless expropriations and demolition orders, work often proceeded

slowly (see Jutikkala, 1968). Sometimes, however, a fire would clear the way for radical planning and in southern Sweden several towns had been damaged or destroyed during the 1611–13 war with Denmark. In these cases it was possible to implement new projects as part of the rebuilding programme.

The most ambitious programme was launched in Stockholm. Planning started as early as the 1620s, when the western part of the mediaeval centre, the Gamla stan of today, was given a new plan after a fire. At the end of the 1630s work continued into the suburbs – Malmarna – and within about ten years the twisting mediaeval street network had been replaced by new plans consisting of straight streets crossing at right angles and, as far as possible, of regular blocks (figure 5.2). For reasons of topography, however, the orientation of the various street systems in the different parts of the town had to be varied. The seventeenth-century street network remained relatively intact until after the Second World War, and even today large parts of it have survived. The city engineer, Anders Torstensson, was probably mainly responsible for the seventeenth-century plans. He also executed plans for Uppsala, Turku (Åbo), Södertälje and other towns, none of which were intended as forts. Torstensson's Uppsala plan, which he produced around 1640, was realized with great consistency and has survived largely unaltered. It seems justifiable to describe Torstensson as a professional town planner, and he was certainly regarded *de facto* as such by his contemporaries (on Torstensson and his work in Stockholm, see Hall, 1970).

As regards planning operations in other towns, a few examples will have to suffice. Göteborg must of course be one of them: it was the most outstanding success among the new seventeenth-century foundations. It was founded around 1620 at the mouth of the Göta river, at the time Sweden's only outlet to the west and thus also providing the only way of reaching western Europe and England by sea

Figure 5.2. Stockholm, a map from around 1645. After 1636 'Malmarna', the districts surrounding 'Staden mellan broarna' (the Town between the Bridges) were either redeveloped or planned afresh. The old winding streets were replaced by street networks as close to a gridiron pattern as the topography permitted. *Source*: Det kongelige bibliotek, Copenhagen.

without having to pay customs duty to Denmark. Göteborg was planned as a trading city and fortress. Inspired by Dutch urban development, the plan has survived largely unchanged except for the closing of a few canals (figure 5.3). Kalmar was also of great interest to the authorities. Like Göteborg it was needed as a trading centre and a border defence. The town had been badly damaged during the 1611–13 war with Denmark, and the idea was to rebuild

it according to a radial plan on Italian Renaissance lines. It is not clear how far this plan was implemented, but it was apparently soon recognized that the site of the town immediately in front of the fortress was strategically unsuitable, and after a fire in 1647 the town was moved a couple of hundred metres to the east. This time the choice was for a gridiron plan, but one which is particularly well proportioned. It is largely intact today (figure 5.4). The new town of

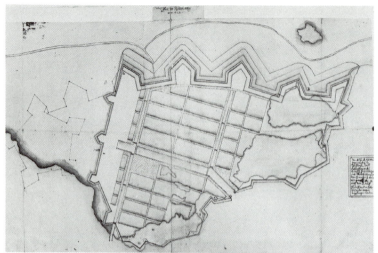

Figure 5.3. Göteborg, the greatest success of seventeenth-century Swedish planning on a map from the early 1620s. The town was probably designed by a Dutch engineer around 1620. The street system remains basically unchanged today (cf. figure 5.33). *Source:* Krigsarkivet, Stockholm.

Vänersborg was given a gridiron plan of a more simple kind (figure 5.5).

These towns are among the more successful projects. Some other plans remained entirely or partly at the drawing-board stage. Jönköping is a case in a point. This town had also been damaged during the 1611–13 war. It was to be rebuilt on a new site according to a plan of the Dutch type rather like the Göteborg plan. But the final result had little in common with this proud vision. In several other older towns, projected plans came to nothing or at least to very little, as in Gävle for example. Here a few new and admittedly important streets were the only outcome of a grandiose lay-out plan. Several coastal towns in Norrland were given plans so simple that their urban structures could easily be thought to have emerged 'spontaneously', and in some cases they were certainly influenced by existing buildings. The same applies to one of the last of the new foundations, namely Strömstad (c. 1670) in the recently acquired Bohus county on the west coast.

The fortified towns which were planned towards the end of the seventeenth century to safeguard the Swedish occupation of the former Danish territories, represented a category of their own. Landskrona (figure 5.6) and Karls-

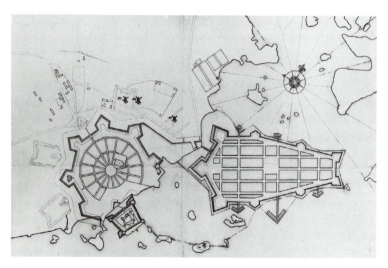

Figure 5.4. During the Middle Ages Kalmar was one of the most important towns in Sweden. In 1611 the town was burnt during the war with Denmark, after which it was replanned as a 'radial' city on the Italian model. It is unclear how far this project was realized. After another fire in 1647 the town was transferred and rebuilt on a new site according to a gridiron plan which still survives fairly intact (cf. figure 5.14). This map from the 1640s shows both projects next to one another. *Source:* Krigsarkivet, Stockholm.

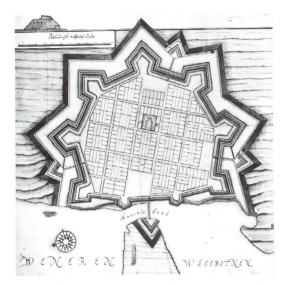

Figure 5.5. Vänersborg was founded in the early 1640s on the Göta Älv river, not far from its outflow from Vänern, the largest lake in Sweden, and thus at an important point in the communications system. The simple gridiron plan was probably drawn by Olof Hansson Örnehufvud, head of the Swedish fortification corps. The planned fortifications were never executed. *Source:* Krigsarkivet, Stockholm.

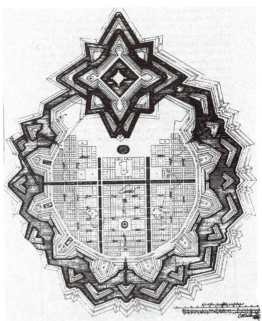

Figure 5.6. For Landskrona – as for Karlskrona – several town and fortification plans were made, inspired by contemporary writings on the subject. The goal was to secure the provinces captured from Denmark. Above, a proposal from 1680 by Erik Dahlberg. *Source:* Åström (1967).

krona were the most important examples. The plans for these towns appear in many variations, but they are often strongly influenced by the fortification and town-planning theories which were then prevalent in continental Europe. The leading Swedish expert on this type of town building was the fortification engineer Erik Dahlberg. Mention should also be made of Hamina (Fredrikshamn) in the Finnish part of the kingdom, after 1721 a border town facing Russia. Because of its strategic site the town was rebuilt on a radial plan, thus becoming the only example in the Nordic countries of a systematically realized plan of the type recommended by many fortification theorists.

All in all it seems justified to regard these seventeenth-century projects as the start of Swedish urban planning history. In this context several towns acquired 'modern' plans, many of which have largely survived and are still functioning. As a result of these activities certain

notions also came to be accepted about how towns should be planned and designed – notions which were not to be seriously questioned until nearly the end of the nineteenth century.

The lively planning of the seventeenth century did not continue in the century that followed. After the death of Karl XII in 1718, the absolute monarchy was replaced by a system whereby power was vested in the Riksdag and its institutions. Among the town dwellers there had always been strong opposition to the costs and inconveniences of planning regulations; the burghers, as one of the four Estates of the Riksdag, now had much better opportunities than before of winning support for their own interests. Thus towns damaged or destroyed by fire were generally rebuilt on their old foundations and with their old street networks. In Skövde in 1759 and in Enköping in 1801, however, new street systems were introduced

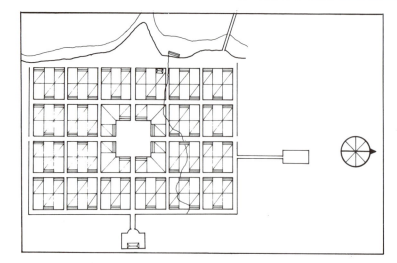

Figure 5.7. Östersund, founded in 1786, and the only Swedish town founded in the eighteenth century. The plan was drawn in 1788 by a local surveyor. The central square is remarkable for its closed corners. Every second plot was intended to be used as a garden without any buildings, partly for reasons of fire security but also as a way of getting the whole area built more quickly. The town was built more or less according to the plan, but the central square has been distorted by later alterations. *Source:* Länsstyrelsens lantmäterienhet, Östersund.

after fires. Skövde's town privileges were threatened, and in order to safeguard them the citizens launched their own planning initiative (Nisser, 1970). In both these cases it was a question of simple surveyor plans. The same applied to Östersund, the only new foundation of the eighteenth century (figure 5.7). More thought seems to have gone into the project for Gävle after a fire in 1776; the author of the plan has clearly tried to adapt it to the local conditions (figure 5.8; Karlström, 1974). In structure the eighteenth-century plans are similar to those of the previous century, except for a tendency to introduce wider streets and green areas, and to locate streets along quays and shorelines.

Even at the beginning of the nineteenth century few if any town plans were made, except when a town had burnt down. In such situations, however, they were customary; in 1828 it was even officially forbidden to start restoring a town after a fire before the government had approved a town plan. An interesting example of such post-fire planning was Nils Ericson's 1834 project for Vänersborg, in which one of the seventeenth-century rows of blocks was left unbuilt, to provide a series of parks and places across the centre of the town (cf. below, p. 181).

Nils Ericson, then active as a canal-builder,

was later to become the leading figure in the construction of the Swedish state railway. Another outstanding engineer of the period was Baltzar von Platen, initiator and guiding hand in building the Göta Kanal. He was also responsible for an original contribution to town planning. In 1823 he executed a town plan for Motala, which was intended to be the chief town on the canal and thus important to communications between the east coast and Göteborg. The main outlines of the plan, with streets radiating from the centre, were realized. Motala was the only urban foundation to be planned during the first half of the nineteenth century, although its town status was not legally acknowledged until some time later.

As well as the ordinary towns, pre-industrial Sweden boasted another type of community which was sometimes subjected to detailed planning, namely the *bruk*, the communities attached to local foundries or ironworks. This applied particularly to the large *bruk* in Uppland. A place of this kind would often consist of a manor house and park, and the community itself with its church and estate office, the houses of the employees neatly lining the main street, the workshops a little way away, the blast furnace, the hammer mill, and the coal depot. Because of his financial resources and because

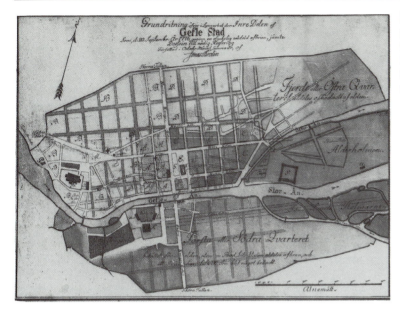

Figure 5.8. Gävle, regulation plan for the reconstruction of the town after the fire of 1776, drawn by the land surveyor Jonas Brolin. *Source:* Gävle stadsingenjörskontor, Gävle.

he owned the community as well, the proprietor could shape the whole complex according to his own wishes. General plans were often made, with a view to achieving a rational and suitably impressive form. It was during the eighteenth and early nineteenth centuries that the *bruk* communities acquired what became their classic design. When the Vallon forges began to give way to new metallurgical processes during the nineteenth century (see below), the traditional ironworks lost their leading position in production. But many of their settings have survived relatively intact, testifying to a desire to co-ordinate planning and building design and thus to create a systematically conceived environment, which in many ways seems to presage the paternalistic model communities of the nineteenth century. Leufsta (figure 5.9) and Forsmark are two of the most interesting examples.

If we turn from planning to the more general regulation of building, we find that Magnus Eriksson's building code was the basic authority up to 1734, but it was supplemented by local rules adapted to local conditions. However, under Johan III (1568–92) the central author-

ities began to take a more serious interest in urban building, and various building regulations were successively introduced, particularly for Stockholm. The main theme in this torrent of decrees was always that wooden houses should be replaced by brick. And the very fact that the message had to be constantly repeated, shows that it was having little effect.

Towards the end of the seventeenth century preparations began for a new general law. It was to include a code of urban building, but in fact nothing came of it, probably largely because the new political situation after the death of Karl XII affected attitudes towards relations between the central and local administrations. And so the individual towns continued to be responsible for the rules on building in the urban setting. Stockholm led the way; the first local building ordinance had been issued as early as 1725, and it was followed by revised and expanded versions. These ordinances gave detailed instructions regarding the distribution of plots and sites, the disposition of streets, the design of houses and so on, but they did not present or prescribe plans or deal with planning issues as such.

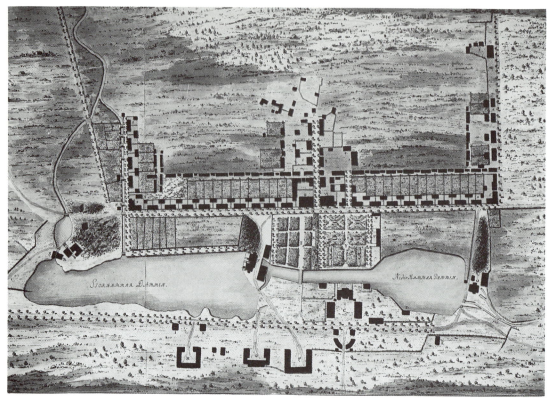

Figure 5.9. Leufsta Bruk in Uppland, section of a map from 1735. The *bruk* was burnt by the Russians in 1719 but was rebuilt during the following decade without any radical alterations to the main pattern of the seventeenth-century plan. Most of the buildings have survived intact. The splendid manor-house is separated from the great garden by a canal. The main street runs at right-angles to the garden's main axis and is lined by dwelling-houses for the smiths. The two large buildings on the main street are the church and the agent's house with the estate office next door. The workshops etc. were located near the system of basins and dams on two sides of the village. *Source*: Kungliga biblioteket, Stockholm.

The example set by Stockholm was not followed immediately. Only a few towns passed building ordinances of their own during the eighteenth century. But fire regulations were becoming customary; the need for these could hardly be questioned when most towns suffered devastating fires every 100 years or so. And it was the Fire Insurance Office, established towards the end of the eighteenth century, which became most involved in building regulations. The connection between cramped and huddled buildings and the rapid spread of fire was obvious. Between 1800 and 1830 a great many Swedish towns introduced building ordinances.

The regulations were chiefly aimed at fire safety and would cover such things as building materials, building height, street width, the regulation of plots, and minimum distances between buildings. But there were no requirements regarding plans for general layout or building expansion.

URBAN PLANNING – THE BREAKTHROUGH 1850–1915

Changes in Society

At the beginning of the period in question, around the middle of the nineteenth century,

Sweden had not yet been greatly affected by industrialization and all the social changes generally embraced by this concept. The economy was still predominantly agrarian, and only one-tenth of the total population lived in towns. Non-agricultural production was largely a question of crafts. The guild system had just been abolished (1846), but Sweden had to wait another eighteen years before a law granting full freedom to trade was passed in 1864. The communications system was still fairly primitive, and a journey between the capital city and the more remote parts of the country could be a matter of weeks.

By the end of the period a great deal of this had changed. By 1910 a quarter of the population was living in towns. Roughly the same number of people were employed in agriculture as in 1850, but their proportion of the total workforce had dropped from over three-quarters to barely half, while the proportion working in industry and the various crafts had risen from less than a tenth to approximately a quarter. Large factories and plants had appeared in many places, and big sections of the railway network had been completed – this last being particularly important in view of the great distance to many outlying parts of the country.

The period between 1800 and 1840 was one of rapid population growth – the most rapid in the history of Sweden – with an increase from 2.4 to 3.5 million. But although this resulted in the emergence of a large impoverished agricultural proletariat living in harsh conditions, urbanization remained at the same level with around 10 per cent of the population living in towns – a level which seems to have been reached as early as the middle of the eighteenth century. By the 1850s, however, the urban population was beginning to increase more rapidly than the population as a whole. A major factor in this context was a rise in urban in-migration, which in turn was due to a combination of push and pull effects: the abolition of trading restrictions, greater freedom to move, better communi-

cations, and a higher level of information and knowledge all encouraged greater mobility in the rural population, while at the same time more jobs became available in the towns (the greater mobility also led to extensive emigration, mainly to the United States). Another important factor in Sweden as elsewhere was the improvement in urban sanitation and hygiene with the consequent decline in mortality rates. Births per annum now outnumbered deaths, and towns were no longer dependent for survival on continual in-migration; their populations could increase independently.

Industrialization in the narrow sense of mechanized factory production did not play a significant role during the early stages of urbanization. The first two export industries to be mechanized were sawmills and iron manufacture, neither of which was town-based. The sawmills accounted for Sweden's most rapidly expanding export product during the second half of the nineteenth century, namely sawn timber. The major foreign market was Great Britain, whose own industrialization had generated extensive building activities, which thus became a motive force in the industrialization of Sweden as well. A great many sawmills were established in the period immediately after 1850, most of them at the mouths of rivers on the Norrland coast. During the later years of our period, a growing proportion of the wood products went into the sulphate and sulphite industries, much of which also came to be located at the mouths of the rivers, often giving rise to new communities.

Around 1900 the iron industry underwent a radical structural reorganization. Many small ironworks were replaced by fewer larger units based on new production techniques (the Bessemer and open-hearth processes). These foundations, which presupposed the presence of good communications, led in many cases to the establishment of new communities. Special mention should be made of Sandviken, a foundation planned by G. F. Göransson who had introduced various modifications to make the Bessemer process commercially viable. The development of the Thomas Gilchrist process was also extremely important in Sweden, as it made it possible to use phosphoric ore and the great ore deposits of Lappland could thus be exploited. In connection with these activities several new communities were established, foremost among them Kiruna, which was eventually granted town status. Apart from the sawmills, however, these various operations were still in their infancy in 1915.

During the second half of the nineteenth century urban-based industries were also gaining in importance, mainly in the production of consumer goods for the domestic market. First to introduce mechanization and mass production was the textile industry, with its chief centres in towns such as Norrköping and Göteborg. From the 1860s onwards steam breweries operating on an industrial scale, and even some steam mills, had been established. During the later years of the century an engineering industry had also started up, part of it new and part the result of improvements in earlier engineering workshops, shipyards and other manufacturing plants. Like the electronics industry at a later date, the mechanical industries were located in towns. Thus, around the beginning of the present century, many Swedish towns were being transformed into manufacturing towns, and industrialization was providing a powerful impulse to urbanization.

Between 1850 and 1910 the urban population increased by one million; by the end of the period 1.4 million people in Sweden were living in towns. Although the rate of increase fluctuated in different regions within this period (Nilsson, 1984), no really radical change occurred in the urban system. Between 1850 and 1910 only five more communities were granted town status. In both 1850 and 1910 Stockholm accounted for just over 25 per cent of the total urban population. Between the same dates the

six towns immediately below the capital city in size in 1850 were growing slightly more quickly (Ahlberg, 1958). The existing housing stock was much too small to cope with the influx of people to the towns, and many of the new immigrants had to crowd together in overpopulated lodgings, or in shanty towns on the city outskirts, or at best in jerry-built tenement housing. Conditions were particularly poor in Stockholm. Various well-intended and sometimes successful attempts were made to find better alternatives, but they remained a very small drop in the bucket. At the same time, though, various accounts of living conditions of the working classes, like earlier studies of urban sanitary conditions did succeed in encouraging a public interest in planning and building.

In earlier periods there had been three main types of building agglomeration outside the towns; agricultural communities, many of them dispersed as a result of extensive land reforms around the end of the eighteenth century; fishing villages; and the *bruk* communities attached to local ironworks. During the second half of the nineteenth century new types of agglomeration began to appear, many of them in connection with railway stations or various industries, and others as suburbs outside the larger cities. For these types of community two new municipal classifications were introduced, namely the *köping* and the *municipalsamhälle*. A *köping* was a municipality with a legal status between that of a town and a 'rural district' (*landskommun* – the basic municipal unit outside the towns). A *municipalsamhälle* was part of a 'rural district' to which the urban ordinances applied, in particular the 1874 building ordinances (see below). One rural district could thus embrace several *municipalsamhällen*. By 1910 about 4 per cent of the population of the country was to be found in these two new types of municipality.

The 1874 Building Ordinances and the 1907 Town Planning Act

We have already noted that local building regulations began to be common in Swedish towns during the first decades of the nineteenth century. During the 1820s, after several severe fires, the Riksdag discussed a general building ordinance, but the proposal was turned down. In 1859 the question of a national building enactment came up again. During the year a bill was moved in the Riksdag by A. W. Edelsvärd, one of the leading engineers and architects of the day, who is chiefly known to posterity as the architect of the station buildings in many Swedish towns. The unplanned building that often grew up round railway stations apparently inspired the motion. A committee rejected in principle the idea of a general building enactment applying to all towns, but it recommended a number of 'basic principles' which should be included in all local building ordinances. One was that plans should be made for the regulation of plots, streets and public places, and another that no building should be allowed without some such plan being approved. Thus the idea was beginning to emerge that planning should be a regular ingredient in municipal operations, and not an extraordinary or exceptional event connected with the foundation of new towns or the rebuilding that followed a fire.

The matter was considered by the various authorities and several objections were raised, not least as regards the weight that was to be given to the town plan. The critical reaction may explain why the whole question was shelved until in 1866 Albert Lindhagen, a justice and government official, was given a free hand to bring his legal expertise to bear on the problem and to revise the committee's proposal. This task must have been attractive to Lindhagen; at the time he was deeply engaged in local government affairs in Stockholm, particularly in the preparations for the general plan for the capital which was published the following year (see below).

In 1874, as part of comprehensive legislation concerning urban conditions, the government[1] issued a set of building ordinances drawn up by Lindhagen, which was both more than and different from a mere revision of the 1859 committee proposal. The 1874 ordinances mark the beginning of a new era. They are not written for the small semi-agrarian towns of the pre-industrial period, but for the large cities of the industrial age. They also represent an enactment which even in a European perspective can be described as both progressive and modern, embodying the notion of the 'good town' that was typical of a whole series of urban planning enterprises at the time (see Hall, 1986).

Significantly it was now made compulsory that towns and other densely populated areas should have a *stadsplan* (town plan) regulating the expansion of the town. This plan should consist of a map showing how a town or a district was to be divided into blocks and streets and other public spaces such as squares and parks, i.e. what we today perhaps would call a lay-out plan. No binding directives regarding the design of buildings could be included in the plan.

We will return later to the detailed regulations in the ordinances regarding the shape of the town plan. But it should be mentioned here that despite the outstanding legal experience of their author the ordinances ignored the problems connected with the legal effects and the implementation of the town plans. Moreover, building ordinances were issued by the government and were not the subject of a joint decision by Riksdag and government together. Hence neither the ordinances themselves nor any related town plans could encroach on the rights accorded to property-owners under the civil law.

Thus the injunction against building in contravention of the town plan was *de facto* limited in its effect. If a property-owner applied for building permission on part of a plot which was designated for a street in the plan, the town was ultimately unable to prevent the building unless it expropriated the ground. And in calculating the compensation for such an action the possible utility of the street to the property-owner himself was not taken into account, which meant that the cost to the town was often disproportionately high. This situation made any long-term planning difficult and encouraged land speculation. Another major weakness in the ordinances which became evident after a time was the lack of any effective legal instrument for preventing dense building outside the area of the plan.

In 1884 a motion was put before the Riksdag describing forcefully and in detail the drawbacks of the current system and recommending new legislation. The proposer, Moritz Rubenson, was secretary of the Stockholm City Council and for many decades a prominent figure in local government. He appears to have been particularly interested in planning and building issues.

The motion met with a positive reception, and an investigative committee was appointed. By 1885 this committee had already produced a report, including a factual review of legislation in other countries and a proposal for a law on town plans and the parcelling of land. Although most of the authorities called upon to comment were essentially positive, the conservative minister of justice decided to shelve the proposal, instead of letting it proceed to the Riksdag as a bill. Another twenty years, several motions and yet another committee of investigation were to pass before a bill regarding a new planning law was finally placed before the Riksdag in 1907, pushed through by certain members who were themselves involved in local government. As in the earlier proposal the ratification of a town plan would mean that the landowner was forbidden to build on land allocated for streets or public places, and that the municipality had the right to purchase such land. The landowners' obligation as regards compensation for street costs, however, had been solved in a new way. In case of exploita-

tion the municipality was first to acquire the land required for a street by purchase or expropriation, after which the plot-owners along the new street were to compensate for the cost. Town plans were to be drawn up not only for towns but also for *köpingar* and *municipalsamhällen*. On the other hand, unlike the 1874 building ordinances, the proposed law included no prescriptions as to the aims or the contents of the plans. Further the municipalities' role in the planning process was strengthened, since it was established in the explanatory exposition of the law that the government would not in future be able to alter plans submitted for ratification; all they could do was to refuse ratification to a plan which they considered to be unsuitable.

During its passage through the Riksdag an important addition was made to the law. On the initiative of a private proposer a provision was included, whereby plans could even prescribe the details of the development on individual properties, such as height, number of floors etc. It is no exaggeration to describe this alteration, which transformed the town-planning law from a law regulating streets and plots into a genuine planning law, as perhaps the most important step in the history of Swedish planning legislation. And yet it passed almost unnoticed. It is doubtful whether even the proposer recognized the full import of his own suggestion. Nor do we know how he got the idea or where it came from.

Actors and Decision Processes

During the later years of the nineteenth century, town-planning issues were handled roughly as follows. First the question was to be raised and a decision taken to produce a plan. An expert was then entrusted with executing the plan. Few towns had anyone on their staff who possessed the necessary competence, and an external consultant would be engaged. When a plan proposal was ready it was submitted for comment to the various boards and committees concerned before being finally discussed and accepted, often in revised form. At this stage it was submitted to the government for approval.

During the period under consideration, i.e. from roughly 1850 to about 1915, the system for handling town-planning issues changed on a couple of occasions as a result of major reforms. The 1862 municipal reform improved the efficiency of municipal operations and new units were established for preparing and deciding various questions. The 1874 building ordi-

nances made it obligatory for towns to produce plans, while rules were also given about decision paths and the design and content of the plans. The 1907 Town Planning Act regulated the legal effects of the town plans, and paved the way for including prescriptions regarding the design of buildings in the plan.

As regards the way in which the planning process was initiated, and by whom, we find that the 1874 ordinances represent a major watershed, in that towns were now enjoined to pro-

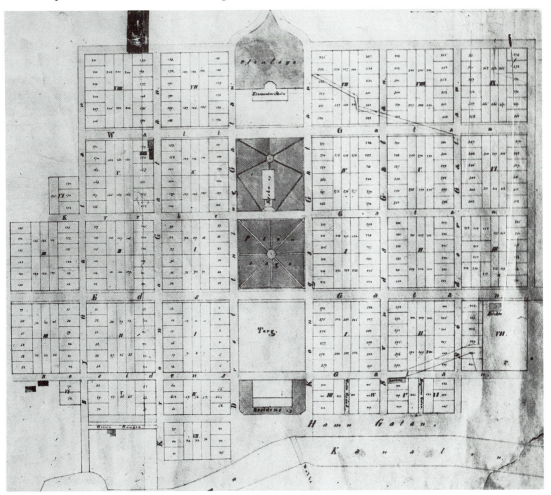

Figure 5.10. Vänersborg, plan drawn by a surveyor under the auspices of canal engineer Nils Ericson for the reconstruction of the town after a fire in 1834. The major change is that a row of blocks through the middle of the town has been replaced by un-built space for reasons of fire security (cf. figure 5.5). At the same time, however, the town acquired an elegant belt of parkland where public buildings could be located. *Source:* Byggnadsnämndens arkiv, Vänersborg.

duce and adopt town plans. Previously such plans were rare except following some devastating fire, as in Vänersborg in 1834 (figure 5.10), Karlstad in 1865 and Gävle in 1869 (figures 5.11 and 5.12) to mention only a few of the most familiar examples. Even after 1875 major fires were often the triggering factor, as in Sundsvall and Umeå in 1888.

Even before the ordinances were passed, however, there were a few cases when planning was initiated although there had been no fire. The two largest cities in the country, Stockholm and Göteborg, are instances of this. As early as 1857 it had been proposed in the Stockholm local council (predecessor of the city council) that a plan should be produced. However, it was only when the city governor (government representative in the capital, roughly equivalent to the prefect in Paris) took action, that work began in 1863, although another seventeen years were to pass before definite plans were ratified (see below). In 1862 a noted town-planning competition was arranged in Göteborg. Only a few years after the great

competition for the Ringstrasse area in Vienna, this was the first such competition in Sweden and it resulted in a town plan ratified in 1866. In both Stockholm and Göteborg the main motive for these planning activities was probably the rapid expansion that was expected, and in both cases influential individuals appear to have been important in pushing action through.

Umeå should also be mentioned in this context; a proposal for extending the town plan was commissioned in 1863 and was approved the following year (Eriksson, 1975). The need to expand was certainly a motive force in this case, but inspiration also seems to have come from Vaasa on the other side of the Gulf of Bothnia, a town which had been moved after a fire in 1852 and rebuilt on a new site according to a 'modern' plan (see pp. 67–68).

The 1874 ordinances launched a wave of intensive planning in Swedish towns. Within a period of five years a large number of plans were ratified. (see graph opposite). These activities were largely impelled by directives from above. In many places however planning discussions

Figure 5.11. Photo of Gävle after the fire of 1869. Great fires were recurrent events in the history of Swedish towns, and an important prerequisite of the regulation plans. *Source:* Gävle kommuns centralarkiv, Gävle.

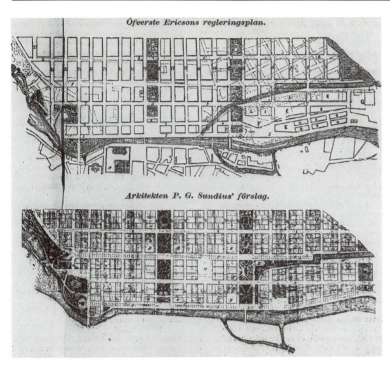

Öfverste Ericsons regleringsplan.

Arkitekten P. G. Sundius' förslag.

Figure 5.12. Gävle. Two alternative proposals for the regulation
plans after the fire of 1869: above,
by the engineer Nils Ericson (cf.
figure 5.10), below, by the
architect P. G. Sundius. The
basic structure is the same in the
two proposals, except that Sundius has one row of blocks less.
Source: Gävle kommuns centralarkiv, Gävle.

continued even after the obligatory plan was
complete, and in the following five-year periods
many plans were ratified as well (see graph).
Obviously a growing number of local government politicians were recognizing that well-
organized urban expansion was impossible
without physical planning, and that plans could
not be established once and for all but must be
adjusted as conditions changed.

A major reason why so many plans had to be
revised and extended was substandard suburban building in many expanding communities
outside the planning zone. In these areas the
ordinances imposed no restrictions and it was
possible to build without permits. With their
poor sanitary conditions and the combination of
overpopulation and poverty these unplanned
shanty towns, usually outside but sometimes
even within the legal urban boundaries, represented a serious problem in many towns. The
need to expand and a wish to inhibit the growth
of substandard suburban areas, were probably
the main motives behind the creation of new

plans. But there were other problems which
also generated a demand for town plans, or
which anyway often came up in planning
discussions, such as the location of railway stations and their connection with a possible har-

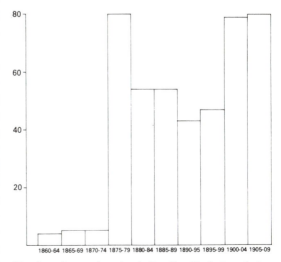

Number of town plans (excluding Stockholm) ratified in
the five-year periods 1860–1909. *Source:* Hall, 1984.

bour and the main part of the town, and the siting of other public buildings. The question of industrial location, on the other hand, still played only a minor role in the planning debate, and it seems to have been generally assumed that any major industrial establishments belonged outside the planned urban areas. But as industrialization proceeded, the question of the location of factories and workshops became increasingly important. And around 1900 that new ideas about town planning began to become more widespread (cf. below). At this time any town that wanted to keep up with developments had to have new plans made, even if their earlier official plans had not yet been realized.

Who was responsible for all these projects? The great majority of the plans were produced by ordinary land surveyors and engineers. The following list from the period 1850–1910 gives some idea of the professional background of the men behind the ratified projects (for sources, see Hall, 1984, pp. 144 *et. seq.*; the table follows the titles appearing on the plans, hence the mixture of titles referring to a position and titles indicating a particular type of competence).

City engineers	50
Other engineers	12
Land surveyors	50
Architects	8
Officers	8
Others of documented occupations	5
No documented occupation	38
Total	171

Thus, together with the city engineers, the land surveyors represented the biggest group. The boundary line between land surveyors and engineers was flexible, however: many city engineers were trained in land surveying, and it was probably by no means unusual for members of the surveyor corps to be appointed city engineers. In other words, the land surveyors were probably more dominant than the figures would suggest.

Of the 171 planners listed, the overwhelming majority had been responsible for a single planning job in one town. Only nine were active in more than two towns (though the statistics are not complete). Thus the great majority of 'planners' cannot have had much experience of planning. Nor does the subject seem to have been included in the training of the relevant professional groups.

The first person who tried to carve out a profile for himself as a professional planner was the architect Per Georg Sundius (1823–1900), who made plans for several towns between the mid-1860s and the early 1880s. He can be described as the first real town planner in Sweden after Anders Torstensson. During the 1870s he was so busy that the authorities in Södertälje threatened to remove him from his job, to compel him to complete the proposal already contracted. Sundius's special interest in planning had probably been roused during a couple of years spent in practice with G. T. Chiewitz, city architect of Turku and author of several Finnish town plans (see chapter 3, p. 68). He may also have been inspired by a visit to the international exhibition in London in 1862.

The next architect to interest himself particularly in planning was Per Olof Hallman (1869–1941), who was active from the 1890s. More even than Sundius, Hallman deserves to be classified as a professional town planner. He made plans for over seventy towns and other communities, he published a great many articles and essays on the subject, he was awarded Sweden's first academic post in the planning field in 1897 (as part-time lecturer at the Royal Institute of Technology), and in 1922 he became Stockholm's first director of town planning. On several occasions Hallman collaborated with Fredrik Sundbärg (1860–1913), who also produced plans of his own. Nils Gellerstedt (1875–1961), by profession a civil engineer, was also the author of a great many plans. His numerous projects included a prize-winning entry in the Canberra competition in 1911; the

Finnish architect Eliel Saarinen was also awarded a prize in this noted competition (see chapter 3, p. 77).

Mention should be made of one more person in this context, although his work belongs largely to a later phase, namely Albert Lilienberg (1879–1967), who worked under Hallman for a while and became the chief city engineer of Göteborg in 1907. Like Hallman he received a great many commissions, and during the second decade of the present century he succeeded his master as the leading debater and writer on planning issues in the country. The international exhibition on urban development, which was part of the Göteborg Jubilee Exhibition in 1923, was largely his work.

In some cases town-planning competitions were arranged in order to generate projects, as in Göteborg in 1862 and 1901, in Karlstad in 1865, in Helsingborg in 1906, in Trollhättan in 1907 and in Stockholm for the Katarina area in 1909. The most important of these, the second Göteborg competition, was won by Hallman together with Fredrik Sundbärg.

Committees were often appointed, but generally to comment on or to choose between proposals made by others. In one case at least a committee of this kind produced its own alternative. This was the committee headed by Albert Lindhagen, who submitted the 1866 proposal for a general plan for Stockholm, the most grandiose Swedish planning project of the nineteenth century.

How were town-planning issues decided in the municipalities? In this context the municipal reform of 1862 represents a major turning-point. After the reform the city council became the highest decision-making authority, but various units with preparatory functions as well as *ad hoc* committees were also involved in the decision process. However a distinction must be made between those occasions when planning was launched after a fire, and other cases. In the first situation there was a compelling reason for getting a plan approved as quickly as possible,

while in the second there was no similar pressure for speed and the decision process was sometimes fairly lengthy, not infrequently dragging on for several years. Detailed studies have been made of two such decision processes, leading in one case to the approval of plans for Stockholm (Selling, 1970; cf. also Hall, 1986) and in the other for Södertälje (Gelotte, 1980).

In the Stockholm example the process can be divided into three phases: first an initial planning phase lasting almost four years (1863–66) during which two proposals were prepared, followed by seven years when work was at a standstill (1866–74), and finally a discussion and decision phase lasting almost another seven years (1874–80). Thus seventeen years passed between the initiation of the planning activities and the final approval of the plans. During the last phase the issue made its slow way through the municipal system, waiting for comments and delayed by alternative proposals, tablings and reservations. The plan for Norrmalm, for example, came before eleven city council meetings during 1877–78. The decision process seems to have been chaotic: the broad outlines became swamped in an endless series of votes about the width and length of streets; majorities were often minute, and varied in composition from one item to the next. And when it came to the handling of planning issues, Södertälje seems to have been a Stockholm in miniature. The idea of a town plan was put forward in the spring of 1875 but the plan itself was finally approved five years later after numerous committees had been appointed, comments submitted and meetings held.

The examples mentioned here are probably fairly representative of the way town-planning issues were handled in Swedish towns at the time. One may well wonder why planning issues aroused so much passion. Several factors probably came into it. First, there was no established party system as yet. Council members could not cite a party line in support of their arguments; on the other hand they were not tied down by such lines and could thus vote freely on every separate question. Secondly, planning was not yet regarded as a task for professional experts. Anybody could – and obviously did – have ideas about how streets should be laid out. General conservatism and opposition to change also came into the picture. And it was always difficult to push through expensive projects which might mean an increase in taxes. The cheaper alternative could generally count on support from the thrifty or the parsimonious, whatever it might mean. Moreover, many people simply opposed the idea that towns should embark on such lengthy undertakings as the execution of town plans.

The decision process was further complicated by speculation. The municipal franchise was graded according to income and capital, and extensive real estate holdings thus gave many votes. Property-owning interests were consequently in a strong position in the various municipal organizations, and at the time it was barely regarded as immoral or even disquieting if people used inside information about the town's plans for their own gain, or even if they sought to favour their own private economic interests when participating in the municipal decision-making process. Further, the significant role often played in the decision process by politicians with leading roles in industry is evident.

Once a town plan had been adopted, it had to be submitted to the government for ratification. The most important element in the subsequent examination was the submission received from the Board of Public Works and Buildings. This Board appears to have shown great interest in the planning proposals, and particularly in seeing that the prescriptions contained in the building ordinances were observed, with regard to such things as street widths, and so on. But other points were also raised, and serious objections were sometimes made to the plans adopted by the towns. In some cases the towns bowed to the authority of the central Board and accepted the changes suggested, but in others the original plan was retained, and it was by no means certain that the government would then follow the recommendations of its own official body. Sometimes town plans were actually ratified in spite of the outright opposition of the Board. Sundsvall provides an example of this. After the fire in 1888 the central office set its face against the town's request to be allowed to retain the old street widths in breach of the building ordinances; the government accepted Sundsvall's point of view.

To make town plans is one thing, to realize them is another. In principle the municipalities had, and have, two alternative ways of dealing with approved plans. One was to leave the initiative to the property-owners and let them determine the speed of implementation. In other words, in the case of built-up areas it was a question of trusting to self-regulation, and in the case of new areas it meant laying out streets, squares etc. as exploitation proceeded. The second was to make an active effort to realize the plan, but even after the 1907 Town Planning Act this required extensive land acquisitions. A property-owner could not and still cannot be forced to implement a plan. Most towns chose the passive line; not without good reason did Sundius declare in a memorandum to his proposal for Södertälje that a 'thoroughgoing fire' was needed before a 'modern' town could be built. In Stockholm, on the contrary, the problem was attacked with great energy; around 1900 the realization of the plans was one of the great municipal campaigns.

Planning Principles and Urban Building Ideas

During the period in question, 1850–1910, two schools of thought involving diametrically opposed sets of planning ideas succeeded one another. The first school, which was predominant until roughly the turn of the century, continued to favour the right-angled pattern of blocks and streets which had been standard in Sweden since the seventeenth century at least, although there had been an increase in scale with broader streets and larger blocks. Naturally planning in the nineteenth century also differed in other ways from that of earlier centuries: for example, new types of building and building complexes such as railway stations now had to be included, and some attempts at zoning were being made. New elements included broad streets with trees down the middle, referred to in the building ordinances as 'esplanades' (see p. 189), as well as public gardens and other planted areas; tree-lined streets and parks had of course existed earlier, but not as part of a mandatory standard. Many features, however, were still in the tradition of earlier planning, for example the rationalistic approach, the desire for order and clarity and the consequent tendency to organize a plan as systematically as possible with the help of straight streets and right-angled blocks, to be divided in turn into standard plots and built to a uniform pattern.

The desire for order and uniformity which also appears in other public spheres during the nineteenth century, is fundamental to the doctrine of urban development underlying the building ordinances of 1874. A paragraph in the ordinances expresses the goal as follows:

A town plan should allow for the space and convenience necessary to mobility and the light and fresh air necessary to health; it should also provide for the greatest possible protection against great fires, and satisfy our sense of beauty with its open spaces, its variety and the neatness of its ornament.

The smooth flow of traffic, a good standard of hygiene, a high level of fire safety, and an attractive and dignified urban landscape were thus proclaimed as the goals to be borne in mind in making an urban plan. The list could well have included the demolition of substandard building, but it was perhaps assumed that this

was implied by the four stated goals. Nor was there any mention of the 'internal security' that was sometimes invoked in other countries (though its importance has been much exaggerated) but which was hardly relevant in Sweden. Nor would such considerations have been appropriate in a statutory text (cf. Hall, 1986).

What, then, was meant by 'beauty' in the context of an urban landscape? This question had been answered by Edelsvärd when as early as 1859 he wrote: 'That which is useful and appropriate to its purpose is also the most beautiful', and: 'How much aesthetic pleasure, how much elevation of the spirit, is thrown away in the confusion, the congestion and the ugliness which still reign in so many of our smaller towns.' It was the conviction of the times that uniformity and rectangularity, and open spaces in the shape of orderly streets, squares and parks between the blocks, helped to enhance a town while also making it a healthier and more functional place. 'Neo-baroque' features such as closing a street perspective with a visual focus, on the other hand, never aroused much interest.

The broad, straight thoroughfare was regarded as a universal means of achieving the stated goals. Such streets allowed optimal traffic flow, they stopped fires from spreading, and they were thought to syphon off insalubrious or infected air. At the same time they were regarded as dignified and aesthetically pleasing. Further, when streets of this kind were cut through the old quarters of a town, they provided an opportunity for demolishing substandard building, although this was hardly a matter of much importance except in Stockholm. The pleasing aspect as well as the sanitary and fire-safety qualities of these streets could also be enhanced by the addition of trees. The building ordinances distinguish between two types of street: the ordinary street which in a new district had to be at least 18 m broad, and the main street or 'esplanade' which was really two streets divided by trees; these were to 'cut across the town, if possible in several places and in several directions'. Ring roads round the edge of the urban area featured in several planning proposals, but they were not made mandatory in the building ordinances (in Norrköping parts of a grand ring road project were actually carried out). It should be noted, however, that the central government's insistence on broad streets was by no means always greeted with unmitigated enthusiasm at the local level, any more than it had been in earlier centuries. As we have seen, Sundsvall succeeded in retaining its old narrower streets after a fire in 1888, claiming that the regular streets in other towns had 'lost their character of commercial vitality'.

Some projects were intended as show-pieces illustrating various ideas about the ideal town. A model plan, dated 1859, for a station community by A. W. Edelsvärd published in Sweden's only technical journal at the time, is an interesting example. Even in a European context the plan is a creditable attempt at designing a rationally organized community (figure 5.13). Of more practical importance, however, was a series of plates published in 1875 as a kind of illustrative complement to the building ordinances. It was compiled by Albert Lindhagen for the government (although the idea may well have been Lindhagen's originally), and sent to all the municipalities and

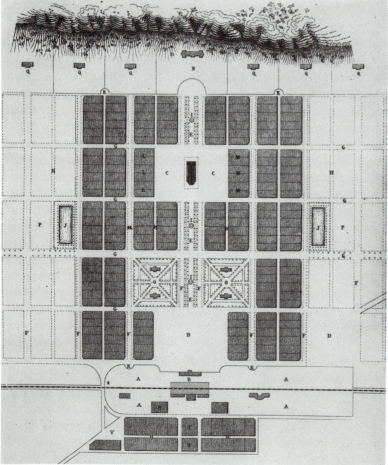

Figure 5.13. A. W. Edelsvärd's proposal for a railway town. Typical of contemporary ideals for urban planning is the great open square in front of the railway station and the tree-lined central thoroughfare, which divides the town symmetrically in two and links squares and parks. The blocks have been given a uniform design and possible extensions of the plan are indicated. Warehouses, workshops etc. are located on the other side of the railway. *Source: Tidskrift för Byggnadskonst och Ingeniörsvetenskap,* 1859.

authorities concerned in order to 'disseminate knowledge of good town planning'. The work included eight Finnish towns, a rather Utopian project for an ideal circular town, and four sheets devoted to detailed suggestions for blocks and plots. The proposal of the Lindhagen committee for Stockholm was certainly another important source of inspiration. The proposal was published together with a detailed explanatory commentary, which can be regarded in turn as a kind of preparatory study for the building ordinances.

Although most nineteenth-century town-planning projects have a number of basic features in common, there are significant differences in quality. Some proposals are carefully prepared; their aim is to achieve functionally optimal solutions while paying due consideration to topography and to appropriate links and relationships between new and existing urban areas. Per Georg Sundius's project belongs to this category (figure 5.12). But others appear to have been knocked together hastily at the drawing-board; stereotyped block networks are scattered around without thought for topography or existing buildings. Not infrequently the new areas are also drawn on a disproportionately large scale, perhaps to make the proposal more attractive to local patriots on the council. The projects for Sigtuna and Kalmar (figure 5.14) are examples of this type.

The ideas which pervaded nineteenth-century planning in Sweden were by no means unique to this country. Similar ideas and ambitions can be found at much the same time, or a little earlier, in most parts of Europe (cf. Hall, 1986). Lindhagen, however, appears to have derived most of his ideas from Finland, and thus indirectly from Russia where a great many towns had been founded, or their plans regulated, during the second half of the eighteenth and the beginning of the nineteenth centuries, often following elegant plans prepared centrally or in line with central directives. In the course of the nineteenth century many towns in Finland

were regulated along similar lines, but their plans were simpler, consisting of right-angled street networks and fairly broad 'esplanades' (on Finnish planning and its links with Russia, see chapter 3, pp. 68–69). Lindhagen was not alone in being inspired by Finnish town planning regulations. As we have seen, Umeå's plan was influenced by the new town plan for Vaasa and Finnish planning also provided an important source of inspiration for Sundius.

The specifically Nordic connotation of the term 'esplanade' goes back to Johan Albrecht Ehrenström's 1812 Helsinki project. Ehrenström included an almost 100-metre broad green belt to separate the wealthy city of brick from the wooden town of the poor, and this was called *Esplanaden* (the esplanade), thus following French usage. Subsequently, however, first in Finland and later in Sweden, the word came to mean a broad thoroughfare with trees down the middle. In Sweden the term became generally accepted only after publication of the building ordinances, but the idea had appeared earlier. The open area that cut through Vänersborg to the width of a block after the fire in 1834 (figure 5.10) recalls the esplanade in Helsinki and was certainly inspired by it, although the Vänersborg version did not function as a physical social barrier like the Finnish prototype. Two similar broad esplanades can be seen in Ericson's and Sundius's 1869 project for Gävle (figure 5.4). One of these was realized according to the original intentions, while the other was replaced by the railway running through the town. After the building ordinances came into effect new esplanades were generally planned on a more modest scale, as broad streets rather than green belts.

It would be interesting to discover just how much impact the plans ratified in the latter part of the nineteenth century had on the physical development of the towns concerned. A well-founded answer to this question would require a lot more studies than are available today. But towns probably vary a great deal in this respect:

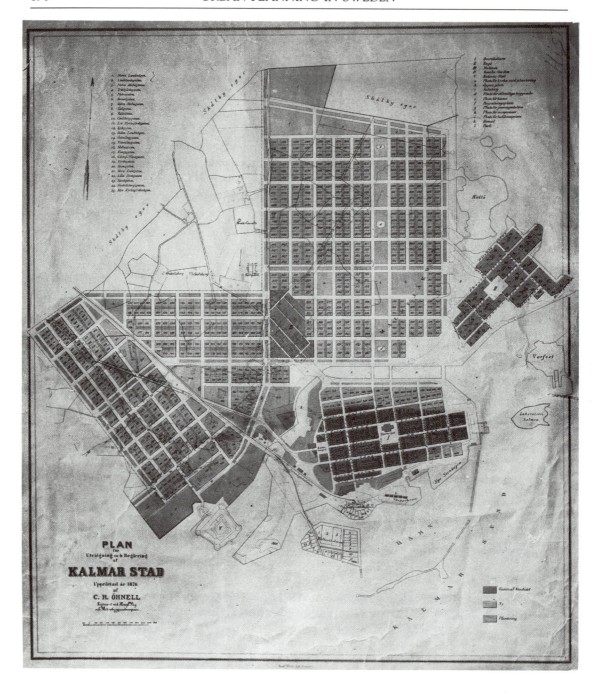

Figure 5.14. Kalmar, town plan from 1876 by an officer attached to the Road and Canal Construction Corps. The plan was a result of the 1874 building ordinances, which made town plans compulsory. Below right, the seventeenth-century town (cf. figure 5.4) with the cathedral. To the north and west an over-dimensioned gridiron street system criss-crossed by 'esplanades'. *Source*: Planarkivet, Statens planverk.

where a town had been totally destroyed by fire, the plans naturally made a great impact; in towns which were expanding fast during the period in question, some districts bear a strong stamp of nineteenth-century planning; and again, in towns which were growing more slowly or not at all, the plans would carry little weight.

Towards the end of the nineteenth century new planning ideas began to attract notice. Their foremost advocate was Per Olof Hallman, whom we have mentioned above. In essays, articles and lectures Hallman attacked the prevailing principles. From his first appearance in a letter to a daily newspaper in 1894, the main lines of his programme are clear. He opens the argument with a question: 'What is urban planning?' Does it mean 'levelling everything regardless, so that planners can lay out all the streets as they want, in neat straight lines, intersected at right angles by side streets just as straight?' He then points out that people in Germany have started to question this way of 'manufacturing' towns, and he mentions the master who throughout his career was to remain his special idol and personal authority, namely Camillo Sitte. He also refers to Karl Henrici and Joseph Stübben. Only a year later, after travelling on the continent, Hallman began to develop the new ideas with great energy and on a more professional basis. He wrote articles in all kinds of publications, and lectured not only to professional colleagues but also to a wider audience.

The new principles made such a strong impact, and implied such a sharp break with previous ideals, that we would be justified in speaking of a new 'school'. The breakthrough came with the competition in 1901 for a town plan for Göteborg, which was won by Hallman and Fredrik Sundbärg together. During the first ten years of the present century Per Olof Hallman dominated town planning in a manner probably unparalleled in Sweden before or since, and he executed plans for a great many towns and other places. Often it was a case of

projects embracing whole towns; Hallman can be said to be the last person to produce overall town plans in the traditional way. Among many examples can be mentioned projects for Kalmar (figure 5.14), Härnösand and Södertälje. In other cases his plans covered particular districts, residential suburbs or new communities. In this last category special mention should be made of the plan executed together with Gustaf Wickman in 1900 for the new mining community of Kiruna (see Brunnström, 1981).

Hallman's proposals are generally based on a careful study of the terrain, and he was probably the first in Sweden to use town plan models. The idea was to adapt the blocks and street networks to the lie of the land, and to exploit the topographical opportunities for planning a varied urban landscape. Long wearisome perspectives were to be avoided; rather, the urban structure should be based on a series of comprehensible and artistically designed spatial entities and pleasing views. A comparison easily suggests itself between a typical Hallman plan and the billowing curves, the often assymmetrical composition, and the 'natural' organic ornament of contemporary Art Noveau architecture.

This programme was naturally less appropriate to the city world of the multi-storey block. Hallman's plans are generally intended for villas or other small-scale building, often with gardens and forecourts. His ideas had much in common with the garden city movement, and one of his major achievements was the 1908 town plan for the oldest part of the Stockholm garden suburb of Enskede (Stavenow-Hidemark, 1971). The plan shows a striving for visual variety based on open places, winding streets and buildings as visual foci (figure 5.15). The enclosed street spaces intended by Hallman were not realized, however, as most of the buildings were free-standing houses instead of the terraces originally proposed. The plan, which is also well designed functionally with differentiated streets and community buildings in the centre, reflected contemporary ideas in

Germany and England and was granted the honour of publication in *Der Städtebau* in 1908, which in turn brought an appreciative comment from Raymond Unwin. Hallman also made plans for some parts of Stockholm's inner city, such as the Rödaberg area (figure 5.17(*b*)), where it had not previously been possible to build because of the rocky terrain. In this case, however, the plan was revised before being implemented. Perhaps the district known as 'Lärkstaden' in Stockholm near Engelbrekt's church provides the most faithful expression of Hallman's intentions.

Although Hallman became the foremost advocate of the new principles, he was not alone in adopting them. Plans of a similar kind were also produced by Fredrik Sundbärg, Nils Gellerstedt and Albert Lilienberg. Among the most satisfying of the communities and districts planned during this period is the Landala dis-

trict in Göteborg with its owner-occupied homes. Here Lilienberg produced a plan which is clear and comprehensible, yet also flexible and varied. The charming overall impression of this piece of small-scale urban planning is greatly enhanced by the standard house type, designed by Carl Westman, which accords so well with the plan.

Although several urban monographs have discussed various of Hallman's projects, no systematic survey has yet been made of the whole of his extensive production, and it is therefore difficult to assess his real impact on Swedish towns. But it is probably true to say that he had more influence as a propagandist and source of inspiration than as the author of completed projects. The First World War put a stop to most building activities, and during the 1920s Hallman's plans were largely overtaken by events: as road traffic increased, the straight

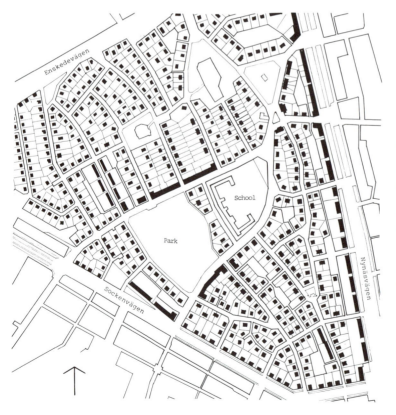

Figure 5.15. Enskede, a suburban district of Stockholm. The street network in the oldest part of this suburb essentially follows Per Olof Hallman's plan from 1908. Hallman had envisaged that most of the buildings would consist of terraced housing, however, and that the streets would thus form an enclosed space. But at the time there was no interest in terraced houses and the area came to consist instead of detached or semi-detached villas. With its streets smoothly adapted to the topography and its series of self-contained gardens within the blocks, the plan provides a happy combination of ideas stemming from Sitte and from English garden cities.

thoroughfare once again came into its own. And both speculators and municipal authorities probably often demanded a more efficient exploitation of the land than Hallman's plans allowed. Nor did his often rather elaborate and sometimes even slightly stereotyped picturesque effects appear to be appreciated in the wave of neo-classicism, which characterized the 1920s, as they once had been.

Albert Lilienberg was much more successful in adapting to changing ideals. As early as 1912 he distanced himself in remarkably categorial terms from the ideas which Hallman represented, and his own plans became stricter and more technical, but also more mechanical. Lilienberg was the first to exploit systematically the opportunity provided by the new Town Planning Act to include building regulations in his plans. It is significant that in 1927, when Hallman's appointment as Director of Town Planning in Stockholm was not renewed, he was succeeded by Lilienberg.

A survey of planning activities may well give a somewhat misleading impression of the actual part played by planning in shaping the physical environment. It should therefore be emphasized that a significant proportion of urban growth was taking place outside the planned areas and was not subject to any kind of public planning.

THE PLANNING OF MODERN SWEDEN

Some Aspects of Social and Economic Development

In Sweden the inter-war years fall into two quite distinct periods, before and after the beginning of the 1930s. The years of international economic crisis at the beginning of the 1920s were followed by a period of economic expansion and growing foreign trade, dominated increasingly by paper and pulp, iron ore and steel, and the mechanical engineering and electronics industries, i.e. just those industries which were to become the basis for Sweden's growing pros-

perity. Universal suffrage had been introduced after the First World War, but had not led to any immediate reforms. The 1920s were a time of weak and frequently changing minority governments.

Like other countries Sweden was badly hit by the economic crisis at the beginning of the 1930s. One important result of this was the political rapprochement between the Social Democrats and the Agrarian Party, which in 1936 finally gave the country a majority government. It was then possible to introduce some social reforms, helped by the continuing economic growth. There was now a strong social democratic emphasis on 'the People's Home' or *Folkhemmet*, marking a shift in interest away from the establishment of a socialist system towards successive improvements in living conditions. Sweden was to be like 'a good home' for its people, providing them with full security and a reasonable standard of living. Economic principles were also invoked: according to the scholars who formed the so-called 'Stockholm school of economics' and, somewhat later, to J. M. Keynes, depression should be countered by expansive policies which generated greater purchasing power for all.

During the 1930s industry overtook agriculture in terms of number employed, and by the end of the decade the service industries had also drawn level. There was a close connection between this development and the rapid urbanization and growth of the urban areas. Twenty-three communities were granted town status between 1911 and 1940, and the town-based population increased from 25 per cent of the total population in 1910 to 30 per cent in 1920, 33 per cent in 1930 and 37.5 per cent in 1940. The proportion of the population living in administratively defined 'urban areas', that is *köpingar* and *municipalsamhällen* (see p. 178), increased more slowly, from 5 per cent in 1910 to 7 per cent in 1940. It was not until after the middle of the 1940s that the combined population of the towns and other 'urban areas' passed the 50 per cent barrier, and another ten years were to pass before half the population was living in towns proper. But if we disregard the legal classifications, and distinguish instead between densely populated and thinly populated areas, the trend assumes another shape: as early as the mid-1930s, more than half the population of the country was living in densely populated areas (figures quoted from *Historisk statistik för Sverige*, I).

When we look back at social developments in Sweden after the Second World War, there seems to be a major break around 1970. The 1950s and 1960s were characterized by rapid growth in productivity due to such factors as good raw material supplies, a quiet labour market with little in the way of serious conflict, the influx of cheap immigrant labour (cheap at any rate to start with), advanced industrial technology, and a continuous easing of customs duties and other barriers to trade. The increase in production contributed to what was virtually the doubling of real wages, the introduction of shorter working hours and longer holidays, new and more comprehensive social insurance, basic allowances to certain categories such as families with children, and the expansion of many parts of the social services.

Particularly during the 1960s it appears that most politicians and business leaders and planners assumed that the economic growth would continue largely uninterrupted throughout the foreseeable future. The prevailing attitude, as somebody succinctly put it, was that 'the future will be like the present, but bigger and better'. But although the curve was expected to continue to climb more or less automatically, it was still felt that developments should be helped along and speeded up by various kinds of rationalization, particularly the merging of smaller units into larger ones. It was an axiom that a larger unit was more efficient and would be more profitable than a small one, and not only in industry. The philosophy of 'big is better', influenced by the goals and methods of business economics, was also applied to municipalities (which were reduced from about 2,500 to 280), to residential areas, to agriculture (for several years running, an average of one farm was being shut down every hour), and to schools, hospitals and prisons. Crucial to this development was the coordinated wage negotiation system and the 'solidaristic wage policy' fostered by the Swedish Trade Union Confederation. Industrial and regional wage differentials were systematically opposed, with the result that company closures and mergers followed one another more quickly than would otherwise have been the case.

With hindsight, what seems particularly noticeable about the 1960s is the basic consensus which persisted despite certain obvious disagreements between industry, the trade unions, the social democratic government and leading opposition politicians, that rationalization and industrial growth would lead to a better society, and that growth in consumption was perhaps the most important criterion by which to judge that society was in fact becoming 'better'. Almost everyone would eventually be living in newly built homes in the major urban areas, and would be able to afford a car and a holiday cottage. Little interest was shown in the possible negative effects of all this in the way of environmental pollution, the squandering of natural resources, the impoverishment of small communities which lost their industries in mergers, the decline of former cultivated areas into scrubland, and so on. In so far as such consequences were noted at all, they were dismissed as a necessary but reasonable price to pay for greater prosperity.

We are therefore justified in speaking of the 'record years' and in identifying a kind of 'sixties ideology' which, as we shall see below, has affected urban planning and development and, consequently, the buildings which we have today. A large proportion of the Swedish population lives, works, or is being cared for in buildings dating from the 1960s and 1970s.

In the early 1970s several of the previous trends were broken, in Sweden as elsewhere. But the break may have been perceived with particular force in Sweden because the preceding expansion had been so rapid. The energy crisis and the rising price of oil became identified in the mind of the general public as the main cause of the change; and it was of course an important factor. But equally important was the fact that industrial development in Sweden had fallen behind, and that the market for several of the previous cornerstones of the country's wealth, such as iron ore, paper pulp and several manufactured products, had declined. The high wage level – there was a 67 per cent increase in labour costs between 1974 and 1976 – was also making Swedish products less competitive, not least on the domestic market. The Swedish ready-made clothing industry, for example, has been almost completely destroyed by the import of cheap products.

The problems were long regarded as a temporary difficulty due to fluctuations in the business cycle; sooner or later everything would return to normal. In other words growth would start up again. In 1976 the first non-socialist government for more than forty years came to power, eager to deny the Social Democrats the opportunity of blaming non-socialist policies of unemployment and stagnating living standards. An attempt was made to maintain demand and employment at a high level by way of deficit budgeting, and problem industries were feather-bedded with the help of government loans and aid on a scale undreamt of before. Unemployment was increasingly masked by a variety of employment schemes. By the end of the 1970s the situation was looking grim, as the budget deficit was swelling rapidly and the national debt was growing.

In this situation the government sought to improve Sweden's competitive status by devaluing the Swedish krona. The most recent and most substantial devaluation followed on the heels of the social democratic election victory in 1982. This drastic remedy, combined with the protracted business boom during the 1980s, resulted in a new economic upswing, but without solving any of the underlying structural problems.

For a long time the state and the municipalities continued to act on the assumption that revenues would go on growing; but earlier commitments were ensuring automatic increases in cost, even without any new reforms. No effective reappraisal of public undertakings had been made during the 1970s, and there was very little during the 1980s either. Another major obstacle to any efficient reorganization of the Swedish economy has been and still is the behaviour of the unions. Spurred on partly by internal rivalry, the unions have succeeded in winning wage increases unmatched by any corresponding improvement in productivity.

Towards the end of the 1980s storm clouds once again began to gather, in the shape of a low rate of growth, a deficit in the balance of trade, a rapid rise in prices and heavy pressure for wage increases, while at the same time the public services were being criticized and questioned in a way that would once have been unthinkable. There is no doubt whatsoever that 'the Swedish model' faces the prospect of a dramatic reappraisal during the 1990s.

From the beginning of 1971 the 'town' was abolished as an administrative unit and all municipalities acquired the same legal status. At the time when the towns ceased to exist on paper, they accounted for 59 per cent of the population of the country. If we disregard administrative boundaries and include as urban areas all agglomerations of at least 200 inhabitants, we find that 65 per cent of the population lived in such areas in 1950, 72.5 per cent in 1960, and 81.5 per cent in 1970. At the beginning of the 1970s the population curve in the urban areas flattened out; by 1980 the proportion was 83 per cent (figures supplied by the Swedish Central Bureau of Statistics).

These general figures naturally conceal big

variations between different regions, different types of place, and different districts in the towns. Thus an increasing proportion of this urban growth has occurred in suburbs which in the larger cities often lie outside the municipal boundaries, while the numbers in the town centres have declined. This trend was particularly marked in Stockholm, where the population of the inner city fell by half between 1950 and 1980, and the combined population of the whole municipality began to decline as early as 1950 (see table 5.1). However, over the last years the decline of the central areas has levelled off and been replaced by an increase (table 5.1), due at any rate partly to the clearances and

renovations of the last few decades, and to the revived attraction of the central districts in the large towns as places to live.

During the later 1960s engineering industry accounted for a little over 40 per cent of Sweden's exports. It has been shown that in all the places which were growing most rapidly during the 1950s and 1960s, there was a strong engineering presence (Nilsson, 1983). Similarly, the growth of the service sector, which during the 1960s overtook industry as regards number employed, has meant that places possessing service institutions, primarily in the public services, are also expanding. It is significant that the urban municipality which grew most rapidly in the late 1980s, namely Uppsala, has an unusually high proportion of public employees, who account for over half the working population of the municipality. In all these ways, developments in Sweden have probably largely coincided with the current trends in the Western world.

Table 5.1 Population trends in Sweden's three largest cities 1950–85 (in thousands).

| | Stockholm | | | |
	Urban core	Inner city	Municipality	Greater Stockholm
1950	19	440	746	1004
1960	11	343	808	1162
1970	8	269	740	1345
1980	4	226	647	1387
1985	4	236	659	1435

| | Göteborg | | | |
	Urban core	Inner city	Municipality	Greater Göteborg
1950	29	266	354	496
1960	21	239	405	565
1970	10	171	452	678
1980	7	138	431	693
1985	7	142	425	704

| | Malmö | | | |
	Urban core	Inner city	Municipality	Greater Malmö
1950	21	144	192	328
1960	16	165	229	369
1970	13	126	266	445
1980	10	97	234	453
1985	11	94	230	458

Source: Population figures from Sveriges officiella statistik. The division between urban core and inner city is tentatively indicated.

Building Legislation and the Planning System in the Twentieth Century

The Development of the Legal Framework

In 1907, as we have seen, Sweden's first Town Planning Act came into operation. At the time it was thought to be progressive and radical. But changes and additions were soon being discussed. For many reasons – rapid urbanization, a growing demand for higher standards of housing and environment, better communications and a gradual shift in attitudes towards the role of the public sector in creating and maintaining the physical social setting – planning and building legislation have been the subject of almost constant investigation and alteration since the beginning of the century. Let us consider some of the main stages in this development.

By the time the Town Planning Act was passed in 1907, the 1874 building ordinances which pre-dated the main wave of urbanization had become out-of-date. A committee was therefore appointed to suggest new ordinances. But almost twenty-five years of discussion and investigation were to pass before new ordinances finally came into effect in 1931, when a new Town Planning Act was also passed. This did not involve any very radical changes. The unstable political situation may have been one reason for the long delay, and for the fact that important problems of outline planning, for instance, were left half solved. At the beginning of the 1940s the investigatory machinery rolled into action again (Government Official Report *SOU*, 1945: 15), and by 1947 it was time for the third generation of building statutes since the beginning of the century. In the 1947 Building Act and building ordinances, regulations for planning and building were brought together. The distinction between the Act and the ordinances reflects a procedural difference: the Act, passed by Riksdag and government together, provided the basic provisions and regulated the exercise of authority, while the building ordinances were issued by the government and dealt mainly with implementation. A major novelty in the 1947 Building Act was that plans were required for the development of any 'densely built-up area', and densely built-up areas were defined as all areas 'requiring special arrangements to provide common amenities', such as arrangements for traffic, water or sewage. This made it easier for the municipalities to control the inception of urban areas as regards both timing and location. The rapid legislation process on this occasion, resulting in fundamental changes, was probably connected with the strong position of the social democratic movement at that time and its belief in planning and public controls.

The 1947 building ordinances were extremely detailed, and they were joined by various provisions and restrictions in other statutes. Complaints about the complications and muddle were legion, and during the 1950s the possibility was examined of simplifying the whole body of building legislation (Government Official Report *SOU*, 1957: 21). This resulted in the 1959 building ordinances. During the 1950s and 1960s various changes were made in the Building Act, to adapt it to the rapid growth of the urban areas and to the large scale of new building. Other new laws also appeared which in various ways affected planning conditions, land use and building (for example the Nature Conservancy Act). One controversial problem concerned the areas which were most attractive for outdoor activities: if these were not to be swallowed up by private building, more effective controls over the rapid spread of second homes would be needed. Towards the end of the 1960s work started on national physical planning (see below), something which had no base in the Building Act.

For these and other reasons a radical revision and coordination of building legislation was becoming increasingly urgent. In 1968 a committee was appointed to look over the planning system and to coordinate all provisions about planning and building in one set of laws. However, the results which were published in 1974 (Government Official Report *SOU*, 1974: 17) did not lead to any legislation, perhaps mainly because the political situation changed with the advent of a non-socialist government in the autumn of 1976. Instead yet another enquiry was launched, resulting in 1979 in a proposal for a new Planning and Building Act (Government Official Report *SOU*, 1979: 65 and 66). After lengthy discussions in all the relevant quarters, which were complicated by several changes in government, the Social Democratic government was finally able to put a bill before the Riksdag in the autumn of 1985 (proposition 1985/86:1). However, the Act contains various controversial points, and it was held up for a long time at the parliamentary committee stage (see *Bostadsutskottets betänkande*, 1986/87: 1). The Conservative Party (*Moderata samlingspartiet*) argued that the Act would give the local government unwarranted new powers at the expense of the individual property-owner and wanted to reject it altogether, while the Liberal Party (*Folkpartiet*) wanted some radical changes introduced. Nonetheless after certain adjustments had been made it was possible to pass the new law with a clear majority in November 1986, after the Social Democrats and the non-socialist Centre Party had reached a compromise. *Plan- och bygglagen* (the Planning and Building Act), in Sweden always referred to as *PBL*, took effect from 1 July 1987.

Municipal Planning Instruments

Ever since the 1874 building ordinances and up to 1987, the *stadsplan* (town plan) had been the basic instrument of planning. However town plans produced in accordance with these ordinances and those produced according to the 1947 Building Act, had little in common with one another apart from their designation. In reality, as a result of changes in both law and praxis, the concept of 'town planning' had shifted away from the division of the planned area into streets and blocks and towards the inclusion of sometimes very detailed directives for land use as well as design of the buildings. A 'town plan' could now sometimes even refer to a single property. The *byggnadsplan* (local building plan) was introduced in 1931 as a simpler alternative to the town plan, aimed mainly at developments in the rural districts.

In the new Planning and Building Act these two planning instruments were replaced by a single instrument, the *detaljplan* (local development plan). Town plans remained in force until they were changed, which implied in principle that a property-owner had the right to build according to a ratified plan, however old it might be. Municipalities have thus had to arrange prohibitions of limited duration, and also ran the risk of having to pay compensation if they wanted to revise plans which new conditions or new values had rendered obsolete. In order to get to grips with this problem, each new

local development plan will have a fixed implementation period of between five and fifteen years. During this period the property-owner's right to implement the plan is guaranteed. After this the plan still applies, but the property-owner no longer has the unconditional right of execution. If the plan is largely unrealized when the time limit runs out, the municipality has the right to acquire the land. This period of implementation is one of the most controversial points in the new Act. One of its refinements is that town plans and local building plans ratified later than 1978 are given five-year periods of implementation, while in the case of older plans the period is regarded as having already run out.

By the 1920s it was obvious that the town planning system needed supplementing by an instrument for outline planning, if the physical expansion of the urban areas was to be controlled rationally and in a longer-term perspective. Fixing in detail the shape of large areas which might not be exploited for several decades was not very efficient, and was anyway more or less impossible. Moreover there was no effective way of preventing urban sprawl on non-planned land, for example in municipalities adjoining the large towns, which meant that many communities subsequently found themselves bearing heavy costs for arranging the necessary roads, water, sewage systems, etc. During the 1920s several new planning instruments were discussed, but were dismissed as being too radical. One result of these discussions, however, was that the 1931 Act included a new instrument for outline planning, known as the *stomplan* (core plan). This instrument proved unwieldy and could be very costly for the town because of the land that had to be acquired, and it thus never had much practical importance.

In 1947 the core plan was replaced by the *generalplan* (masterplan), whose purpose is to provide a general guide to land use for various purposes. Ratified master plans carry certain legal consequences; building permits, for instance, cannot be given in contravention of the intentions of the plan. But not even this planning instrument has acquired the importance intended, and very few master plans have been ratified. Obviously the municipalities have not wanted to circumscribe their own future freedom of action by seeking ratification for their outline plans.

The new Planning and Building Act includes one general municipal planning instrument, namely the *översiktsplan* (structure plan) for the municipality as a whole. According to the new Act every municipality must have such a plan. On its passage through the Riksdag the provisions of the law with respect to this instrument were so modified that it is doubtful whether we can still speak of planning: a 'structure plan' is supposed to specify such interests as 'should be' considered in decisions on land use.

A new instrument which came in with the Planning and Building Act should also be mentioned here, namely *områdesbestämmelser* (local provisions). These, which are approved in essentially the same way as the local development plans, cover such things as rules for considering building permits, developments outside the local development plan, and so on.

Municipal Outline Planning

Municipal planning as applying to the layout and design of residential areas and suburbs, and to clearance and city renewal, calls for sections of their own. Under the present heading we shall briefly consider municipal outline planning (drawing largely on Rudberg, 1981 and 1985 and Folkesdotter, 1987).

As long ago as the 1930s individual towns were making master plans. A notable pioneering effort was Albert Lilienberg's master plan for Stockholm's inner city in 1928, and Bärnhard Sandström's for Borås in 1930. Both were largely concerned with traffic problems. The official introduction of the master plan as a planning instrument in the 1947 Building Act stimulated approaches of this kind, although as

we have seen the plans were not usually ratified and sometimes were not even brought before the Municipal Council for approval. In the first case, i.e. if a plan was approved but not ratified, it became a municipal programme but without the special legal consequences of a ratified master plan, while in the second case it constituted more of a survey to which attention could subsequently be paid as seemed appropriate. We can see an example of this second course of action in the many years of planning activity in Stockholm. This was the biggest initiative of its kind in Sweden, resulting in 1952 in a printed volume running to almost 500 pages but leading to no political decisions (cf. figure 5.16; see also Sidenbladh, 1981).

The purpose of the master plan, as formulated in the building legislation, was to identify the land requirements for dwellings, industry, traffic, recreation etc., which were likely to follow from expected developments, and thus to provide a basis for local development planning. By the middle of the 1960s most towns probably had master plans for certain areas, and in many of them work was in progress on new plans, which tended to be more and more grandiose as the decade drew to a close. At first the projects were frequently commissioned from external consultants, who often had little intimate knowledge of the special problems of the municipality concerned. The plan was often a very standardized and doctrinaire product and there was little impetus for incorporating its intentions into the local development plans. During the 1960s it became more usual for municipal officials to assume responsibility for planning activities, and the plans were consequently more firmly entrenched in local conditions.

At the beginning of the 1970s municipal planning was confronted with new tasks. First, the national physical planning system was making new demands on the municipalities. Secondly, the freedom to build in thinly populated areas was abolished in 1972, which meant that build-

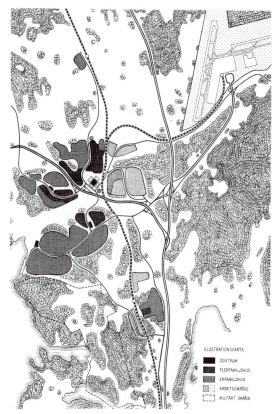

ILLUSTRATIONSKARTA

CENTRUM
FLERFAMILJSHUS
ENFAMILJSHUS
ARBETSOMRÅDE
MILITÄRT OMRÅDE

Figure 5.16. Märsta, master plan from 1960. The centre is surrounded by residential areas situated on higher ground. The major development of Märsta on the northern side of Stockholm was contingent on the proximity of Arlanda, Stockholm's international airport, which was inaugurated that year. (Centrum = centre; Flerfamiljshus = apartment houses; Enfamiljshus = single-family houses; Arbetsområde = commercial and industrial area; Militärt område = military area) *Source:* Åström (1967).

ing permits were needed for all projects apart from agricultural structures, so that all municipalities had to decide what kind of development they wanted in different parts of their area, i.e. they had to embark on some kind of planning for the whole municipality. For these and other reasons the central planning authority, the National Board of Physical Planning and Building, launched two new types of plan, the *markdispositionsplan* (indicative municipal land-use plan) and the *kommunöversikt* (indicative

municipal plan), neither of which were incorporated in the building legislation. The comprehensive municipal land-use plan covers the entire municipal area and indicates the intended use of its different parts. The indicative municipal plan supplements the land-use plan and provides guidelines for the issue of building permits in light of various interests, including such national interests as the conservation of special cultural monuments or environments, or areas of outstanding natural beauty, or the needs of recreation, agriculture and forestry, and the protection of beaches. Plans of this kind have been made in almost all the Swedish municipalities. Although often prepared by external consultants they are more integrated into the day-to-day work of detailed planning and building permits than were the old master plans. The new 'structure plan' which was introduced with the Planning and Building Act is intended to replace these two types of plans.

If any plan designer is to be mentioned individually, it must be the Hungarian architect Fred Forbat. Forbat settled in Sweden in 1938 after working in Germany (under Walter Gropius) and elsewhere, and became the author of normative master plans, in particular a project for Skövde in 1949. Typical of Forbat's plans was a scientific approach which included a critical discussion of the background, a well-prepared analysis of the problems and an account of alternatives, and a lucid presentation of the material and the various proposals. He devoted a good deal of interest to the question of design of the built environment. Forbat also contributed to various publications on outline planning. Uno Åhrén also played a crucial role during the initial period of this planning, but mainly as an investigator, opinion leader and teacher. Quantitatively speaking, the greatest contribution to planning during the 1950s was made by the 'Vattenbyggnadsbyrån', where the architect Sune Lindström was the name best known to the public. More recently this role has been largely taken over by 'K-Konsult', a large consultancy firm owned by the municipal organizations.

Outline planning was undertaken in several countries in the inter-war years, and the contact network over the borders seems to have been well developed. The Bauausstellung in Berlin in 1931 provided a kind of overview of what had been done in towns such as Berlin, Hamburg and Frankfurt over the previous decade. In Sweden, Fred Forbat introduced what he had learnt in Germany, Hungary and the Soviet Union; like Uno Åhrén, he had also been involved in CIAM. Since the war English planning has been a source of inspiration. As early as 1945 the planner Otto Danneskiold-Samsoe published a book entitled *Nutida engelsk samhällsplanering* (Contemporary Community Planning in England). American traffic planning has also affected developments in Sweden.

Regional Planning

In Sweden 'regional planning' has usually referred to planning undertaken by several municipalities together in order to solve their common problems. As long ago as the 1930s Stockholm and its municipal suburbs formed a regional planning association, but it never acquired any very great practical importance. With the 1947 Building Act, the *regionplan* (regional plan) was established as an official planning instrument. Two or more municipalities can draw up a regional plan together, to be ratified by the government. The regional plan is intended to serve as a guide to local planning, but it has no real legal consequences. This planning instrument has never acquired much practical importance either, and only a few plans have even been made. Among these are plans for Eskilstuna, Kalmar, Göteborg, Borås and Sundsvall and their satellite municipalities. Three regional plans have been ratified for the Stockholm area (1958, 1973 and 1978). None of the plans, however, appear to have made much impact. Much discussed was the 1966 draft re-

gional plan for Greater Stockholm; it was a typical 'sixties' vision of a metropolis with ring-roads and intersecting multi-lane motorways. Intermunicipal collaboration in the Stockholm region has been less visionary but more successful in other spheres: working through the County Council, Greater Stockholm's municipalities have jointly succeeded in solving many of the problems that plague big city regions all over the world: local communications, housing, medical care, and so on. The County Council is now ultimately responsible when it comes to regional planning in Greater Stockholm.

The regional planning instrument has been retained, albeit somewhat revised, in the new Planning and Building Act.

Organization of the Planning System

Twentieth-century Swedish planning law has been guided by the principle that physical planning should be primarily a municipal concern, and there has been much talk of the 'municipal planning monopoly'. It has been felt that the state should play a more passive role in the planning process, basically limiting itself to checking that current regulations are obeyed and that municipal plans do not conflict with other legitimate interests.

Within the municipality the Building Board appointed by the Municipal Council has a special responsibility for building activities in that it has the deciding role in granting building permits. In planning, the Board functions as a preparing committee. It deals with the drafting and publication of plan proposals; these have to be on show to the public for a certain length of time, and anyone has the right to make his or her opinions or comments known. After this the Board submits the proposals with its own report to the Municipal Executive Board and thence to the Council for their final approval. The Municipal Executive Board or some particular organ has, however, often acted as principal for the comprehensive municipal planning of the last few decades. In the new Planning and Building Act the municipalities are granted greater freedom to deal with planning issues.

The politically appointed building boards naturally depend on expert officials to deal with planning and building issues. Towards the end of the last century and at the beginning of the present one, an increasing number of towns were acquiring town architects, mainly to deal with building permits and municipal building projects, but also to handle planning issues. In the early years of the century special positions were created in Stockholm and Göteborg to deal with planning issues, and from then on the number of officials concerned with planning continued to increase in both cities. Between 1921 and 1954 Stockholm even had a special Town Planning Board. However, as late as the mid-1940s many towns were still without professional planners, and planning issues were generally handled by the town architects. Today most of the larger municipalities have special planning officers, and in some cases even a special department.

Town plans and local building plans had to be ratified by the County Administration Board (until 1959 the government) to acquire legal effect. The Board could not alter a plan, simply refuse to ratify it. State control over municipal planning – what form it should take and how far it should go – has been one of the hottest topics in the various twentieth-century investigations and reports on planning. In recent years it has been widely held within different political camps that municipal independence should be strengthened, and the state ratification process has consequently been abolished in the new Planning and Building Act. The municipalities are thus acquiring full sovereignty over planning issues, which is one of the most important changes introduced by the new law. However, it is intended that even in future the County Administration Board should play an important part in planning, but only as a consultative and coordinating body. In principle the Board can

intervene with compulsory effect only if a municipal plan is thought to threaten environmental and other national interests, or if plans touch on intermunicipal interests, or if a development is considered unsuitable from the point of view of health or safety. Only the future will show whether, without any real power, these boards can act as an efficacious corrective to municipal shortsightedness. It should be added that the position of the County Administration Board as an organ of state control has already been weakened, in that their executive committees are appointed by the County Council, i.e. by the regional municipal body. Previously the County Governor, appointed by the government, had the last word on policy making in the County Administration Board.

What expertise has been available to the County Administration Board? Over the first fifty years or so of the present century, a system of 'county architects' was gradually being developed. The architects were accountable to the National Board of Public Building. These architects fulfilled a variety of functions, but perhaps the most important came to be the provision of expertise to the County Administration Board on planning issues. At the beginning of the 1970s the boards were reorganized and allotted special planning departments; the county architect became head of what is known as the 'planning unit'. The planning department also includes a regional economic unit, a nature conservancy unit, a surveying unit and a county custodian for historical sites.

At the beginning of this century the Board of Public Works and Buildings was the country's central organ for the administration of building. The Board also exercised certain control functions and, as we have seen, scrutinized the planning issues on which the government required reports. After the reorganization in 1918 its name was changed to Byggnadsstyrelsen (the National Board of Public Building), but the administrative and control functions were still retained within the one authority. The idea of separating the two functions was frequently discussed, however, until planning questions were finally removed from the National Board of Public Building in 1967 and transferred to a separate body, the Statens planverk (the National Board of Physical Planning and Building). This board produces no plans of its own, but it acts as the supervisory authority for planning activities, and as such is responsible for norms and guidelines. In 1988, the board was merged with the National Housing Board to create a new authority called Boverket (National Board of Housing, Building and Planning), which was moved to Karlskrona in southern Sweden in 1989.

The Planning Profession

In 1923 an international exhibition of urban development was arranged in Göteborg as part of the great exhibition to celebrate the 300th anniversary of the foundation of the city. The organization of the urban development section, the brainchild of Albert Lilienberg, was influenced by the exhibitions held in Germany before the war under Werner Hegemann. The editing of the international edition of the Göteborg exhibition catalogue was also entrusted to Hegemann. The exhibition appears to have assumed a retrospective stance, concentrating more on summarizing the achievements of the recent past rather than opening up future prospects. This was in striking contrast to the now far more famous 1930 Stockholm exhibition, which signalled the breakthrough of functionalism in Sweden. But even if the Göteborg exhibition did not play a major part in transmitting new ideas, it was a significant expression of the importance of planning in the urban environment.

At the time of the Göteborg exhibition it was still unusual for anyone to engage in planning as a full-time job. Over the next few decades the number of full-time planners seems to have risen rather slowly but the amount of time spent on planning matters by many consulting architects and engineers and by officials at the state and municipal levels was gradually increasing. It was primarily architects who were engaged in producing not only local development plans but also in making outline plans based on forecasts and economic and social considerations (for a while the building ordinances even included a provision that town plans and master plans could be made only by those with qualifications from a college of technology). If social or behavioural scientists became involved at all, it was generally in a subordinate role or to deal with complementary surveys. One of the main reasons for the predominance of architects was that the National Board of Public Building functioned as the central planning authority; many of its leading posts were held by architects, and until 1957 with one exception its director generals were architects too. Another factor may have been that for a long time there was no university course of study suited to future planners. And, as public employees or private consultants, architects still dominate physical planning today, while planning constitutes one of the main tasks occupying architects as a professional body. Thus in 1976 over 200 private and public architects were employed in physical planning at the outline level, and about 240 in planning at the local development level. This can be compared with the barely 700 practising architects engaged on building plans (Folkesdotter, 1987). There are no certain figures to tell us how many people engaged in physical planning today are not trained as either architects or engineers, but they are probably relatively few.

Most planners have thus been trained in the architectural departments of the colleges of technology. But the attention paid to planning in these departments was somewhat sparse, at least until the end of the 1940s when the first chair in urban development was established at the Royal Institute of Technology in Stockholm. Since then the time devoted to planning has increased at the colleges of technology, but generally in the shape of specialized courses within the architectural programme. The idea of a special planning course has been discussed on several occasions. In 1970 a cross-disciplinary course in regional planning was launched at the Royal Institute of Technology in Stockholm, but it has been difficult to decide on the right form for its activities. At present its future is under debate. The first and hitherto the only planning course on the social science and arts side was started at Stockholm University in 1977 within the Department of Human Geography.

In Stockholm there is also the Nordic Planning Postgraduate Institute, or Nordplan, a joint Nordic institute for the advanced training of community planners, established in 1969. Its courses, with their emphasis on discussion, field trips and project work, are aimed at planners of different backgrounds but with several years professional experience behind them. The one-year postgraduate course at the School of Architecture at the Academy of Fine Arts is organized along similar lines. This course is mainly intended for architects, but is open to other professional categories associated with building. Under the two professors Göran Lindahl and John Sjöström land-use and rehabilitation plans for several towns and urban areas during the 1960s and 1970s were discussed. As a result of these activities at the School of Architecture it became more widely understood that planning need not always be concerned with expansion and the creation of new structures, but that it is a powerful tool for maintaining and exploiting what is of value in existing structures as well.

In 1947 the *Föreningen för samhällsplanering* (Society for Community Planning) was founded. It is an organization open to anyone interested in its aims, and is thus not a professional body of the same kind as the Royal Town Planning Institute in England for instance. The society publishes a journal, *Plan*, which includes articles on various topics connected with planning. The articles are generally quite short, rarely criticizing or challenging the established ideas of the profession. Since the mid-1970s, it has been possible to find a more provocative approach in the journal *Arkitektur*, which because of its larger format can also publish longer articles with more illustrations. A good deal of material on planning has also appeared in the journals of the National Association of Swedish Architects (SAR): *Arkitekten* (until 1969) and *Arkitekttidningen* (from 1970).

Many people's names have been associated with the evolution of the Swedish planning system; some have been particularly important as opinion leaders and initiators. If Per Olof Hallman and Albert Lilienberg established planning as a professional occupation in the public mind during the first decades of the twentieth century, Uno Åhrén can be said to have played a similar part during the 1930s and 1940s. In 1932 he became town planning director in Göteborg, where he succeeded Albert Lilienberg, and in 1947 he became Sweden's first professor of urban development. In addition he participated in various investigations and appeared frequently in print (Rudberg, 1981). Gustaf Linden, who was head of the Town Planning Office of the National Board of Public Building during the 1930s, also made an important contribution (Mårtelius, 1982). One more name that should be mentioned in this context must be Lennart Holm. Trained as an architect, Holm represents better than anyone else the close connection between planning, Social Democratic housing policy, the creation of building norms, and housing research. During the 1970s and 1980s Holm headed the National Board of Physical Planning and Building. Pugnacious in debate he is always prepared to fight back whenever the purpose or powers of planning are attacked.

Something should also be said about attitudes to planning, and the way in which these have changed. During the 1930s and 1940s a Social

Democratic enthusiasm for the planned economy together with the technological optimism of the functionalists helped to create a climate which encouraged confidence in the possibilities of planning – an optimism that peaked during the 1960s. It was thought that almost everything was accessible to planning, and hardly anyone doubted that the 'right' plan could always be found. This meant that alternative possibilities were not always considered, or the full complexity of the problems recognized; nor was it always realized that the roles the built environment is called upon to fulfil can sometimes conflict with one another (cf. Linn, 1984). Further, it was not thought to be either necessary or desirable to engage the ordinary citizen in the planning process; his needs could surely be surveyed and identified by investigations.

As in other countries critical voices began to be raised during the later 1960s against expert-dominated planning. At the same time urbanization and national income were stagnating and changing the role and conditions of planning: today the planner is not expected to see himself simply as the supplier of ready-made solutions; it is also his job to survey the consequences of different alternatives and to inform about them. One of the main purposes of the new Planning and Building Act is supposed to be just this: to strengthen the position of the ordinary citizens in the planning process. The future alone will show whether it succeeds. So far, several cases suggest that the result will be the opposite.

Lastly, voices can be heard in Sweden as in several other countries, questioning the need for planning altogether, and seeking to reduce the power of the public authorities to control land use in this way. These ideas are gaining in popularity particularly in the Conservative Party, at present the largest of the non-socialist opposition parties. The party's opposition to the new Act has been largely dictated by ideas of this kind.

National Physical Planning

Finally a few words should be said about national physical planning. By the late 1950s several industries were becoming too big to be located in the interior of Sweden, either because of transport problems or because dumping would be on such a scale that only the sea could cope with it. During the late 1950s and the 1960s there were several notably large-scale industrial establishments on the coast, in areas which were important and attractive for outdoor recreation (for example Stenungsund, Mönsterås, Väröbacka and Brofjorden). The municipalities concerned generally reacted very positively to these projects, and made no bones about adopting the requisite local development plans. Rather naturally, they did not feel any responsibility for providing the population of the large cities with recreation areas, nor were there any effective instruments for weighing such interests against one another at a national planning level, or for redirecting industrial establishments to alternative sites.

Demands for some kind of national planning were becoming increasingly vociferous, and towards the end of the decade various government surveys were launched. On the one hand they were to take stock of areas of interest in a recreational, conservationist, cultural, or historical context, and on the other to examine the land-use requirements of the polluting industries. The results were published in 1971 in the report *Hushållning med mark och vatten* (The conservation of land and water resources, Government Official Report *SOU*, 1971: 75). After submitting the report to various authorities and organizations for comment, the government brought in a bill the following year, laying down guidelines for the management and conservation of the country's natural resources. There then followed the 'programming and planning phases', during which the intentions of the national planning initiative were to be translated at the regional and municipal levels into concrete plans and programmes of action.

National planning had come into being largely in response to the heavy pressure of industrial exploitation during the 1960s; when few large expansion projects remained, national planning lost much of its impetus. However, it has had one result of lasting value, namely the surveys which it generated and which opened people's eyes in the counties and municipalities to the importance of many areas in the contexts mentioned above. One of the principles behind the new Planning and Building Act was to introduce a basic ecological approach: the conservation and management of land, air and water was to be one of the major tasks of the planning system. To this end a proposal was submitted along with the Planning and Building Act for a Nature Conservancy Act. The two acts together are to guarantee that the intentions of the physical national planning programme are realized. However, serious criticism has been raised regarding the rules for compensation and other aspects of the new legislation, and initiated opponents have claimed that the new laws will ultimately provide less opportunity for protecting the natural environment than before.

Residential Areas and Suburbs

During the later years of the nineteenth century various types of suburban development were appearing on the outskirts of the larger Swedish towns. Because of the requirements of the building ordinances as regards planning and minimum standards, simple housing intended for the poorest groups in society was often located outside the town boundary and beyond the reach of any plans. Further, towards the end of the century the more privileged classes began to move away from the congested conditions of the old central districts into single-family homes on virgin ground. Thus several suburbs grew up, some more elegant than others. The most distinguished were Saltsjöbaden and Djursholm, to the south-east and north of Stockholm. Rail-

ways were constructed to both these communities when they were built. A feature common to all the different types of suburb was the absence of public control. In the first stages at least, it was a question of private development companies, and as a rule there does not seem to have been any planning apart from simple plans for parcelling sites. The only major move towards planning and building a suburb under municipal auspices before the First World War was at Enskede, south of Stockholm (cf. above, p. 191), where building began in 1907. It was here that the *tomträtt*, a system of leaseholding, was adopted for the first time on any great scale, i.e. the town surrendered the ground on long-term leases but retained ownership.

The Inter-War Years: The 'Storgård' and Functionalism

During the First World War housing production in Swedish towns declined sharply, while building costs shot up. In 1917, as part of a policy to combat unemployment, the Riksdag and government launched an emergency programme to support the equivalent of one-quarter of pre-war production by granting loans and subsidies primarily to municipal companies. At the same time a system of rent control was introduced. The programme also reflected a certain acceptance of the concept of community housing. At the beginning of the 1920s, however, both the system of state subsidies and the rent controls were abolished. Thus most new housing was once again being produced by speculative private builders just as it had been before the war.

Nonetheless several towns – Stockholm and Göteborg in particular – did a good deal to improve the quality of the housing stock by planning and adopting a number of building provisions. The creation in 1923 of the National Association of Tenants' Savings and Building Society (HSB) was also an important factor here. HSB promoted the cause of nonspeculative building and urged that all housing should be supplied with modern facilities. Most important of all, it demonstrated in its own production that these goals could be realized within the prevailing economic system.

The town plans were generally made by consultants. Only a few of the larger towns appear to have produced most of their plans themselves. Several of the consultants had their own businesses, but architects employed by the state or the municipality often accepted planning commissions. As city engineer of Göteborg, Albert Lilienberg had such an extensive private practice that his new post as town-planning director in Stockholm was made conditional on the discontinuation of his private commissions.

In an aesthetic context, urban development during the 1920s exhibits traces both of nineteenth-century classicism with its emphasis on straight axes and visual foci and monumental places, and of the small-scale planning of the early twentieth century with its interest in variety and intimate spatial solutions. The work of Fritz Schumacher and Heinrich Tessenow should be mentioned here, as possible foreign models and parallels. Almost without exception the interiors of the blocks were now left open. This paved the way for the model which Björn Linn has called the *storgård*, whose development he has surveyed in a comparison of several countries (Linn, 1974). The *storgård* as Linn defines it is an enclosed or semi-open block round a fairly large common courtyard, where the whole complex is perceived as a single unit. In its pure form the *storgård* presupposes a single builder. The equivalent term in English is perhaps *court*, as used in the names given to many blocks of this kind. In several parts of Europe – and Linn quotes examples from Germany, Austria, Holland and Denmark – *storgård* blocks were built to a high architectural standard during the 1920s, as part of a programme of community housing under municipal auspices. Sweden has relatively few examples of orthodox *storgård* blocks, mainly because there

were still no municipal or public utility companies able to undertake the building of a whole block in this way. Most new building in Sweden was still effected plot by plot, by individual developers.

The development of idle land in the larger towns continued during the 1920s. In Stockholm's inner city some land was now built on which had not been fully developed before because of the awkward terrain. One example is the Rödaberg area, which is generally regarded today as one of the finest parts of the inner city. The first proposal, basically designed as a garden suburb, was produced in 1907 by Per Olof Hallman. During the 1920s the plan was revised and simplified by the architect Sigurd Lewerentz; the central axis was given greater emphasis, but Hallman's adjustments to the peculiarities of the terrain were retained (figure 5.17(*b*)). There are few city districts in Sweden which can compare with this one in its combination of monumentality and clarity on the one hand, and an intimate spatial conception on the other.

Many of the houses in Rödaberg area were built by HSB, and the standard was high for those times. However, we cannot call this a *storgård* district in the strictest sense of the term, i.e. uniform buildings occupying a whole block, since several builders were involved in each block. But in other parts of the Stockholm inner city the *storgård* model did appear, for instance at Helgalunden (figure 5.17(*a*)) and at Draget by Blecktornsparken on Södermalm, which was planned at the beginning of the 1920s. Skilful exploitation of the terrain and a modest scale of building have combined to create an intimate small-town idyll in the heart of the city, where the visitor immediately feels at home. The *storgård* blocks built by HSB have a different air. Here the buildings are generally heavier and more formal, as at Metern on Södermalm built in 1926 (figure 5.17(*a*)) or at Färjan on Kungsholmen in 1929–30, both designed by HSB's director Sven Wallander.

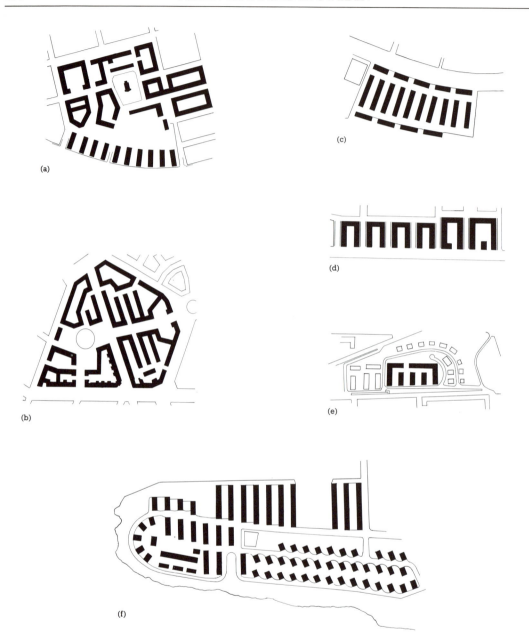

Figure 5.17. Stockholm town planning patterns I. (*a*) Helgalunden (mid-1920s, the lamella blocks in the southern part of area a few years later); (*b*) the Rödaberg area (1920s); (*c*) the Eriksdal area (early 1930s); (*d*) Norr Mälarstrand (around 1930); (*e*) Kvarteret Marmorn (around 1930); (*f*) Fredhäll (1930s); (*g*) Kristineberg (1930s); (*h*) Gärdet (1930s); (*i*) Traneberg (1930s); (*j*) Kungsklippan (mid-1930s); (*k*) Hjorthagen (mid-1930s); (*l*) Reimersholme (early 1940s); (*m*); Gröndal (mid-1940s). Scale approximately 1:14,000. North uppermost with some minor deviations. The dates refer to the development of the main part of the respective areas; in some cases the plans are earlier, and important additions were made later. *Drawing*: Karl Almgren.

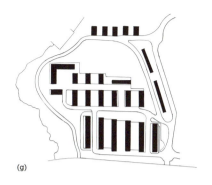

(g)

(j)

(k)

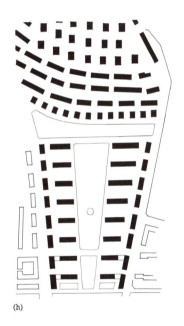

(h)

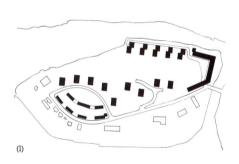

(l)

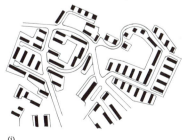

(i)

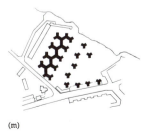

(m)

In Göteborg a type of workers' housing predominated that is unique to the town. Known as the *landshövdingehus*, it has a ground floor in brick with two upper storeys in wood – this type of house goes back to the time when a provincial governor or *landshövding* (hence the name) granted a dispensation allowing wooden houses to exceed the permitted two storeys. During the 1920s several well-designed areas were built largely under municipal auspices on the *storgård* model, for example at Bagaregården, where the original plan is the work of Albert Lilienberg. Malmö and Västerås also have interesting examples of the *storgård*. The idea persisted into the next decade. In Göteborg a town plan was approved in 1934 for the development of an estate known as Gubberoparken. This area of parkland was flanked on three sides by great unbroken blocks, although a doctrinaire lamella block plan had been considered. The park, and the slight curve in one of the surrounding blocks, create an impression of rhythm and variety despite the large scale of the solution.

Thus the 'closed' street and the enclosed block were fundamental features of 1920s planning. But from the middle of the decade things began to change (the seminal work on this process is Råberg, 1970). Le Corbusier's message as manifest in *'L'esprit nouveau'* also reached Sweden, and several of the younger architects read his work and discussed his *Plan Voisin*. Le Corbusier provided the ideological groundwork, but did not really supply any models suitable to everyday Swedish building. These came rather from the Germany of the Weimar Republic, from the new *Siedlungen* in Berlin, Frankfurt and Dessau. Several Swedish architects also took part in CIAM's activities, and a congress held in Frankfurt in 1929 on the theme of *'Die Wohnung für das Existenzminimum'* was particularly important. The housing exhibitions in Stuttgart in 1927 and in Berlin in 1931 also made a considerable impact. The second of these, for example, was visited by four members and six officials of Stockholm's Real Estate Board.

Most energetic in introducing the new ideas, and frequently and sharply attacking 'dilettantism' and 'all the artistic paraphernalia' of town planning, was Uno Åhrén. 'It is high time', he wrote in one of his polemical articles in 1928, 'to introduce exact methods into urban development.' The subjectivist art of urban building should be replaced by an exact urban development science. 'The town is not a sculpture in which we happen to wander around; it is an apparatus, organized so as best to meet the needs of our lives.' (Quotations from an article in *Byggmästaren*, 1928; on Åhrén, see Rudberg, 1981.)

Two noted competitions in Stockholm played an important part in the breakthrough for the new planning principles, namely the Kristineberg competition in 1927 and the Gärdet competition in 1929. The latter particularly evoked several proposals based on the new principles, i.e. the closed blocks had been replaced by rows of uniform and parallel lamella houses, combined with adaptation to the character of the landscape. First prize was awarded for a proposal based on a relatively traditional grouping of large buildings, albeit in many cases the blocks were open. This award was heavily criticized in radical circles, and in 1930 the plan was revised in line with the recommendations of the critics (figure 5.17(*h*)). In that same year two projects from the Stockholm Town Planning Office were approved, both of which marked a breakthrough for 'functionalist' planning. These were the plans for Eriksdal and Fredhäll-Kristineberg (figure 5.17 (*c*), (*f*), (*g*)). Both consist of parallel lamella houses.

The year 1930 was also the year of the Stockholm Exhibition, which both then and later was regarded as an epoch-making event. The man behind it, and who subsequently superintended it, was Gregor Paulsson, later professor of art history and the main author of a famous work on the Swedish town, *Svensk stad*. The exhibition was imbued with an optimistic belief in the future, but it was also something of a provocation, calling in question many accepted notions. One contribution that greatly added to the festive effect was the architecture of Gunnar Asplund. The exhibition heralded a breakthrough for the functionalist design principles whose aim was to weed out traditional ornamentation and to discover forms expressive of function and construction. The housing section, for example, included box-shaped houses with no ornamentation and flat roofs. In the context of urban development, the exhibition served to confirm even more strongly the new principles which already were becoming widely accepted.

The ideas that had imbued the Stockholm Exhibition were developed further in a collective manifesto issued in 1932 with the challenging title *Acceptera* (Accept!). The authors included Gregor Paulsson, Uno Åhrén and Sven Markelius. Key passages were concerned with town planning. 'It is now imperative to demand that a residential area be so planned that every dwelling has sufficient access to sun and air . . .' Social justice demands that dwellings should be regarded as people's homes and not as 'motifs in the townscape'. As we must demand homes that are equally healthy for all, the authors continued, a housing district should be judged by its worst houses and not by its best. This calls for an open building mode with parallel rows, orientated according to the sun. This meant an east-west orientation for flats with windows on both sides, and a north-south orientation for others.

Thus the orientation of the building was linked to the idea of flats with windows on both sides, which in turn affected the depth of the buildings. The design of the houses was also the subject of lively debate, and in 1932 the city of Stockholm announced a special thematic competition for cheaper housing for 'the less well-to-do'. Two alternatives finally emerged from these discussions: the deep block and the narrow block. The principle behind the second of these was the functionalists' cherished notion

that all flats should have two outside walls to allow for adequate airing and for light from two directions. Thus there could be two flats only on every landing, and since the flats were to be small, the houses had to be narrow. This meant that lifts were out of the question for reasons of cost; at the same time no house without a lift was permitted to have more than three storeys. These conditions produced the three-storey narrow lamella block, about 8 or 9 metres deep. Between the town proper and the belt of garden suburbs several areas were built with houses of this kind in parallel rows during the 1930s on land owned by the town, for example at Bromma (figure 5.18).

This type of house had an enthusiastic advocate in Axel Dahlberg of the Real Estate Board which did much to ensure its success (figure 5.19). But the deep block also had its supporters, in particular Sven Wallander of HSB who claimed that the larger house permitted not only cheaper flats but also amenities such as lifts, utility rooms and so on. Moreover, a bathroom in every flat was the HSB rule, and this was not always possible in the narrow blocks. Several variations of the deep-block theme were employed during the last phase of expansion in Stockholm's inner city. HSB's high-rise houses at Kungsklippan on Kungsholmen are a high-class example (figure 5.17(*j*)). Despite lack of space and awkward terrain these tall houses do not appear congested; on the contrary, they add a dimension of light and space to the Stockholm skyline.

It should be remembered, however, that the type and forms of planning and housing advocated by the functionalists in the inter-war years remained a big-city – even a Stockholm – phenomenon. During the 1930s several lamella housing estates were built in Malmö, but the houses were generally higher and deeper than in Stockholm. In Göteborg there are a few examples of orthodox functionalist planning, for instance Söderlingska ängen, where the *landshövdinge* houses have been given the look

Figure 5.18. Riksby, Abrahamsberg and Åkeslund in Stockholm, three residential areas in the district of Bromma, largely developed during the early 1940s. These areas reflect the planning patterns advocated in the 1930s, although the building blocks do not represent the narrowest type. *Photo:* Oscar Bladh.

that was then in fashion. Towards the end of the 1930s building began at Övre Johanneberg, following a town plan produced under Uno Åhrén, with large high-rise lamella blocks somewhat reminiscent of HSB's houses in Stockholm.

During this period a great many single-family homes were naturally also being built. In some of the larger towns, particularly in Stockholm, several housing estates consisting of *egna hem* (small standardized owner-occupied houses mainly for low-income families who often did the building themselves) came into being under the auspices of the municipality of Stockholm. Examples can be seen at Tallkrogen, Norra Ängby and Enskede. With their small scale and

their many gardens these areas possess undeniable environmental qualities.

But the small houses built as part of public planning schemes represented only a tiny part of the total production. Far more were the result of various kinds of private enterprise, ranging from the regular operations of development companies to the subdivision of single plots. To a great extent this building occurred in outlying municipalities, which legally speaking were *landskommuner* (rural districts) and were thus without either the administrative resources or the legal means to control the development. If rail communications made planned suburban development possible, it was the car and the bus

Figure 5.19. Axel Dahlberg was the head of the Stockholm Real Estate Office 1933–45. His devotion to the narrow lamella block provoked this cartoon in the daily newspaper *Svenska Dagbladet* in 1939.

that made possible what we know as urban sprawl.

Decades of Growth: Service Suburbs and the 'Million Homes' Programme

Housing production in the post-war period has been influenced to a great extent by two fundamental ideas, both of which can be said to stem from the pioneers of the 1920s and 1930s: first, that a good home is the irrefutable right of all citizens regardless of income, and secondly that optimal solutions to the design of flats, dwelling-houses and urban districts do exist and are accessible to research.

Let us look first at housing policy. Better housing for the people at large was a key element in the message of the functionalists, and

one that found response in the increasingly powerful labour movement. Communication between the social democratic movement and the functionalist architects was facilitated by the fact that several of these architects were or became socialists. Housing policy principles were debated and analysed by the *Bostadssociala utredningen* (Housing Commission) appointed in 1933, one of whose members was Uno Åhrén. The Commission's two final reports were published in 1945 and 1947 (Government Official Reports *SOU*, 1945:63 and 1947:26). In these the broad outlines of a programme were presented, whereby overcrowding and the housing shortage would be remedied, and a clearance campaign would abolish much of the older housing stock. However, it was to prove much more difficult to remedy the housing shortage than the Commission had envisaged, which was one of the main reasons why the clearance campaign came to nothing (see below, p. 232).

But another of the Commission's major recommendations was realized, namely that the state and the municipalities should be largely responsible for the provision of housing, the state by way of rent subsidies and tertiary credits, and the municipalities by assuming responsibility for planning and the provision of land, and by establishing public utility companies as developers and owner-administrators. These ideas have generated an extensive administrative apparatus, with a central authority, the National Housing Board, and regional bodies, the County Housing Boards, as well as a great many public utility and co-operative housing companies with their own national organizations. This system has facilitated efficient production, but it has also led to inflexibility and bureaucratic blockages (see Dahlman and Gärdborn, 1975). The fact that the whole apparatus of housing policy was geared to the building of flats for example, was probably one of the main reasons why so few small houses were built during the 1950s and

1960s, despite heavy demand for just this type of housing.

One fundamental principle of Swedish housing policy during the late 1940s deserves particular mention. In contrast to many other countries it was decided not to build special areas for low-income groups; instead a system of general production support was introduced, available to any construction that meets the quality norms and does not exceed the established cost limits. Moreover, with the help of housing grants, child benefits etc., low-income households have been able to seek houses in the 'normal' stock. Despite these measures it has not been possible to prevent certain areas becoming dominated by low-income families and those with social problems.

Thus far housing policy. The functionalists were also keen advocates of research in order to discover normative solutions, and before the Stockholm Exhibition some investigatory work was done on the subject of planning and housing. But it was not until the end of the 1930s that building research was seriously launched, and then with two main thrusts: one concerned with the dwelling function, aimed at improving the layout and equipment of dwelling units, and the other geared to the rationalization of production with the help of standardization and industrial prefabrication. During the 1940s a permanent state building research organ was established, predecessor of the present Swedish Council for Building Research and the Building Research Institute. Housing policy considerations and the results of the various research and development projects provided a basis for national building norms and loan terms. As early as 1942 directives were issued regarding the minimum standards for government loans. A more comprehensive set of rules was published in *God bostad* (Good housing) 1954 (revised 1960 and 1964). Since 1976 the rules have been included in *Svensk byggnorm* (Swedish building norms). One of the conditions qualifying for a government subsidy or loan was

fulfilment of these norms, which meant that they were endowed with considerable force.

The growing engagement in housing production of the central and local authorities naturally also affected the focus and forms of the planning system. The mandatory local development plans often constituted the last stage which was tackled once the layout of the new development had been determined. This last was generally the result of negotiations between landowners, developers and the municipality. And the public utility housing companies were now acting increasingly as developers. Moreover, many of the larger towns owned much of the land which was to be developed for housing, and the idea gradually gained ground that all housing development should take place on municipal land. The municipalities were thus often able to exercise considerable influence, not only because of the planning monopoly but also through their housing companies and through their ownership of the land which provided them with an effective control instrument even when the ground was surrendered to private companies.

It is not really possible, at least not at the present stage of research, to generalize about how the design of the larger residential areas evolved. The planning process probably followed a different course in different projects and different municipalities. But particularly during the 1950s there was often scope for independent contributions both to planning and to the design of the buildings. A fairly common procedure would probably be that the municipal planning authority produced a synoptic proposal regarding land use in the area, after which the developer's architectural consultant was responsible for the local development and building plans. Finally the municipality executed and approved the town plan required by the building permit system.

Turning now to planning principles and urban patterns, we find that by the late 1930s doubts were being expressed about the functionalist ideal of uniform parallel lamella houses orientated according to the sun. The absence of perceived spaces or of any sense of neighbourhood to give the area an identity and to provide safe playgrounds and meeting-places, was all too evident. The idea of the community centre and the neighbourhood unit was all the rage in the 1940s. Before the war Swedish planners had already begun to look for models and professional contacts in Great Britain and the United States rather than in Germany, and this shift in focus was consolidated during and after the Second World War. One result of this was that Lewis Mumford's *The Culture of Cities*, published in Swedish in 1942, came to play much the same role in the 1940s that Le Corbusier's works had done in the 1920s: it acted as a kind of manifesto, stimulating the mind and triggering debate with its provocative flow of ideas and categorical simplifications. Paradoxically Mumford became far more influential in Sweden and the Nordic countries than at home in the United States.

Thus, just as Mumford filled the same role in the 1940s that Le Corbusier had filled in the 1920s, so now English planning and particularly Patrick Abercrombie's 1943 and 1944 plans for Greater London and the first New Towns, played the part that the German *Siedlungen* had played in the earlier period, namely as tangible models which could inspire practical solutions. Otto Danneskiold-Samsoe's *Nutida engelsk samhällsplanering* (Contemporary English Community Planning) has already been mentioned. This work had been commissioned by the Town Planning Committee in Stockholm and was published in 1945 with a foreword by the new town planning director Sven Markelius. Markelius had been one of the pioneers of functionalism, but the 1940s produced no new generation of pioneers and the new principles were being advocated by people who had been active as long ago as the 1920s. The new ideas were obviously regarded not as a break with the functionalists, but as a

further development of their programme.

It was in Stockholm that the most important and comprehensive planning activities of the 1940s occurred (see Sidenbladh, 1981). To the south of the inner city several new districts were built under municipal auspices and linked to the centre by extended tramways. (It was decided in 1941 that these should be reconstructed to the standard of the underground system, and the improvements were started in 1945.) The narrow-block model, albeit chunkier in appearance than in the 1930s, dominates these areas, although houses both deeper and taller have also been included. The plan designs are much more varied than during the earlier period, particularly towards the end of the decade, and there are even some attempts at traffic separation, with pedestrian walkways and access roads into the residential streets. The suburbs of the 1940s were envisaged as neighbourhood units, and a sociological study was conducted in Hägerstensåsen and Hökmossen (1949–50) to see whether the social goals embraced by the plans had been realized. The results showed that communication between the residents in these districts was by no means as extensive as the advocates of neighbourhood planning had hoped (Dahlström, 1951).

A housing exhibition which attracted considerable attention was held in Göteborg in 1945 in the newly built area of Norra Guldheden, where narrow blocks alternated with an intermediate form between the *maison rayonnant* (see below) and the tower block. The arrangement of the houses is determined by steeply undulating terrain and is much more informal than in the typical 1930s areas (figure 5.20). The architects were Gunnar Wejke and Kjell Ödéen. Torpa, which was built a year or two later, consists basically of parallel narrow blocks, but monotony has been avoided by allowing some irregularity in the arrangement of the buildings and by grouping the houses round an open space. In both these districts attempts were made to stimulate social contact

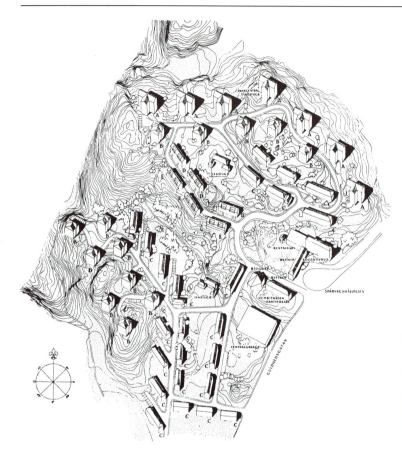

Figure 5.20. Guldheden, a residential area in Göteborg designed by Gunnar Wejke and Kjell Ödeen 1944–45, and erected as part of a housing exhibition in 1945. Because of the difficult topographical conditions, the large tower blocks were eminently suitable. *Source: Byggmästaren* 1945.

by including various kinds of community and leisure amenities. Among other districts built during the 1940s and inspired by the concept of the neighbourhood unit are Södra Guldheden in Göteborg, Friluftsstaden in Malmö, Slottsvången in Helsingborg, and Sandvången in Landskrona.

The residential areas of the 1930s were generally provided with ample commercial services in the shape of small shops at ground-floor level in the dwelling houses. During the 1940s planners sought to collect shops and other service units in squares, preferably free from traffic, and for this kind of amenity the 'centre' became the accepted designation. Early examples of this kind of centre were built at Hägerstensåsen and Hökarängen in southern Stockholm. These cen-

tres were intended to serve their own districts only. The first attempt to create a centre capable of serving several surrounding districts was at Kärrtorp built by the municipal company Svenska bostäder.

But the most notable undertaking along these lines was at Årsta, immediately south of central Stockholm, where an ambitious attempt was made to realize the idea of the community centre. Once again the driving-force was Uno Åhrén. The cooperative housing company Svenska Riksbyggen had been given the task of developing parts of Årsta, and when Åhrén became director of the company in 1942 he decided that Årsta should not be a mere 'dormitory town'. Rather, the new project was to prove that centres of this kind could succeed not only commercially but also socially and could provide facilities for a wide range of activities. The image projected by this centre owes much to the architectural design of Erik and Tore Ahlsén, whose solution is certainly well-conceived: within a relatively small space a variety of buildings and functions have been arranged in an informal and imaginative way, to create a friendly atmosphere and to encourage social contact (figure 5.21). But soon after the opening in 1953 it became clear that the social

activities envisaged were not being realized, perhaps because the city centre was so close, and that it was proving difficult to cover the running costs of the various amenities. Thus Årsta centre became a warning rather than a model; in later centres commercial operations would dominate. Although Årsta centre may be the most coherent attempt to build a community centre, other projects have naturally been influenced by similar ideas. An early example is Guldhedstorget in Göteborg, in the Norra

Figure 5.21. Årsta centre, designed by Erik and Tore Ahlsén and inaugurated in 1953. Årsta was the most ambitious attempt in Sweden to create a 'community centre'. The idea was to design and combine the buildings in such a way as to encourage the residents to meet and partake in various activities. (1) and (2) cinema; (3) and (20) dwellings; (5) restaurant; (6), (8) and (18) shops and officespace; (7) square; (9), (10) and (12) entrances, vestibules etc.; (11) café; (13) theatre; (14) and (15) library; (16) studios; (17) concert hall. *Source: Arkitektur* 1980.

Guldheden district which has been mentioned above.

One of the main problems facing the planners during the 1940s was to find a way of combining the advantages of the deep and narrow blocks, i.e. to retain the better lighting of the narrow building with the better service facilities of the deep blocks. One solution to this problem was the tower block, which is essentially a 'cut-off' deep lamella block, in which four flats can have windows in two directions. The most noted example of this solution is the development on Danviksklippan in Stockholm (1943–45), planned by Sven Backström and Leif Reinius. The area consists of nine houses of eight to ten

storeys. Here the special advantage of tower blocks, i.e. that they can be happily accommodated on undulating ground, has been skilfully exploited. From a distance the houses rise in monolithic blocks from the rocky cliff, of which they seem to be a part.

Another answer to the problem was the *maison rayonnant* or star-shaped house, which appears to have been a Swedish innovation. By building three wings radiating from a central stair-well, it was possible to have three flats on each storey with windows in three directions. Star-shaped houses could also be joined together to form a courtyard. This model appeared for the first time at Gröndal in Stock-

Figure 5.22. Rosta, a residential area in Örebro designed by the architects Backström and Reinius for the municipal housing company. Here the star pattern was employed for first time on a grand scale. The estate was completed in 1952. *Photo*: Oscar Bladh.

holm, in a group of three- or four-storey houses. Again the architects were Backström and Reinius.

The star pattern was employed, sometimes on a grander scale, in several residential developments around 1950, for instance by the same architects at Rosta in Örebro (1948–52, figure 5.22). Long rows of houses were grouped round a series of broad green spaces; small courtyards are created through the 'points' of the star. Rosta, which was built by the Örebro municipal housing company, was a unique undertaking which attracted a good deal of attention. It was followed a couple of years later by Baronbackarna, planned by Per-Axel Ekholm and Sidney White. This estate consisted of three-storey lamella houses arranged in a meander-like chain, forming large traffic-free courts on the inner side, opening on to a green central area, and courtyards on the outer side suitable as parking space. These estates, both of which were preceded by architectural competitions, established Örebro's reputation as the model town of Sweden's housing policy – a reputation confirmed by later projects (see Egerö, 1979).

In medium-sized towns such as Örebro the new residential areas built during the 1950s were functionally and topographically in the nature of extensions to the existing urban structure. But in the 1940s Stockholm was already acquiring new districts of such a size and location as to deserve the designation suburbs, although they were in fact within the municipal boundaries. Towards the end of the decade the capital city was preparing to go a step further and to launch new developments which, in Swedish population terms, would rank as towns rather than suburbs. The prototype was the English New Town. In Stockholm this model was adapted to the local requirements and dubbed the 'ABC community' (A, B and C are the first letters in the Swedish words meaning workplace, dwelling and centre). The new suburbs were not to be dormitory towns with shopping centres; they were to be communities with individual profiles, where it would be possible to work as well as to live.

The first of these satellite towns was Vällingby (figure 5.28(a)). Stockholm had long owned a large piece of land located about 10 kilometres west of the city centre in an outlying municipality, which after much ado the city had succeeded in incorporating. Here, linked to the centre of town by the underground railway, a series of suburbs was planned on wooded and agricultural land. Apart from Vällingby it included Blackeberg, Grimsta and Råcksta. Planning activities continued for much of the 1940s. The final plans were accepted at the beginning of the 1950s; building also began during this period. As town planning director Sven Markelius was ultimately responsible for the project. Master plans were produced in Stockholm's Town Planning Office under his direction. It also seems to have been his idea that Vällingby should be the centre, built on a bigger scale than the other suburbs and with a large centre catering for them all. The plans for the Vällingby centre were produced by Backström and Reinius.

Several housing companies were involved in the development of Vällingby, which meant that various architects had a say in the detailed planning, and particularly in the design of the buildings. Thus many planners and decision-makers have contributed to the shaping of Vällingby, and anyone looking at a map or an aerial view of the area (figure 5.23) will find it difficult to discern a single design concept underlying the complex as a whole. On the other hand there is plenty of variety in the urban landscape, and each 'neighbourhood' has its own particular character. We could perhaps speak of three neighbourhood levels: the local and individually designed group of buildings; the suburb; and the satellite town in its entirety.

A comparison with older areas, and even with more recent ones, clearly reveals Vällingby's special character. Vällingby differs from the

Figure 5.23. Vällingby, an attempt in Stockholm to create within the city boundaries an equivalent to the English New Towns. The photograph shows the centre and the surrounding buildings, which exhibit a considerable variety as regards plan and house type. Development continued for most of the 1950s. Chief architect of the master plan was Sven Markelius. *Photo*: Stig Gustavsson.

preceding suburbs not only in size but also because the houses are more varied and more informally grouped. At the same time it differs from suburbs built ten years or so later, in that the houses are not yet so big or the production methods so rationalized as to disallow this freedom in forms and orientations. Vällingby also maintains a pleasant balance between built and open spaces: the houses are sufficiently close to one another to create spatial coherence and a certain atmosphere of 'town', and yet they are scattered enough to retain something of the original topography and natural landscape. Similar features often reappear in the residential areas of the 1950s.

As we have seen, Vällingby and its neighbours were not supposed to form a dormitory town, and in time various activities were in fact attracted to the areas allotted as workplaces. But it turned out that a minority of those employed in these workplaces lived in the Vällingby area. This was partly due to the housing shortage, which made it difficult for people to move house when they changed jobs, but with

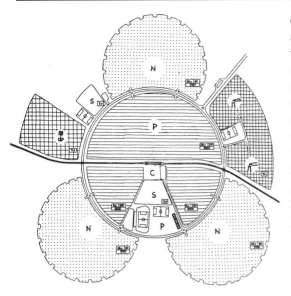

Figure 5.24. Rough model for the development of satellite communities in the Stockholm region according to the ideas prevalent around 1950. Lined area intended for blocks of flats and dotted areas for one-family houses. The chequered area to the right was intended for industrial purposes and to the left for small gardens for the residents in the suburb. C. The centre with underground station and stores and public services. N. Neighbourhood centre with shops and services. S. Primary school. P. Larger playground. *Source: Det framtida Stockholm.*

development there should be a centre, preferably with an underground station, and this is where department stores, shops, public services (schools, library, church, facilities for health and medical care etc.) and facilities for social activities are located. The centre should be approached as far as possible by pedestrian walkways. Buildings are arranged fairly close together with blocks of flats round the centre itself, and single-family homes further out. A green-belt should separate one suburb from the next. The model was subsequently modified, partly to adapt to increases in motor traffic. But by and large it continued to apply. In the twenty years or so after the mid-1950s, approximately one such suburb was completed each year. From the beginning of the period special mention should be made of Farsta, to the south of central Stockholm. This development is a few years younger than Vällingby and the houses there are larger, but like Vällingby it has a centre scaled to cater for a group of suburbs.

As a result of new legislation (the *Lex Boll-mora*) it became possible after 1961 for Stockholm's municipal housing companies to build in the outlying municipalities and thus to plan new residential areas further out of town. However, several of Stockholm's suburban municipalities undertook extensive housing construction projects of their own. Special mention should be made of Täby, which was responsible for one of the most noted undertakings of the 1950s. Around the middle of the decade a group of architects under Sune Lindström produced a proposal for a satellite town to consist of tall fifteen-storey tower blocks grouped in an oval (Näsbydal), together with two tall, long, half-moon buildings and two similar lower ones surrounding a courtyard (Grindtorp). This project was realized at the beginning of the 1960s, largely in line with the original proposal (figure 5.25). At the same time Lindström was planning the Täby centre nearby, to include a twenty-five-storey bow-shaped slab-type block, providing a powerful focus in the urban landscape.

hindsight we can also see that it was a little illogical to try to counteract commuting while also building the latest type of transport system nicely scaled to commuting requirements. And, sure enough, in later suburban developments, plans for including workplaces were either modified or abandoned. Also, in 1951 radical plans for redeveloping the city centre were launched in Stockholm, and the drive to relocate workplaces to the outskirts presumably lost much of its impetus.

With the Vällingby project the principles for subsequent suburban building were established. In its theoretical ideal form the model was presented in the above-mentioned 1952 master plan for Stockholm. In the middle of the

Figure 5.25. Näsbydal (in the foreground) and Grindtorp, two residential areas in the municipality of Täby on the northern outskirts of Greater Stockholm. These developments were carried out in 1958–66, largely according to Sune Lindström's ideas. Photographer unknown.

However, the height was reduced to seventeen storeys before the plan was ratified, which meant that much of the intended effect was lost. Lindström's enormous complex – which comes closer to Le Corbusier's visions than anything else in Sweden – shows that even very large volumes can express a cogent design. But buildings on this scale have remained the exception in Swedish urban development. One other unique and famous project should be mentioned here, and one which represents Täby's opposite pole, namely Ralph Erskine's Brittgården in Tibro. This estate, where construction began in 1960, consists of low buildings,

arranged close together and richly varied. Around this time the uniformity of prefabrication was beginning to spread through Swedish building industry. But as in both earlier and later projects Erskine showed his ability to discover unconventional solutions.

During the 1950s two large suburban areas were built in Göteborg, Kortedala and Biskopsgården (see Andersson, 1975), both connected to the centre by tramway. Both were intended as purely residential suburbs, but building standards were to be high. The municipal planning authority made a rough layout plan showing the design of the future dwelling areas, after which the developers – including both public utility and private companies – were to be responsible for the detailed development planning. This resulted in considerable variety in house types and plans. Because of the undulating ground Kortedala seems even less subject to a single overall design than Vällingby. But there is at least one coherent unit, along Gregorianska gatan, where a row of three-storey houses resembling a ring-wall encloses a green area and triangular tower blocks (figure 5.26). The southern part of Biskopsgården (figure 5.27) is built on the same lines as Kortedala, i.e. with a combination of three-storey narrow blocks and tower blocks. The northern part, built towards the end of the 1950s, consists mainly of slab houses, i.e. broader and higher houses with load-bearing party walls in cast-in-situ concrete. This has resulted in a more rigid pattern; instead of letting the houses adapt to the terrain, the terrain has been blasted to adapt it to the buildings.

During the Second World War housing construction remained at a low ebb. After a temporary peak during the first post-war years, the volume of production increased fairly slowly and only in the mid-1950s did it reach the pre-war level. This comparatively low rate of growth was desired by the government, which wanted capital and labour to be used primarily for the rapid expansion of industry. But industrial growth combined with rationalizations in agriculture resulted in big population transfers, which further hastened the already high rate of urbanization. Demands for more spacious dwelling units – part of the continual rise in living standards – were also affecting the demand for housing, while at the same time the market mechanisms had been neutralized by rent controls. The housing shortage in the larger towns became increasingly serious, representing a political handicap to the Social Democrats which the opposition parties did not fail to exploit. Hundreds of thousands of people were on the waiting lists for houses in Stockholm

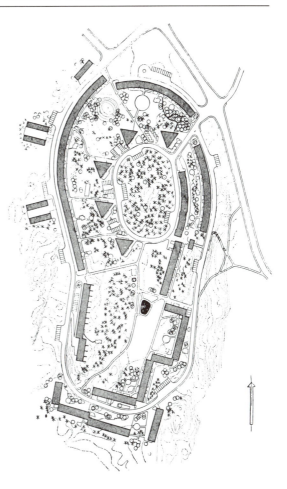

Figure 5.26. Part of Kortedala, a residential district in Göteborg developed during the 1950s. This particular area was designed by Sven Brolid and Jan Wallinder. A hilly area with tower blocks is surrounded by lower lamella blocks. Source: Byggmästaren, 1957.

alone, and many young families were without homes of their own. At one election after another the government was blamed for failing to cope with this fundamental need in the welfare society, despite its ambitious notions about a planned economy. The housing issue was particularly embarrassing in the 1964 election, in which the Social Democrats did not do very well. All this explains why in 1967 the govern-

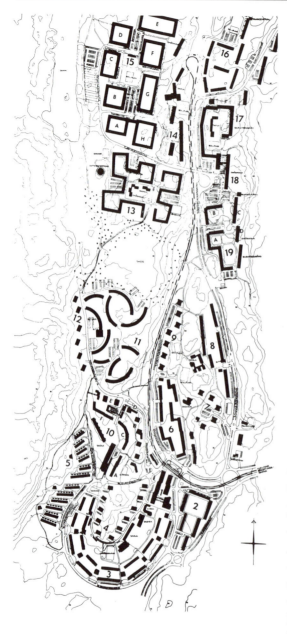

Figure 5.27. Biskopsgården, a residential district on the outskirts of Göteborg, developed during the 1950s. The southern section, which is the oldest, consists of narrow lamella blocks and tower blocks happily adapted to the terrain in a way that creates an impression of variety. The northern sections are characterized by more formally grouped and broader blocks. *Source: Byggmästaren,* 1959.

ment launched its 'Million Homes' programme, promising that by 1975 a million new dwelling units would have been built. The level of production, already high, culminated around 1970 when in relation to the size of its population Sweden had the highest housing production in the world.

As we have seen, suburbs planned during the 1950s were often noted for variation and attention to detail. When the level of production had to be increased and the houses built on an even bigger scale, there was less scope for architectural design. This was not thought to be particularly important – if indeed it was noticed at all. There was little interest in the external setting or the visual qualities of the residential areas. Housing production was regarded primarily as a question of technology and economics, not of architecture. What a good home should look like had been established in the national norms; provided these were fulfilled, by definition the standard would be acceptable. This meant that all efforts could be concentrated instead on improving the speed and efficiency of production. Many architects saw themselves as coordinators rather than designers. Around 1960 ideas about 'production-related planning' began to circulate. A major planning goal, perhaps even sometimes *the* planning goal, was to design areas that lent themselves best to 'rational' building. And since the building industry was becoming increasingly dominated by large development corporations which manufactured their own materials and had their own industrialized methods, the new residential areas had to be designed to suit the system of the particular builder concerned. The end result of this industrialized planning can be seen in the large uniform buildings surrounded by empty space and multi-storey parking.

The pattern had evolved gradually. Suburbs were built during the early 1960s which, despite their standardized housing, were not monotonous. Bredäng in Stockholm, for which plans were finalized in 1961–62 by the architects Höjer and Ljungqvist, is a good example (figure 5.28(*b*)). The terrain has been sensitively exploited, so that particularly in the summer the visitor is hardly aware of the predominance of the large parallel blocks. The centre is also successful, both visually and functionally, even though the 'underground' has been carried over the central zone on a low bridge, to unfortunate effect.

Bredäng, built on municipal land within the city limits, was the first in a series of new suburbs built during the 1960s and 1970s to the south-west of Stockholm. A slightly more recent and even larger-scale project is Skärholmen (figure 5.28(*c*)), built on municipal land which had been incorporated as late as 1963. The Skärholmen plan still clearly includes some attempt at creating a comprehensible urban form and at introducing a certain amount of variation. It has a very large centre, which was intended to cater for the whole south-western region of Greater Stockholm and which at the time was one of the largest of its kind in Europe.

Skärholmen was the target for a good deal of harsh criticism, which in retrospect may seem excessive. But the next step had already been taken: from the mid-1960s onwards a series of large residential areas, the corner-stones of the 'Million Homes' programme, were built. As these standardized giants were assembled largely from prefabricated panels, all design considerations were abandoned. The overriding goal was development in large units and quick rational construction. The design of the setting in which these houses appeared was determined not by the needs of the future residents, but by the requirements of the cranes and lorries shuttling back and forth as building proceeded. In some places the negative consequences of this are particularly noticeable, for example at Hallunda and Norsborg, two parts of an area developed mainly by public utility housing companies to the south-west of the Stockholm municipal boundaries. Massive prefabricated houses have been unimaginatively assembled in

rows on what used to be pastureland, creating an environment that lacks any visual quality or stimulating variety, anything which could generate a local identity. Because the buildings are so big they have been spread out so that plot ratios will not be too high, which means that many people have to walk a long way to the shops or to the communications in the centre. Other areas often quoted as examples of the shortcomings of 1960s planning are Tensta in Stockholm (figure 5.28(*d*)), Bergsjön and the Angered group of suburbs in Göteborg (figure 5.29), and Rosengård in Malmö (figure 5.30). Rosengård suffers from an additional drawback in the busy arterial road which cuts across the area.

Obviously suburbs of this kind are not attractive; only those who had no alternative moved there, and many of these unwilling residents looked upon it as a temporary expedient only. Turnover was high; most long-stay residents were immigrants or problem families, and the reputation of the area thus continued to deteriorate.

Quite suddenly around 1970, apparently to the surprise of planners and builders, the housing shortage gave way to a housing surplus. Apart from the enormous number of houses that had been produced, various circumstances combined to achieve this result, including stagnating growth in the densely populated areas, and a substantial rise in housing costs due in part to a reassessment and reduction in state subsidies to housing construction. But the poor quality so blatantly evident in many of the new areas also played its part. For much of the 1970s many houses in these areas were half empty. In 1975 for example there were 25,000 vacant dwelling units in the country, and most of these were in gigantic and sterile developments of the 1960s.

There has been much debate in Sweden over the last ten years or so, as to whether the housing projects of the 1960s can be regarded as the ultimate consequence of 1930s functionalist

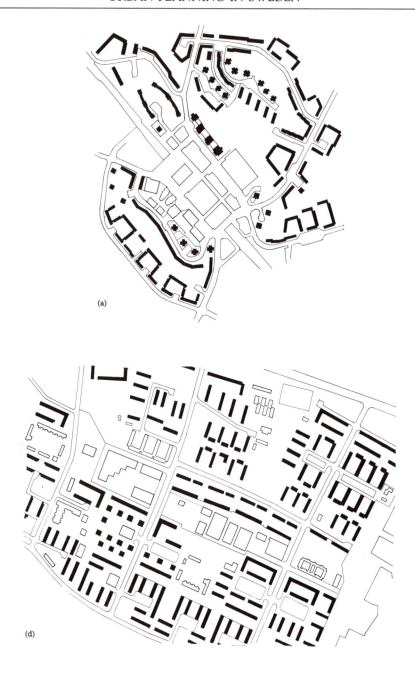

(a)

(d)

Figure 5.28. Stockholm town planning patterns II. (*a*) Vällingby (early 1950s); (*b*) Bredäng (early 1960s); (*c*) Skärholmen (mid-1960s); (*d*) Tensta (mid-1960s); (*e*) Kista (around 1970); (*f*) Dalen (late 1970s). Scale approximately 1:12,000. North uppermost with some minor deviations. *Drawing:* Karl Almgren.

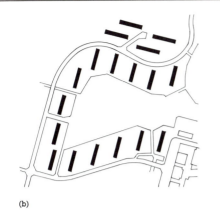

(b)

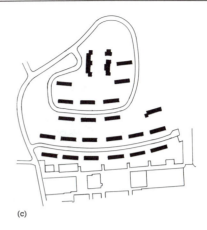

(c)

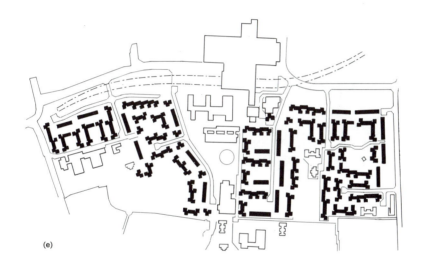

(e)

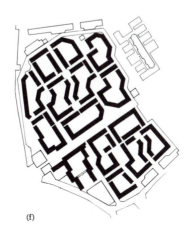

(f)

Figure 5.29. Hammarkullen, Göteborg, a striking example of the 'concrete suburbs' of the late 1960s. *Photo:* Jens S. Jensen.

thinking. Industrialized building methods, and the emphasis on technical and economic aspects, were certainly a crucial element in the functionalist programme, so there is a line of development that can be traced from the early 1930s to the late 1960s. But this is a long way from saying that the functionalists are responsible for the failures of the later period. Behind Norsborg, Angered and their fellows lay a whole series of factors, of which the national legacy of ideas from the 1930s may have been one. Moreover, the manifestos and programmes of the functionalists were a response to the conditions of the 1920s and 1930s, and must be judged in that light. That they may

seem inappropriate or questionable in a completely different situation is hardly surprising.

The 1970s: Reappraisal and Small House Construction

The 1970s heralded a radical reappraisal of Swedish housing policy. For the first time since the 1930s vacant flats were available even in the big city regions, which allowed the consumer a certain freedom of choice. From around 1975 there was a marked drop in total housing production, while the building of one-family homes was increasing in both relative and absolute terms. There was thus a dramatic shift in the relative numbers of multi-family units and small houses. In 1970 this last category represented about one-quarter of total production; by the end of the decade it accounted for three-quarters.

During the 1960s housing corporations knew that they could always find customers, whatever they produced; now, in the 1970s, they were compelled to think in terms of attractive environments. Kista (figure 5.28(*e*)) is an example of the new approach. Built towards the end of the decade, this project – consisting of Kista and its neighbouring suburbs – was built on the last large piece of land available for development within the Stockholm boundaries. The regular arrangement of uniform houses is a thing of the past. Instead an effort has been made to vary house types and planning patterns. An even more advanced example can be seen at Skarp-näck, a 1980s development built on an abandoned airfield in southern Stockholm. Kista harks back to the 'ABC' idea, in that the plans allowed a good deal of space for workplaces, which have proved attractive not least because of the excellent communications including underground, motorways and easy access to Arlanda airport.

Thus, for several reasons, the 1970s was the decade of the small house in Sweden. To begin with, many people wanted to be able to step out

Figure 5.30. Rosengård in Malmö has not undeservedly come to be regarded as one of the foremost examples of the large-scale stereotyped urban development of the 1960s. For the 1986 Housing Fair in Malmö (*Bo86*) attempts were made to reverse the continuing decline of the area by investing huge sums in improving both the indoor and outdoor environment. Similar campaigns are being planned or are already under way elsewhere. *Photo*: Lars Mongs.

of their own front door at ground level, to have a little garden, or to own and maintain their homes themselves. Secondly, the exclusive concentration on multi-family homes during the two previous decades had left a large unsatisfied demand for small houses. And last but not least the tax system favoured the small house-owner: as interest on loans was tax deductible, the progressive tax system meant that the higher income-earners enjoyed a greater tax benefit.

Towards the end of the 1960s and at the beginning of the 1970s several large areas for small houses were planned, often in fairly peripheral locations on the outskirts of the larger towns (Jonsson, 1985). These areas were usually surrounded by broad feeder roads, from which access roads led to the houses. The overall design is often monotonous, with closely packed houses arranged in unimaginative regular patterns reminiscent of American suburban areas (figure 5.31). The demand for such homes was so great that there was never any difficulty

Figure 5.31. Staffanstorp. Several one-family house districts from the late 1960s and 1970s are characterized by the same monotony in planning patterns and building designs as many American suburbs. *Photo*: Lars Mongs.

in selling them. But there were exceptions to this uniformity. At Esperanza, an area of terraced housing in Landskrona, Ralph Erskine showed that very slight adjustments in the orientation of the streets can mean a great deal: his work here (1969–70) adjoins an older area with a right-angled street network; with the help of a few twists and turns in the pattern, the monotony has been broken.

The criticism of the residential areas of the late 1960s was also directed at small-house building, and during the following decade more care was generally taken to ensure variety in the appearance of buildings and spatial arrangements, and in the grouping of houses to allow

for privacy, wind conditions, and so on. Whereas before it was often possible to implement a plan by the inclusion of any type of house of a suitable size, the idea now was to harmonize the design of the houses and the overall plan. A combination of intimacy and variety was sought. Sometimes multi-family houses were combined with single-family homes, and often also homes of different sizes, so that areas would not acquire a homogeneous social character.

As we have seen above (p. 196), there has recently been a sharp decline in the population in the more central districts of many large cities. This trend began in the city centres, but during the 1950s and 1960s it extended to the residential areas built in the inter-war years, and it became difficult to maintain the necessary public and private services as the population base declined. The municipalities were eager to check this trend, which meant that existing infrastructures were not being fully utilized and even that towns risked losing taxpayers to neighbouring municipalities. Thus over the last fifteen years or so one of the main tasks confronting town planners has been to find ways of dealing with this situation. One approach has been by way of clearance and redevelopment (see below, p. 237). Another, which it has sometimes been possible to combine with clearance, was to exploit previously unbuilt areas: it may be a case of land released from some other use, perhaps because of the transfer or discontinuation of institutions or industries, or of green open spaces – and here there would often be powerful opposition from the people already living there. As a rule these 'concentration' projects have been on a relatively small scale, but not always. Ekensberg in Stockholm built in a former shipyard area is an example of a fairly large project of this kind.

Clearance and City Redevelopment

Although to a lesser extent than in England, for example, the breakthrough for modern planning in Sweden is related to what is known broadly as the clearance problem, i.e. an ambition to replace technically and hygienically defective housing by something more appropriate to modern standards. As we have seen, the first major planning project in Stockholm in the last century concerned the general regulation of the Old City, Gamla stan. Towards the end of the nineteenth and the beginning of the present century there was a good deal of new building in the larger Swedish towns, sometimes on virgin ground and sometimes following the demolition of older buildings. However, such renewal generally came about as a private initiative, and

the prime goal was profitable investment rather than 'clearance' as such. Although there was written and spoken evidence that a large section of the urban population was living in slum-like conditions and much was heard of the need for clearance, there was still no support for any major social effort to improve the housing stock.

Not until the 1930s, when functionalism had already begun to make its mark and the Social Democrats had managed to form a government on a stable basis, was there any serious consideration of large-scale public clearance operations (on the clearance issue see Lindahl, 1969, and Folkesdotter's contribution to *Stadsförnyelse*, 1981). The requirements regarding 'acceptable standards' were becoming more stringent, and one of the main tasks that the Housing Committee (see p. 213) had to undertake, was to provide the guidelines for extensive clearance operations. These appeared in the Committee's second report (SOU, 1947: 26). While the main argument for clearance earlier had stemmed from the technical and hygienic defects of the houses themselves, the Committee now largely motivated its recommendations on town planning grounds: most existing urban building was ripe for clearance, it was claimed, because streets were too narrow, land was over-exploited, light conditions were poor, and functional differentiation inadequate. Clearance thus motivated could not be conducted property by property, or even block by block, and it was therefore necessary for the local government to assume the overriding responsibility. Nor should major clearance operations be pre-empted or obstructed by individual improvements or sporadic clearances. The Committee also invoked employment policy as a further motivation for the kind of large-scale planning operations now being recommended (Folkesdotter, 1981).

The Housing Committee imagined that most of this clearance programme could be completed within fifteen years. Because of the housing shortage, however, it was impossible to embark on the wholesale demolition of houses, and because of the situation on the labour market the government in fact tried to restrain building operations rather than investing in clearance as part of their employment policy. Thus large all-embracing clearance operations were the exception rather than the rule. The most important of these was the clearance of the Söder district in Gävle. In the later 1950s in a large and fairly central district, old wooden houses which had escaped the fire of 1869 (see above) were replaced by buildings more reminiscent of the suburban style. The main difference, compared with the usual contemporary suburban residential areas, is that the houses, some of which are noticeably tall, are arranged in closer groupings, and there are more premises for commercial operations. During the final phase of this clearance programme it was decided to save a few blocks on grounds of cultural and historical interest, and these today constitute the urban reserve of Gamla Gävle. Perhaps the main reason why the first major clearance operation of this type occurred in Gävle, was that the town had an energetic Municipal Real Estate Director who succeeded with great skill in solving all the economic and administrative problems.

The redevelopment operations of the 1950s and 1960s (see Lindahl *et al.*, 1971 and Folkesdotter and Vidén, 1974) concentrated instead on the city centres, whose structure was often still adapted to the needs of a bygone age. Streets were narrow and plots frequently small. Several factors combined to compel a change. As the cities expanded, the pressure of the growing numbers of city dwellers using the centres became more marked. But perhaps even more important was the restructuring of activities traditionally belonging to city centres, in particular the retail trade. Small shops offering personal service and an often narrow line of goods were beginning to face competition from large foodstores and department stores. The

trend was accelerated by a regulation introduced in 1953 which prevented manufacturers and wholesalers from fixing retail prices. This stimulated price competition, as was intended, which in turn encouraged rationalization and a trend towards larger units and national chains. The older small-scale buildings were not at all suitable for department stores and other large operations. New premises were regarded as necessary to rational and efficient business. Similar processes were also at work in other city-centre operations such as banks, offices and the public administration. Here, too, new work forms led to a demand for new premises.

Another important factor involving change was the rapid increase in car traffic. In 1945 there were about 50,000 private cars in Sweden. By 1960 there were 1.2 million, by 1970 2.3 million, and by 1980 2.9 million. Conditions became intolerable as this swelling stream of cars had to be absorbed into central areas whose street networks were generally on a scale suited to the needs of the pre-industrial town. Most towns lacked ringroads, so that even through-traffic had to traverse the heart of the city. There were few segregated parking places; cars had to be parked in the streets, thus making it even more difficult to drive there.

A third factor was the ambition of local politicians and officials. As we have seen, the 1950s and – even more – the 1960s were a period of optimism and confidence in the future, not least among the decision-makers in Sweden's towns. Population figures were rising steeply, faster even than the forecasts had proclaimed. Naturally this created problems, but it also implied a challenge: even quite small towns began to have big-city dreams. It has been claimed that if all the growth forecasts of the 1960s had proved correct, the population of the country would have doubled and doubled again by the year 2000. The stage was set for a vigorous and expansive policy. In municipal circles a particularly urgent goal was to transform the old urban cores into attractive modern centres, efficient and easily accessible. Given an attract-ive centre, business and other activities would be drawn to a city; without such a centre, the business would go to a rival place. It thus be-hoved every town to be farsighted, and to go one better than any comparable urban neigh-bour. This approach was typical of both the Social Democrats and the non-socialist parties, although the Social Democrats generally appear to have been the party most firmly geared to change.

Nor were there any powerful forces or restric-tions ranged against such radical renewal. Ex-isting buildings were generally of little econo-mic value; at the same time land values were high, due to the expected new development. Many property-owners obviously hoped to ex-ploit the increase in land values, either by sell-ing or by demolishing and rebuilding. Thus all those involved – politicians, centrally based companies, and property-owners – were pulling in the same direction.

No particular environmental or cultural value was usually assigned to the old buildings; on the contrary they were often regarded as a substan-dard element in the environment which it would be as well to abolish. The bodies concerned with cultural conservation still limited their interest to isolated objects of great historical or aes-thetic value. Nor does financing appear to have represented any serious restriction, at least not until the end of the 1960s – partly because the banks themselves were often directly involved, seeking to solve their own space problems. Since it was easier to demolish business prem-ises than dwellings in Sweden, with its housing shortage, the fact that relatively few people actually lived in the central districts also helped to pave the way for demolitions.

As this situation developed, it led to the transformation of many Swedish town centres – most dramatically in Stockholm. Since the late 1920s plans had been afoot for a radical renewal of the central business district. Work began in 1951 and more than 400 properties, many of

them in good condition, were demolished and replaced by about 100 new buildings (figure 5.32). At the same time many streets were widened and underground railways and traffic tunnels were constructed, all with a view to creating an efficiently functioning CBD (see also Hall, 1985).

In the provincial towns it was not possible to advance so relentlessly, but progressive local politicians did their best to follow the example of the capital city. Sometimes total renewal was limited to a few central blocks, while surround-ing areas were sporadically redeveloped. Only exceptionally was there any radical broadening of the streets in the urban core itself; instead an effort was made to carry traffic round the cen-tral areas or on ringroads further out. The new buildings were rarely much taller than the old ones (particularly in towns where the older buildings were brick). Nonetheless floorspace has often been greatly increased by the addition of basement storeys, by building over court-yards, and by reducing the height and increasing the number of storeys. One new property often, although not always, replaced several older ones (figure 5.34). The townscape changed in that the old varied street façades with houses of different shapes and sizes were replaced by new frontages, which appear more monotonous if for no other reason than because they consist of fewer houses.

How, then, did the decision-making and implementation processes work during this redevelopment of Sweden's town centres? In Stockholm the municipality was actively en-gaged during the 1950s and 1960s. Intentions for the new city centre were revised several times in structure plans (mainly 'City 62' and 'City 67'), but the final result must be regarded as the product of a long sequence of compromises and *ad hoc* decisions rather than the result of any initial planning vision. From the start the princi-ple was adopted that the municipality should acquire by purchase or expropriation posses-sion of any sites that might be affected by the

Figure 5.32. Demolitions in the centre of Stockholm 1951–87. Areas marked in black, demolished before or during 1975, hatched areas demolished after 1975. The concentrated area in the south was mainly demolished under municipal auspices during the 1950s and 1960s, while many of the more scattered demolitions were carried out by private interests during the 1970s and 1980s and were largely motivated by neglect, in itself a result of the municipality's plans. *Source*: Hall (1985) (updated). *Drawing*: Dieter Künkel; supplementary data supplied by Susanna Järnare and Johanna Karlin.

city redevelopment scheme. A new law known as the *Lex Norrmalm* was introduced for the purpose, providing the municipality with extensive expropriation rights. The idea was that the municipality acquired all the property in a block, demolished the buildings, and carried out any necessary technical work such as the construction of tunnels. The plots, combined into larger units, were then disposed of again but now as leasehold land. The system worked so long as there were firms interested in building on the conditions offered, but by the end of the 1960s large sections of the centre had been demolished without the municipality having been able to find prospective builders (for a more detailed account see Hall, 1985).

In the provinces the municipalities generally assumed a more passive role, although the situation varied from town to town. Masterplans for the centre were generally made, with a

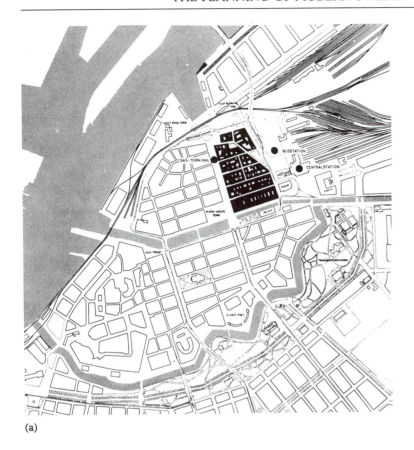

(a)

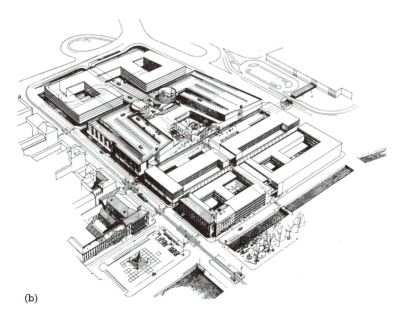

(b)

Figure 5.33. City centre redevelopment in Göteborg. (*a*) Central Göteborg in the 1960s with the area which was redeveloped marked in black (cf. figure 5.3). (*b*) Perspective drawing in a plan from 1965 showing the new central district, Östra Nordstan. This new centre was successful, but it also meant that parts of the old office and retail business district were emptied of qualified activities. Similar processes can be observed in Stockholm. *Source:* Åström (1967).

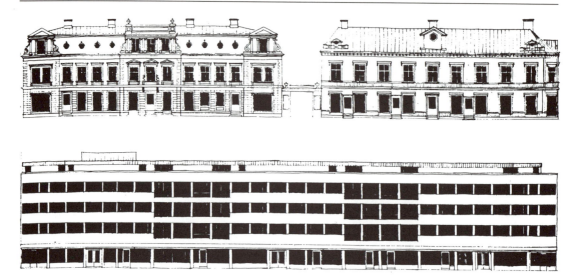

Figure 5.34. Gävle, the block Klipparen before and after renewal around 1960. The block faces the central 'esplanade' (cf. figure 5.12). *Source*: Lindahl *et al.* (1971).

view to controlling subsequent developments. Not uncommonly these plans were commissioned from consultants in Stockholm, which meant that the solutions were often somewhat arbitrary. The plans generally implied radical alterations and, particularly during the 1960s, also extensive adaptation to motor traffic. The plan was an impelling factor, but whether or not the development was realized depended on the property-owner's resources and attitudes. The forces for change were the speculative building and construction companies, or companies seeking premises for their own operations, or the municipalities themselves. Usually the developer owned the land; it was probably an exception for buildings in provincial town centres to be built on land leased from the municipality.

Towards the end of the 1960s, when every self-respecting municipality had manged to produce impressive plans for further rapid expansion, the trend went into reverse. The rate of urban growth declined dramatically, and problems began to appear in the Swedish economy

(cf. above p. 195). At the same time public opinion was being roused against the rough handling meted out to existing townscapes, with its heavy bias in favour of motor traffic. As a result of this and other factors, the transformation of the town centres often came to a halt half way through. New plans with a more conservationist bent began to appear around this time. In Stockholm the 1975 city plan proposal marks an almost complete stop to the old comprehensive ambitions.

A good many older buildings were still left at the beginning of the 1970s in the central districts of some Swedish towns. But as later events have proved, they had not really been saved. The great 1960s planning projects which disallowed improvements and the care of existing buildings and held out the prospect of huge profits later, meant that many houses were left to the ravages of urban blight. This was particularly obvious in Stockholm, but was noticeable in most expanding provincial towns as well. This is one – if not the only – reason why even during the last fifteen or so years a great many buildings have still been demolished, but now generally un-accompanied by the protests that were so common around 1970. The firm and widespread belief that the wave of demolition in the heart of Swedish towns drew to a close as the 1960s ended is thus a misconception.

If we now turn to the course of urban housing clearance in Sweden, we would find that little happened during the 1950s, apart from a few sporadic operations under private auspices and one or two slightly larger municipal undertakings. At the same time, because of plans for future clearance schemes, property-owners did not want to maintain their houses, and indeed were often forbidden to do so. Many houses which might have been brought up to an acceptable standard without too much trouble, were instead left to decay for decades.

During the 1960s redevelopment operations were on the increase, generally involving total clearance, i.e. demolition and new building. Roughly speaking about 10,000 dwelling units a year disappeared in this way over a ten-year period (see also Schönbeck, 1983). The most dramatic changes were made in Göteborg, which possessed several relatively central districts consisting mainly of the *landshövdinge* houses described above (p. 210). In several of these areas the old three-storey buildings were destroyed, to be replaced by tall tenement blocks (for example Majorna, and at the beginning of the 1970s Annedal and Landala). The new town plans showed little interest in design. The urban changes were promoted and stage-managed by the municipality of Göteborg itself. Since the floorspace ratio had previously been fairly low, and since few people were living in the old-fashioned buildings it was possible to increase the resident population greatly as a result of the clearance operations. The local politicians saw this as a matter of urgency; the provision of housing on attractive sites would, they hoped, put a stop to emigration to neighbouring municipalities. Stockholm's brick buildings were less susceptible to clearance

plans, but in many parts of the inner city individual properties were redeveloped, generally on the initiative of private owners.

In Göteborg the systematic destruction of the *landshövdinge* houses aroused increasing opposition, and elsewhere too people began to question whether demolition was the best approach to redevelopment problems. In Stockholm discussions and investigations during the late 1960s about the development of Mariaberget and Katarinaberget to the south of Gamla stan proved to be something of a turning-point. In 1968 a Clearance Committee was appointed by the government. One of the issues it was asked to address was whether the wave of clearances expected during the 1970s could not be partly conducted in the shape of modernizations. In their final reports (*SOU*, 1971:63 and 64) the committee suggested changing national loan conditions in such a way as to encourage repair and renovation. During the 1970s and 1980s clearance operations have been dominated by renovation, though often of an unnecessarily heavy-handed kind which has spoilt much of the historical value of the buildings, but there have also been extensive demolitions, mainly as a result of various small scattered redevelopment operations.

During the later 1980s a good many redevelopment schemes have been part of a 'ROT' programme (ROT = *Reparation, Ombyggnad, Tillbyggnad*, or repair, renovation, extension). To qualify for a loan under this programme, however, radical and costly undertakings are often required, which sometimes means that the previous tenants cannot continue to live in the house. Many multi-family blocks and small houses characteristic of earlier periods have been spoilt, perhaps by the addition of insulation and new façade cladding in materials differing from the original. For these and other reasons the ROT programme has been the subject of much controversy, but a detailed account of the debate would be outside the range of the present book.

SOME RECENT TRENDS

If the study of planning history has anything to teach us, it must be that things seldom turn out as we might expect at any given moment. The unexpected is always lurking round the next corner. In Sweden it is particularly difficult to predict the next developments in planning and the built environment, as the consequences of the 1987 Planning and Building Act are still uncertain and controversial. We shall not tempt providence here by even trying to predict the next moves.

However, a few words should be said about present trends. The climate has changed a great deal since the middle of the 1970s. Then, as stagnation hit the heavily populated regions and many industries were in decline, there was a widespread belief that the age of the planner and developer was over. Modern Sweden had been built, and all that remained to do was maintenance, a certain amount of clearance and a little additional building. The great projects of the 1960s like the Stockholm ring road were dismissed as examples of the deficient realism of the previous period.

The mood of the 1980s is quite different. The main metropolitan regions – and Greater Stockholm in particular – are growing rapidly again. Industry has reported good profits several years running and stock prices are rising. Sweden is building, perhaps as never before; demand is outrunning the available labour and the capacity of the developers, with a consequent increase in prices. The despondency of the 1970s has given way to optimism and confidence in the future. Property, particularly in central locations, has become an attractive investment, often subject to short-term speculation. A great many major investments in new city centre building are probably encouraged by a tax system which favours saving in the form of retirement pensions, which means in turn that insurance companies have plenty of capital which by law has to be invested in real estate.

Several of the great 1960s projects have been revived, for example the Stockholm ring road which is now being supported even by those who say they want to reduce traffic in the inner city. Other traffic plans include a 'Scandinavian link' from Norway through Sweden and Denmark to the Continent. Consequently the vexed question of a bridge over Öresund has been brought up again and a definite decision may be made within a year or two, unless there is a new economic downturn or if the cross-party green lobby succeeds in arousing enough opposition to the link, because of the extra traffic concentration in several regions already under heavy pressure.

The term 'post-industrialism' is being bandied about, often with rather ill-defined connotations. Although new technology may have radically altered production processes, we still live in a highly industrialized society.

But the expression 'post-industrial' does seem particularly apt in the context of planning and urban development. One of the most important issues facing physical planners over the last ten or fifteen years has been the re-use of land released for new development as a result of changes in manufacturing and communications systems – changes associated with 'post-industrial' times. In particular the great harbours and railyards of the industrial age have enabled post-industrial developments to rise in central locations. Where great cranes once clattered and railway trucks creaked along, where countless workers trooped to work – there the dwellings and offices of today are going up. The foremost international example is Docklands in London. But several similar projects, albeit on a smaller scale, are also under way in the North. In Göteborg offices and housing are to be built in a vast harbour and dock area; the resemblance to Docklands is striking. Malmö and Helsingborg also have well-advanced plans for re-equipping and revitalizing their sea-fronts; so too do Copenhagen and several Norwegian towns.

In Stockholm it is particularly the railway

hich has released most land. What was once a large railyard on Södermalm is being rebuilt as a residential area; and it is typical that one of the foremost post-modernistic architects, Ricardo Bofill, is being involved in part of the design (figure 5.35). At the very heart of the city new decks are being built over the central railway station area, making a piece of land 700 m × 140 m available for exploitation. Offices, a conference centre and a hotel are being planned. The urban landscape in this part of the inner city will be radically altered, perhaps even more dramatically than neighbouring Norrmalm during the redevelopments of the 1950s and 1960s. And this still represents only a fraction of the present building activities in Stockholm; several other projects are at the planning stage or are already being realized, among them further examples of that post-industrial monument par excellence, the great international hotel. At the same time the search is on for yet more free land, particularly in the central districts, which could be used for residential building. Green areas which used to be regarded as vital oases are no longer sacrosanct.

Office skyscrapers, hotels and conference centres are by no means exclusive to Stockholm; all the major provincial towns try to keep up as well as they can. It seems that every town with any self-respect has to have its own skyscraper, even if it remains the only one, to assert its 'urban image'. Nor is the added density to existing residential building a purely Stockholm phenomenon.

To return to Stockholm, however: there is a strong tendency for high-tech industry head offices and consultancy firms to look for sites to the north of the city. This is where the highly qualified workforce tends to live, and this is the area closest to the region's international airport, Arlanda. The motorway between Stockholm and Arlanda is the strongest locational magnet in the region; great new developments are appearing each year and, if the present trend is maintained, the time cannot be far off when the road will be flanked by a more or less continuous ribbon of commercial building. Several major multi-purpose projects are also under way: business campuses and a new 'town' to be known as Arlanda City, which are all being tailor-made to meet the requirements of post-industrial production, and all located so that it will be possible to fix meetings with foreign business colleagues 'five minutes after passport control', to quote the project's own manifesto. In the light of this development it is obvious that the location of the international airport was the most important decision in the development history of Greater Stockholm, far more important than any regional plan.

This development is reinforcing the existing imbalance within the region: in the suburban municipalities on this side of town housing is better, jobs are more interesting, wages higher, and municipal taxes considerably lower than on the southern side. And in the national perspective there is also an imbalance between the Stockholm region as a whole and the rest of the country. Should Stockholm's present expansion be restrained or encouraged? Both alternatives have their champions: either, they say, Sweden's future prosperity needs a Stockholm which can grow unchecked to become a metropolitan region of international stature; or, the others warn, the rest of the country will be drained of qualified activities.

A distinguishing feature of present-day planning and building is the generally higher pretentions to quality in environmental and architectural design compared with the 1960s; planning is not only post-industrial but also post-modern. This applies as we have seen to much housing production and even to many office-building projects. A good environment, it is thought, encourages a qualified workforce to develop its 'creativity', as well as adding to the 'corporate image'. The Arlanda City manifesto declares that the town should 'give the impression of being a very special place'; before any new project starts, the question should be

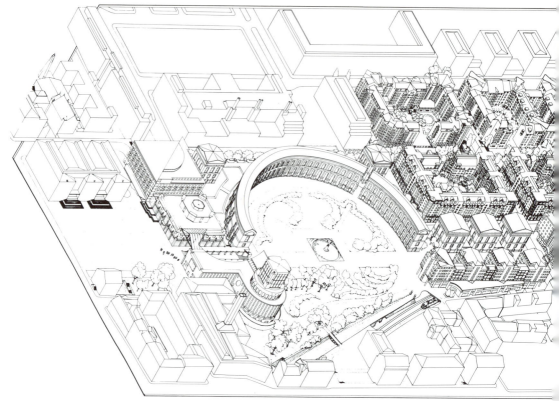

Figure 5.35. The area known as Södra station in central Stockholm. Perspective drawing by Jan Inge-Hagström showing how the district will appear when it is completed in the early 1990s. The large curved building has been designed by Ricardo Bofill. *Source:* Stadsbyggnadskontoret, Stockholm.

asked: 'Has this got that "little bit extra" which can make Arlanda City a perfect composition?'

Another characteristic feature of present-day planning and building is that, far more than before, it is based on industry's conditions, while the borderline between public and private investment is tending to weaken. In many large current projects, public and private interests are so intertwined that the steering and controlling functions of the political institutions are rendered ineffective, and it is often impossible to say who is actually responsible for decisions. Thus in the Arlanda City manifesto it is logical – as well as absurd – to call for 'a new form of municipal government in which business also has the voting power and responsibility for issues affecting development opportunities in their "own" municipality'.

What is becoming known as 'consortium planning', whereby leading representatives of the municipality and industry negotiate with one another to agree on large and important projects, thus reducing the planning and political process to an empty formality, became increasingly common towards the end of the 1980s. In the typical case a consortium, consisting of building contractors and insurance companies, negotiates with the municipality. The consortium provides something which the municipality wants, while the municipality exploits its planning monopoly in granting generous building permits, and the insurance company takes care of the financing. This kind of agreement makes inevitably for secrecy. The prime example is the gigantic sports arena in Stockholm, the Globe, built in the shape of a

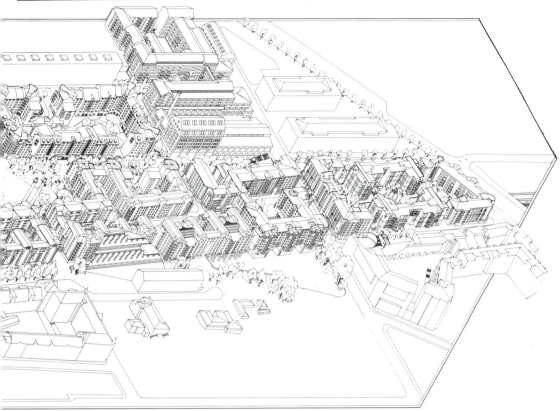

enormous globe and visible from many places in the city. A consortium built the arena and presented it to the municipality in exchange for the rights to transform an area around the arena into a large office and retail centre.

To the politicians and planners of the 1960s it was self-evident that planning should steer developments, and not the other way round. But planning today is not a question of drawing up grand visions of the future, but simply of investigating and coordinating, or even just registering decisions already made. It is a sign of the times that the National Board of Physical Planning and Building has been merged with another authority and is now located a long way away from Stockholm (see above, p. 203). This cannot perhaps be compared with Margaret Thatcher's abolition of the Greater London Council, but it is an indication of similar trends and values.

Who are we planning for today – if we can speak of planning at all? The spontaneous answer might be largely for a fairly small group of well-educated and competent people in the prime of life, not hampered by time-consuming family obligations – the group known in Britain and the United States as 'dinkies' (double income, no kids). The overriding goal that is cited for Arlanda City is to create 'a beautiful working environment for great young brains'.

It would be misleading to generalize from such declarations, or even from projects like Arlanda City. And yet, despite the evident ambitions regarding environmental and architectural quality, present-day planning does seem to lack something of the social commitment, the visions of a better and more equitable society, which used to mark the urban development debate in Sweden. 'Human' needs, like re-equipping the many shabby schools throughout the country, have been overshadowed by spectacular multi-billion projects.

But if the 1980s in many ways resembled the 1960s, perhaps the 1990s will be more like the 1970s. Perhaps in ten years time the grandiose projects of today will have found their way into the curio cabinets of planning history.

NOTE

1. Following the constitutional reform of 1809, and until 1974, government decisions were reached by the King in Council, referred to as *Kungl Maj:t* or His Majesty. Without any accompanying change in the letter of the law, the *de facto* right of decision gradually shifted from the person of the monarch to the council; at the same time parliamentary practice was evolving. In the 1975 constitutional reform parliamentarianism was confirmed by law and the monarch's part in government decisions ceased. After that, the government is officially referred to as *regeringen*. Both *Kungl Maj:t* and *regeringen* have been translated here as the government.

ANNOTATED BIBLIOGRAPHY

The aim of this bibliography is to present the literature on which the chapter is based, and also to provide a survey of Swedish research on planning history. The publication of the book has been delayed for various reasons. Since the manuscript was completed, further publications have appeared which it has thus not been possible to refer to in the text.

The only survey of Swedish town planning from the Middle Ages to the present day is Åström (1967, published in Swedish and English editions). The emphasis of the book is on the twentieth century, while descriptions of earlier developments are brief and in some cases questionable. The author's discussion of the present century bears a strong imprint of ideas and values current at the time of writing.

Urban Development and Planning before 1850

Basic surveys on urban development in the Nordic countries are provided in Authén Blom (ed.) (1977), I–III. The first part deals with the Middle Ages, the second with the seventeenth and eighteenth centuries, and the third with the first phase of industrialism. The sections on Sweden have been written by Hans Andersson, Birgitta Ericsson and Bo Öhngren.

The comprehensive work on Swedish town planning during the seventeenth century is Eimer (1961).

Jutikkala (1968) is mainly concerned with the legal and administrative aspects of the town regulations. Nisser (1970) provides, albeit only in essay form, an excellent overview of developments in town planning during the eighteenth century.

Urban Planning – the Breakthrough 1850–1915

The first part of this section, 'Changes in society', is based mainly on Carlsson and Rosén (1980). The second part of this work, which is written by Sten Carlsson, is by far the best available survey of modern Swedish history. Nilsson (1984) is concerned with urban development during the period in question.

The rest of the section is an abbreviated and slightly revised version of an essay published in Hall (ed.) (1984). In the notes to this essay sources are reported, and a comprehensive survey of the literature is provided. Göran Lindahl's seminal survey of town planning during the period concerned (Lindahl, 1965), however, deserves particular mention. Other useful works are the monographs on Gävle (Karlström, 1974), Kiruna (Brunnström, 1981), Sandviken (Carlestam, 1986), Stockholm (Selling, 1970 and Johansson, 1987), Södertälje (Gelotte, 1980) and Umeå (Eriksson, 1975).

Some Aspects of Social and Economic Developments

Carlsson and Rosén (1980) provide a comprehensive exposition of social developments in Sweden during the present century, with extensive bibliographical references. The section draws heavily on this book. The perspective on the 1950s and 1960s is, however, preliminary and personal; the period has not yet been the subject of any comprehensive research. But similar views can be found in other works, for example Elander (1978).

The development of urban areas during the 20th century is described and analysed in Nilsson (1983). Falk (1976) should also be mentioned in this context. Åman (1968) is a condensed but very informative survey of the character of twentieth-century towns.

Building Legislation and the Planning System in the Twentieth Century

Reports submitted by government-appointed committees are generally published in the series *Statens offentliga utredningar* (abbreviated *SOU*) numbered consecutively each year. Legislative developments can be followed in detail in these reports and in the published proceedings of the Riksdag. The major survey of the 1947 planning legislation in a legal perspective is Bexelius, Nordenstam and Körlof (1970) and earlier editions. Similar commentaries on the 1907 Town Planning Act and the 1931 legislation are Westring (1908) and Forssman (1932).

Comprehensive physical planning is discussed in Folkesdotter (1987). A concentrated exposition of the origins and evolution of synoptic planning is provided by Rudberg (1985). Important perspectives on comprehensive planning are also to be found in the same author's book on Uno Åhrén (1981). Thomas J. Anton provides in American a picture of the special problems of the Stockholm region (1975).

Among surveys of community planning in Sweden, Tobé (1972) and Svensson and Thufvesson (1973) can be mentioned. National physical planning is also described in *Fysisk riksplanering* (1985, and earlier editions) published by the Ministry of Housing and the National Board of Physical Planning and Building. This booklet is also published in English: *National Physical Planning* (1981 and earlier editions).

Residential Areas and Suburbs

An excellent survey of housing construction from the 1920s onwards is provided in the essays by Olle Svedberg, Eva Rudberg and Bengt O. H. Johansson in *Funktionalismens genombrott och kris, Svensk bostadsbyggande 1930–80* (1980). The first version of this book, which appeared in 1976, was provoked by an exhibition in Munich: *Aufbruch und Krise des Funktionalismus, Bauen und Wohnen in Schweden 1930–80* (1976). Planning and building in Sweden during the present century have also been the subject of a special number of *Process: Architecture* (No. 68, 1986), entitled 'Swedish Contemporary Architecture'. The concise yet comprehensive text was written by Kristina Berglund.

Some important works have appeared on various aspects of twentieth-century housing construction. Eva Rudberg's study of Uno Åhrén has already been mentioned. The seminal work on the housing districts of the 1920s is Linn (1974). Functionalism's breakthrough is treated in Råberg (1970). Mention should also be made of Dahlman and Gärdborn (1975), a critical analysis of housing construction in an organization theory perspective. Strömberg (1984) should also be mentioned in this connection.

Åke Daun has collected a number of essays and papers on post-war housing (1983).

A great deal has been written on planning and housing construction in Stockholm during the present century. The exhaustive work is Sidenbladh (1981). The author was long active in Stockholm's planning system, for more than ten years as head of the town planning office. His exposition is detailed and reliable, but naturally the importance and consequences of planning are not questioned. Another important work is Johansson (1974), which discusses among other things the effects of land ownership and communications on the internal differentiation of the Stockholm region. Greater Stockholm is depicted here as a product of market forces rather than of planning. This viewpoint characterizes the same author's recently (1987) published building history of Stockholm. The outstanding architectural guide to Stockholm by Henrik O. Andersson and Fredric Bedoire should also be mentioned. After running into several editions in Swedish, it has now been published in English (1988). Among other works, mention should be made of 1976 issue of the yearbook *Sankt Eriks årsbok*, which contains several essays on the Stockholm suburbs, and Goldfield (1979).

Various studies have been made of housing construction in individual towns. Of these, mention should be made of Andersson (1977) on Göteborg, and Bergold (1985) on Uppsala. Both studies have a primarily architecture-historical orientation, but they also describe the background in social history and housing policy. Two shorter studies are Gejvall-Seger (1976) on Norrköping and *Bygga skånska städer* (1975) on towns in the southern province of Skåne. As we have seen, Örebro has acquired a reputation as something of a model town with respect to housing policy, as a result of several noted residential areas that have been built there. Housing policy in Örebro has been scrutinized in Egerö (1979) and Strömberg (1984).

The planning of residential areas devoted to single-family homes has aroused much less interest in Sweden, both in reality and in writing, than areas with blocks of flats. The garden suburbs built at the beginning of the century, however, have been discussed in a planning perspective by Stavenow-Hidemark (1971). The story of the detached single-family house between 1950 and 1980 is told in Jonsson (1985). The description concentrates largely on the houses themselves; the overall plans are mentioned only briefly. A similar work on terraced housing is Arén (1980).

Clearance and Urban Renewal

Göran Lindahl has described the main outlines of the clearance problem in the present century in an essay published in 1969. *Stadsförnyelse – kontinuitet, gemenskap, inflytande* (*SOU*, 1981:100), published by the Committee for Urban Renewal, includes a series of essays on urban renewal and urban development in a variety of perspectives. Of particular interest is Gärd Folkesdotter's contribution. The same author's study (1981) of the social housing committee and the clearance problem should also be mentioned. A good survey of the clearance issue is provided in Schönbeck (1983, unpublished).

Finally, on the subject of urban renewal the present author has published a number of essays on the redevelopment of Stockholm city centre, collected in Hall (1985). Parts of the book are in English. The section in the present chapter on the transformation of the city centre is an abbreviated version of pp. 145–153 in this work. And these pages are in turn are based largely on Lindahl *et al.* (1971). Folkesdotter (1974) and Folkesdotter and Vidén (1974) are also important in this context. It should also be mentioned that Göran Sidenbladh (cf. above) has recently published his views on the redevelopment of the Stockholm city centre (1985).

REFERENCES

Ahlberg, Gösta (1958) *Stockholms befolkningsutveckling efter 1850*. Stockholm: Stockholms kommunalförvaltning.

Åman, Anders (1968) Städer som Karlskoga. *Arkitektur*, Nos 5/6.

Améen, Lennart (1964) *Stadsbebyggelse och domänstruktur, Svensk stadsutveckling i relation till ägoförhållanden och administrativa gränser*. Lund: Gleerups.

Andersson, Birgitta (1977) *Idealbostad eller nödbostad? Det moderna flerfamiljshusets arkitekturutveckling studerad i Göteborg*. Göteborg: Chalmers tekniska högskola.

Andersson, Henric O. and Bedoire, Fredric (1988) *Stockholm – Architecture and Townscape*. Stockholm: Prisma.

Anton, Thomas J. (1975) *Governing Greater Stockholm, A Study of Policy Development and System Change*. Berkeley: University of California Press.

Arén, Hans 1980 *Radhuset som folkbostad*. Göteborg: Chalmers tekniska högskola.

Åström, Kell (1967) *Svensk stadsplanering*. Stockholm: Byggmästarens förlag.

Åström, Kell (1967) *City Planning in Sweden*. Stockholm: The Swedish Institute.

Aufbruch und Krise des Funktionalismus, Bauen und Wohnen in Schweden 1930–80. (1976) Stockholm: Sveriges arkitekturmuseum.

Authén Blom, Grethe (ed.) (1977) *Urbaniseringsprocessen i Norden*, I–III. Oslo: Universitetsförlaget.

Berglund, Kristina (1986) Swedish Contemporary Architecture. *Process: Architecture*, No. 68.

Bergold, Carl Erik (1985) *Bostadsbyggande i Uppsala 1900–1950 – en aspekt på folkhemmets framväxt*. Uppsala: Acta Universitatis Upsaliensis.

Bexelius, A., Nordenstam, A. and Körlof, V. (1970) *Byggnadslagstiftningen*, 5th ed. Stockholm: P. A. Nordstedt & Söners förlag.

Brunnström, Lasse (1981) *Kiruna – ett samhällsbygge i sekelskiftets Sverige*, I. Umeå: Norrländska städer och kulturmiljöer.

Bygga skånska städer, Aspekter på stadsarkitektur efter 1850. (1975) Malmö: Sydsvenska Dagbladet.

Carlestam, Gösta (1986) *Samhällsbyggarna vid Storsjön, En plats i utkanten blir en stad i världen*. Gävle: Statens institut för byggnadsforskning.

Carlsson, Sten and Rosén, Jerker (1980) *Svensk historia, 2, Tiden efter 1718*. Stockholm: Esselte studium.

Dahlman, Carsten & Gärdborn, Ingemar (1975) *Utvecklingsproblem i Bygg-Sverige*. Stockholm: Statens råd för byggnadsforskning.

Dahlström, Edmund (1951) *Trivsel i Söderort*. Stockholm: Stockholms kommunalförvaltning.

Danneskiold–Samsoe, Otto (1945) *Nutida engelsk samhällsplanering*. Stockholm: Forum.

Daun, Åke (1983) *Ethnology Housing and Communication Studies 1972–83*. Stockholm: Institutet för folklivsforskning.

Egerö, Bertil (1979) *En mönsterstad granskas, Bostadsplanering i Örebro 1945–75*. Stockholm: Byggforskningsrådet.

Eimer, Gerhard (1961) *Die Stadtplanung im schwedischen Ostseereich 1600–1715*. Stockholm: Svenska bokförlaget.

Elander, Ingemar (1978) *Det nödvändiga och det önskvärda: en studie av socialdemokratisk ideologi och regionalpolitik 1940–72*. Stockholm: Arkiv för studier i arbetarrörelsens historia.

Eriksson, Karin (1975) *Studier i Umeå stads byggnadshistoria, Från 1621 till omkring 1895*. Umeå: Acta universitatis Umensis.

Falk, Thomas (1976) *Urban Sweden, Changes in the Distribution of Population – the 1960s in Focus*. Stockholm: The Economic Research Institute.

Folkesdotter, Gärd (1974) *Stadskärnans behandling under 20 år*. Stockholm: Byggforskningen.

Folkesdotter, Gärd (1981) '*Störtas skall det gamla snart i gruset'*, *Bostadssociala utredningens syn på äldre bebyggelse*. Gävle: Statens institut för byggnadsforskning.

Folkesdotter, Gärd (1987) *Nyttans tjänare och skönhetens riddare*, *Hur arkitekter som författare till översiktliga planer 1947–74 förhållit sig till professionens överordnade värden*. Gävle: Statens institut för byggnadsforskning.

Folkesdotter, Gärd and Vidén, Sonja (1974) *Stadsomvandling i plan och verklighet*. Stockholm: Byggforskningen.

Forssman, Hilding (1932) *Stadsplanelagen jämte byggnadsstadgan*. *Stockholm: P. A. Nordstedt & Söners Förlag*.

Funktionalismens genombrott och kris, Svensk bostadsbyggande 1930–80. (1980) Stockholm: Arkitekturmuseet.

Fysisk riksplanering. (1985) Stockholm: Statens planverk.

Gejvall-Seger, Birgit (1976) Stadsplanering och bebyggelseutveckling i Norrköping 1719–1970, *Norrköpings historia*, VI(16). Norrköping: Norrköpings kommuns historiekommitté.

Gelotte, Göran (1980) *Stadsplaner och bebyggelsetyper i Södertälje intill år 1910*. Stockholm: Stockholm University.

Generalplan för Stockholm. (1958) Stockholm: P. A. Nordstedt & Söners förlag.

Goldfield, David R. (1979) Suburban development in Stockholm and the United States: a comparison of form and function, in Hammarström, Ingrid and Hall, Thomas (eds), *Growth and Transformation of the Modern City*. Stockholm: Almquist & Wiksell International.

Hall, Thomas (1970) Anders Torstensson och Södermalm. *Konsthistorisk tidskrift*, No. 34.

Hall, Thomas (1978) *Mittelalterliche Stadtgrundrisse, Versuch einer Übersicht der Entwicklung in Deutschland und Frankreich*. Stockholm: Almquist & Wiksell International.

Hall, Thomas (1984) Stadsplanering i vardande, Kring lagstiftning, beslutsprocess och planeringsidéer 1860–1910, in Hall, Thomas (ed.) *Städer i utveckling, Tolv studier kring stadsförändringar tillägnade Ingrid Hammarström*. Stockholm: Svensk stadsmiljö.

Hall, Thomas (1985) '*i nationell skala . . .*' *Studier kring cityplaneringen i Stockholm. 'on a national scale . . .*', *Studies on the Redevelopment of Stockholm's City Center*. Stockholm: Svensk stadsmiljö.

Hall, Thomas (1986) *Planung europäischer Hauptstädte, Zur Entwicklung des Städtebaues im 19. Jahrhundert*. Stockholm: Almquist & Wiksell.

Historisk statistik för Sverige, I, 2nd ed. Stockholm: Statistiska centralbyrån, 1969.

Johansson, Ingemar (1974) *Den stadslösa storstaden, Förortsbildning och bebyggelseomvandling kring Stockholm 1870–1970*. Stockholm: Statens råd för byggnadsforskning.

Johansson, Ingemar (1987) *Stor-Stockholms bebyggelsehistoria, Markpolitik, planering och byggande under sju sekler*. Stockholm: Gidlunds.

Jonsson, Leif (1985) *Från egnahem till villa, Enfamiljshuset i Sverige*. Stockholm: Liber.

Jutikkala, Eino (1968) Town Planning in Sweden and Finland until the middle of the nineteenth century. *Scandinavian Economic History Review*, No. 16.

Karlström, Ture (1974) *Gävle stadsbild, Bebyggelsehistoria och samhällsplanering till 1900-talets början*. Gävle: Flanör bokhandel.

Lindahl, Göran (1965) Karlstad 1865: stadsbyggande för hundra år sedan. *Värmland förr och nu*, No. 63.

Lindahl, Göran (1969) Saneringsfrågan – en kritisk översikt. *Stadsvård*. Stockholm: Svenska kommunaltekniska föreningen.

Lindahl, Göran *et al.* (1971) Centrumkvarterens öde: återblick på 50- och 60-talen i svenska städer. *Arkitektur*, No. 5.

Linn, Björn (1974) *Storgårdskvarteret, Ett bebyggelsemönsters bakgrund och karaktär*. Stockholm: Statens institut för byggnadsforskning.

Linn, Björn (1984) De renhjärtade, de vilsekomna. *Arkitektur*, No. 4.

Mårtelius, Johan (1982) Gustaf. Linden och hans drabanter. *Arkitekturmuseet årsbok*.

Mumford, Lewis (1938) *The Culture of Cities*. London: Secker and Warburg.

National Physical Planning. (1981) Stockholm: Ministry of Housing and Physical Planning and National Board of Physical Planning and Building.

Nilsson, Lars (1983) En översikt över den svenska tätortsutvecklingen 1920–1975. *Studia Historica Jyväskyläensia*, 27. Jyväskylä: Jyväskylän Yliopisto.

Nilsson, Lars (1984) Öst och väst i Sveriges urbana historia 1800–1900, Försök till en teori om ojämn urbanutveckling, in Hall, Thomas (ed.) *Städer i utveckling, Tolv studier kring stadsförändringar tillägnade Ingrid Hammarström*. Stockholm: Svensk stadsmiljö.

Nisser, Marie (1970) Stadsplanering i svenska riket 1700–1809, in Zeitler, Rudolf (ed.), *Sju uppsatser i svensk arkitekturhistoria*. Uppsala: Acta Universitatis Upsaliensis.

Paulsson, Gregor (1950 and 1953) *Svensk stad* I–III. Stockholm: Albert Bonniers förlag.

Råberg, Per G. (1970) *Funktionalistiskt genombrott*. Stockholm: Sveriges arkitekturmuseum.

Rudberg, Eva (1981) *Uno Åhrén, En föregångsman inom 1900-talets arkitektur och samhällsplanering*. Stockholm: Almquist & Wiksell International.

Rudberg, Eva (1985) *Från mönsterplan till kommunöversikt, Den fysiska översiktsplaneringens framväxt i Sverige*. Stockholm: Statens råd för byggnadsforskning.

Sankt Eriks årsbok (1976).

Schönbeck, Boris (1983) *Stadsförnyelse i Sverige*. Unpublished.

Selling, Gösta (1970) *Esplanadsystemet och Albert Lindhagen, Stadsplanering i Stockholm åren 1857–1887*. Stockholm: Stockholms kommuns monografiserie.

Sidenbladh, Göran (1981) *Planering för Stockholm 1923–1958*. Stockholm: Liber förlag.

Sidenbladh, Göran (1985) *Norrmalm förnyat 1951–1981*. Stockholm: Liber.

Stadsförnyelse – kontinuitet, gemenskap, inflytande (*SOU*, 1981: 100).

Stavenow-Hidemark, Elisabet (1971) *Villabebyggelse i Sverige 1900–1925*. Stockholm: Nordiska museet.

Strömberg, Thord (1984) *Kommunsocialismen inför verkligheten* Örebro: Örebro Studies.

Sutcliffe, Anthony (1979) Environmental control and planning in European Capitals 1850–1914: London, Paris and Berlin, in Hammarström, Ingrid and Hall, Thomas (eds.), *Growth and Transformation of the Modern City*. Stockholm: Almquist & Wiksell International.

Svenson, Göte and Thufvesson, Bengt (1973) *Hur planeras Sverige?* Stockholm: Allmänna förlaget.

Tobé, Erik (1972) *Kommunal planering*. Stockholm: Almquist & Wiksell.

Westring, Hjalmar (1908) *Lagen angående stadsplan och tomtindelning*. Stockholm: P. A. Nordstedt & Söners förlag.

6

CONCLUDING REMARKS:
IS THERE A NORDIC
PLANNING TRADITION?

Thomas Hall

In this book the planning histories of the Nordic countries have been presented in separate chapters. In conclusion let us look briefly at developments in a Nordic perspective and compare these with what was happening in the rest of Europe.

In this context we can disregard mediaeval urban development. We need only note that the picture was by no means the same in the four Nordic countries: in Sweden the urban system developed later than in Denmark and Norway, and in Finland there was only one mediaeval town of any importance, namely Turku (Åbo). Swedish mediaeval towns were also more influenced by German urban culture than were the Norwegian or the Danish.

THE EMERGENCE OF PLANNING

Throughout the North the seventeenth century was a period of intensive urban building, promoted by the respective governments with mercantilist zeal and an eye to military and defensive strategies. In the Danish-Norwegian kingdom, Christian IV (1588–1648) was particularly active in founding towns, among others Christiania (figure 4.4) and Christiansand in

Norway and Kristianstad in present-day Sweden. His projects also include the Christianshavn district in Copenhagen (figure 2.2(*a*)). In Sweden-Finland an even more comprehensive series of foundations and regulation plans was launched in the 1620s, continuing for more than fifty years on a scale unparalleled elsewhere at the time. The plans followed the patterns currently popular in Europe, with plain gridiron solutions or simplified versions of plans recommended in contemporary treatises on architecture and the art of fortification. In Sweden in particular the more remote provincial towns were often planned on extremely simple lines, while generally speaking ambitions were perhaps slightly higher in Denmark-Norway. However, towns such as Trondheim (figure 4.5) or Göteborg (figure 5.3), or the new districts in Copenhagen (figure 2.2), show that even in the North plans of a very high quality were sometimes produced.

Compared with the feverish urban activity of the seventeenth century in the two Nordic kingdoms, the eighteenth century looks much quieter. But new ideas were nonetheless beginning to creep into the regulation plans and into the few new foundations. For instance, more effort was being made to increase fire protection by planning for green spaces and broad streets.

During the early years of the nineteenth century the main developments were taking place in Finland, now a grand duchy under the Russian Tsar. The most important project was in Turku, which had been destroyed by fire in 1827 and was now being rebuilt. The irregular mediaeval street network was replaced by a gridiron plan with 18 m broad streets. Open spaces between the houses and 'esplanades' were also intended to give greater protection from fire. Over the following decades several other Finnish towns were replanned on similar lines, and the principles were codified in a General Building Ordinance in 1846. Ever since the late 1760s a great many towns in Russia had been founded or redeveloped, often according to quite sophisticated plans, and developments in Finland should be seen as part of this whole movement, albeit on a somewhat simpler level.

Nothing in the other Nordic countries during the first half of the nineteenth century could compare with these plans. But, as in Finland, the provincial towns of Norway and Sweden were built almost exclusively of wood, and devastating fires were thus a constant threat. Thinning out the buildings was one way of reducing the risk that a fire would spread, and the advocates of town planning saw it chiefly as a means to greater fire safety – an emphasis which is probably unique to the North. In Sweden it was decreed in 1828 that no town should be rebuilt after a fire until a new town plan had been approved, and in 1845 a new law was promulgated in Norway, whereby all new or rebuilt towns must consist of a rectangular street network. To modern eyes, such provisions were to have fatal consequences particularly in many Norwegian towns. But the idea that houses should be neatly arranged in straight rows, and not scattered here and there along winding streets, was axiomatic to the nineteenth-century planner.

By the middle of the nineteenth century England had reached a milestone in its urban history: half the population of the country was now living in towns. Among the Nordic countries at the same date town dwellers represented between ten and twenty per cent of the total population. But the second half of the nineteenth century was characterized by rapid urbanization, and the urban population more than doubled. New areas had to be exploited and older urban districts as far as possible modernized and regulated. Furthermore a great many new urbanized areas were growing up, particularly around railway stations – areas which were in fact outside the established urban system.

The problems were similar, albeit to a varying extent and in different guises, in all the Nordic countries. The Swedish Building Ordinances of 1874, which enjoined towns to prepare town plans and gave detailed instructions as to how this should be done, represent one ambitious attempt to tackle them. The newly regulated Finnish towns furnished a model, and particular attention was paid to laying out 'esplanades', i.e. broad streets divided down the middle by a row of trees (see above, p. 189). Several Finnish and a few Swedish towns still have splendid examples of this type of thoroughfare, which was never adopted in Denmark or Norway.

The later nineteenth century was a time when liberal values were in the ascendant in the North, which probably explains why no planning legislation was introduced in Denmark until the 1920s, and why Finland and Norway long remained content with their nineteenth-century planning statutes. Nor did the 1874 Swedish Building Ordinances have the intended effect. However, in 1907 Sweden acquired a new Town Planning Act – the first real planning law in the North – which with full legal effect prohibited any building in conflict with the town plan. It even allowed for directives regarding the design of individual properties.

Shortly before the end of the century voices

began to be raised in the North against gridiron planning, first in Sweden and a little later in Finland. The new ideas inspired mainly by Camillo Sitte, called instead for greater sensitivity in adjusting to the topography, for more visual variety and aesthetically planned spatial entities. The new principles were soon accepted throughout the North, particularly after several notable town planning competitions.

Inspiration from Germany and Austria was combined with ideas culled from the English experience. The main theme of Ebenezer Howard's *Garden Cities of To-Morrow* is of course the prevention of urban sprawl by laying out new communities that combined the advantages of town and country; they should not be allowed to grow beyond a certain predetermined size and should be surrounded by a rural zone. Howard included numerous calculations in his book, to show that the garden city was a realistic proposition both economically and socially. He was much less interested in its physical appearance. Thus Raymond Unwin and Barry Parker, the two architects working at Letchworth, the first garden city, had free hands when it came to transforming Howard's principles into concrete reality.

The publicity surrounding Letchworth and Unwin's writings together helped to spread the idea of the garden city, not least in the North. Here, the term referred mainly to residential suburbs with an architecturally planned environment and often of some social pretensions, rather than to communities of the type envisaged by Howard. Around 1910 areas labelled 'garden city' were being planned in all the Nordic countries (see figures 3.8, 4.17 and 5.15). Common to many of them is a high standard of design; but they are not really garden cities in Howard's sense. Massive urbanization was barely beginning in the North, and the right conditions for Howard's ideas did not therefore exist. It was the architectural shape of Letchworth, and even more of Hampstead Garden Suburb, which Nordic visitors found useful and attractive, not the basic concept of Howard's programme.

At the beginning of the 1920s Sweden was the only Nordic country with laws allowing for some municipal control over the design of buildings, and even the Swedish Planning Act was weak on many points. Between the wars there was much debate in all four countries about how to structure planning and building legislation with the result that new laws were passed in Norway in 1924, in Denmark in 1925 and 1938, and in Finland and Sweden in 1932. The status of planning was thus successively improved, often as one country invoked the laws and findings of its neighbours. Whereas before building layout and design had been regulated exclusively by general building provisions, the idea now was to make it possible to control developments more flexibly by way of plans that would be binding on landowners. The various acts also addressed the question of the financial relations between municipalities and landowners.

The concept of town planning as a distinct field of knowledge calling for a certain amount of specialization, goes back in the North to the turn of the century. During the 1920s town planning was confirmed as a distinct area of competence and knowledge, for example by the establishment of the National Association for Town Planning in 1919 in Norway and of the Danish Town Planning Research and Teaching Institute in 1922, and by the mounting of an urban planning exhibition in Göteborg in 1923. By this time the capital cities had already established posts for dealing with planning issues, and other towns began to introduce similar posts around this time. Courses in urban development were started in the schools of architecture.

During the second two decades of the century the recognition was spreading in the North that the rational development of a society called for overall planning in a long-term perspective, planning which could provide guidelines for developing the system of communications, and for considering land use and the location of various operations and activities. But the legislation of the interwar years included no effective institution for planning of this kind. Nonetheless several interesting and progressive general and regional planning studies were undertaken. The 1908 competition for Greater Copenhagen provided a major impulse. Eliel Saarinen's 1915 plans for Munkkiniemi-Haaga (figure 3.9) and his Greater Helsinki plan of 1918 (figure 3.10) aroused considerable interest, but both were more in the nature of large-scale development plans. Albert Lilienberg's 1928 general plan for Stockholm was probably the first Nordic plan to focus on traffic issues. A high point was reached in Nordic planning history with Harald Hals's regional planning study for Greater Oslo in 1929. This resulted in a large book covering all topics relevant to the development of the region, and based on a thorough acquaintance with the contemporary international planning debate. A proposal for a regional plan was prepared on a basis of the book – just at the time that the famous Regional Plan for New York was being produced – but it had no legal standing. Some other towns were also making studies for general and in some case regional plans on a more modest scale. All these activities outside the legally regulated planning system were without binding effect, but nonetheless sometimes influenced developments.

Nordic architecture in the 1920s was often characterized by unbroken façades, well-defined forms, and tastefully inserted classicizing accents. In planning, too, we find a classicizing trend: the Sitte school's emphasis on visual foci was not abandoned, but streets were now more likely to represent axial monumentality rather than intimacy and variety. Closed street spaces and enclosed blocks were still the given solution when planning blocks of flats, but there were no longer any *gårdshus* (dwelling-house within a courtyard).

Most urban expansion in the North in the years between the wars occurred in estates of single-family homes. It was generally a question of purely commercial plot sales, without any particular social or aesthetic pretensions, and often without any public planning. In the larger towns a good many apartment blocks were also the subject of speculative building. When social democrat politicians in the big cities of the North addressed the problem of workers' housing, they thought like their counterparts in other European countries in terms of multi-family houses – for economic reasons, to minimize the land used, and perhaps too because it seemed 'bourgeois' to live in a villa. Thus investment in public and co-operative housing was geared mainly to flats, often in whole blocks of a uniform type with a carefully designed courtyard. This model, known in the North as the *storgård* (see above, p. 207), can be found in some larger towns (see figures 4.18 and 5.17(*a*)), though there are no really characteristic examples in Finland.

In the Nordic countries the concept of 'functionalism' is commonly used to describe the predominant trend in design during the 1930s. The formative impulses – chief among them Le Corbusier – reached these countries around the middle of the 1920s, and the first real functionalist buildings appeared towards the end of that decade. The 'revolution' revealed at the Stockholm Exhibition in 1930 appears less dramatic now than it did to its pioneers: in their Nordic versions the classicism of the 1920s and the functionalism of the 1930s have in fact certain structural features in common.

But 'functionalism' does not only imply a style; it also suggests a new view of the role of the architect: his task is no longer primarily aesthetic, he is also expected to be a technician who serves the community by producing scientifically sound solutions to divers problems of design and planning. In Denmark, Norway and Sweden many of the leading functionalists were also socialists, preaching their views of society and architecture with equal enthusiasm and combativeness. In Norway and Sweden a constructure relationship developed between the radical architects and leading representatives of the social democratic parties, and when the latter came to power at the beginning of the 1930s the functionalists acquired considerable influence over national housing policy. In Denmark the relationship between social democracy and functionalism was not as strong. In Finland where political life was dominated by right-wing groups there was no social democratic victory, and Finnish architects apart from Aalto were more inclined towards a bourgeois stance. But functionalism was still accepted as a symbol of the progressive inclinations of the young republic. Thus functionalism was able to survive in the North when its development in Germany was brutally terminated by the Nazi takeover.

To architects eager to participate in building the new society, town planning and designing good cheap housing for the workers offered a particularly urgent challenge. And they found their models in the *Siedlungen* that were being built in Berlin, Frankfurt and other German towns. A forum for international contact and the exchange of ideas was created in CIAM, in which several Nordic architects were involved. At the second meeting of the organization in Frankfurt in 1929 in connection with the exhibition 'Die Wohnung für das Existenzminimum', all the Nordic countries were represented.

The cornerstone of the functionalist town planning and building programme was the free-standing lamella house, arranged in such a way as to provide every flat with maximum sunshine. Such flats would not only be healthy but would also be equal in quality, thus promoting greater democracy in the way people live. The most consistent example of this programme in the North can be seen in the areas of 'narrow blocks' in Stockholm (figures 5.17(*a*) and 5.18), where the strictly parallel arrangement creates a more rationalistic impression than their prototypes in Germany; the architectural language of these estates suggests the inspiration of Mies

and Gropius rather than Taut and Scharoun. Apart from the narrow blocks, taller houses were also built in other parts of Stockholm on a larger scale but in open lamella configurations. Even high-rise building stems from functionalist theory. Gropius – and also of course Le Corbusier – assumed that given a certain level of exploitation, there would be more light for a few high-rise houses than for a lot of low-rise buildings.

In the rest of the North there was neither the same sympathy nor the same conditions for functionalism in its purest form. In Norway a number of similar projects were planned, but most remained at the blueprint stage (see figure 4.19). Copenhagen has lamella areas of various kinds, some in an obviously functionalist mould, but most of the dwellings were in smaller houses and in a more traditional style. In Finland Alvar Aalto produced a personal version of the *Siedlung* model in his famous project for Sunila (figure 3.14), with buildings adapted organically to the natural surroundings in a way that heralded the Finnish 'forest town'. An example of functionalist planning of a more purist kind was produced for the Olympic Village (figure 3.15).

POST-WAR SUBURBS AND REDEVELOPMENT

Since the mid-nineteenth century a constant stream of technological and cultural impulses had been reaching the North from Germany. The Nazi takeover and the German occupation of Norway and Denmark accelerated a reorientation towards England and the United States evident not least in the planning field. Lewis Mumford's *The Culture of Cities*, which aroused little interest in the author's own country at first, became something of a cult book for a whole generation of Nordic planners; the book was published in Swedish in 1942 and in Finnish in 1946. Significantly, the Finnish edition included Patrick Abercrombie's *Greater*

London Plan, which also aroused considerable interest and debate in the North. The negative epithet 'dormitory town' had been adopted for the *Siedlung*-inspired suburbs of the 1930s, and now the idea in the North was to create residential areas in which social networks could evolve. 'Neighbourhood unit' and 'community centre' were the new buzz words; every unit was to have a centre with shops and premises for social and cultural activities. Plans were also beginning to be made for the segregation of traffic. Radburn provided a model noted even in the North.

Around 1950 satellite suburbs inspired by the English New Town model were being planned in the Nordic capitals, most notably Tapiola outside Helsinki (figure 3.18), Lambertseter in Oslo (figure 4.24) and Vällingby in Stockholm (figures 5.23 and 5.28(*a*)). They all have a centre, and are in turn divided into smaller neighbourhood units. Common to them all is the sense of 'houses in parkland', the idea being that the buildings should be informally located in some sort of landscape setting. Vällingby was intended to provide workplaces for a large proportion of its population, while the others were built more as purely residential suburbs. The success of these areas depended to a great extent on the architectural design of the buildings. The functionalist mould had now been abandoned, and considerable variety and diversity in form and colour were being employed. This 'realistic' style is related to what is known in England as the 'new empiricism'.

These developments established a pattern for the larger cities: expansion would take the form of new clearly defined units. During the 1950s and early 1960s new suburbs were generally built with an eye to the topography and with houses of modest dimensions and architectural variety. In Finland the evocative term 'forest town' is used to describe the kind of organic integration with the natural landscape that was typical of areas being built around 1960.

But during the rest of the 1960s the trend was towards standardized larger-scale housing, and topography tended to be adapted to the buildings rather than the other way round. Several factors contributed to this development. Rapid urbanization and growing demands for more space and a high housing standard had resulted in a disturbing housing shortage in larger cities all over the North. House construction was being industrialized and prefabrication becoming increasingly common. In Sweden particularly there was a conviction that once the ideal design of a flat had been scientifically determined, it was simply a question of multiplying these ideal units in blocks that could be mass-produced in more or less the same way as cars. The 'house-in-the-parkland' model was no longer so popular and many people were calling for a new type of urban development with closed blocks and a traditional arrangement of streets; such an environment, it was claimed, would be better suited to a more diversified social life. Such ideas, which gained the support of many sociologists, were particularly common in Finland, and during the late 1960s the 'forest town' came in for a good deal of criticism. Carefully prepared plans of the gridiron type were introduced instead. The drawback was that ideas of this kind could be used to justify stereotyped solutions, of which Tensta in Stockholm is a prime example (figure 5.28(*d*)).

Suburbs dominated by vast buildings whose architecture could in some cases perhaps be described as structuralist or brutalist but which generally represents nothing more than a jaded late modernism, are particularly common in Sweden. But the larger towns in all the Nordic countries possess areas of this kind, often the source of social problems.

However, it should be mentioned in all fairness that stereotyped tower-block estates are not specific to Sweden or to the North: in many parts of Eastern and Western Europe, densely built high-rise estates of standardized design appeared during the 1960s and 1970s, but lacking the surrounding open spaces and the high-quality flats which were still undeniably a positive feature of the Nordic model, and often without any accompanying centre or adequate communications, which are usual in the North.

During the 1970s a dramatic shift occurred throughout the North: the production of high-rise blocks ceased almost entirely (in all the Nordic countries except Sweden this type of housing still accounts for only a tiny proportion of the housing stock) and the provision of residential areas of varied and carefully considered design became the chief concern.

Planning legislation has been debated vigorously and more or less continually in the Nordic countries, resulting in countless small changes as well as in new laws in Denmark in 1949 and 1970, in Finland in 1959 (a new act was prepared in the 1980s, but the work came to nothing; instead the old act will be reformed piecemeal), in Norway in 1965 and 1985, and in Sweden in 1947 and 1986. The idea has been to improve the efficiency of local development planning and to extend its range beyond existing 'densely built areas', to create instruments for structure planning at the municipal and regional levels, and – in the case of the most recent legislation – to reinforce public participation in the planning process. In Denmark and Norway in particular some sort of legal means of controlling building on agricultural land was also urgently advocated.

XClearance and street regulation have been important issues in the planning debate ever since the seventeenth century, but the demands have never been as vociferous as during the functionalist period. According to the radical architects of the 1930s almost all inner-city buildings earlier than the 1920s were due for clearance to make way for free-standing lammela housing (see figure 4.19). Perhaps it is not surprising that in their new-born enthusiasm they advocated radical solutions; but it is more remarkable that their attitude towards older buildings became the generally accepted view in the North for more than thirty years. For several decades the 'clearance problem' was a burn-ing topic, and there would have been more municipal action if it had not been necessary to concentrate available resources on new production in order to cope with the housing shortage. But even if – with a few exceptions – none of the major clearance projects were actually carried out, there was nothing to stop innumerable lesser depredations. When a new attitude began to emerge towards the end of the 1960s, many late nineteenth-century districts had already suffered severe damage either from urban blight due to prospective clearances or from demolition and insensitive new building. The Finnish wooden towns, which were still relatively intact as late as the 1950s, were a particularly glaring example. And the danger is far from over: a new wave of demolition seems to be sweeping over the North, and clearance for redevelopment is often ruthlessly imposed. At the same time the higher standard of housing that results means higher living costs, and thus – despite fine words about social improvements – the kind of gentrification process which is becoming increasingly common throughout the Western world.

Clearance in the city centres is something else again. Its purpose is to provide modern premises for offices and for a variety of commercial and other activities, as well as making the urban core more easily accessible to cars. Stockholm is the prime example in the North, and indeed in Europe as a whole, of the vast transformation of a city centre under the auspices of the municipality (see figure 5.32). Several provincial towns followed Stockholm's example, so far as they could (see figures 5.33 and 5.34). In all the Nordic countries, perhaps particularly in Denmark, similar interventions have been planned but have not in fact been as fully implemented as in Sweden, probably because economic conditions have not been so favourable to radical changes. It should be noted, however, that Helsinki chose another approach: in order to reduce the pressure on the old city centre the Finns have built a satellite centre, Pasila (figure 3.32), three kilometres north of the CBD, on much the same principles as were applied at La Défence outside Paris.

During the 1960s Nordic planners 'regarded a steadily rising standard of living as almost a law of nature', as the authors of the Danish chapter have put it. It was a question of investing in continuing urbanization and motorization. But by the 1970s urban growth was stagnating and economic growth falling off; there were energy problems, although to a lesser extent in Norway which benefited from the oil crisis. All the established holy cows of planning were being challenged by environmental groups, by the press, and by young architects. Clearances were damned as vandalism, the new residential environments as inhuman, the redeveloped central areas as sterile and over-commercialized, and the traffic arteries as a health hazard.

The 1970s were also characterized by scrapped plans and half-finished ring roads, and a laborious reorientation of the planning machinery towards a more conservationist approach. And a new attitude was emerging: even in the North planning was becoming in Gordon Cherry's words 'pragmatic and reactive, instead of normative and prescriptive' (Cherry, 1980).

THE PLANNING APPARATUS IN THE NORDIC COUNTRIES

From this sketchy outline of planning history, let us try to pinpoint the status of planning in the Nordic countries. Public control exercised by a professional bureaucracy is well established in the North, and has been at least since the seventeenth century. During the nineteenth century a system of municipal administration also evolved which, for the times, was both standardized and effective. In both these respects the North differs from England, for example. Furthermore over the last fifty years or so political life in Denmark, Norway and Sweden has been dominated by social democratic parties which

have seen no ideological objection to the social control of land use and similar interests. The conditions for effective planning should have been favourable – perhaps more favourable – than anywhere else in the Western world.

Any discussion of the importance of planning in the North comes up against the problems of definition mentioned in the introduction to chapter 5. We can either regard all deliberations and decisions that affect the shaping of an environment as part of a lengthy planning process, or we can reserve the term 'planning' for cases in which a single individual or a group of people with genuinely free hands produce a blueprint for the exploitation and building of a particular area, starting from certain principles and ideas regarding the design of the physical environment. And here we can limit planning exclusively to planning under public auspices, or we can include cases in which the developers are responsible for the planning as such, either themselves or through the offices of an independent consultant.

Let us consider physical local development planning as affecting the location and design of buildings. A principle common to all the Nordic countries as manifest in their twentieth-century planning legislation, concerns the so-called 'municipal planning monopoly', whereby legally binding physical plans must be approved by the municipalities before being ratified by the state institutions. Another principle, which has become generally accepted since the war, makes such plans mandatory for the building of any 'densely built areas'. This gives the municipalities the right to veto any undesirable building projects, but no power to compel a landowner to do anything which he regards as incompatible with his own interests. In other words the landowner has retained considerable power despite the municipal planning monopoly, and the production of a town plan has often been preceded by negotiations between municipality and landowners. It has also been quite common for the landowners/developers to produce plans of their own and then to submit these to the municipality for approval. In order to increase their control over building developments many municipalities, particularly in the larger towns, have made extensive land purchases, and it has thus been possible for densely built areas to grow to a large extent on municipal land. But not even this could guarantee the municipal plan-makers any real influence over the arrangement and design of the buildings. The main lines for the design of a residential area, for example, have often been established at an early stage in agreements between the municipal bodies and the relevant companies, which have also been responsible for the actual planning. When it has finally come to producing the plans required by the law, little more than the formalities remain to be settled. Thus legally regulated planning provides no guarantee in itself that society can control building developments, even though the planning monopoly provides a strong bargaining counter.

Further, the social control of building developments can operate either by way of general rules, or through plans created individually for specific environments. The nineteenth-century laws and building ordinances represented the first approach, while the planning legislation of the twentieth century is geared essentially to the second. But over the last fifty years or so the design of the built environment has come to be regulated by a rising tide of national norms and rules – in all the Nordic countries to some extent, but particularly in Sweden. Thus the scope for individual design has been further reduced. The planner's task has come to consist increasingly of co-ordinating the various requirements ensuring that production will be able to run smoothly, and checking that all the norms are being met. Thus the existence of documents designated as 'plans' is no guarantee that there has been any planning worthy of the name. This applies particularly to the 1960s, and probably to Sweden more than to the other Nordic countries. But

the general trend should not blind us to the numerous exceptions, occasions when municipalities or developers have shown great interest in creating a good environment, or when the planner has had the status and capacity to promote a line of his own. Since the later 1970s concern for design has been growing, and aesthetic values again carry more weight.

Municipal planning as affecting land use, infrastructural investment, and the location of industrial and commercial operations has been touched upon only briefly in the main texts. An important condition for such planning has been the series of municipal mergers in the Nordic countries during the 1960s and 1970s, which radically reduced the number of municipalities. The idea was that every municipality should consist of a central place and its surrounding rural area.

There has, at least sporadically, been an ambition in all the Nordic countries at the national level to create a municipal and regional system of structure planning. All four countries have tried out various kinds of legal planning institutes in this context. But when it has come to the point, the municipalities have shown little interest in tying themselves down to binding long-term plans. After all, planning always involves striking a balance between often incompatible interests, which means that politicians frequently find it prudent to postpone unnecessary decisions until after a coming election – and then probably until after the next and the next. Furthermore the chance of being able to realize a plan which conflicts with the wishes of a landowner, for example, has remained small and is always costly. Many overall plans have therefore taken the form of studies or trend projections rather than of directives actually intended to steer developments. If a company with ample resources wants to establish itself in conflict with a plan, the municipality concerned has rarely objected. And then of course the ambitions of the individual municipalities quite often conflict with one another, or with regional or even national interests. One step forward is thus often followed by two steps back. For example, with its 1947 Building Act Sweden spearheaded the idea of legally defined municipal structure planning, but by the time the Riksdag held its final debate on the new national Planning and Building Act in the autumn of 1986, the municipal structure plan had been stripped of all its legal force and effect and reduced to the status of a purely investigative document – which must be described as a pretty meagre result.

Nor does Nordic regional planning, as described in the different chapters here, emerge as much of a success story; in fact it serves to confirm Gordon Cherry's observation that non-federal countries 'which have developed forms of local government over many years', seldom succeed in establishing effective regional planning. 'Regional planning is really regional management and relations between institutions of government are crucial; when the keynote of these relations is independence rather than interdependence, effective regional planning is impossible' (Cherry, 1980).

Thus it proved difficult or even impossible to find an appropriate form for structure planning in the North, despite some shining examples of farsighted and well elaborated projects. We can look at a few attempts which have little in common apart from their ingenuity and the fact that they aroused interest throughout the North without ever acquiring legal force. At the start of the reconstruction period in Finland, several general and regional plans were produced under Aalto's versatile guidance, among them the Antler Plan for Rovaniemi, the master plan for Imatra (figure 3.16) and the regional plan for Norrland (figure 3.17). No other Nordic regional plan has achieved such fame as the 1947 Finger Plan for Copenhagen. The town was to expand in finger-like ribbons along radial highways and railway lines, while the areas in between would be left green (figure 2.15), thus offering an exciting alternative to London's

green belt and New Towns. In Sweden mention must be made of the extremely comprehensive and carefully elaborated 1951 master plan for Stockholm, and Fred Forbat's various influential plans for several provincial towns. Nor should we forget the 1966 draft regional plan for greater Stockholm, coloured by the idea of the town as a vast production and traffic apparatus, and imbued with technological enthusiasm and an uncompromising approach recalling Garnier and Le Corbusier.

To summarize: planning has hardly acquired the importance in Nordic social development that might have been expected in view of what has been said about the apparently favourable circumstances. When it comes to the point the various decision-makers have not been able – or perhaps have not wanted – to steer societal development in conflict with the market forces. Sailing freely with the wind seemed preferable to trying to tack against it. And yet apart from the United Kingdom it is in the Nordic countries that we find the most highly developed planning systems of any Western democracies. The relatively subordinate role of planning in southern Europe emerges with all clarity from a perusal of *Planning and Urban Growth in Southern Europe* (Wynn, 1984). The kind of extensive illegal building that often conflicts with official plans and which seems to be widespread in several Mediterranian countries, would be difficult to envisage in the North.

Another feature common to the Nordic countries is the dominating position of the architect in all physical planning. When it comes to planning in the sense of designing, this is not particularly remarkable, but Nordic architects have also kept a firm hold on structure planning. One reason for this may be that structure planning has evolved as a complement to the physical local development plan, and that structure planning is concerned with cartographical analysis and methods of presentation. Presumably geographers, sociologists and cultural historians will play an increasingly active part in future planning. No equivalent to the British Royal Town Planning Institute has been established in the North.

IS THERE A NORDIC PLANNING TRADITION?

Let us look finally at post-war relations between the Nordic countries in planning contexts. An extremely important factor is the common language: apart from the Finnish speakers, Nordic architects and planners have been able to communicate with one another in their mother tongue, and even the Finnish speakers have generally been able to speak and read Swedish without much trouble. Further, in many respects social development in the four countries has followed a similar course, steered by politicians upholding related ideologies and guided by similar goals. The extensive harmonization of Nordic legislation has also been important, and over the last few decades the 'North' has even become something of a battle-cry: Nordic collaboration has been encouraged by politicians, authorities and organizations in all sorts of ways.

Thus it is not surprising that communication between Nordic planners has been highly developed, particularly during the 1950s and 1960s. For a long time, for example, Nordic planning meetings were being held every other year. The co-ordination of higher education in the relevant fields which was established in 1969 in Nordplan (see above, p. 204) has naturally also helped to promote Nordic collaboration.

It is one thing to declare that close contact exists between the Nordic countries, and quite another to identify what exactly this has meant in concrete terms. It is not easy to try to distinguish what is the result of conscious aims and efforts, and what is contingent on contemporary trends, common external impulses, or other similar factors. Nonetheless it is clear that Nordic planners have found inspiration and moral support in working along similar lines in planning and designing their suburbs, and in tackling traffic problems and clearances etc. One field in which they have benefited more concretely from one another's experiences has been legislation; the Swedish acts of 1907 and 1947 in particular provided models for the other countries.

Parallel developments in the Nordic countries have been repeatedly emphasized above. But naturally there are also important differences due to economic, social, historical and not least geographical and topographical conditions.

Differences in housing policy and decision processes can be disregarded here, since these have only been touched upon briefly in the national chapters. But even when it comes to the form of the various plans, each country has its own profile, and such differences are naturally a major source of inspiration and the constructive exchange of ideas and experiences. Sweden and Denmark can perhaps be regarded here as each other's antipoles: Sweden has pushed technochratic rationalism close to the limits in its large-scale high-rise suburbs. Denmark has generally built on a smaller scale, and even during the functionalist period it aimed at more variety and tradition in the design of buildings. In many ways Finland has followed the Swedish model, but on various occasions has also been inspired by the Danish alternative. In some ways, however, Finland stands alone, not least in having had an Alvar Aalto with the capacity and status to follow his own line in a way that is unique in the North. And Aalto is not the only one to have commanded respect for individual efforts; there has certainly been more scope for personal design in Finland, at any rate compared with Norway and Sweden. Norway has largely followed in Sweden's footsteps, but by no means slavishly or uncritically. Towards the end of the 1960s Norwegian interest in Swedish planning declined and, unlike Sweden, Norway never lost sight of the human element in both scale and setting.

The Nordic countries have found inspiration not only in each other's experiences, but also to a very great extent outside the North. David Goldfield has said that international planning ideas 'had easier entrée into professional and political circles in Sweden than they did in the States, where planning in the Cold War era carried connotations of a manipulative and vaguely totalitarian régime' (Goldfield, 1979). This can be extended to apply to the North as a whole. Perhaps we can simply say that a certain receptiveness to international planning ideas is a distinguishing feature of Nordic urban development.

Thus we have seen how Nordic plan-makers around the turn of the century and for some years afterwards knew their Sitte, their Stübben and their Unwin, and how their plans were clearly inspired by German and English models. During the 1920s and 1930s it was Le Corbusier, CIAM and the radical German architects who counted. The masters of functionalism were replaced during the 1940s by Lewis Mumford and Patrick Abercrombie, and England's New Towns were held up as ideals and adapted to the nature of suburbs like Vällingby and Lambertseter. Other projects which aroused great interest in the North were Lijnbaan in Rotterdam and the new centre in Coventry; these provided models for the redevelopment of centres and the creation of pedestrian precincts.

The 1950s is probably the only period when the North became a place of pilgrimage for international planners. However, the interest aroused by Vällingby in particular was hardly due to any new Nordic thinking; it was rather that the North had proved receptive to ideas prevalent at the time and that it had the opportunity to realize them – which it did with considerable architectural skill – before England's New Town programme had really started to take shape. A general interest in the Nordic welfare model certainly contributed to the attention these projects aroused. From the 1950s onwards Finnish plans – and particularly Aalto's work – have also attracted international interest on account of their high architectural quality.

During the 1960s the North showed less interest in ideas outside its borders. This may have been partly because there were now no international figures of the standing of a Le Corbusier or an Abercrombie. But it was apparently also because the North, and Sweden in particular, was convinced of its own position at the forefront of developments, with more to teach than to learn from others. Nevertheless American traffic planning and urban development drew considerable interest, and many Northerners went to North America to study what was being done there.

From the 1970s onwards we can perhaps identify a new wave of internationalism, with a growing interest in foreign publications and models.

I would like to close with a few words on current trends in the North. As elsewhere, the 1980s meant a return of optimism and confidence in the future. Investment in building is booming, particularly in the city centres. Space released by industrial closures or the closing of harbours and railyards is being exploited for offices, hotels and luxury housing aimed at people with the money to pay for it. The central municipalities in the large metropolitan regions are eager to reverse the decline in their populations by attracting high income earners and tax payers. The old duality between the authorities on the one hand and private developers on the other has either softened or ceased altogether: many projects today are pure joint ventures involving public bodies and private enterprise. An increasing amount of planning also occurs within consortia of this kind, efficiently hidden from view. Aesthetic ambitions are often high in a spirit of post-modernism, but results frequently seem rather forced.

In many parts of the Western world at the

present time people appear to regard public planning as an intrinsically negative activity – as something that hampers development and restricts private initiative. Such reactions have occurred – and can still occur – in the North. But in this part of the world such hostility to planning is, hopefully, a transient phenomenon. There is pretty broad agreement that the physical environment – buildings, cultivated land and the natural landscape – are a common resource that cannot be handed over *carte blanche* to the care of private individuals or companies, and that the long-term ecological management of land, air and water is un-thinkable without an effective social-planning apparatus.

REFERENCES

Cherry, Gordon E. (1980) Introduction: aspects of twentieth-century planning, in Cherry, Gorden E. (ed.) *Shaping an Urban World*. London: Mansell.

Goldfield, David R. (1979) Suburban development in Stockholm and the United States: a comparison of form and function, in Hammarström, Ingrid and Hall, Thomas (eds.) *Growth and Transformation of the Modern City*. Stockholm: Almquist & Wiksell International.

Wynn, Martin (ed.) (1984) *Planning and Urban Growth in Southern Europe*. London: Mansell.

SUBJECT INDEX

ABC-community 219, 228
airports 37, 164, 200, 228, 239
architects' associations 20, 87, 88, 204
axial composition 29, 30, 69, 74, 76, 78, 82, 133, 138, 141, 145, 207

Bauhaus 23
block of flats, see under housing
Bruk 174–6, 178
Building Ordinances of 1856 (Finland) 65, 74, 80, 100
Byggnadsstadga, 1874 års, (Building Ordinances of 1874, Sweden) 178–83, 186–90, 196–8, 206, 248

CBD and central areas 18, 19, 23, 36, 37, 46, 47, 55, 79, 81, 91, 103, 104, 130, 133, 137, 143–5, 151–4, 156, 163, 232–6, 238, 253
CIAM 84, 201, 210, 251, 258
classicism 12, 23, 24, 29, 30, 61, 65, 80, 83, 98, 101, 143, 207
community action, *see* public participation under planning and building
community centres 216, 217, 252
competitions 17, 25, 28–30, 39, 52, 53, 71, 77, 81, 82, 95–7, 100, 112, 137, 138,

141, 142, 151, 152, 156, 157, 163, 182, 184, 185, 191, 210, 219, 250
congresses, *see* planning and building
conservation planning, *see* preservation planning
'consortium planning' 240, 241, 258
constructivism 98, 107, 108
courtyards (*cf Storgård* under house types) 17, 23, 39, 250
cultivated land, preservation of, see farmland preservation

Danish Town Planning Institute (*Dansk byplan-laboratorium*) 21, 27, 249
'dormitory suburbs' 35, 36, 42, 216, 219, 220, 252

ecological planning 53, 55, 164, 258
esplanades 65, 67–9, 187, 189, 190, 248
exhibitions:
Århus 1909 20
Berlin 1931 201, 210
Göteborg 1923 185, 203
Göteborg 1945 215, 216
London 1862 184
Malmö 1986 229
Odense 1988 53
Stockholm 1930 142, 203, 210, 211, 214, 250
Stuttgart 1927 210

façade patterns 80, 145
farmland preservation 30, 52, 149, 151, 158, 253
'Finger plan' 30–2, 34, 36, 37, 42, 256
fires and town regulations 9, 65–8, 70, 118, 120, 121, 129, 130, 132, 134, 135, 138, 169–76, 179, 181–3, 185–9, 191, 248
functionalism 21, 23, 24, 36, 84, 100, 139, 142, 159, 203, 210–15, 225, 228, 231, 250–3, 257
fortified towns 9, 14–17, 61, 118–20, 170–3

garden cities and garden suburbs 16, 18, 29, 44, 48, 74, 76–8, 83, 136, 138, 154, 191, 192, 206, 249
garden city movement 16, 29, 76, 136–8, 154, 191, 249
gentrification 44, 52, 253
government's role in the planning process 21, 23, 30, 63, 64, 69, 70, 86, 91, 98, 104, 174, 175, 180, 186, 201, 202, 206, 232, 247
green areas 23, 26, 27, 31, 32, 36, 52, 89, 91, 147, 174, 189, 221, 239, 248, 256
gridiron plans 8, 9, 12, 19, 20, 44, 61, 65, 68–71, 87, 95, 98, 101, 105, 109, 118, 119,

gridiron plans – *cont.*
    129–31, 134, 136, 143, 171,
    172, 190, 247–9, 252
Greater London Council 241
Greater London Plan 86, 147,
    215, 251, 252

harbours 9, 12, 14, 16, 17, 19,
    20, 29, 35, 37, 47, 49, 120,
    238
house types and
    building-musters
    blocks of flats, general
        15–18, 23–5, 27, 29, 32,
        41, 53, 132, 139, 143, 149,
        159, 160, 191, 210–31, 237,
        250–3
    high-rise developments 32,
        76, 98, 108–11, 141, 149,
        158, 159, 161, 211, 212,
        221, 222, 251, 253, 257
    lamellas 23, 85, 91, 95, 100,
        101, 142, 143, 210–13, 219,
        224, 251
    Landshövdingehus 210, 211,
        237
    maison rayonnant
        (star-shaped houses) 215,
        218, 219
    single-family houses 18, 21,
        23, 27, 29, 32, 34, 35, 41,
        48, 53, 71–6, 96, 105–7,
        141, 149, 154, 159, 191,
        192, 212, 221, 228–30, 250
    Storgård 84, 207, 210, 250
    tower blocks 215, 218, 223,
        224, 252
Housing
    cooperatives 16, 25, 142, 147,
        149, 206, 207, 211–13, 250
    flats *vs* houses debate 101,
        105, 158, 159, 228, 229,
        250
    general on policy and reform
        16, 21, 48, 82, 83–6, 93,
        97, 106, 110, 139, 142, 147,
        159, 167, 178, 206, 213,
        214
    philanthropic 16, 178
    public and non-profit (council
        housing) 21, 23, 25, 30, 32,

39, 42, 89, 92, 138, 139,
    206, 210–32, 237
    rent control 206, 223
    working-class 15, 16, 20, 44,
        69, 72, 78, 82, 83, 85, 102,
        134, 210, 250, 251

incorporations 17, 25, 43, 79,
    80, 122, 150, 156, 219,
    225
industrial development, sites
    for 30, 34, 37, 44, 45, 69,
    70, 77, 84, 85, 148, 149
industrialization 13, 14, 17, 30,
    34, 35, 63, 123–6, 140, 177,
    178, 184, 193–6
industrialized building
    production 30, 35, 39, 44,
    86, 93, 97, 105, 107, 159,
    222, 224, 225, 228, 252
influence on Nordic planning
    American 46, 87, 88, 96, 141,
        146, 154, 201, 215, 229,
        230, 251, 258
    Austrian 71, 76, 78, 136, 191,
        207, 249, 250, 258
    British 17, 21, 23, 29, 30, 33,
        44, 136–42, 147, 191–3,
        201, 215, 238, 249, 251,
        252, 256, 258
    Dutch 9, 23, 147, 171, 172,
        207, 251, 258
    French 141, 210, 239, 250,
        256, 258
    German 8, 17, 18, 23, 76, 86,
        134, 136, 143, 191, 192,
        203, 207, 210, 215, 247,
        249, 251, 258
    Japanese 96, 108
    Russian 61, 68, 69, 189, 248
influences and contacts,
        inter-Nordic 71, 80, 93, 96,
        98, 101, 104, 106, 132, 134,
        137, 138, 141, 142, 147,
        156, 182, 184, 189, 207,
        248, 257, 258
inner cities policies, *see* CBD
    and central areas

land policy 14, 25, 63, 86, 92,
    101, 170, 206, 214, 234

landscape considerations in
    planning 68, 71, 75, 85, 90,
    93, 94, 107, 108, 131, 138,
    141, 143, 149, 220, 252
Landshövdingehus, see house
    types
Lex Bolmora 221
Lex Norrmalm 234

medieval towns 6–8, 60,
    116–18, 120, 152, 168, 169,
    247
million homes programme 213,
    224, 225
model plans and communities
    68, 170, 172, 173, 175, 188,
    189
motor traffic, *see* traffic and
    communication systems
municipal decision-making
    process 180–6, 214, 254, 255
municipal master plans 17, 18,
    28, 31, 42, 46, 49, 53, 77,
    78, 88, 91, 104, 141,
    148–50, 154, 156, 159, 179,
    185, 199, 200, 221, 250
municipal system 28, 36, 129,
    147, 178, 180, 181, 185,
    193, 194, 212, 255

national physical planning 36,
    48, 155, 197, 205, 206
nature conservation 27, 197,
    205, 206, 259
neighbourhood units 30, 78, 86,
    90, 111, 149, 150, 159, 215,
    216, 219, 252
new towns 30, 89, 147, 215,
    219, 220, 252, 256, 258
Nordplan 1, 155, 204, 257

parks 16, 20, 25, 27, 52, 133,
    134, 139, 148, 157, 174,
    181, 187, 188, 210
party politics and planning 142,
    197, 198, 204, 205, 213,
    223, 231, 233, 250, 251,
    254
pedestrian precincts 32, 35, 46,
    47, 94, 98, 147, 151, 152,
    163, 216, 258

planning and building
  associations and societies (*cf*
    architects' associations) 20,
    21, 27, 82, 83, 89, 139, 147,
    204, 249
  authorities, national 21, 48,
    61, 64–6, 71, 91, 102, 103,
    143, 145, 147, 200, 202–4,
    213, 241
  congresses and conferences
    146, 147, 210, 251
  education 1, 21, 65, 68, 85,
    86, 137, 155, 162, 191, 203,
    204, 249, 253, 257
  goals 97, 98, 141, 173,
    187–93, 214, 224, 232, 233,
    241
  journals 76, 96, 97, 142, 188,
    204
  legislation 14, 16, 21, 25,
    30–2, 36, 39, 48, 65, 68,
    70, 72, 80, 91, 92, 104, 118,
    129, 130, 132, 134, 135,
    140, 141, 147, 154, 155,
    158, 161, 169, 175, 176,
    179–88, 193–206, 248, 249,
    253, 255, 256, 258
  public participation 39, 41,
    44, 47, 48, 52, 53, 101, 145,
    146, 159, 161–3, 205, 254
  research 21, 158, 159, 163,
    204, 205, 214, 250
planning instruments and
  planning system
  general 21, 30, 48, 49, 64, 80,
    91, 92, 120, 140, 141,
    196–8, 255, 256
  local and municipal level 21,
    48, 63, 69, 70, 74, 80, 81,
    90, 91, 106, 129, 141, 151,
    154, 155, 158, 162, 175,
    179–86, 198–203, 214,
    233, 248, 250, 254, 255,
    256
  regional level 27, 48, 88, 89,
    91, 92, 99, 146, 147, 154–6,
    164, 201, 250, 255, 256
planning profession 65, 69, 71,
    73, 81, 85, 137–41, 147,
    155, 170, 184–6, 200,
    203–5, 249, 256

Plan-och bygglagen (PBL)
  (Planning and Building
  Act, Sweden) 197–202,
  205, 206, 238, 256, 257
Plan Voisin 210
population trends, *see* urban
  growth
preservation planning 33, 44,
  47, 48, 53, 55, 101, 151,
  153, 161, 162, 164, 233,
  236, 254
public participation in planning,
  see planning and building
public transportation, *see* traffic
  and communication
  systems

radial plans 61, 69, 171, 173
railways, *see* traffic and
  communication systems
redevelopment and
  rehabilitation
  city centres 16, 18, 19, 24, 27,
    31, 33, 37, 44, 48, 96, 100,
    101, 103, 104, 142, 143,
    151–4, 163, 221, 232–7,
    239, 253, 258
  general 25, 31, 39, 44, 48, 52,
    96, 100, 101, 121, 141, 142,
    151–4, 163, 169–71, 231,
    232, 248, 253
  industrial sites, harbours *etc*
    for new purposes 49, 109,
    110, 163, 231, 238, 239,
    258
  residential areas 23, 25, 31,
    39, 51, 52, 100–2, 134, 142,
    151, 156, 161–3, 229, 231,
    232, 237, 253
  regional plans (see also 'Finger
    plan') 26, 27, 31, 36–8, 45,
    48, 49, 53, 87–9, 141, 142,
    146, 147, 149, 150, 154–6,
    164, 201, 256
  regional public transport
    systems, *see* traffic and
    communication systems
  ring roads, *see* traffic and
    communication systems
  Royal Town Planning Institute
    204, 257

satellite towns 34, 78, 89, 128,
  147–50, 156, 219, 221, 253
second home development 30,
  36, 197
settlements, non-agrarian
  (industrial, in connection
  with railway-junctions etc;
  cf Bruk) 9, 11, 12, 14, 20,
  21, 27, 28, 35, 68, 74, 75,
  86, 98, 122–8, 140, 154,
  177, 178
shanty towns 70, 72, 84, 178,
  183, 206
shopping centres, *see* suburban
  centres
slum clearance, *see*
  redevelopment of
  residential areas
social problems 47, 52, 80, 214,
  225
social segregation 39, 41, 42,
  47, 55, 68, 78, 126, 132,
  178, 183, 214
Stadsplanelag, 1907 års (1907
  Town Planning Act,
  Sweden) 179–81, 186, 193,
  196, 248, 257
Der Städtebau 192
Storgård, *see* house types and
  building musters
street breakthroughs 18, 19, 24,
  25, 27, 32, 33, 35, 43, 44,
  47
suburban centres 30, 31, 36, 43,
  46, 47, 49, 53, 148, 149,
  156, 157, 159, 216, 225,
  252–4
suburban development 15, 20,
  25, 27, 30, 32–9, 43, 44,
  72, 73, 77, 78, 80, 83, 85,
  92–4, 97–9, 122, 125–8,
  141, 147–50, 159, 160, 191,
  192, 206, 212, 215, 216,
  219–29, 252, 257

Tennessee Valley project 146
town foundations and town
  charter grants 7–9, 11, 12,
  19, 29, 63, 116–19, 122,
  131, 140, 154, 168–74, 177,
  178, 193, 247

traffic and communication
systems
general 11, 14, 21, 35, 37, 38,
45, 53, 63, 91, 121, 122,
125, 141, 142, 147, 148,
153, 154, 164, 177, 187,
212, 228, 232, 233
motorization 21, 30, 35, 36,
42, 43, 151, 212, 232, 236,
253, 254
motorways and urban roads
27, 31, 35, 37, 43, 49, 87,
90, 103, 148, 150, 154, 164,
201, 228
parking 30, 31, 35, 36, 100,
103, 224
railways 12–14, 16, 17,
19–21, 27, 28, 35, 63, 78,
122, 125, 163, 174, 177, 179,
183, 187–9, 238, 248, 258
regional public transport
systems 52, 53, 78, 147,
201

ring roads 16, 27, 28, 30, 37,
148, 154, 159, 188, 201,
232, 233, 238, 254
traffic separation 34, 39, 47,
94–6, 111, 142, 143, 160,
163, 215, 221, 252
tramways and local
trackbound communication
systems 17, 18, 26, 27, 30,
32, 37, 39, 55, 78, 142, 148,
149, 206, 212, 215, 219,
222, 228, 253

urban growth and population
trends 11, 14, 20–2, 36, 47,
53, 55, 62, 63, 68, 86,
91–3, 98, 105, 120, 122–9,
132, 141, 147, 148, 150,
154, 156, 157, 163, 177,
178, 193–6, 223, 232, 248,
252, 254
urban space design 11, 12, 16,
20, 21, 23, 24, 29, 30, 32,

39, 46, 52, 53, 66–8, 71,
73, 75, 77, 81, 82, 91, 93,
96, 95, 100, 103, 108, 109,
120, 131, 133, 138, 139,
141, 143–5, 158–60, 175,
187–92, 207–30, 232,
239–41, 249–52, 257
urban system 12–14, 22, 48,
61–4, 92, 117, 122, 126,
168, 170, 193, 194

war damages and
reconstruction 9, 87, 88,
91, 119, 143–7, 170–2,
176
wooden towns 61, 84, 95, 96,
100, 101, 119–21, 125, 129,
132, 134, 135, 140, 141,
151, 152, 161, 169, 175,
189, 232, 248, 253

zoning 18, 30, 31, 35–7, 39,
104, 187

INDEX OF TOWNS AND AREAS

Åbo, *see* Turku
Ærøskøbing 47
Ålborg 6, 8, 9, 13, 14, 18, *19*,
 21, *22*, 27, 32, 34, *43*, 44,
 53
 Hasseris 18, 27
Ålesund 120, 125, *135*, 136
Als, island of *34*, 35
Alta 146
Amsterdam 84
Åndalsnes 143
Årdal 154
Arendal 120, *130*, *131*
Århus 6, 7, 13, 14, 18, 20, 21,
 22, 27, *28*, 32–5, *42*, 43,
 44, 47, 53
 Håndværkerparken *44*
 Lisbjerg 43, 53
 Tranbjerg 43, 53
Arlanda city 239–41

Bergen 116, *117*, *118*, 119,
 120, 125, 129, 134, *136*,
 137, 138, 142, 147, 149–53,
 159, *161*, 162
 Fyllingsdalen 150
 Nordnes 147
 Selegrend 159, *161*
 Vågen *118*, 120, *136*, *137*,
 138, 152
Berlin 76, 84, 201, 210, 251
Björneborg, *see* Pori
Bodø 131, 143, 145
Borås 199, 201
Borgå, *see* Porvoo
Borgund 116, *117*

Bournville 77
Brahestad, *see* Raahe
Budapest 77

Canberra 77, 184
Christiania, *see* Oslo
Christiansand, *see* Kristiansand
Christiansfeld *11*
Cologne 76
Copenhagen 7–9, *10*, 11–14,
 15, 16, *17*, 18, 21, *22*, 23,
 24–6, 27, 30, *31*, *32*, 35–7,
 38, 39, *40*, *41*, 42, 47–9,
 50, *51*, 55, 84, 96, 238, 247,
 250, 251, 256
Albertslund 39, *40*, 52, 96
Amager 24, 37, 39
Bakkehusene 23, *24*
Ballerup 32, 42
Bellahøj *24*, 32
Bispebjerg 23, *24*
Brønsparken 23, *24*
Christianshavn 9, *10*, 16, 25,
 247
Farum *41*, 52
Frederiksberg 11, 16, 48, *52*
Frederiksværk 9
Frederiksstaden 9, *10*
Gadekæret 39, *40*
Galgebakken 39, *40*
Gladsaxe *32*, 52
Grøndals vænge *24*
Høje Tåstrup 37, 49, *50*, 52
Hornbækhus 23
Hyldespjældet *40*
Ishøj 34, *40*

Køge Bay area 37, *38*, 39,
 42, 52, 55
Lyngby 32, 37, 49
Nørrebro *51*
Ryparken 23, *24*
Solbjerg Have *52*
Skråplanet 41
Søndergård Park 32
Tinggården, *see* Køge
Vejlebroparken *40*
Tingbjerg 32
Vesterbro 37, 55
Vesterport 16, *25*
Vibevænget 23, *24*
Voldparken *32*
Coventry 147, 258
Crawley 147

Dessau 23, 210
Djursholm 206
Drammen 120, 130, 163

Ekenäs, *see* Tammisaari
Elverum 143
Enköping 173
Esbjerg 19, *20*, 27, 29, 53, 55
Eskilstuna 201
Espoo (Esbo) *62*, *90*, *97*, 98,
 106, 108, *109*
 Kivenlahti (Stensvik) 108,
 109
 Leppävaara (Alberga) *106*
 Olari (Olars) 96, *97*, 98
 Tapiola (Hagalund) 89, *90*,
 91, 93–5, 106, 252
 Westend 108

Fladstrand 12
Forsmark 175
Frankfurt 201, 210, 251
Fredericia 9, *10*, 27, 45, 53
Frederikshavn 12
Frederiksholm 9
Fredrikshald, *see* Halden
Fredrikshamn, *see* Hamina
Fredrikstad *117*, 118, *119*

Gävle 172, 174, *175*, *182*, *183*,
  189, 232, *236*
Gjøvik 131, *132*
Glomfjord 154
Göteborg 32, 80, 169–71, *172*,
  174, 178, 182, 185, 191,
  192, 201–4, 206, 207, 210,
  211, 215, *216*, 217, 222,
  223, *224*, 225, *228*, *235*,
  237, 238, 247, 249
  Angered 225, 228
  Biskopsgården 222, 223, *224*
  Guldheden 215, *216*, 217,
    218
  Hammarkullen *228*
  Kortadala 222, *223*
  Landala 192, 237
  Östra Nordstan *235*
Grindsted 28

Haderslev 6
Halden (Fredrikshald) *117*, 119
Hamar 116, *117*, 122, 131, 141
Hamburg 37, 201
Hämeenlinna (Tavastehus) 61,
  62, 63, 64, 68
Hamina (Fredrikshamn) 61,
  62, 64, 173
Hammerfest 120, *146*
Hamstead Garden Suburb, *see*
  London
Hanstholm 29, 30, 47
Harlow 147
Härnösand 191
Haslev 28
Haugesund 125, 131, *132*, 163
Havnbjerg 35
Hedeby 6, 7
Heinola *62*, 64
Helsingsborg 8, 37, 185, 216,
  238

Helsingør 8, 21, 34, 37, 47, 49
Helsinki (Helsingfors) 47, 60,
  61, *62*, 63–5, 69, 71, *72–5*,
  76, *77*, 78, *79*, 80, *81*, 82,
  83, *86*, 89, 91–3, *94*, 101,
  102, *103*, 104, *105*, 106,
  107, 108, *110*, *111*, 250,
  252, 253
  Eira 71, 73
  Haaga (Haga) 73, *74*, *77*,
    78–80
  Kannelmäki (Gamlas) *107*
  Käpylä (Kottby) *83*, *86*, 101,
    102
  Katajanokka (Skatudden)
    108, *110*
  Koivukylä, *see* Vantaa
  Konala (Kånala) 106
  Kulosaari (Brändö) 74, *75*,
    76
  Kumpula (Gumtäkt) 101
  Laajasalo (Degerö) 94
  Lehtisaari (Lövö) 94
  Malminkartano (Malmgård)
    110, 111
  Munkkiniemi (Munksnäs)
    77, 78–80, 250
  Olympic Village 85, *86*, 93,
    251
  Palisa (Fredriksberg, Böle)
    79, 110, *111*, 254
  Pihlajamäki (Rönnbacka)
    93, *94*
  Punkimäki (Bocksbacka)
    107
  Sofianlehto (Sofielund) *105*,
    106
  Suutarila (Skomakarböle)
    106
  Tapiola, *see* Espoo
  Töölö (Tölö) 71, *72*, *73*, 80
  Vallila (Vallgård) 80, 102
  Viapori (Sveaborg) 61, 76
Herning 19, *45*, 53
Hillerød 8, *46*
Hirtshals *29*, 45
Hjørring 45
Holbæk 53
Holstebro 45, 46
Hønefoss 131, 141
Horsens 20, 27, 55

Hørsholm 11
Horten 158
Høyanger 140
Husnes 154

Imatra *62*, *88*, 256

Jakobstad, *see* Pietarsaari
Joensuu *62*, 76
Jönköping 172
Jyväskylä *62*, 64, 76, *95*
  Haukkala (Kortepohja) 95,
    96

Kajaani (Kajana) *62*, 64
Käkisalmi (Kexholm) *62*, 64
Kalmar 169, 171, *172*, 189,
  190, 191, 201
Kalundborg 7
Karleby, *see* Kokkola
Karlskrona 172, 173
Karlstad 182, 185
Karmøy 154
Kaskinen (Kaskö) *62*, 64
Kemi *62*, 68, 96
Kiruna 178
Køge 49, 53, *54*, 55, 106
  Hastrup vest 55
  Lynggården, Ølby *54*
  Tinggården, Herfølge *54*,
    55, 102
Kokemäki (Kumo) *62*, 87
Kokkola (Karleby) 61, *62*, 64, 98
Kolding 45
Kongsberg *117*, 119, 122
Kotka *62*, 84
Kragerø *117*, 120, *121*
Kristiania, *see* Oslo
Kristiansand (Christiansand)
  117, 119, 125, 134, 147,
  150, 247
Kristianstad 9, 247
Kristiansund 120, 143, *145*
Kristinestad
  (Kristiinankaupunki) 61,
  62, 64
Kulosaari, *see* Helsinki
Kuopio *62*, 64, 76

Landskrona 8, 172, *173*, 216,
  230

Langesø 35
Lappeenranta (Villmanstrand) 62, 64
Larvik 117, 120, 158
Letchworth 77, 136, 249
Leufsta Bruk (Lövstabruk) 175, 176
Levanger 130
London 147, 184, 215, 238, 241, 252, 256
  Hampstead Garden Suburb 76, 77, 136, 249
Loviisa (Lovisa) 61, 62, 64
Lübeck 7, 8
Lund 7, 8

Maarianhamina (Mariehamn) 62, 68
Malmö 7, 8, 37, 210, 211, 216, 229, 238
  Rosengård 225, 229
Mandal 120
Märsta 200
Middelfart 20
Mikkeli (St Michel) 62, 64, 76
Milton Keynes 33, 44
Mo i Rana 154
Molde 120, 143, 144, 145
Mönsterås 205
Moscow 69
Mosjøen 154
Moss 120
Motala 174

Naantali (Nådendal) 61, 62, 64
Næstved 6, 34
Namsos 143, 145
Nancy 80
Narvik 141, 143
New York 88, 250
Nordborg 34, 35
Norrköping 178, 188
Notodden 140
Nurmes 62, 68, 69, 70, 95
Nya Lödöse 169
Nyborg 7, 12
Nykarleby, see Uusikaarlepyy
Nyköbing Mors 20
Nyslott, see Savonlinna
Nystad, see Uusikaupunki
Nysted 20

Odda 140
Odense 6, 8, 12–14, 18, 21, 22, 27, 33, 34, 35, 43, 44, 53
  H. C. Andersen-quarter 33, 44
Örebro 218, 219
  Baronbackarna 219
  Rosta 218, 219
Oslo (Christiania, Kristiania) 47, 84, 104, 116, 117, 118, 119, 122, 124–9, 132, 133, 134, 138, 139, 141, 142, 143, 147, 148, 149, 151, 152, 154, 155, 156, 158, 159, 160, 161, 162, 163–5, 247, 250, 252
  Aker 141, 148
  Ammerud 149
  Baerum 141
  Blindern 142
  Bøler-Bogerud 149
  Enerhaugen 161
  Grünerløkka 134, 142, 143, 162
  Holmlia 160, 162
  Homannsbyen 134
  Kalbakken 149
  Lambertseter 149, 252, 258
  Manglerud 149
  Piperviken 142, 154, 163
  Rødtvedt 149
  Romsås 160
  Sagene 139
  St Hanshaugen 134
  Skøyen-Opppsal 149
  Torshov 139
  Tveita 149
  Ullevål Hageby 138
  Veitvedt 149
  Vestre Vika 142, 151

Östersund 174
Otaniemi (Otnäs) 91
Oulu (Uleåborg) 62, 64, 111

Paris 78, 80, 182, 254
  La Défense 254
Pelkosenniemi 89
Pietarsaari (Jakobstad) 62, 64, 102
Pori (Björneborg) 62, 64, 68, 69

Port Sunlight 77
Porvoo (Borgå) 61, 62, 64
Potsdam 80
Præstø 20

Raahe (Brahestad) 61, 62, 64
Radburn 252
Randers 6, 7, 8, 20, 27, 47
Rauma (Raumo) 61, 62, 64, 102
Reval, see Tallinn
Ribe 6–8, 47
Riihimäki 62, 80
Ringsted 28, 29
Risør 120, 129, 130, 131
Rjukan 140
Røros 117, 119
Roskilde 6, 7, 12, 34, 46, 49
Rotterdam 147, 258
  Lijnbaan 147, 258
Rovaniemi 62, 87, 256

Saltsjöbaden 206
Sandefjord 158
Sandnes 158, 163
Sandviken 177
St Michel, see Mikkeli
St Petersburg 65, 68, 69
Sarpsborg 116, 117, 122
Sauda 140
Savonlinna (Nyslott) 61, 62, 64
Schleswig 7
Sigtuna 189
Silkeborg 12, 19
Skanderborg 8
Skien 116, 117, 163
Skjern 28
Skövde 173, 174, 200
Slagelse 7
Södertälje 170, 184–6, 191
Søndersborg 35
Sortvala (Sordavala) 62, 64, 68
Sorø 9
Staffanstorp 230
Stavanger 116, 117, 122, 151, 152, 153, 158, 163
Steinkjer 143
Stenungsund 205
Stevenage 147
Stockholm 32, 37, 47, 60, 61, 65, 84, 104, 134, 147, 151,

Stockholm – *cont.*
  155, 167–70, *171*, 175, 176,
  179, 180, 182, 184–7, 189,
  191, *192*, 193, 196, 199,
  200–4, 207, *208*, *209*, 210,
  211, *212*, 214–16, 218, 219,
  220, *221*, 223–5, *226*, *227*,
  228, 231, 233, *234*, 235–9,
  240, *241*, 250, 251–3, 256
Abrahamsberg 212
Åkeslund *212*
Årsta 216, *217*
Bredäng 224, 225, *227*
Bromma 211, *212*
Danviksklippan 218
Dalen *227*
Enskede 191, *192*, 206, 212
Farsta 221
Fredhäll *208*
Gärdet *209*, 210
Gröndal *209*, 218
Hägerstensåsen 215, 216
Helgalunden 207, *208*
Hjorthagen *209*
Järvafältet 96
Kista *227*, 228
Kristineberg *209*, 210
Kungsholmen 207, 211
Kungsklippan *209*, 211
Norsborg 225, 228
Reimersholme *209*
Riksby *212*
Rödaberg area 192, 207, *208*
Skärholmen 225, *227*

Tensta 225, *226*, 252
Traneberg *209*
Vällingby 219, *220*, 221, 223,
  226, 252, 258
Strömstad 172
Struer 45
Stuttgart 210
Sundsvall 182, 186, 188, 201
Sunila *84*, 85, 91, 93, 251
Sunndalsøra 154
Svaneke 47
Svolvær 141

Täby 221, *222*
  Grindtorp 221, *222*
  Näsbydal 221, *222*
Tallinn (Reval) 60
Tammisaari (Ekenäs) 61, *62*, 64
Tampere (Tammerfors) *62*, 64,
  69, 76, 80, 81, 97, 100
Tapiola, *see* Espoo
Tavastehus, *see* Hämeenlinna
Thy 47
Tibro 222
Tønder 47
Tønsberg 116, *117*, 125, 158
Tornio (Torneå) *62*, 64
Trollhättan 185
Tromsø 120, 141, 159
Trondheim 116, *117*, 119, *120*,
  125, 129, 137, 141, 142,
  147, 156, *157*, 158, 162,
  163, 247
  Heimdal 156, *157*

Midtbyen 156
Møllenberg 162
Rosenborg 162
Turku (Åbo) 60, 61, *62*, 64,
  65, *66*, 67–9, 76, 80, 81,
  95, 100, 170, 184, 247, 248

Uleåborg, *see* Oulu
Umeå 182, 189
Uppsala 170, 196
Uusikaarlepyy (Nykarleby) *62*,
  64
Uusikaupunki (Nystad) *62*, 64,
  68

Vaasa (Vasa) *62*, 64, 65, *67*,
  68, 76, 182, 189
Vänersborg 172, *173*, 174, *181*,
  182, 189
Vantaa (Vanda) *62*, *99*
  Koivukylä (Björkby) 98, *99*
Varde 12
Vardø *117*, 120
Väröbacka 205
Västerås 210
Vejle 20, 45
Vienna 16, 76, 84, 182
Viipuri (Viborg) 60, 61, *62*, 64,
  80, 81
Villmanstrand, *see*
  Lappeenranta
Visby 169
Vordingborg 7
Voss 143

INDEX OF PERSONS

Aalto, Alvar 84–9, 91, 96, 98, 101, 103, 108, 111, 251, 256–8
Abercrombie, Patrick 86, 215, 251, 258
Adlercreutz, Erik 107
Ahlsén, Erik and Tore 217
Ahola, Pentti 94, 106
Åhrén, Uno 200, 201, 204, 210, 211, 213, 216
Alexander II 63
Alexander, Christopher 96
Ambt, Charles 17
Andersson, Per 151
Andersson & Skjånes 156
Arnfred, Jens 54
Arnfred, Thyge 40, 41, 52
Asmervik, Sigmund 157
Asplund, Gunnar 211

Backström & Reinius 219
Bauman, Paul 23
Bendtsen, Ivar 23, 25
Bergersen, Øystein 156
Bergsgard, Unnleiv 158
Berlage, Hendrik Petrus 23
Birch, Ole 40
Bjerre, Aage 17, 18
Blegvad, Jacob 50, 52
Blomstedt, Aulis 96
Blomstedt, P. E. 94, 103
Bofill, Ricardo 239, 240
Brahe, Per 61
Brandt, G. N. 21
Bredsdorff, Peter 96
Brinckmann, Albert Erich 80

Brolid, Sven 223
Brolin, Jonas 175
Brunila, Birger 76, 80, 83

Chadwick, Edwin 16
Chermayeff, Serge 96
Chiewitz, Georg Theodor 68, 184
Christian IV 8, 118, 119, 150, 247
Christiansen, Alex 159
Christiansen, Knud H. 29
Cicignon, Jean Caspar de 119, 120, 156
Cubus (architect's office) 159, 161

Dahlberg, Axel 211, 213
Dahlberg, Erik 173, 175
Danneskiold-Samsoe, Otto 210, 215
Draiby, Roy 38

Edelfeldt, Albert 68
Edelsvärd, Adolf Wilhelm 68, 179, 187, 188
EELT (architect's office) 96
Ehrenström, Johan Albrecht 189
Ehrensvärd, Augustin 61, 76
Ekelund, Hilding 81, 82, 85, 86
Ekholm, Per-Axel 219
Engel, Carl Ludvig 65–7, 69, 109
Ericson, Nils 174, 181, 183, 189

Eriksson, Magnus 175
Erskine, Ralph 222, 230

Fischer, Egil 25
Fisker, Kay 28
Forbat, Fred 200, 201, 256
Forchhammer, Olaf 25
Forshaw, J. H. 86
Frederik II 118, 119
Frederik III 119
Frosterus, Sigurd 76

Garnier, Tony 256
Geddes, Patrick 21, 136, 139, 140, 142, 147
Gellerstedt, Nils 184, 192
Gjortz, A. 135
Göransson, G. F. 177
Gropius, Walter 200, 251
Gullichsen, Kristian 106

Hallman, Per Olof 71, 184, 185, 191–3, 204, 207
Hals, Harald 137, 141, 142, 250
Hanssen, Jacob 144, 145
Hansen, Knud 23
Hansen, Svend 44
Hastie, William 69
Haussmann, Georges-Eugène 78, 82
Hedén, Einar 151
Hegemann, Werner 203
Heiberg, Edward 23
Helander, Vilhelm 107, 108, 110

Henningsen, Thorkild 23
Henrici, Karl 137, 191
Hertzen, Heikki von 89, 91
Hielm, Birger 131
Hoff, Oscar 138
Hoff & Windinge 32
Höjer & Ljungqvist 225
Holm, Lennart 204
Hornemann, Emil 16
Howard, Ebenezer 77, 78, 83,
  136, 141, 249
Hultberg, Resen, Throne-Holst
  & Boguslawski 160

Jallinoja, Reijo 97, 105, 106
Jarva, Risto 98
Järvinen, Simo 97, 98
Johnsen, Yngvar 155
Jonsen, Michael Sten 54
Jung, Bertel 71, 73, 76, 78, 79
Juul Møller & Agertoft 32

Kairamo, Erkki 106, 108
Kallio, Oiva 81
Kauria, Risto 98
Keynes, John Maynard 193
Kielland, Jacob Christie 147
Kivinen, Olli 93, 94, 96, 100
Krag, Preben 154
Krier, Leon and Robert 52

Le Corbusier 141, 210, 215,
  222, 250, 251, 256, 258
Léger, Fernand 85
Leiviskä, Juha 107
Lewerentz, Sigurd 207
Lilienberg, Albert 138, 185,
  192, 193, 199, 203, 204, 207,
  210, 250
Lilius, Henrik 101
Lindahl, Göran 204
Linden, Gustaf 204
Lindgren, Armas 73
Lindhagen, Albert 134, 179,
  185, 188, 189
Lindström, Sune 200, 221,
  222
Linn, Björn 207
Linstow, Hans Ditlev 133
LPO (architect's office) 163
Lundsten, Bengt 95

Marcussen, Hanne 40
Markelius, Sven 211, 215, 219
Meldahl, Ferdinand 15
Meurman, Otto-I. 78, 80, 86,
  90, 93
Mies van der Rohe, Ludwig
  96, 108, 251
Mohr, Bjarne Lous 146
Møller Jensen, Viggo 40, 41, 52
Mosso, Leonardo 85
Mumford, Lewis 86, 88, 146,
  147, 215, 251, 258

Nesse, Olav 151
Nobel, O. K. 25
Nörgaard, Ole 96
Norrmén, Herman 71
Nurmela, Matti 106
Nyrop, Martin 16
Nyström, Gustaf 71, 72
Nyvig, Anders 156

Ödéen, Kjell 215, 216
Öhman, Ferdinand 70
Örnehufvud, Olof Hansson
  173

Pakkala, Pekka 108, 110
Parker, Barry 77, 136, 249
Paulsson, Gregor 210, 211
Pedersen, Sverre 137, 141, 143
Petersen, Carl 25
Pietilä, Reima 93
Platen, Baltzar von 174
Plesner, Ulrik 16
Poulsen, Alex 32

Raimoranta, Kari 106
Rasmussen, Holger 25
Rasmussen, Steen Eiler 29, 32
Rinnan, Frode 149
Rinnan, Tveten & Colbiørnsen
  149
Rivertz, Kristian 139
Rolfsen, Erik 148
Rubenson, Moritz 180
Ruusuvuori, Aarno 96

Saarinen, Eliel 76–82, 103,
  185, 250
Samuelson, Karl 138

Sandström, Bärnard 199
Scharoun, Hans 251
Schou, Charles I. 16
Schumacher, Fritz 207
Seidelin, Conrad 15
Setterberg, Carl Axel 67
Sitte, Camillo 16, 18, 71, 73,
  76, 78, 80, 136, 192, 249, 258
Sjöström, Einar 78
Sjöström, John 204
Skaarup & Jespersen 156
Sonck, Lars 71–6, 103
Sørensen, C. Th. 23
Stenius, M. G. 77
Storgaard, J. P. 40
Strengell, Gustaf 76, 80, 82
Strintz, Carl 18
Stübben, Joseph 71, 86, 191,
  258
Sundbärg, Fredrik 184, 185,
  191, 192
Sundius, Per (or Petter) Georg
  183, 184, 186, 189
Sundman, Mikael 108, 110
Svensson, Knud 96
Sørensen, C. Th. 23

Tasa, Jyrki 106
Taut, Bruno 251
Telje, Torp & Aasen 163
Tessenow, Heinrich 83, 207
Thomsen, Edvard 25, 32
Toivonen, Akseli 83
Torp, Hjalmar 139
Torp, Niels 163
Torstensson, Anders 170, 184
Turtola, Risto 98

Uggla, John 80
Ulrik, Frederik Ferdinand 16
Unwin, Raymond 16, 76–8,
  136, 192, 249, 258
Utzon, Jørn 34, 106

Välikangas, Martti 83, 85,
  86
Valjakka, Eero 97, 98
Vandkunsten (architect's
  office) 52, 54, 55, 106
Vibild, Karsten 54
Vormala, Timo 106

Wagner, Otto 76, 78
Wallander, Sven 207, 211, 223
Wejke, Gunnar 215, 216

Westman, Carl 192
White, Sidney 219
Wickberg, Nils Erik 69, 101, 111

Wickman, Gustaf 191
Wolf, Paul 83
Wright, Henry 88